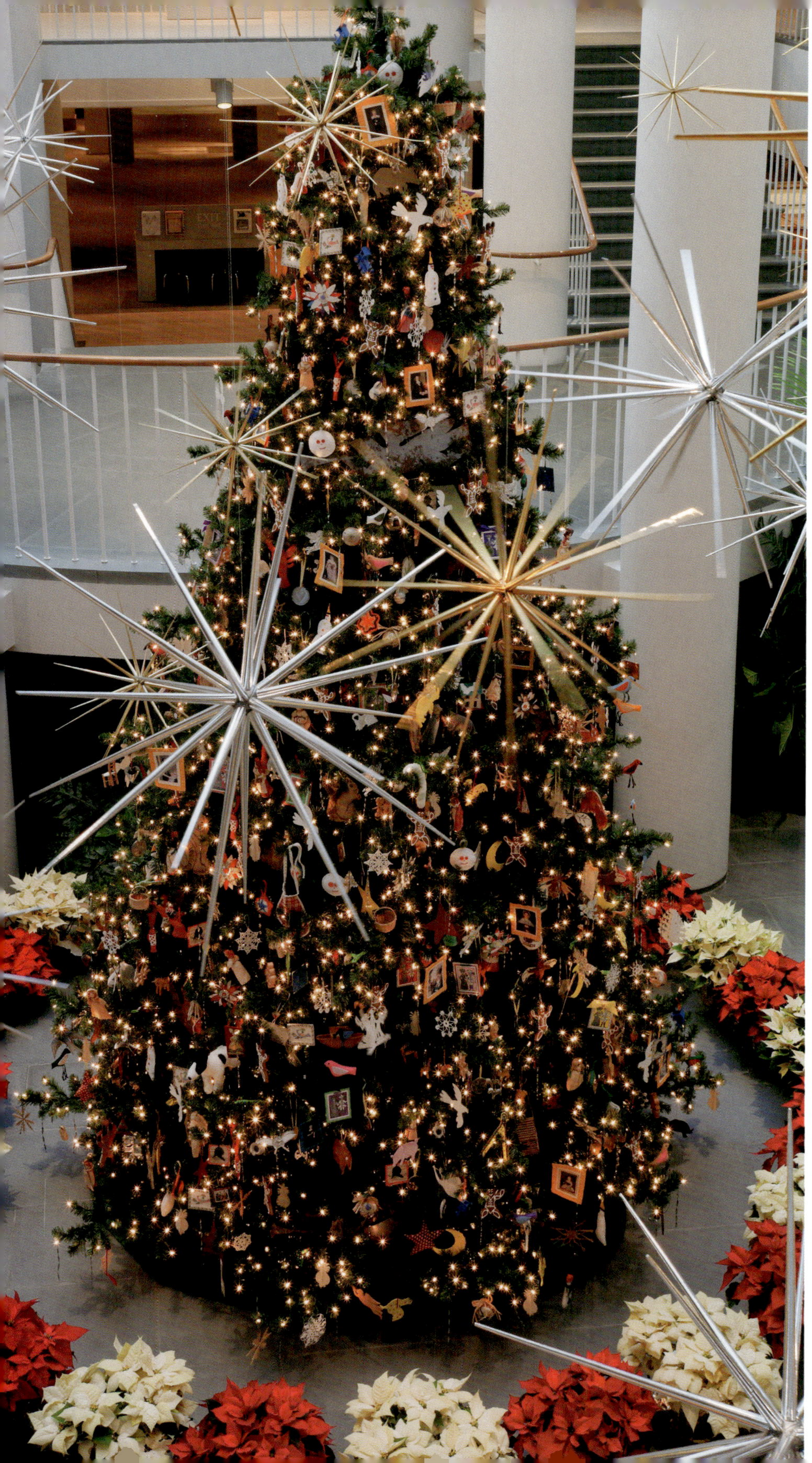

The Art-full Tree

ORNAMENTS TO MAKE
Inspired by the
Abby Aldrich Rockefeller
Folk Art Museum

by Jan Gilliam and
Christina Westenberger

Photography by Tom Green

Colonial Williamsburg
The Colonial Williamsburg Foundation
Williamsburg, Virginia

To all the guests who have visited or will visit
the Abby Aldrich Rockefeller Folk Art Museum during the holiday season
to enjoy the decorated tree.

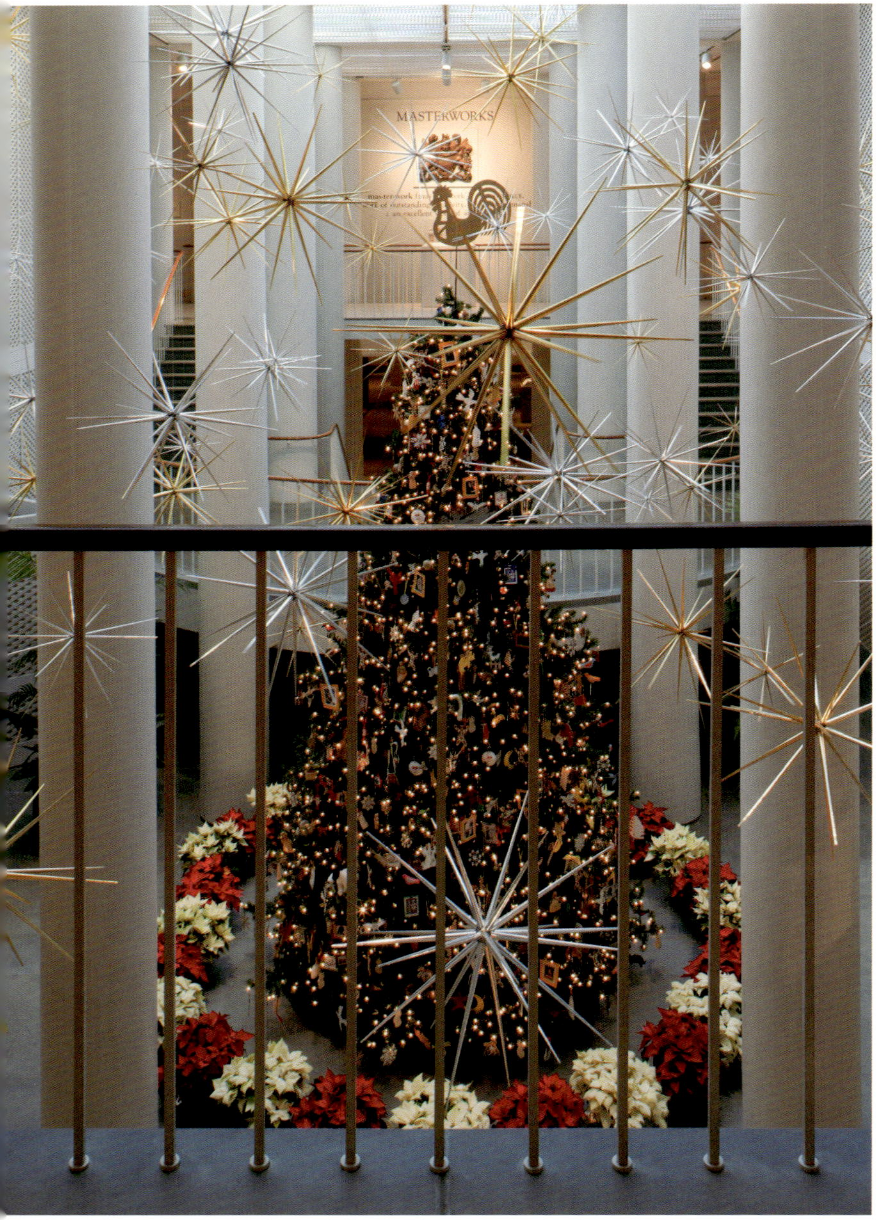

20 19 18 17 16 15 14 13 12 11 1 2 3 4 5 6 7 8 9

Printed in Singapore

Library of Congress Cataloging-in-Publication Data

Gilliam, Jan Kirsten.
The Art-full tree : ornaments to make inspired by the Abby Aldrich Rockefeller Folk Art Museum / by Jan Gilliam and Christina Westenberger ; photography by Tom Green, Hans Lorenz, and Craig McDougal.
p. cm.
ISBN 978-0-87935-249-3 (pbk. : alk. paper) 1. Christmas tree ornaments. 2. Folk art--Virginia--Williamsburg. 3. Abby Aldrich Rockefeller Folk Art Collection. I. Westenberger, Christina, 1969- II. Abby Aldrich Rockefeller Folk Art Collection. III. Title.
TT900.C4G487 2011
745.594'12--dc22
2011007727

Designed by Helen M. Olds

Additional photography by Hans Lorenz and Craig McDougal

Drawings of stitches by Elizabeth Eaton

The Colonial Williamsburg Foundation
PO Box 1776
Williamsburg, VA 23187-1776
www.history.org

Contents

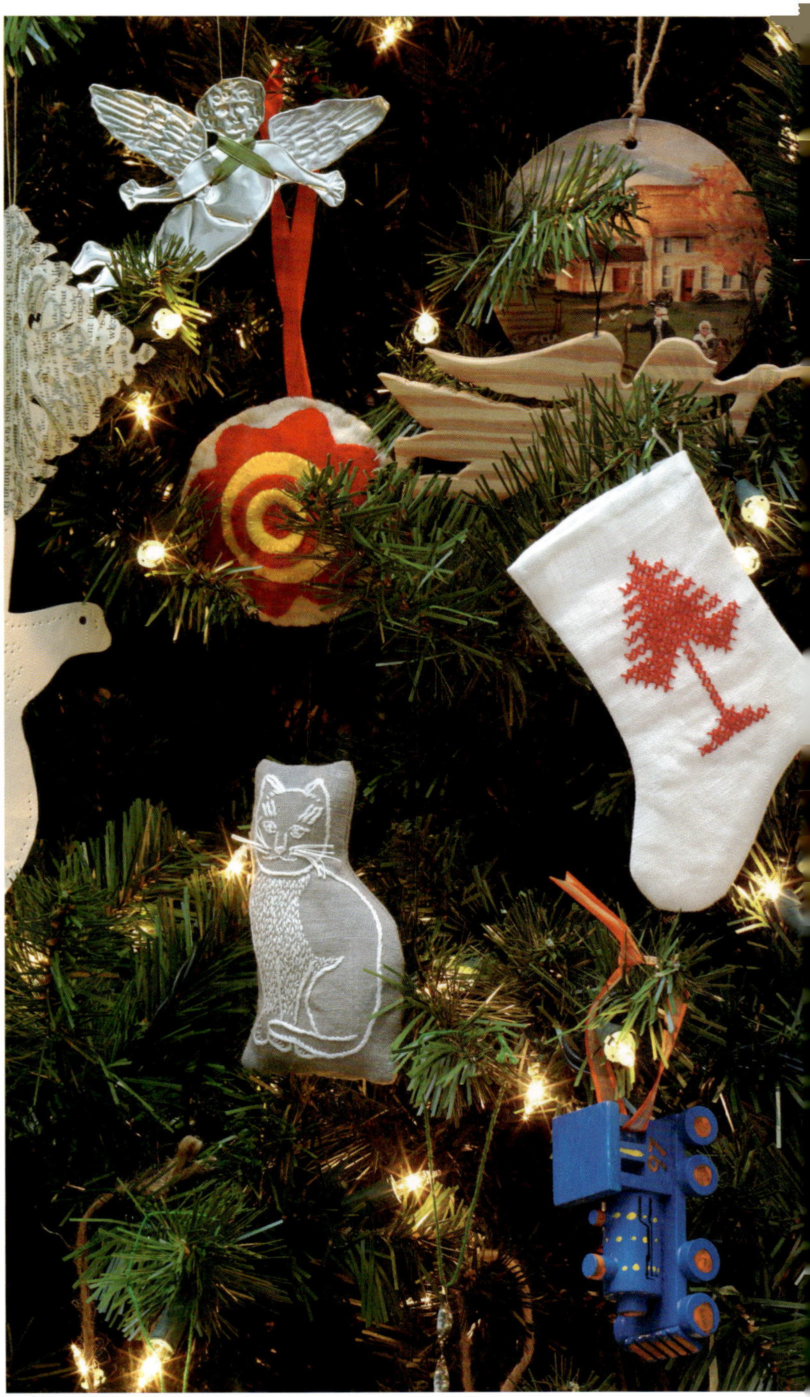

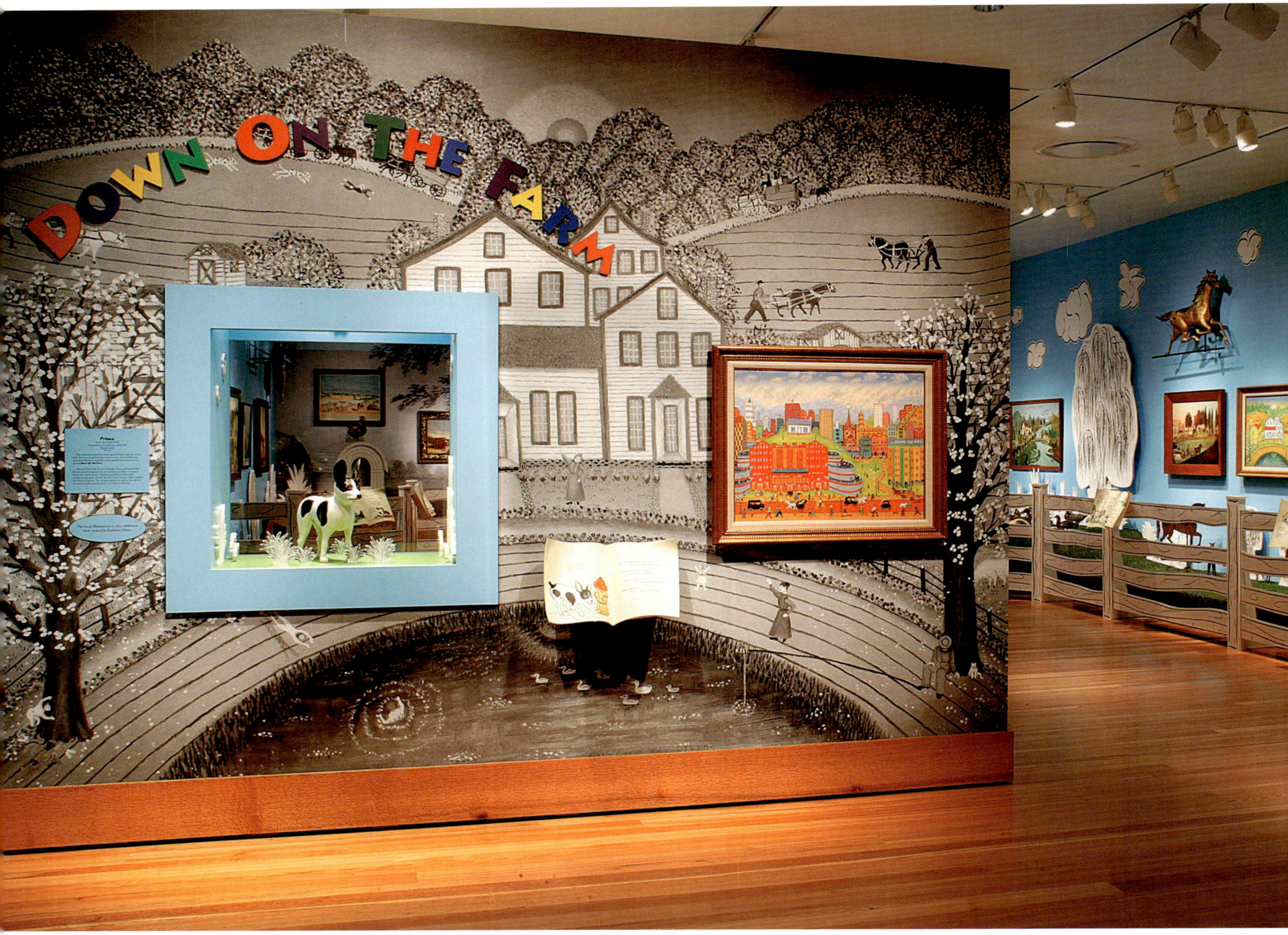
DOWN ON THE FARM

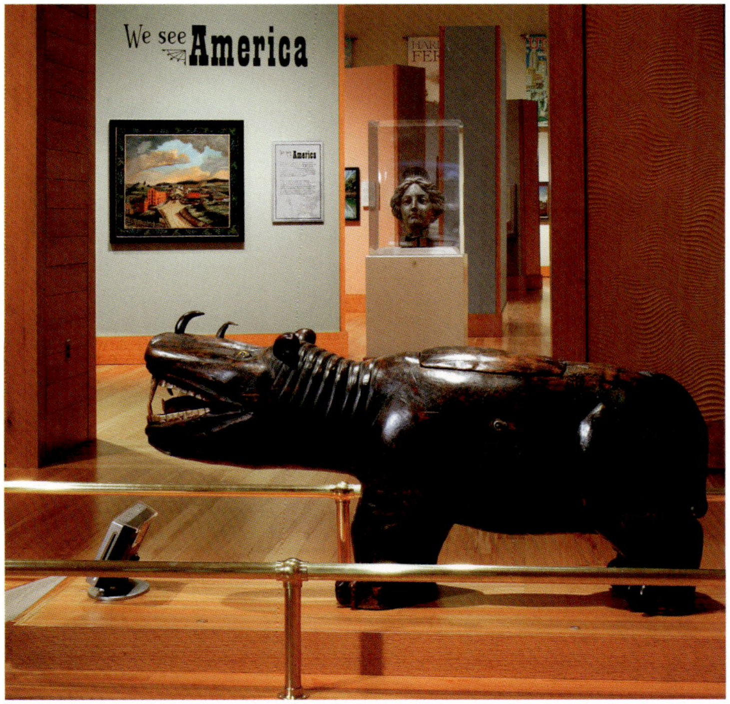

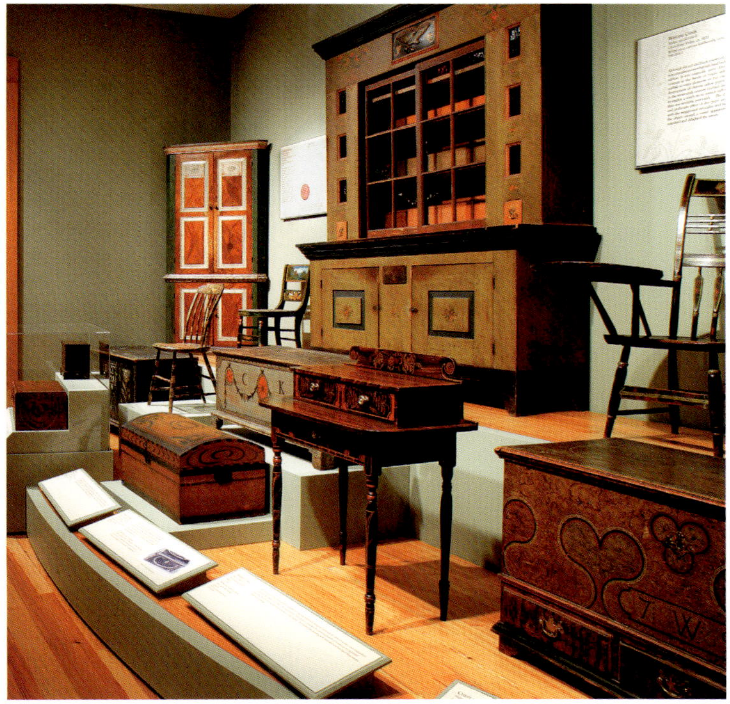

A Folk Art Tradition

What inspires you?

For us, it is the wonderful collection of American folk art that we have the privilege of working with every day. The Abby Aldrich Rockefeller Folk Art Museum collects and exhibits some of the best American folk art in the country. Abby Aldrich Rockefeller started collecting in the 1920s. At the time, there was little interest in folk art and not much information. Mrs. Rockefeller pioneered the effort to win appreciation for the work of the common man (and woman) and anonymously lent her collection to exhibitions that brought folk art to the public's attention. During her lifetime, she displayed the art in her home in New York as well as in Bassett Hall, the home of the Rockefellers in Williamsburg. By the time of her death in 1948, she had acquired over four hundred pieces ranging from oil portraits to needlework to sculpture. She left the collection to the Colonial Williamsburg Foundation, and it forms the core of today's collection, which now numbers over four thousand pieces.

After his wife's death, John D. Rockefeller Jr. provided the funds to build a museum that would allow the collection to be seen by all visitors to Williamsburg. The Abby Aldrich Rockefeller Folk Art Collection opened in 1957 and was the first museum in the country dedicated to the display of American folk art. Over the years, guests have enjoyed hundreds of exhibitions highlighting all aspects of the collection.

A particularly large number of guests visit between Thanksgiving and New Year's. All of Colonial Williamsburg's exhibition sites get decked out for the holidays, and the museum is no exception. One of the most beloved traditions is the large Christmas tree in the museum lobby decorated solely with handmade ornaments. At first, staff and volunteers created the ornaments—some based on objects in the collection and some based on the skills each person brought to the table. From there the tree blossomed. Guests started leaving their own handmade ornaments on the tree. Visitors came back year after year to enjoy the tree and admire the handiwork. In 1975, then First Lady Betty Ford asked the museum staff to provide ornaments for the White House tree in the Blue Room. Staff, volunteers, and members of the local community, honored by the request, created almost three thousand handmade ornaments.

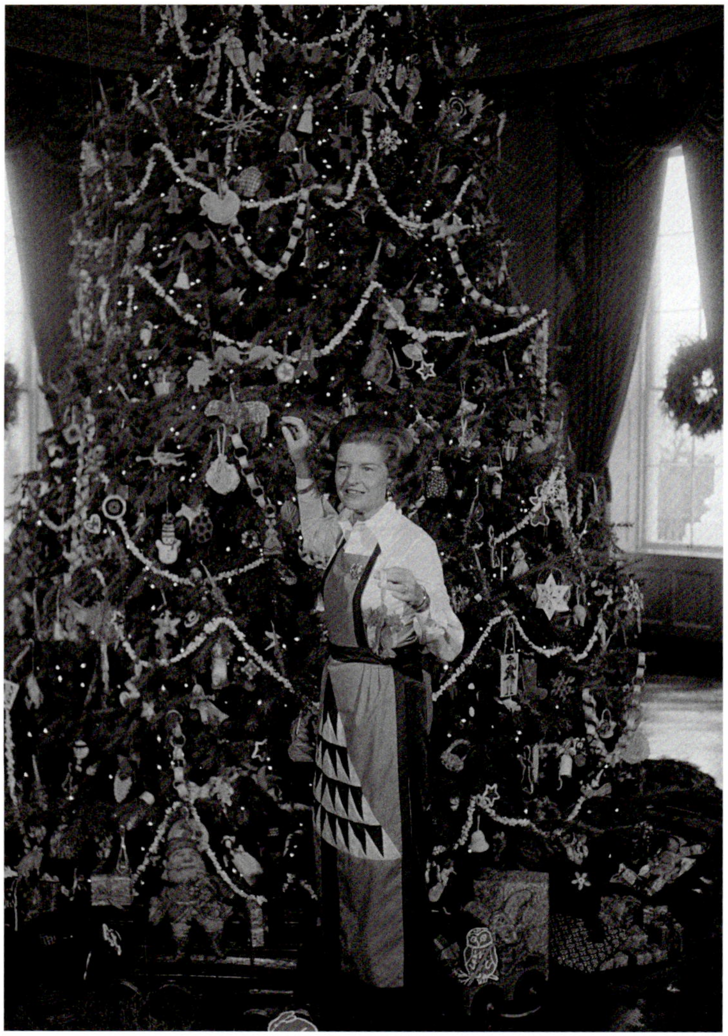

White House 1975

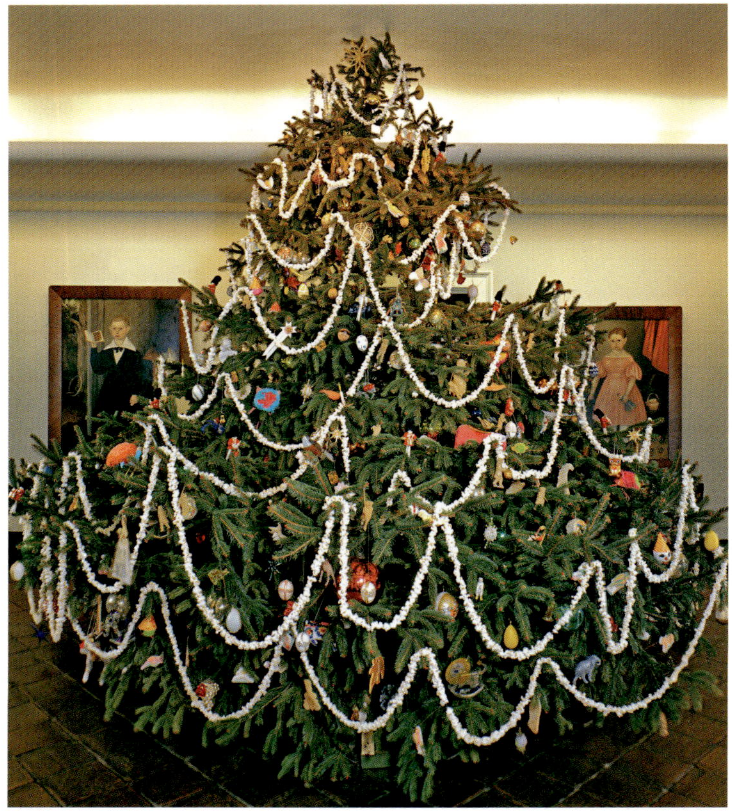

1963

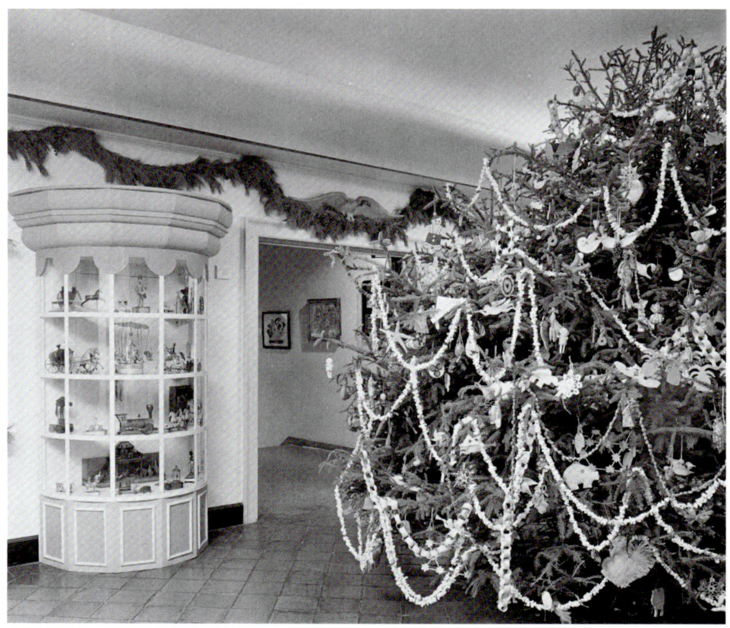

1977

With the move of the Folk Art Museum to its new building in 2007, the tree has a more prominent place in a wonderful sky-lit central area. The two-story center court allows for a sixteen-foot tree that showcases handmade ornaments both new and old. The tree is topped with a handmade replica of the museum's logo, a rooster weather vane from the collection. With over one thousand ornaments, it takes two days and lots of hands to get the tree ready.

All the projects in this book have been inspired by pieces in the collection. Of course, of the four thousand art objects, we could select only a small fraction. That was our hardest chore. Every time we thought we had our selections, we would walk through a gallery or into storage and a new idea would come to mind. Inspiration overwhelmed us! As we started to create the ornaments, we found some ideas worked better than others, so we shelved some ideas and carried on with others. It was exciting to see the art we admired translated into a new form of art. We came to appreciate the original art even more as we took inspiration from it. Since understanding the art is critical to the success of our projects, we have included full-color images of the art as well as information about the pieces. We were inspired by looking at the objects, but we also found that sometimes the stories behind the pieces or something about the artist or the construction or even the owner made a difference in our reaction to the piece. Knowing that the little girl in a portrait died young or that the artist painted images based on her childhood gave us an additional perspective from which to consider the art.

One of the great things about working on this book was the creative process. The different projects included here are the results of hours of trial and error. But, what we have included is not the only approach. We encourage you to make these projects your own. Be inspired! Maybe you will change the color or the size or the material. Maybe you don't have the supplies on our list in hand, and maybe other materials you do have will work just as well. Maybe you have seen art at another museum that captured your imagination. There are countless ornaments waiting to be created. As you get caught up in the creative process, have fun. We did.

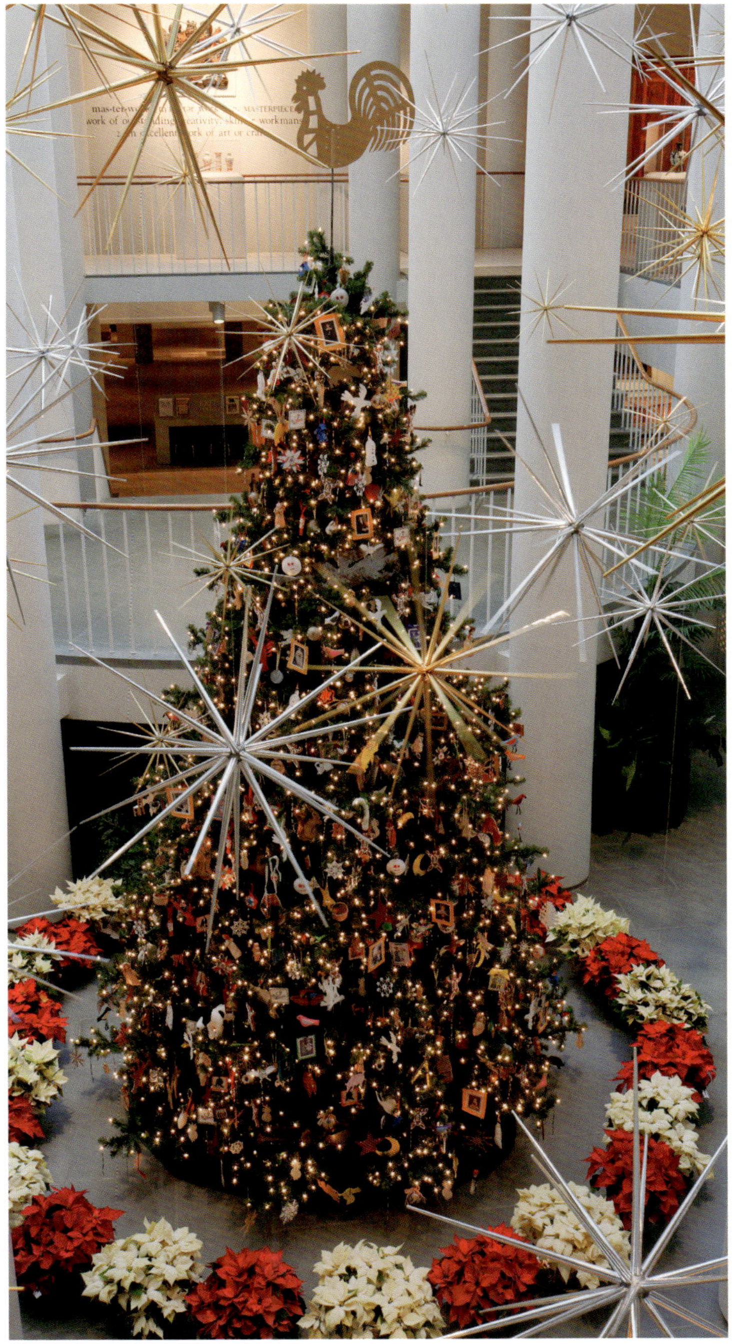

2010

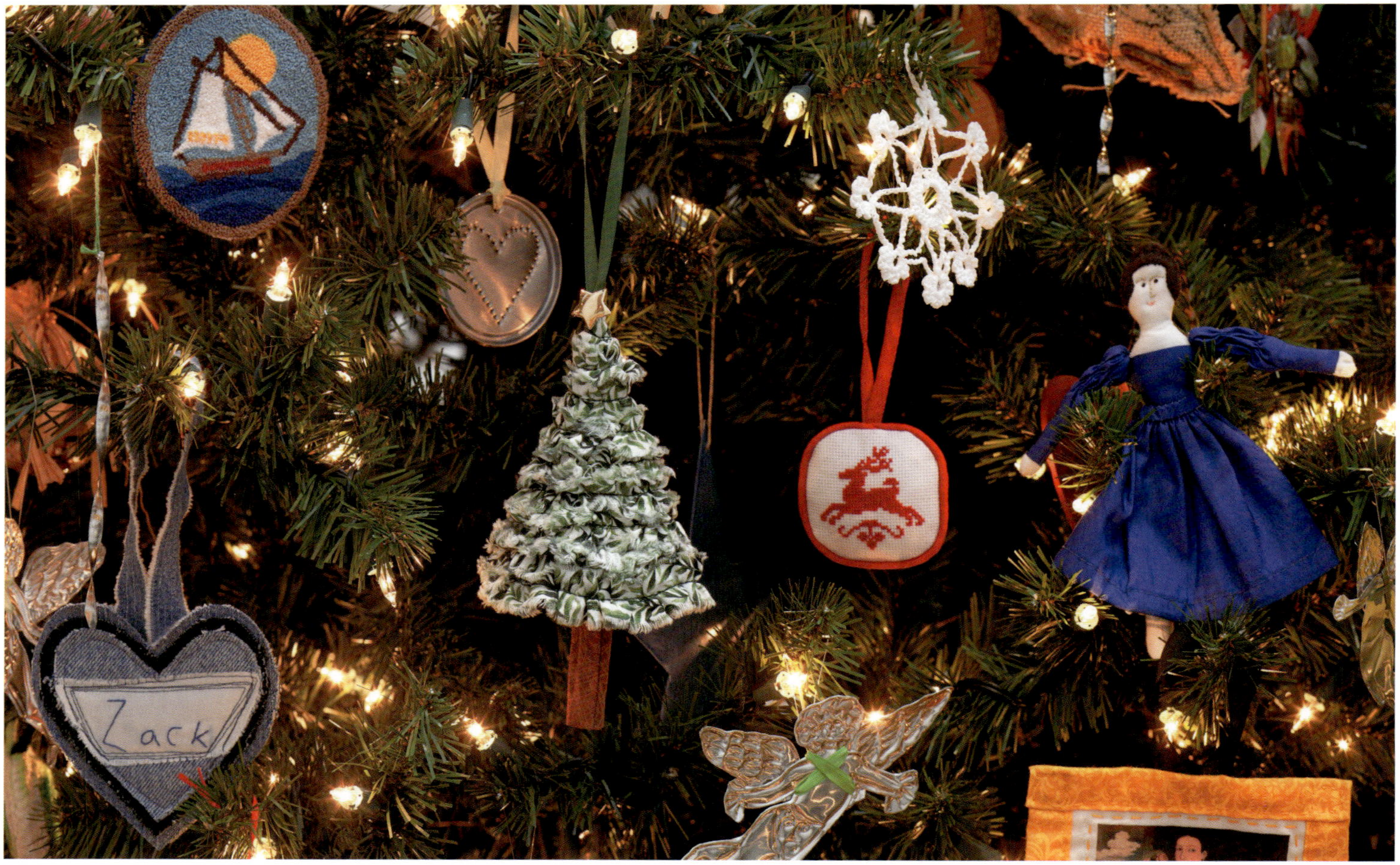

Before You Begin

INSTRUCTIONS

The instructions for each project begin with a list of items you will need in the order in which you will need them. This list is followed by detailed instructions and illustrations on how to create the project. Read through the list and the instructions before beginning.

You can make your ornament just like ours or add your own touches. Change the colors, add different embellishments, use different materials.

When gathering your supplies, if you don't have exactly what is suggested, consider alternatives that you might have on hand. Floss can be substituted for wool, for example, and some fabrics can be substituted for others.

IDEAS

For each project, we give suggestions on ways to alter it. While working through the projects, we thought of lots of things to try differently. The ideas sections (in red type) propose some of our favorite variations. We are sure there are others, so be creative!

TEMPLATES

To make many of the ornaments, you will need to use the templates that appear in the back of the book. If needed, the template will be identified in the materials list for each project.

We have included full-size templates that can be photocopied or traced directly from the pages. In most instances, a paper copy of the template is fine, but, if you prefer heavier paper or cardboard (like a cereal box), that will work too and last longer if you want to make multiples of the same project. Take note in the instructions though: some projects will require paper because you will need the thinness or transparency of it.

The way that you use the template will depend on the material with which you are working. If you are working with paper, cloth, or plastic, trace the template onto the paper, cloth, or plastic. If you are working with felt, pin the paper template to the felt. With foil, tape the paper template to the foil. Additional information for using the templates will be given in the project instructions as necessary.

THREADS

Throughout the book, there are several types of thread and yarn used. These are standard types found at most fabric or craft stores. We use regular sewing thread (listed as "thread"), embroidery floss (listed as "floss"), quilting thread, and wool yarn.

The floss and the yarn are made of multiple strands that can be separated. When the floss is used for sewing (as in the felt projects), use two of the six strands that make up the floss. For the cross-stitching projects, also use two strands. For the punch-needle projects, use three strands. For the needlepoint projects, use one strand of the three making up a piece of wool yarn.

Using the floss for sewing and cross-stitching: Cut a length of floss about a yard long, roughly two arms' length. Pull one strand from the six strands. Fold it in half (this gives you the two strands), and thread both ends into the needle. When you begin the first stitch, bring the needle up through the cloth but don't pull the thread all the way through. As you push the needle back down through the cloth, catch the loop and your thread is secure. Weave your loose thread ends in on the back of your stitching when you begin with the next strand of floss.

Using the floss for punch-needle projects: Follow the directions on the punch-needle packaging.

Using the wool yarn: Cut a length of yarn about 18 inches, roughly one arm's length. Pull one strand from the three strands. When you begin stitching, push the needle up from the back of the fabric but hold about ½ inch of the yarn on the back of the canvas. Catch this piece within the first few stitches. When you are at the end of the strand, pull through to the back side and thread the needle through a row of stitches to secure.

A guide for all of the stitches used in the projects is at the back of the book.

CANVAS FOR NEEDLEPOINT PROJECTS

For the needlepoint projects, prepare your canvas by placing masking tape along the four edges to keep the canvas from unraveling as you work.

The instructions will tell you to trim the canvas when finishing the project. To do this, cut off the excess canvas making sure to leave about six holes beyond the worked area for the seam.

METAL FOIL

Metal foil (36-gauge tooling foil) is fun to work with and renders a wonderful final product. It can be purchased from art supply stores.

Although the foil can be cut with regular scissors, we recommend using embroidery scissors as they give the cut edge an attractive slight curve. The foil also will sharpen your scissors as you cut!

The foil can be manipulated easily, but keep in mind that it is metal and the edges can be sharp, so be careful.

We use aluminum and copper foils in the projects. We experimented with brass foil but found it more difficult to work with. If you don't have access to metal foil, try using a clean pie tin.

FELT

Felt can be purchased off the bolt or in 9 x 12–inch pieces. Either will work for these projects.

When cutting the felt for a project, it is best to cut one piece at a time. If you stack the felt to cut out multiple pieces of the same template, the layers tend to shift, so the pieces may end up not being the same size.

Using two strands of floss when sewing felt pieces together gives the stitching more weight so that it becomes a decorative element of the finished product as well as holding the pieces together. You can experiment with one or three strands if you like.

BIRDS AND TREE

Eddie Arning (1898–1993), Austin, Texas, 1969, oil pastel and pencil on paper, 19 5/8" x 25 3/4", gift of Dr. and Mrs. Alexander Sackton, 1984.201.2

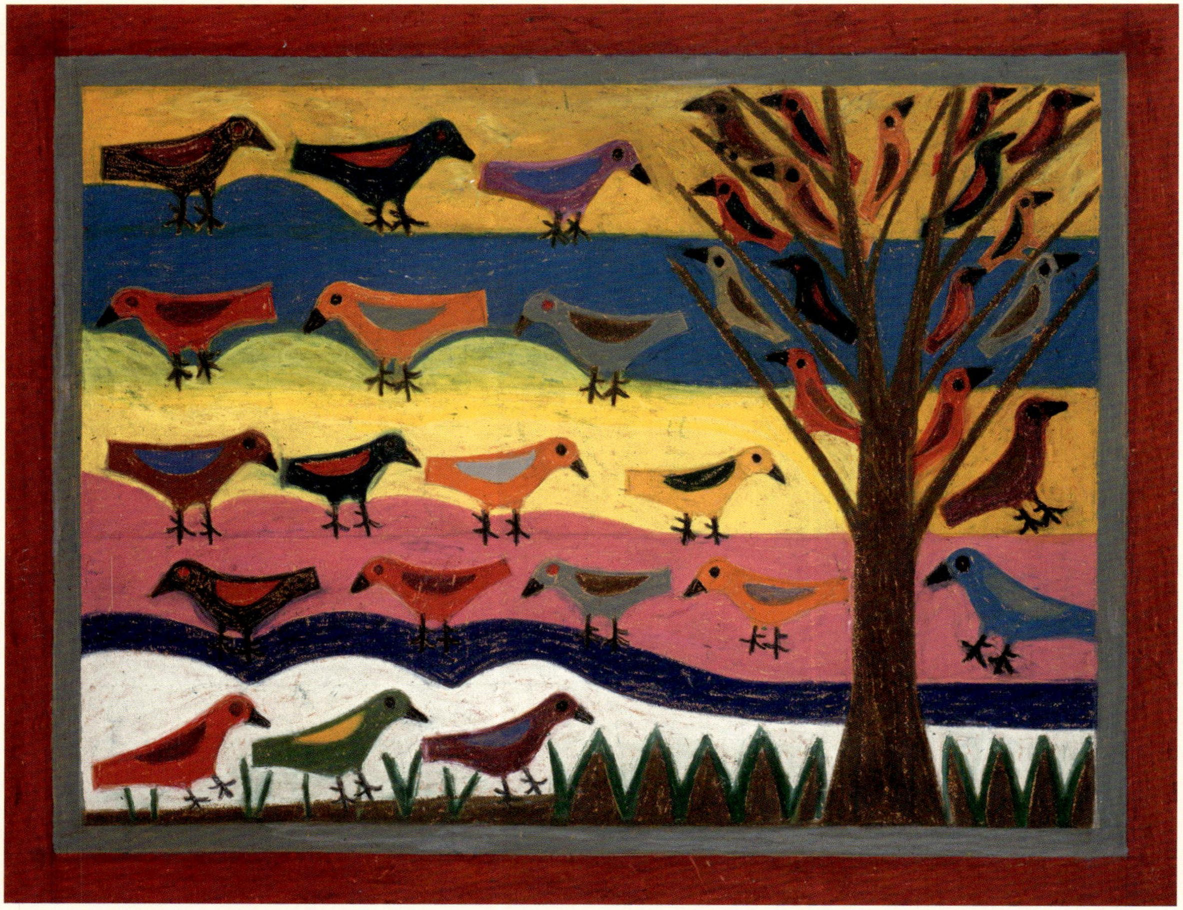

This colorful oil pastel drawing was created by Eddie Arning when he was in his early seventies. His inspiration was an illustration by an eleven year old that appeared in *McCall's* magazine. That picture was titled "Leaves," but Arning chose to interpret the shapes as birds.

Drawing was not a lifelong ambition for Arning. He spent most of his adult life in mental institutions suffering from depression and withdrawal. It wasn't until 1964, when Arning was in his sixties, that an aide, Helen Mayfield, introduced the artist to coloring and drawing. Arning filled paper after paper with crayon drawings. Some pieces depicted farm animals and objects that he remembered from his childhood. Arning liked to collect things, including illustrations and advertisements from magazines. He used these as inspiration for much of his art. He didn't copy the pictures but rather interpreted them to suit his own sense of color, arrangement, and ideas. In 1969, he switched from crayons to oil pastels. For almost ten years, he continued to create his art, ultimately producing over two thousand works.

The artist died in 1993. Today, his art is exhibited in galleries and museums including the Abby Aldrich Rockefeller Folk Art Museum, the Smithsonian, and the Museum of American Folk Art in New York. The Abby Aldrich Rockefeller Folk Art Museum owns twelve drawings by Arning, all of them donated in 1984 by Dr. and Mrs. Alexander Sackton, who knew Arning personally and admired his work.

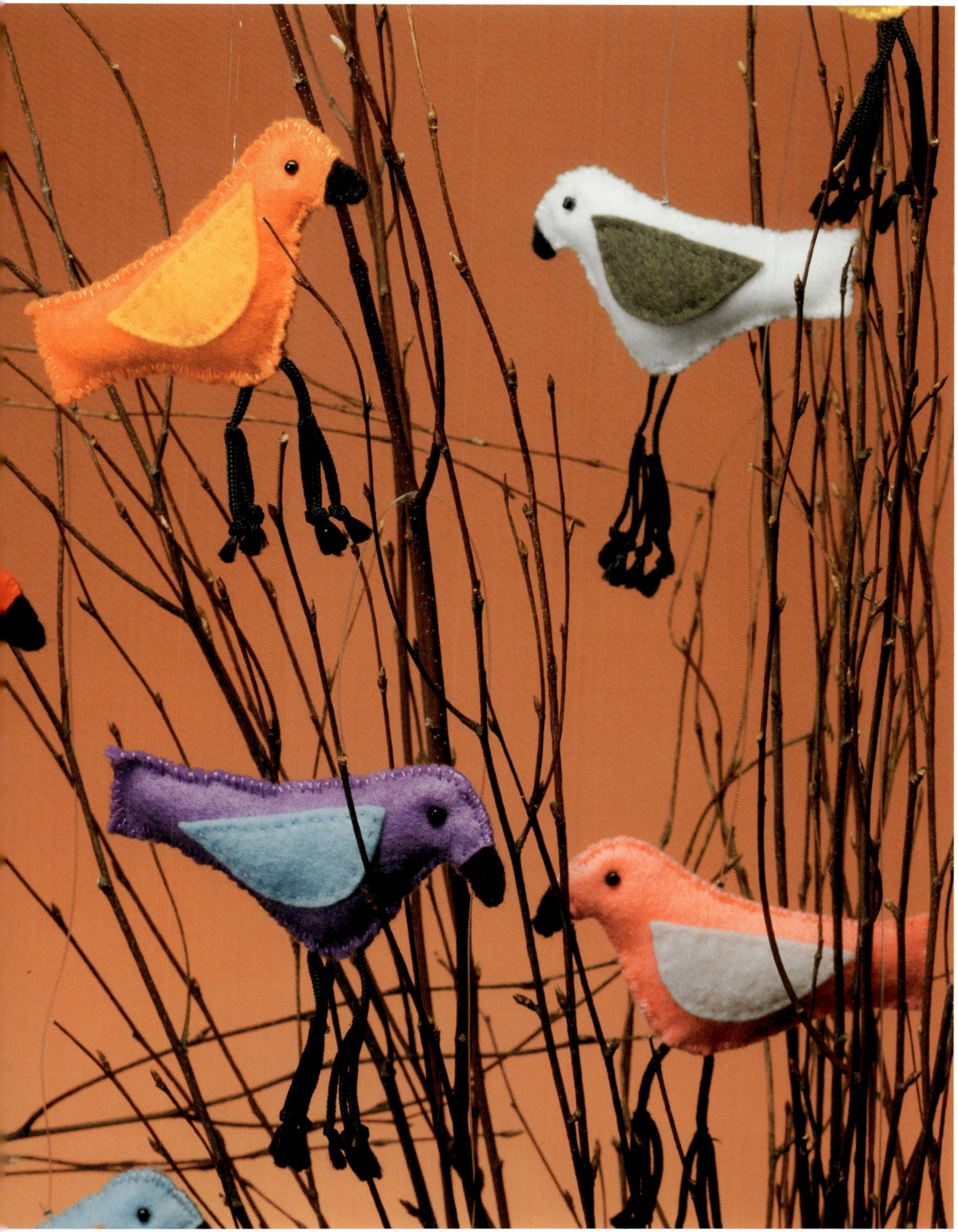

Felt Birds

ARNING WAS INSPIRED BY OTHER PEOPLE'S WORK, AND SO IT SEEMS NATURAL FOR HIS WORK TO INSPIRE US. WE COULD NOT RESIST THE CHARM AND COLOR OF HIS BIRDS. THEY SEEM READY TO JUMP OFF THE PAPER AND ONTO THE TREE. ANY COLORS WORK FOR THIS PROJECT.

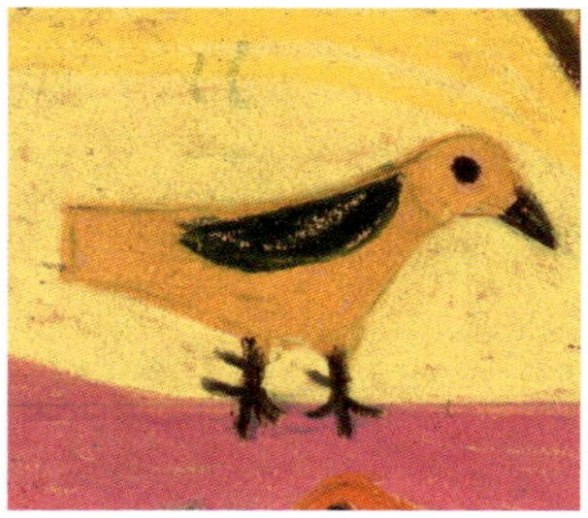

WHAT YOU NEED:

- Beak, body, and wing templates (page 128)
- Black cord
- Ruler
- Scissors
- Needle
- Black thread
- Black felt
- Two contrasting colors of felt (other than black)
- Matching floss
- Pins
- Stuffing
- Four black glass beads, size E
- Two crimp beads, 2 mm
- Fishing line, 18 inches long
- Pliers

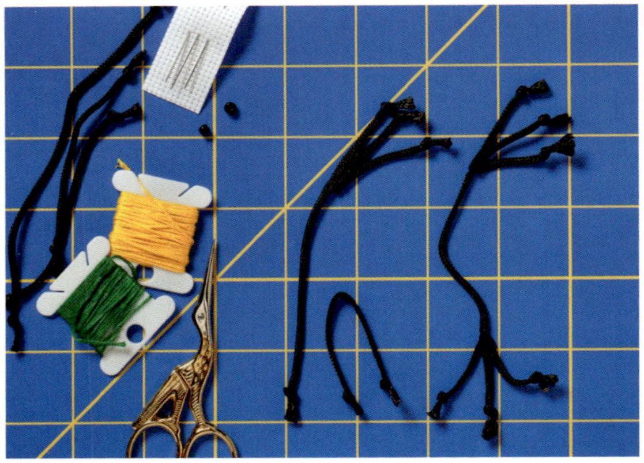

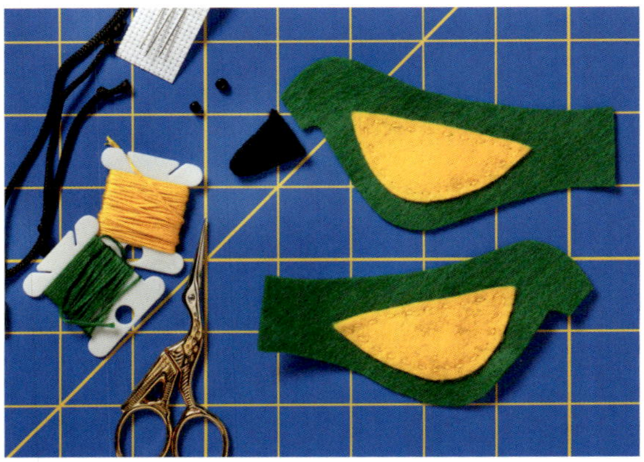

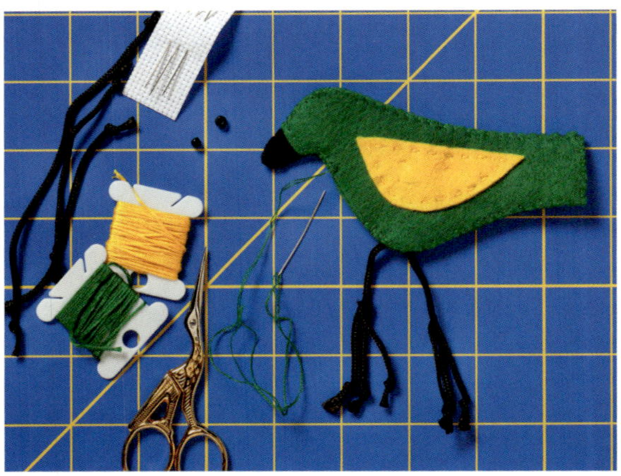

INSTRUCTIONS:

Make the legs first: Tie a knot in the end of the black cord. Measure 4 inches, tie another knot, and snip. Set aside the 4-inch cord for the moment. Again, tie a knot in the end of the cord, but measure 2 inches this time, tie another knot, and snip. Repeat so that you have two 2-inch cords. Attach the 2-inch cords to the 4-inch cord: Fold one of the 2-inch cords in half, match up the knots with one of the knots on the 4-inch cord, and stitch together at the fold. Attach the second 2-inch cord at the other end of the 4-inch cord. Set aside.

Using the templates, cut two black felt beaks, two bird bodies of one color of felt, and two wings of a contrasting color. Stitch the beaks together with black thread using a whipstitch. Stitch one wing to each of the bird bodies with matching floss using the running stitch.

Place the bird bodies wrong side together and pin. With matching floss, begin at the front of the bird tummy and whipstitch together. When you reach the middle of the tummy, stop and fold the legs in half. Tuck fold just inside the bird and stitch into place. Continue to whipstitch around the bird to the beak. Slip the beak into the bird up to the dotted line shown on the template and stitch together. You may need to add a couple of extra stitches to cover up any beak black. Stuff. Stitch closed.

For the finishing touch, add the eyes (black beads): Using the floss that matches the felt body color, pull the threaded needle through all layers at the place you would like the eyes to be. As the needle comes out one side, thread on one bead. Take the needle back through all the layers at a point right next to where the needle came through and thread on the other bead. Go through both beads once more pulling tight and knot.

Repeat all for the second bird.

To create the hanger, place a crimp bead onto the fishing line. With the crimp bead hanging loosely on the line for the moment, push the end of the fishing line through the very top of the bird's back just under the stitching, insert the end of the fishing line back through the crimp bead, and close with pliers. Snip excess line. Repeat on the other end of the line with the second bird.

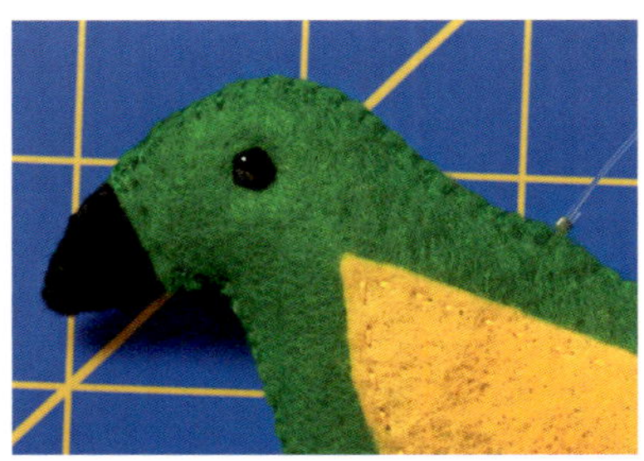

IDEAS: CREATE SEVERAL INDIVIDUAL BIRDS AND MAKE A COLORFUL MOBILE. LOOKING FOR A KID-FRIENDLY PROJECT? MAKE THESE BIRDS OUT OF PAPER.

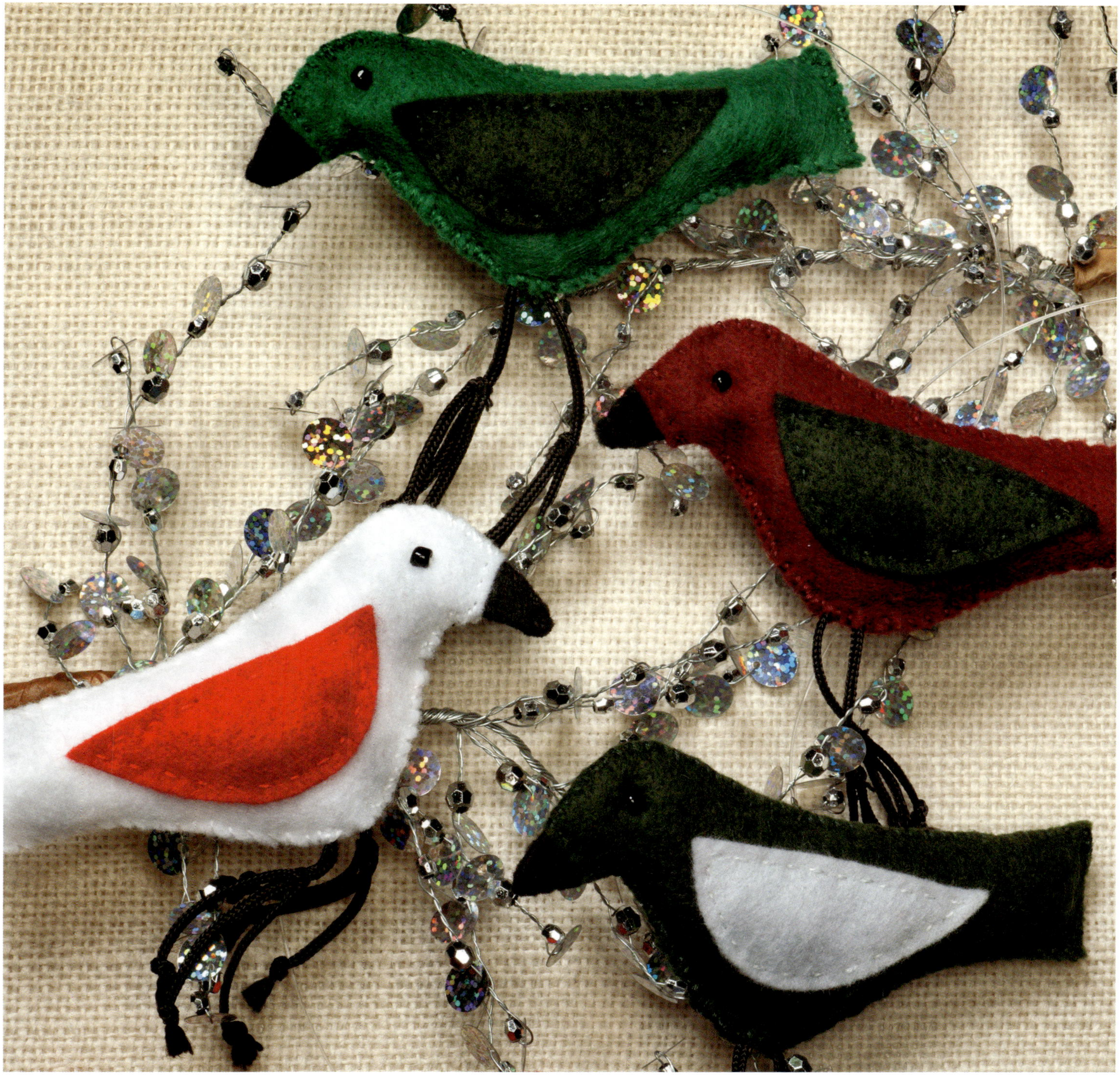

FROG

Miles Burkholder Carpenter (1889–1985), Waverly, Virginia, 1982, wood and paint, 12" long, 1996.701.1

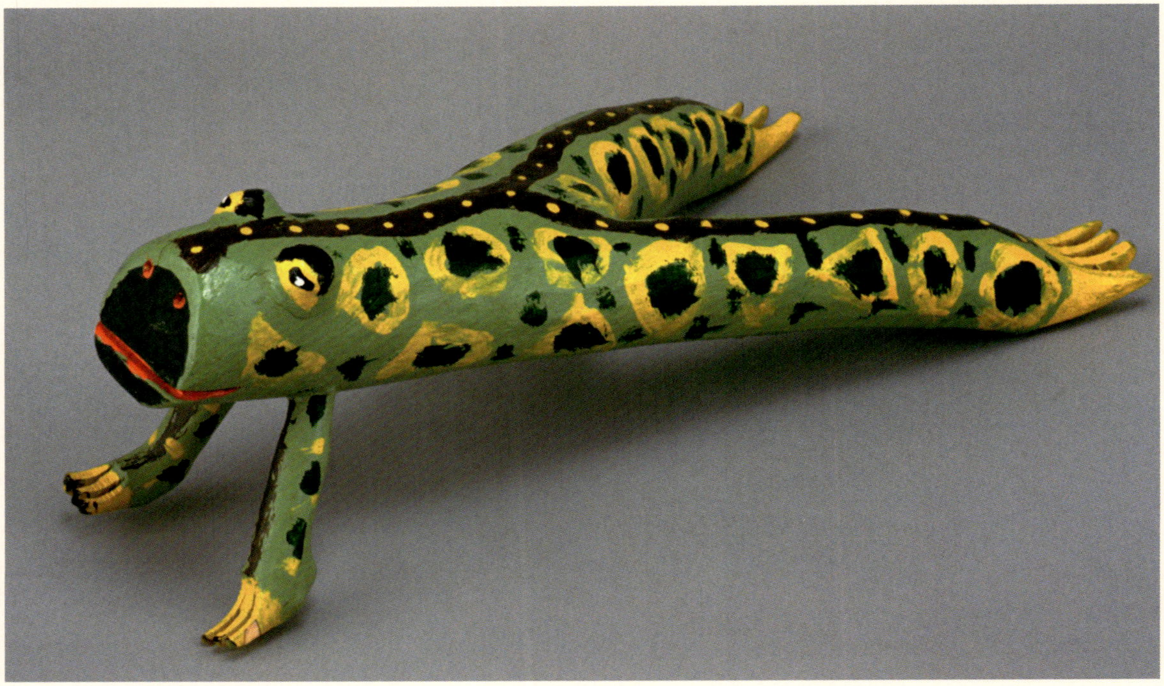

Wood was a material well used by the artist Miles Carpenter. Many of his pieces were created from found pieces of wood—fallen tree limbs, dug-up roots, and simple sticks. In each random piece, he found a creature waiting to emerge. The frog is readily identifiable. The artist's imagination and skill bring it to life.

Carpenter, born in Pennsylvania, grew up working in the family sawmill. Once married, he moved to Waverly, Virginia, in 1910 and set up in the same trade. With the advent of World War II, work at the sawmill declined and prompted Carpenter to begin creating his carvings from the odd bits of wood left around. Once production picked back up at the mill, he put the carving aside. In 1955, after retiring, he took it up again for pleasure. He also set up a roadside stand from which he sold ice and homegrown vegetables. Eleven years later, after his wife died, he set to whittling and painting more often. He displayed the pieces for sale in the back of his truck next to his stand.

Carpenter died in 1985. Today, he is known for his imaginative creations that include not only frogs but also biblical figures, politicians, and monsters, these last truly inspired by the unique twists and gnarls found in roots and branches.

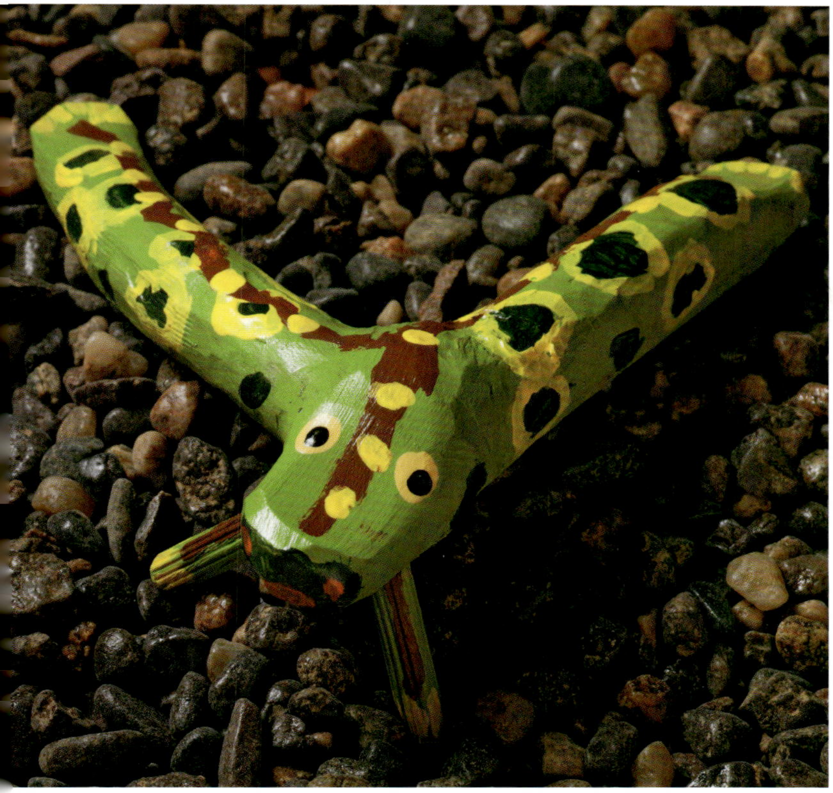

Wooden Frog

MILES CARPENTER WAS INSPIRED BY WOOD HE FOUND LYING ABOUT. TAKE THE WHOLE FAMILY OUTDOORS IN SEARCH OF THE PERFECT FROG BODY BRANCH.

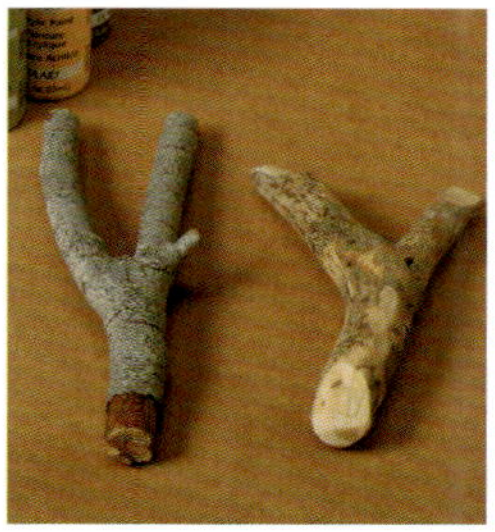

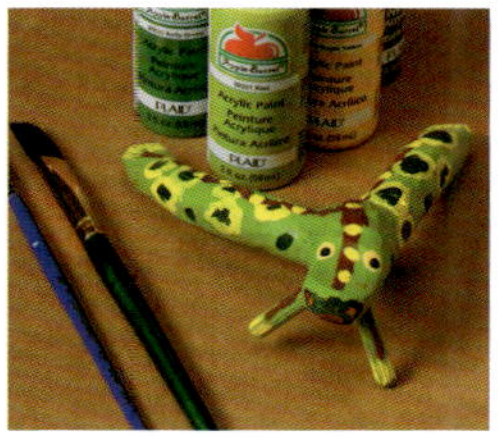

WHAT YOU NEED:

- Thick Y-shaped branch (one that won't snap apart)
- Pruning snips
- Sandpaper or hand sander
- Two 3/8-inch dowel pins, 2 inches long
- Drill with 3/8-inch drill bit
- Wood glue
- White spray paint
- Paintbrushes
- Acrylic paints in several colors (we used Apple Barrel colors leaf green, hunter green, canary yellow, nutmeg brown, cardinal crimson, and black)
- Spray shellac

INSTRUCTIONS:

Prepare your branch: With pruning snips, trim the branch to bring out the frog shape. Remove the bark and sand the entire branch smooth. Flatten the tips of the branch for the legs so that it will rest flat on a surface.

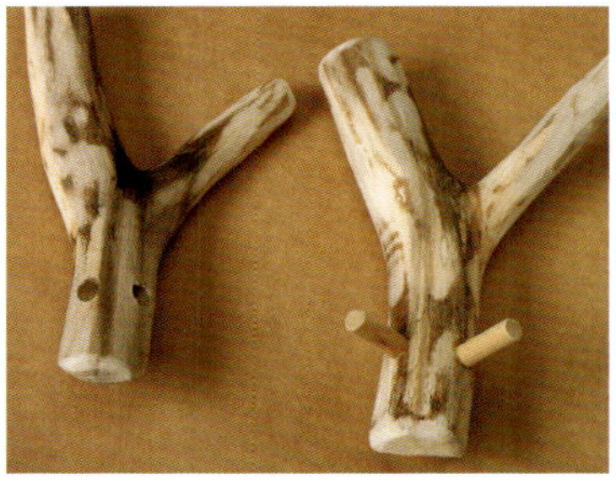

Construct the frog: On the underside of the branch, between the back legs and head, drill two holes. Fill the holes with wood glue and insert the 2-inch dowel pins to create the front legs. Allow the glue to dry.

Once the glue has dried, spray-paint the entire piece white.

Paint the frog: Begin with the base coat and cover the entire branch. Let that dry, and then continue with other colors, letting them dry between layers. Once you are satisfied with the look, let it dry completely. Then give the frog a coat of spray shellac following the manufacturer's instructions.

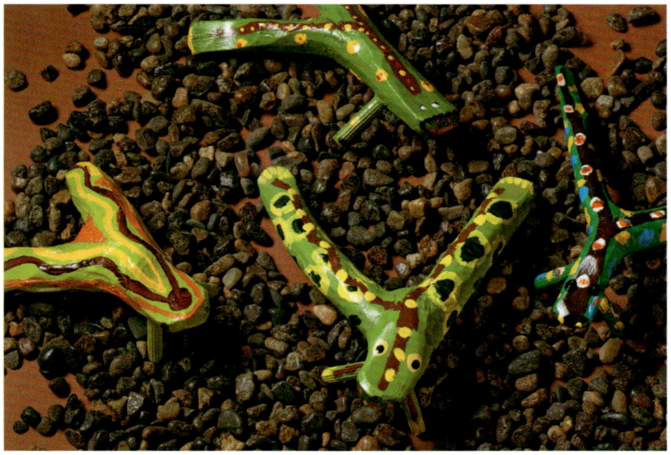

IDEAS: IN YOUR SEARCH FOR THE FROG BODY, KEEP AN OPEN MIND. THE WOOD MIGHT HAVE A DIFFERENT ANIMAL OR PROJECT HIDDEN WITHIN. BE INSPIRED BY WHAT YOU SEE AS YOU LOOK AT THE BRANCHES AND ROOTS. DOES A FROG REALLY HAVE TO BE GREEN? WHEN YOU PAINT YOUR FROG, YOU CAN FOLLOW THE LEAD OF MILES CARPENTER OR DECIDE ON YOUR OWN COLORS AND PATTERN.

SILHOUETTE OF ELIZABETH EDWARDS VAN VOORHIS

William King, New England, probably 1805–1809, cut paper backed with black fabric, 4 5/8" x 3 3/4", gift of Mary B. and William Lehman Guyton, 1999.306.14

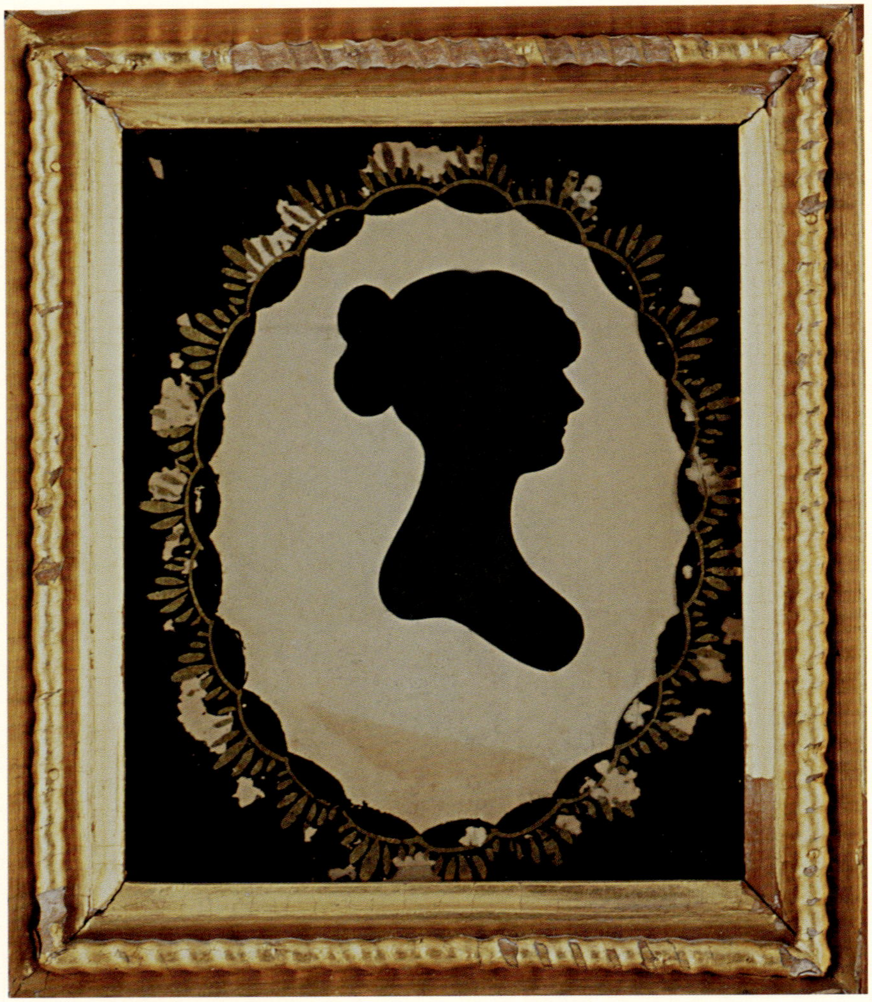

Although we know the name of the sitter in this silhouette portrait, the family context has been lost. A brief, handwritten note on the back of the piece tells us only that Elizabeth was somebody's great-grandmother. Just this simple outline of her has survived the times.

A silhouette, unlike a fully detailed portrait, puts the emphasis on the outline of the person. The profile typically appears in black set against or within a contrasting background. Tracing the outline of a cast shadow onto paper is an easy method that has been practiced for centuries. These solid, "filled" images were appropriately called "shades" or "shadows" in the eighteenth and early nineteenth centuries.

There are two basic types of cutouts: the cut-and-paste and the hollow-cut. The first is as it seems. The drawn profile is cut along the outline and then pasted onto a background. The second method, of which Elizabeth's is one example, involves cutting into the paper and creating a hole in the shape of the profile. This sheet is then backed with paper of a contrasting color that shows through the hole, so the profile deceptively appears to be in the contrasting paper. Hollow-cutting was actually the more popular of the two techniques in the nineteenth century. Silhouettes were at their peak in the early nineteenth century. They were created by both professionals and amateurs.

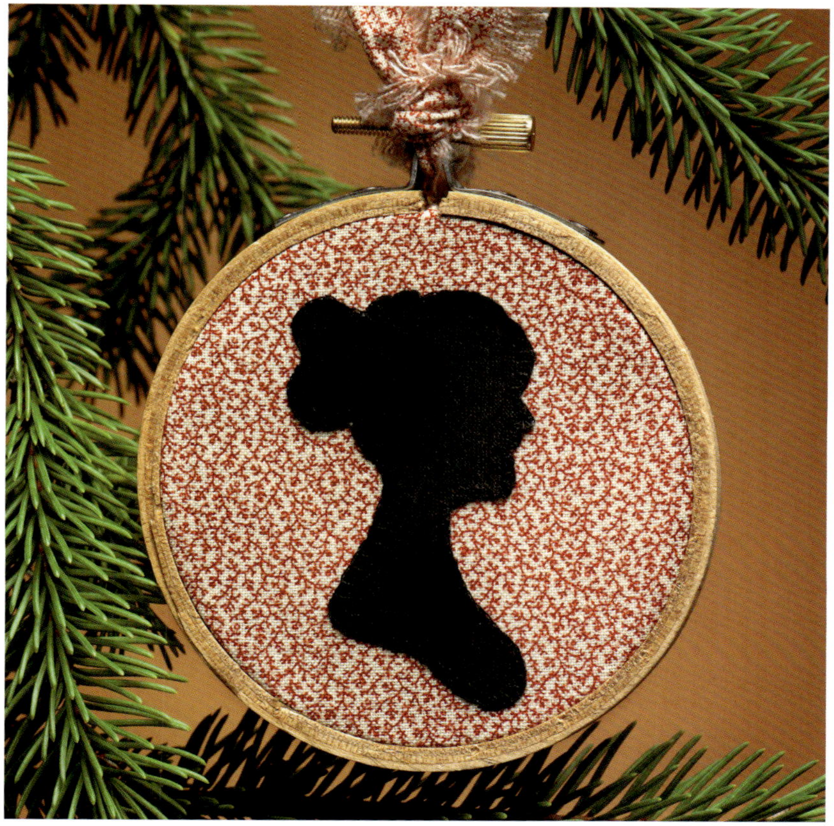

Fabric Silhouette

SILHOUETTES HAVE A SIMPLE AND PERSONAL CHARM MAKING THEM A LOVELY WAY TO REMEMBER SOMEONE AT THE HOLIDAYS. ALTHOUGH SILHOUETTES WERE TRADITIONALLY CRAFTED IN PAPER, THIS ORNAMENT CAPTURES THE LOOK IN A DIFFERENT MEDIUM.

WHAT YOU NEED:

Silhouette template (page 137)
Pins
Black fusible woven interfacing
Matching floss
Embroidery scissors
Iron
Ironing board
Printed cotton fabric, 5 x 5 inches and 1 x 5 inches
3-inch wooden embroidery hoop
Needle

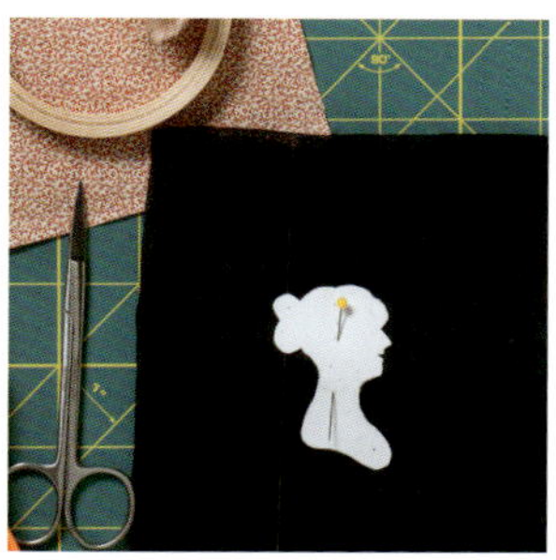

INSTRUCTIONS:

Using the template, cut a silhouette from the interfacing.

Following the manufacturer's instructions for the interfacing, iron the interfacing silhouette to the center of the square piece of cotton fabric.

Place the fabric in the embroidery hoop centering the silhouette with the screw at the top. With one thread of the floss, blanket-stitch around the silhouette. Pull the fabric tight in the hoop, and then trim excess cloth.

Tie the strip of cotton fabric to the top of the embroidery hoop, and tie the two ends together to create a loop for hanging.

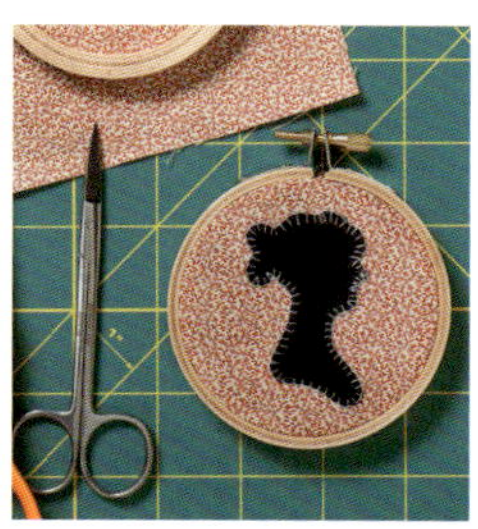

IDEAS: YOU CAN MAKE THIS ORNAMENT MORE PERSONAL BY USING AN INDIVIDUAL'S ACTUAL LIKENESS. HERE'S HOW TO DO IT: HAVE THE PERSON STAND IN FRONT OF A NEUTRAL BACKGROUND FACING SIDEWAYS SO YOU GET A GOOD VIEW OF THE PROFILE. TAKE A PICTURE WITH A DIGITAL CAMERA. DOWNLOAD THE PHOTO AND PRINT IT OUT IN BLACK AND WHITE OR GRAYSCALE. FILL IN THE OUTLINE OF THE PROFILE WITH PENCIL OR PEN. IF IT IS THE RIGHT SIZE, USE IT AS THE TEMPLATE. USE A PHOTOCOPIER TO MAKE IT LARGER OR SMALLER. YOU CAN ALSO USE OLD PHOTOS. PHOTOCOPY THEM AND FOLLOW THE SAME PROCESS. THINK ABOUT SELECTING A FABRIC THAT MIGHT REFLECT SOMETHING ABOUT THE SITTER.

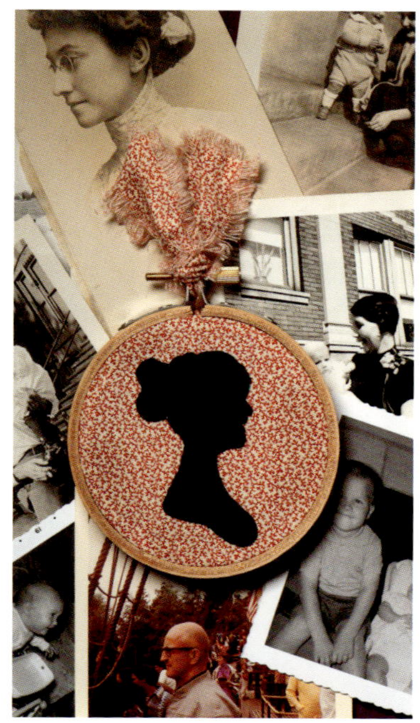

DEER WEATHER VANE

probably Pennsylvania, possibly 1890–1910,
iron and paint, 20 3/4" x 32 1/4" x 3/4",
gift of Abby Aldrich Rockefeller, 1931.800.5

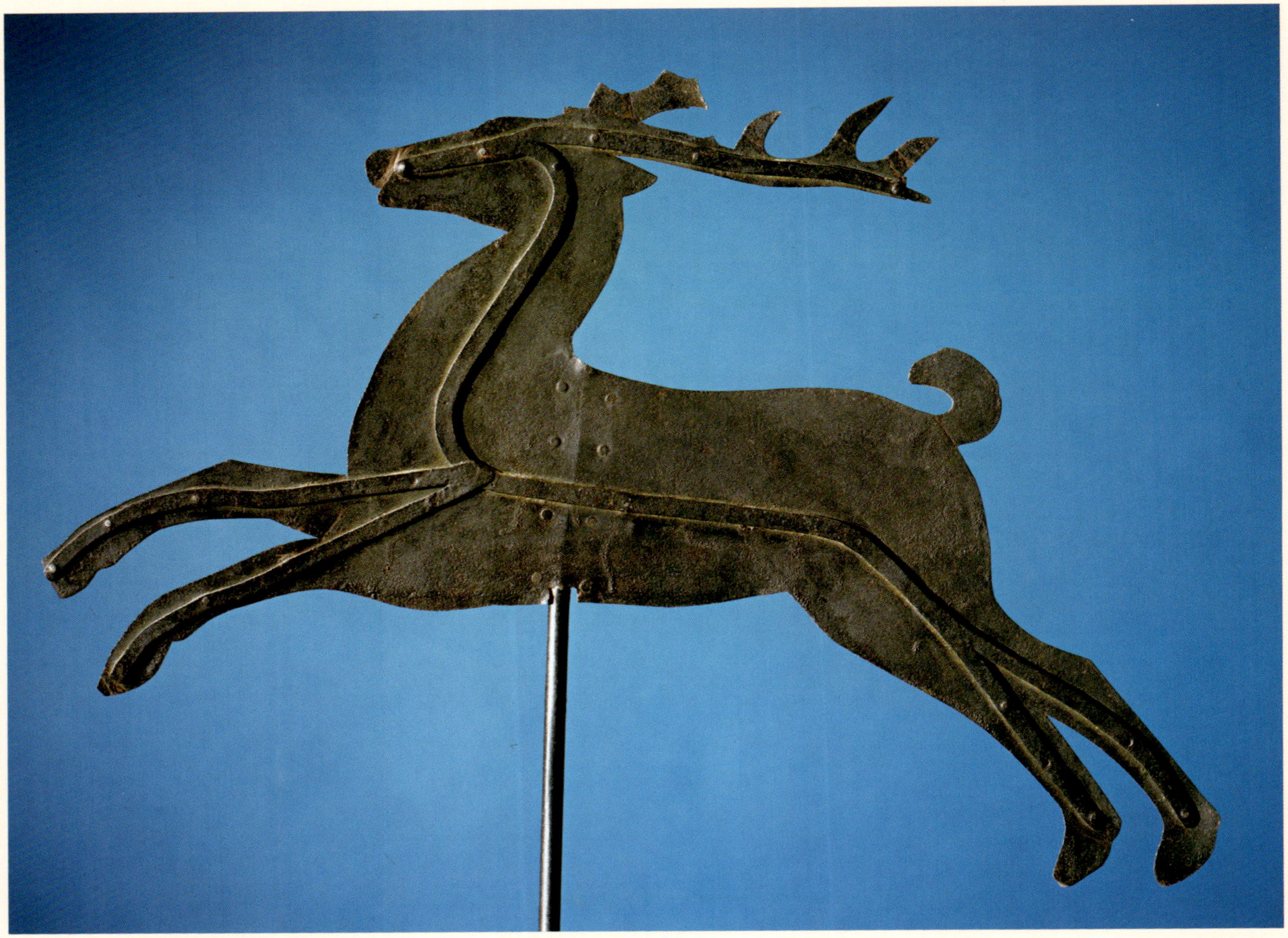

The unknown maker of this weather vane expertly captured the spirit of the running deer. As a weather vane, the deer would have been placed atop a building, so details were not important. What you see with weather vanes is the shape standing out against the sky. This figure was a popular design made commercially as well as by individuals skilled in metalworking. This deer was made from sheet iron and reinforced with banding that in itself gives it an abstract artistic quality.

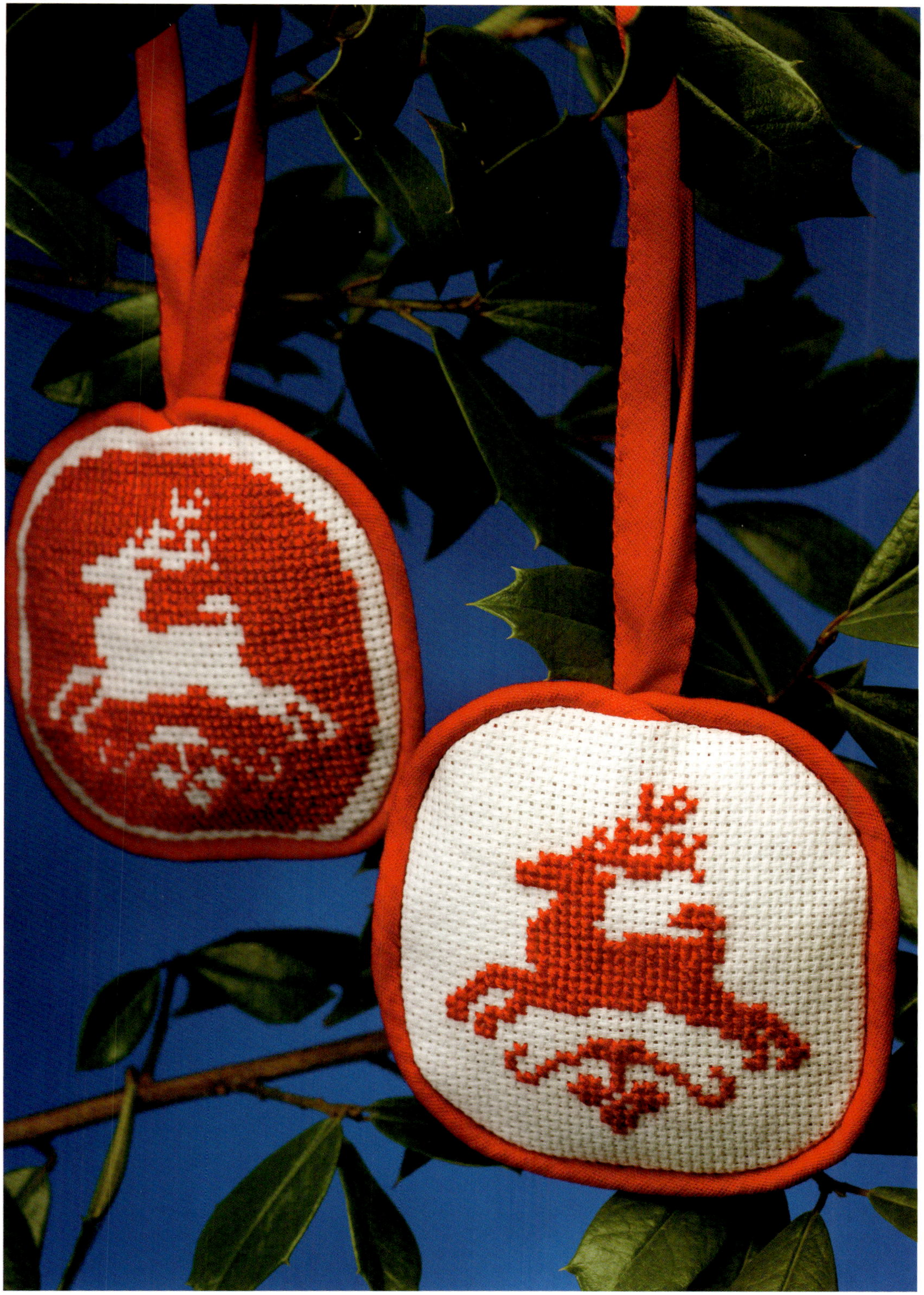

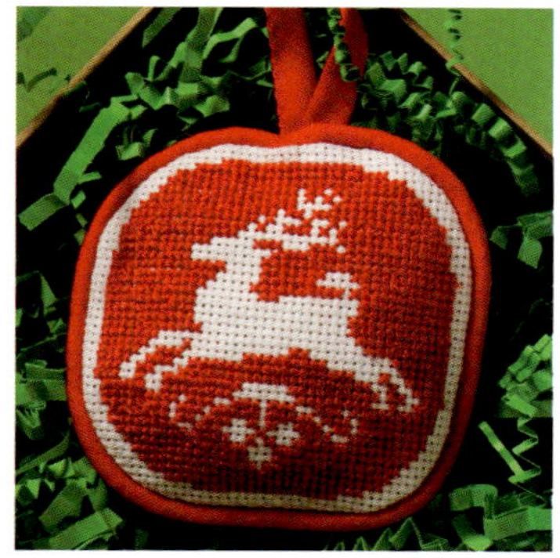

Cross-Stitch Reindeer

Although the original deer was most likely associated with hunting and wildlife, we couldn't help but think of eight tiny reindeer.

WHAT YOU NEED:

Charted design

18-count white Aida cloth, 5 x 5 inches

4-inch embroidery hoop

Cross-stitch needle

Red bias tape maxi piping, 11 inches long

Matching floss

Matching thread

Red cotton fabric, 4 x 4 inches

Pins

Needle

Scissors

Stuffing

Red single-fold bias tape, 9 inches long

Note: You may wish to make your own piping and bias tape based on the color of the floss you use.

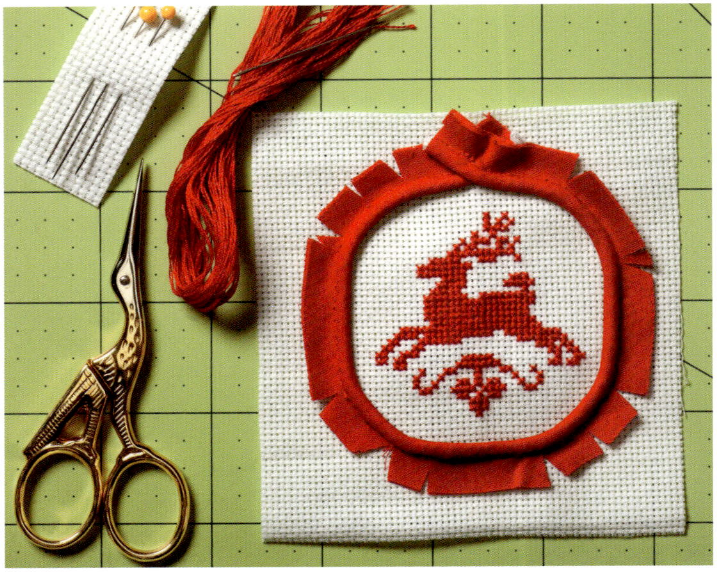

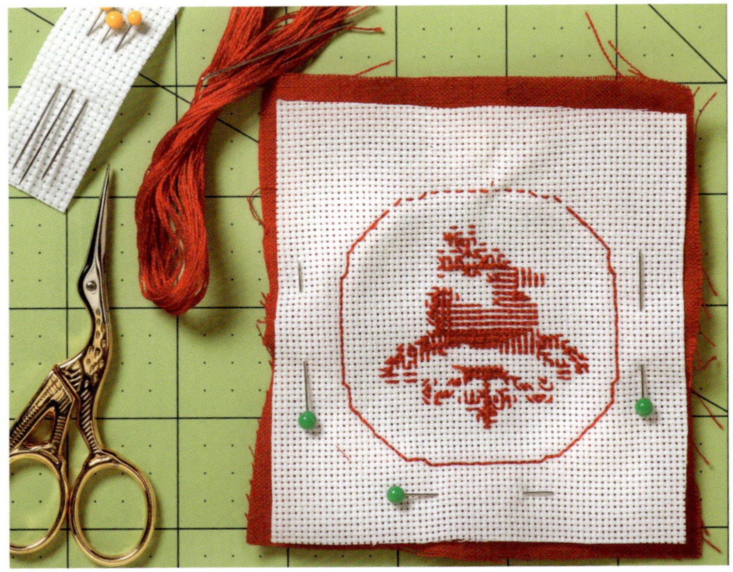

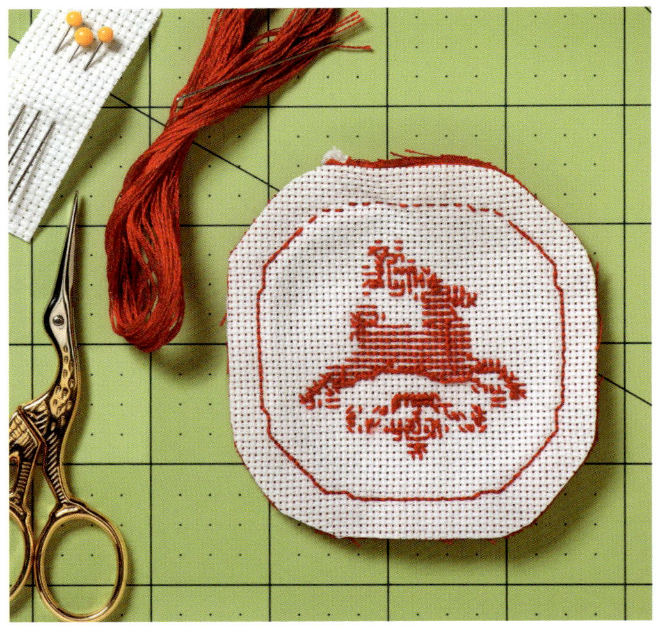

INSTRUCTIONS:

Center the Aida cloth in the embroidery hoop and, referring to the charted design, create the cross-stitch on the Aida cloth with the floss. Start the stitches at the center of the reindeer.

Once the cross-stitching is complete, remove the piece from the hoop and hand stitch, with matching thread, the piping to the Aida cloth using the running stitch and following the line as noted on the charted design. Carefully overlap the piping at the top of the ornament.

Place the cotton fabric with the right side to the right side of the Aida cloth. Use pins to hold in place. With needle and thread, stitch the cotton fabric to the Aida cloth using the piping stitches as a guide. Note the beginning and ending stitches on the charted design; these points allow an opening at the top of the ornament for turning. Once the backing has been stitched to the Aida cloth, trim a 1/4-inch border around the ornament, snip curves, and turn right side out. Stuff loosely.

To make the hanger, fold the bias tape in half lengthwise and whipstitch the edges together with the matching thread. Make a loop to form the hanger, and stitch the hanger to the center of the turned ornament. Close the opening using a slip stitch.

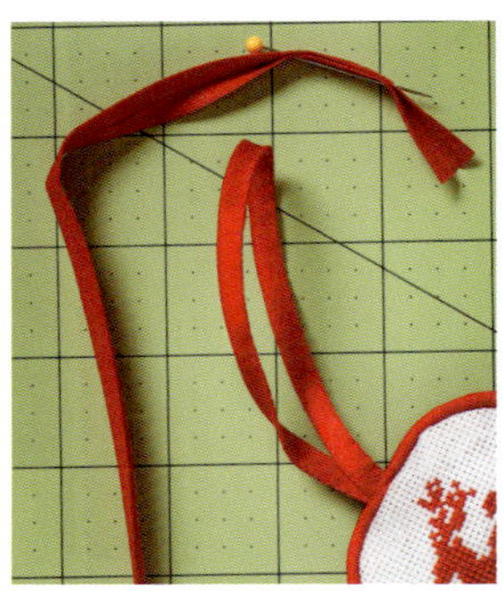

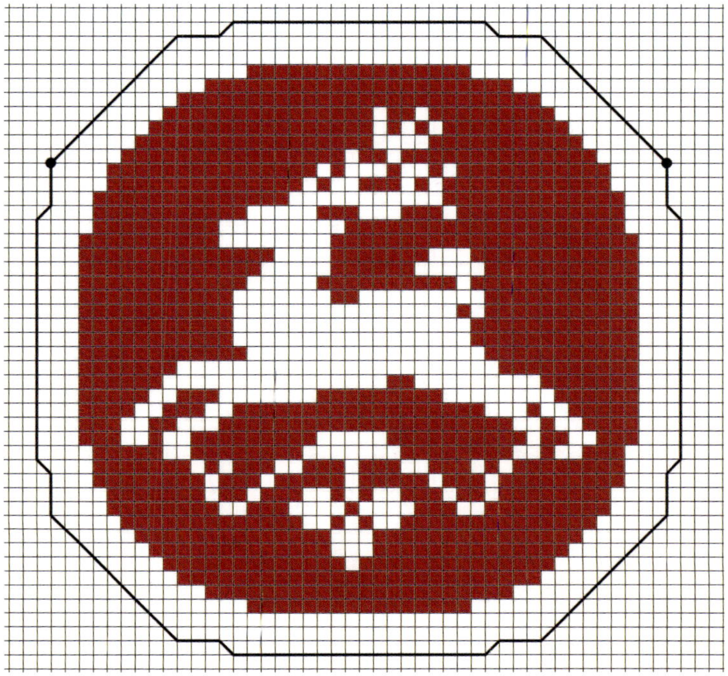

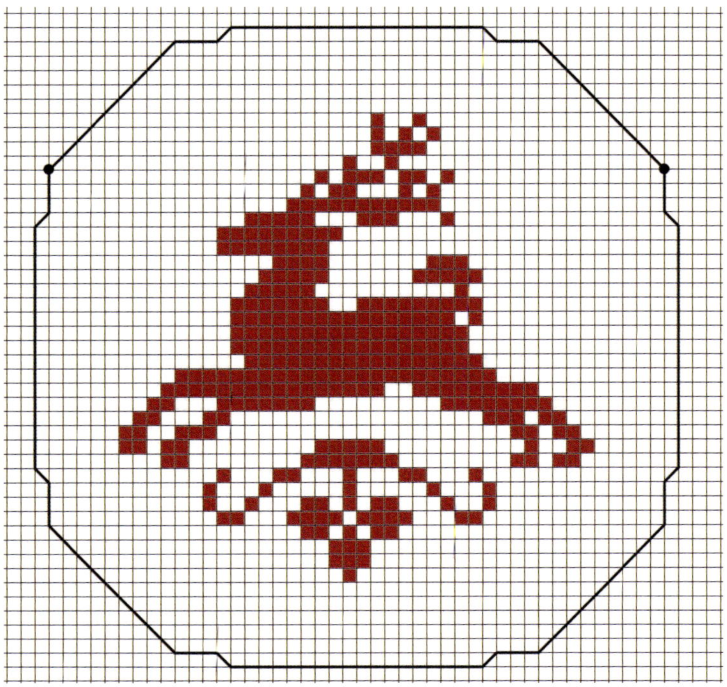

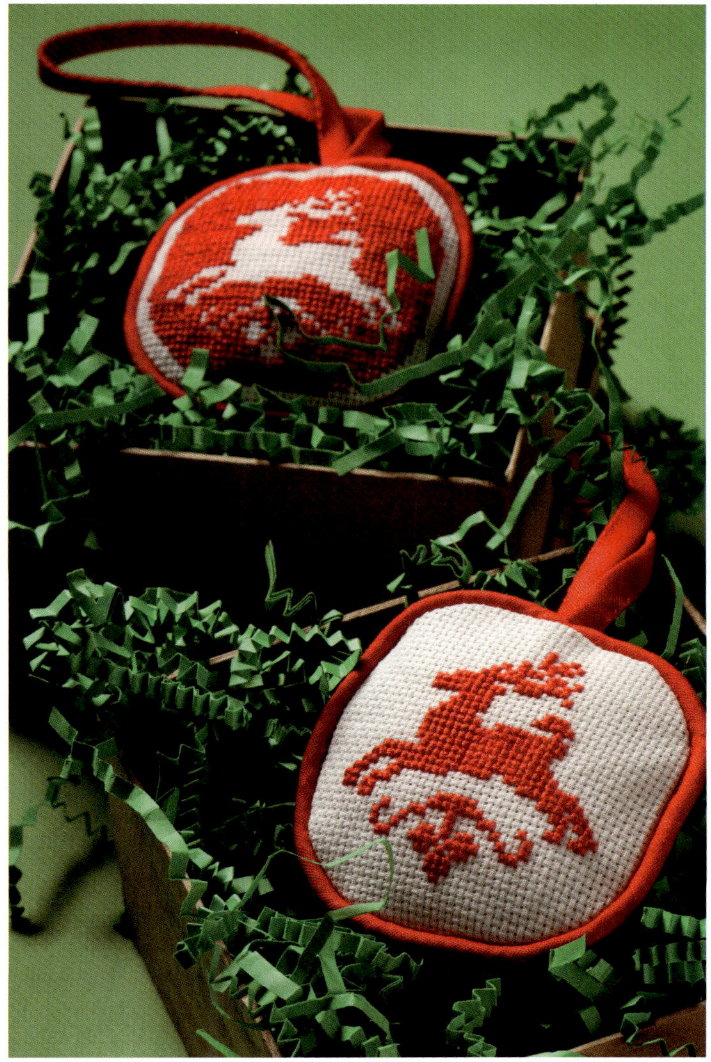

IDEAS: MAKE THE ORNAMENT REVERSIBLE BY CROSS-STITCHING AIDA CLOTH FOR BOTH THE FRONT AND THE BACK. YOU COULD MAKE THE FRONT AND THE BACK DIFFERENT BY CROSS-STITCHING THE POSITIVE DESIGN FOR ONE SIDE AND THE NEGATIVE FOR THE OTHER. ANOTHER VARIATION IS TO STITCH A PIN TO THE BACK TO MAKE A FESTIVE BROOCH RATHER THAN ADD A HANGER FOR AN ORNAMENT.

GERMAN BUILDING SETS

Germany, 1840–1890, paint and wood, range: 1 3/4" x 1 3/4" to 6" x 3", 1971-874 and 1952.1200.71

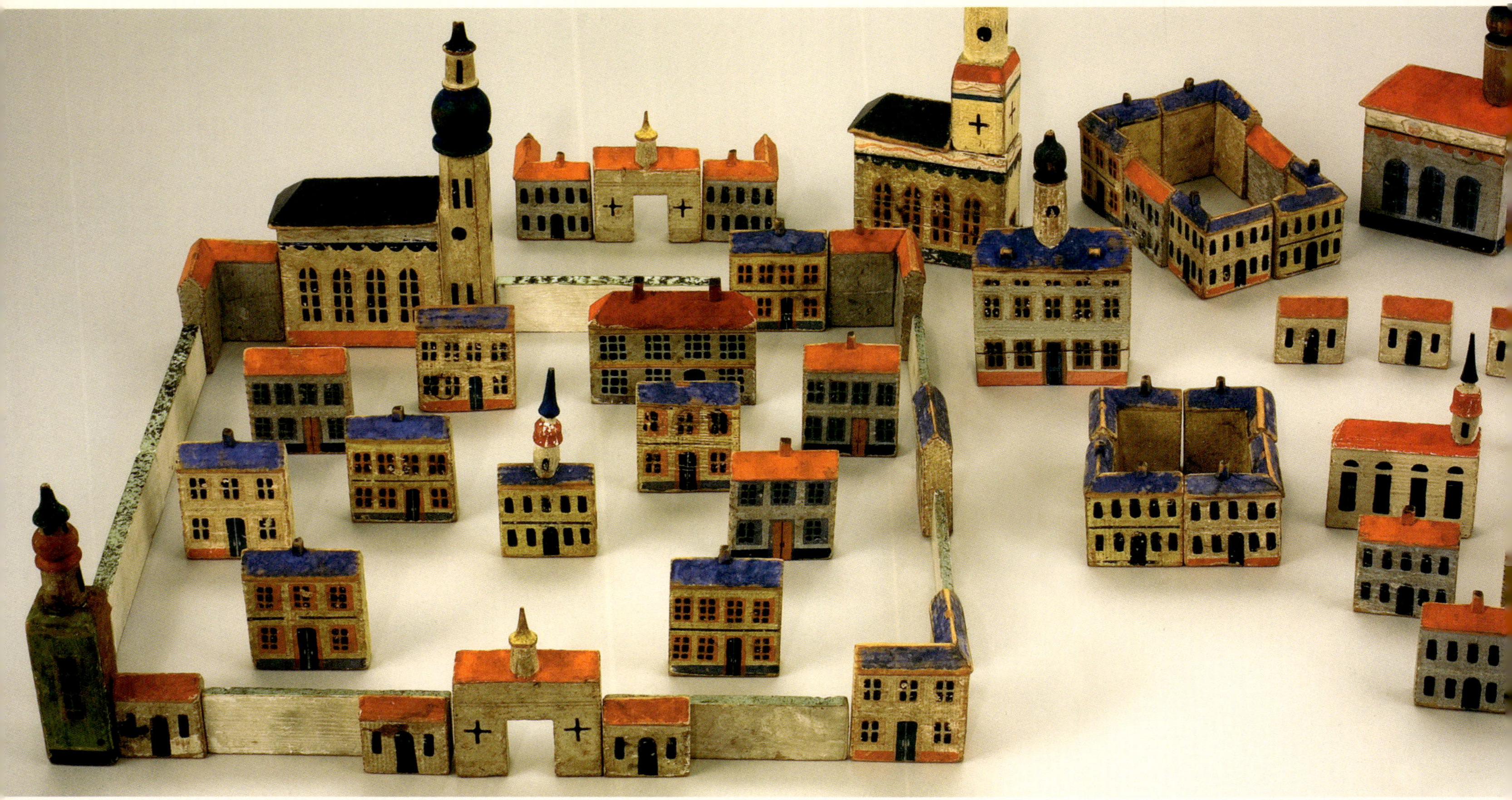

For most of the nineteenth century, Germany was the toy center of the world. The country was known for its production of wooden toys that could be made in vast quantities at little expense. Many of the wooden toys were made by individuals in their homes. A whole family might be involved in the production from carving the pieces to painting the details. The family's output would be picked up and sent to a warehouse for packing and shipping to all parts of the world. Illustrated catalogs were available to shopkeepers so that they could select which items they wished to import. The Folk Art Museum owns one of these catalogs printed in the 1840s.

Sets of toys, like Noah's ark, farms, castles, and villages, were popular playthings. You could purchase a small set of just five or six buildings or a much larger set that allowed you to build an entire walled city. The pieces were painted in bright colors and represented churches and one- and two-story buildings that could be houses, stores, or whatever a child wanted them to be. The buildings had a European style, but to most kids the style didn't matter: it was the ability to have fun and to build your own town.

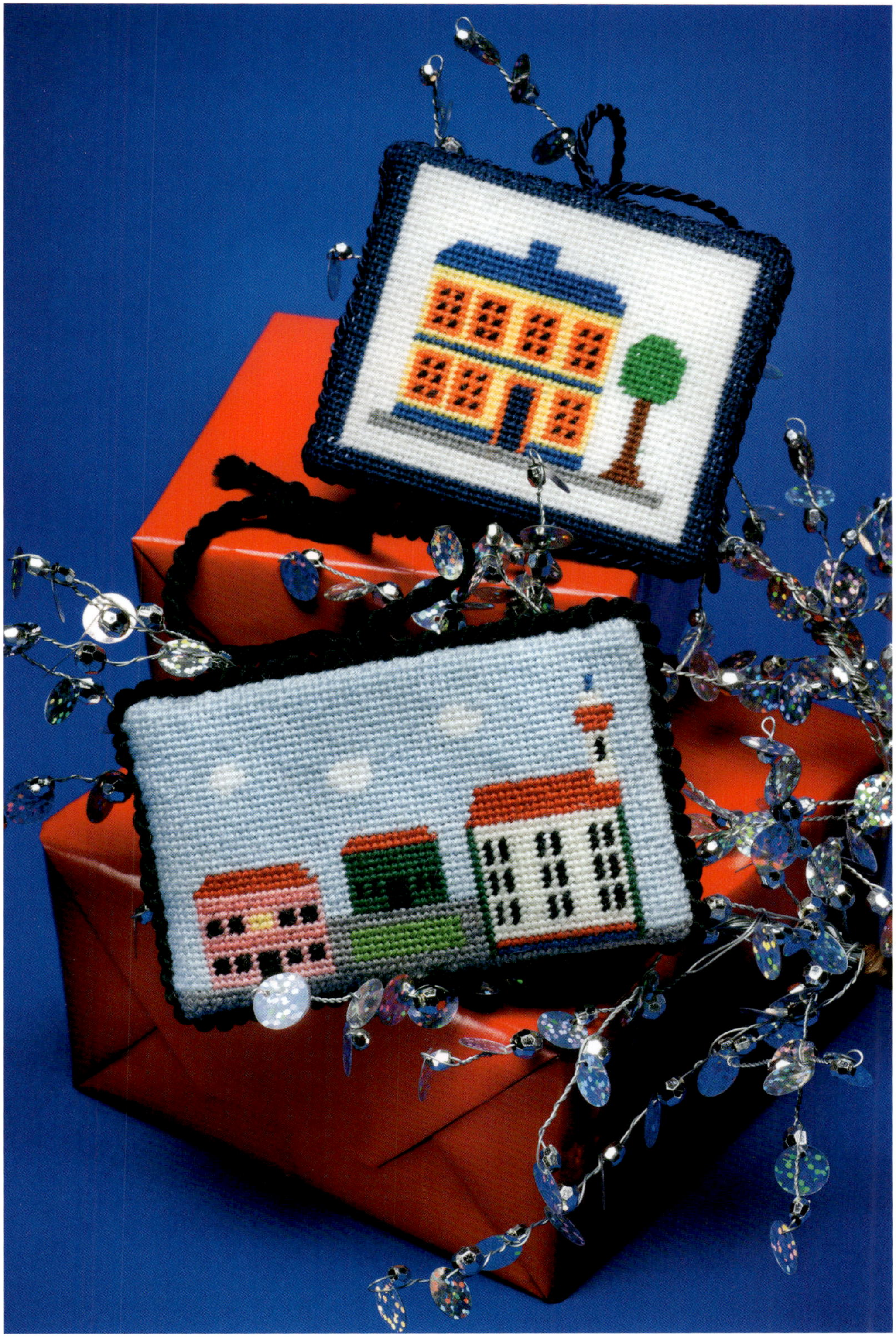

Needlepoint Toy Buildings

THE COLORFUL BUILDINGS IN A VARIETY OF SHAPES GOT US THINKING ABOUT HOW WE WOULD SET THEM UP TO MAKE A TOWN. WITH NEEDLEPOINT, WE CREATED SMALL SCENES USING THE BUILDINGS.

WHAT YOU NEED:

- Charted designs
- 18-gauge canvas, 6 x 6 1/2 inches for the single building and 5 1/2 x 7 inches for the multiple buildings
- Masking tape
- Tapestry needle, #22
- Persian yarn: light blue, dark blue, orange, yellow, gray, green, and brown for the single building; red, dark pink, light pink, yellow, black, green, light green, blue, white, gray, and sky blue for the multiple buildings
- Scissors
- Mat board
- Strapping tape
- Cotton fabric for backing, 4 x 4 1/2 inches for the single building and 4 x 5 1/2 inches for the multiple buildings
- Matching thread
- Needle
- Thin blue cord, 20 inches long
- Matching thread
- Thin black cord, 22 inches long
- Matching thread
- Ruler

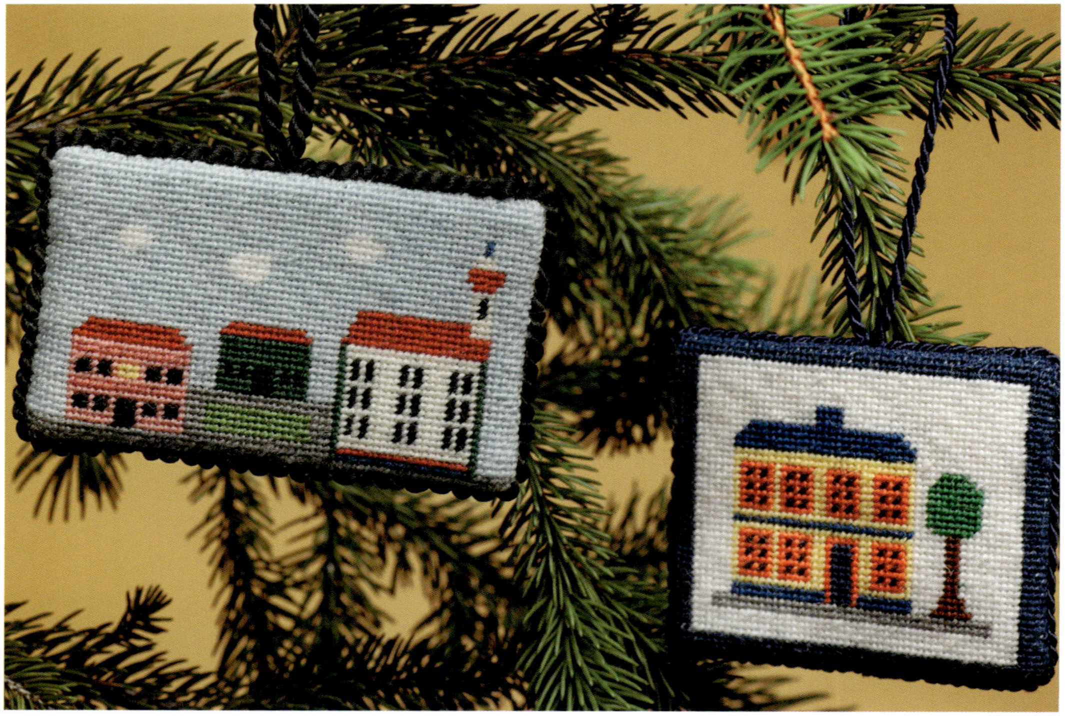

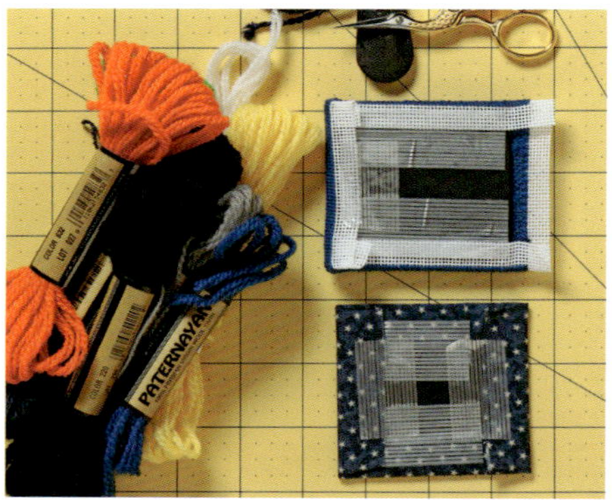

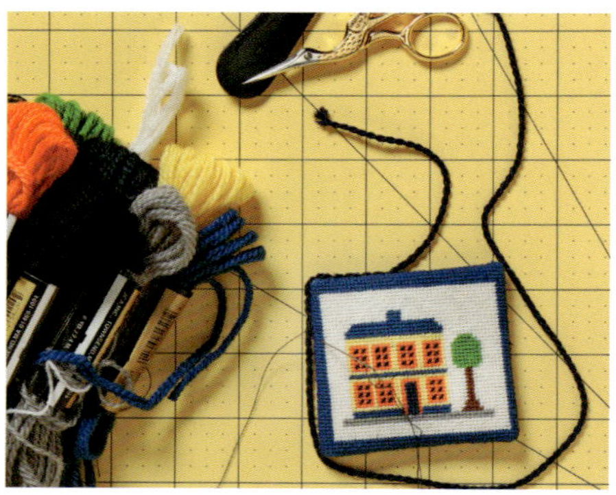

INSTRUCTIONS:

Note: These instructions apply to both needlepoints.

Prepare your canvas by placing masking tape along the four edges to keep it from unraveling as you work. Referring to the charted design, begin with the lower left corner of the building. Stitch colors according to the chart in tent stitch. After the design is complete, fill in the background with tent stitch.

Once the needlepoint is complete, trim the canvas leaving six empty holes from the stitched area on each of the four sides. Set the canvas aside.

Cut the mat board. For the single building, cut a piece $2\frac{3}{4} \times 2\frac{1}{2}$ inches and a piece $3 \times 2\frac{5}{8}$ inches. For the multiple buildings, cut a piece $2 \times 3\frac{1}{2}$ inches and $2\frac{1}{4} \times 3\frac{3}{4}$ inches. Lay the needlepoint canvas right side down. Place the smaller piece of mat board in the center of the canvas. Pull the top and bottom edges of the canvas over the mat board and tape in place with the strapping tape. Then fold in the two side edges and tape. Set this aside.

Lay the backing fabric right side down. Place the larger piece of mat board in the center. Fold the top and bottom edges of the fabric over the mat board and tape in place with the strapping tape. Then fold in the sides and tape.

Hold the two pieces of covered mat board firmly together, mat boards facing in, making sure to line up all edges, and whipstitch them together. Pull the stitches firmly so as to pull the two pieces together as tightly as possible.

Add the cord using matching thread: Use the blue cord for the single building and the black cord for the multiple buildings. Measure 4 inches down from the end of the cord and start attaching the cord to the needlepoint at that point, allowing those 4 inches to hang loose. Begin sewing the cord to the center top of the canvas along the edge to cover the whipstitching. Sew the cord all the way around. When you get back to the top, cross one end in front of the other and do a final stitch around both pieces of cord. Measure out another 4 inches of loose cord and cut it. Knot the two ends of the cord together to form the hanging loop.

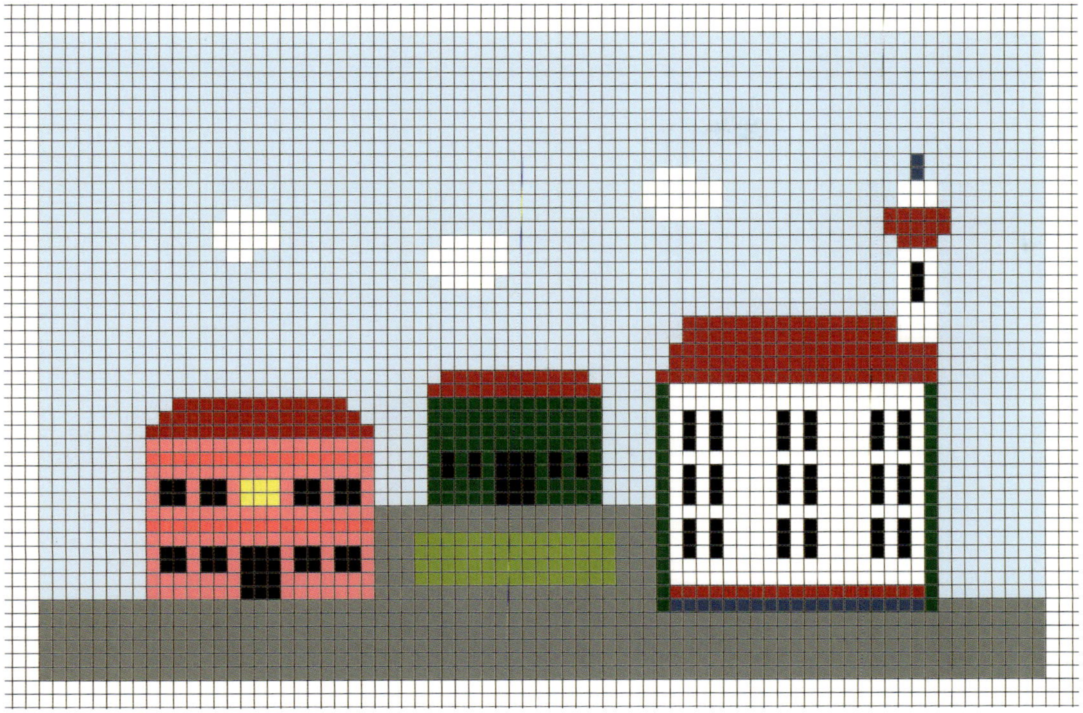

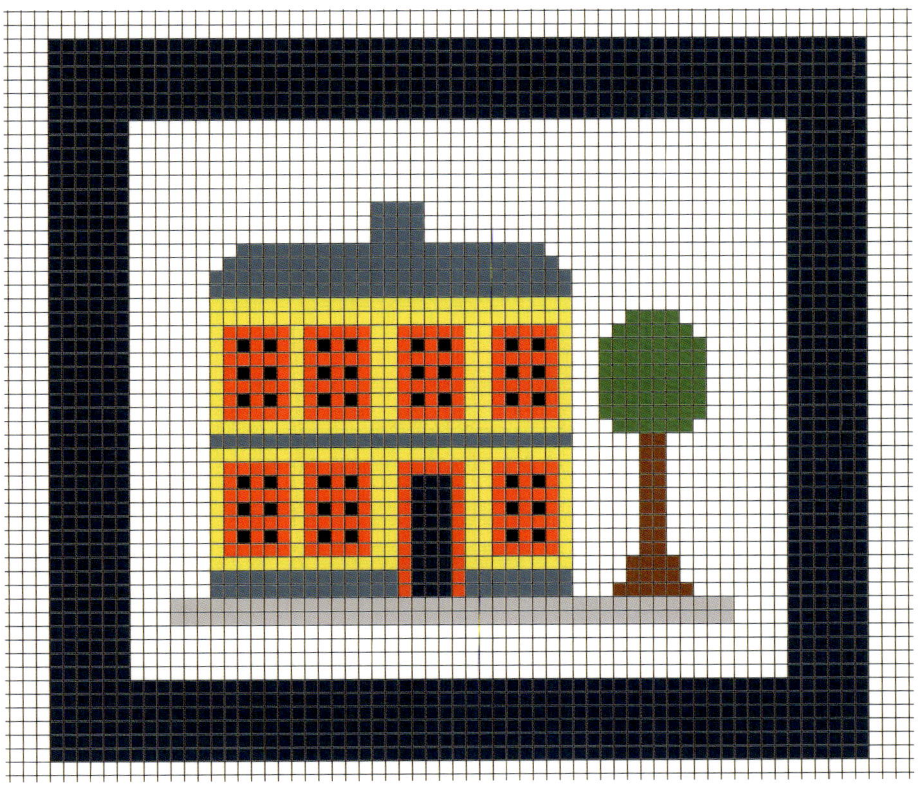

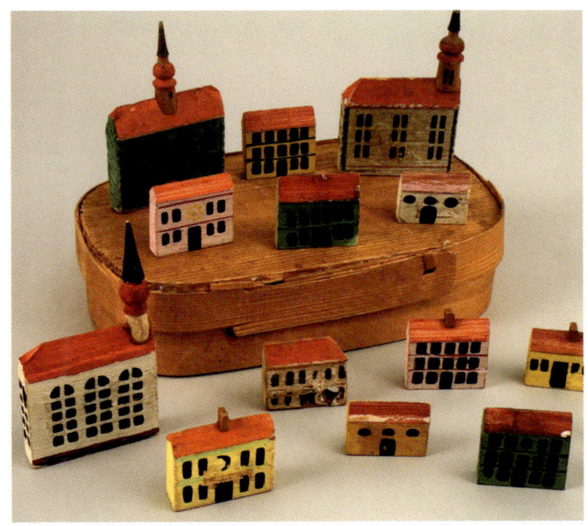

IDEAS: THE TOY BUILDINGS LEND THEMSELVES TO A VARIETY OF OPTIONS. CHANGE THE COLORS, CHANGE THE PLACES ON THE DESIGN, ADD MORE, OR CREATE A WHOLE TOWN.

BUGGY RIDE

Mattie Lou O'Kelley (1908–1997), Georgia, 1989,
paint on canvas, 24" x 36", gift of Dr. and Mrs. T. Marshall Hahn Jr.,
2001.101.22

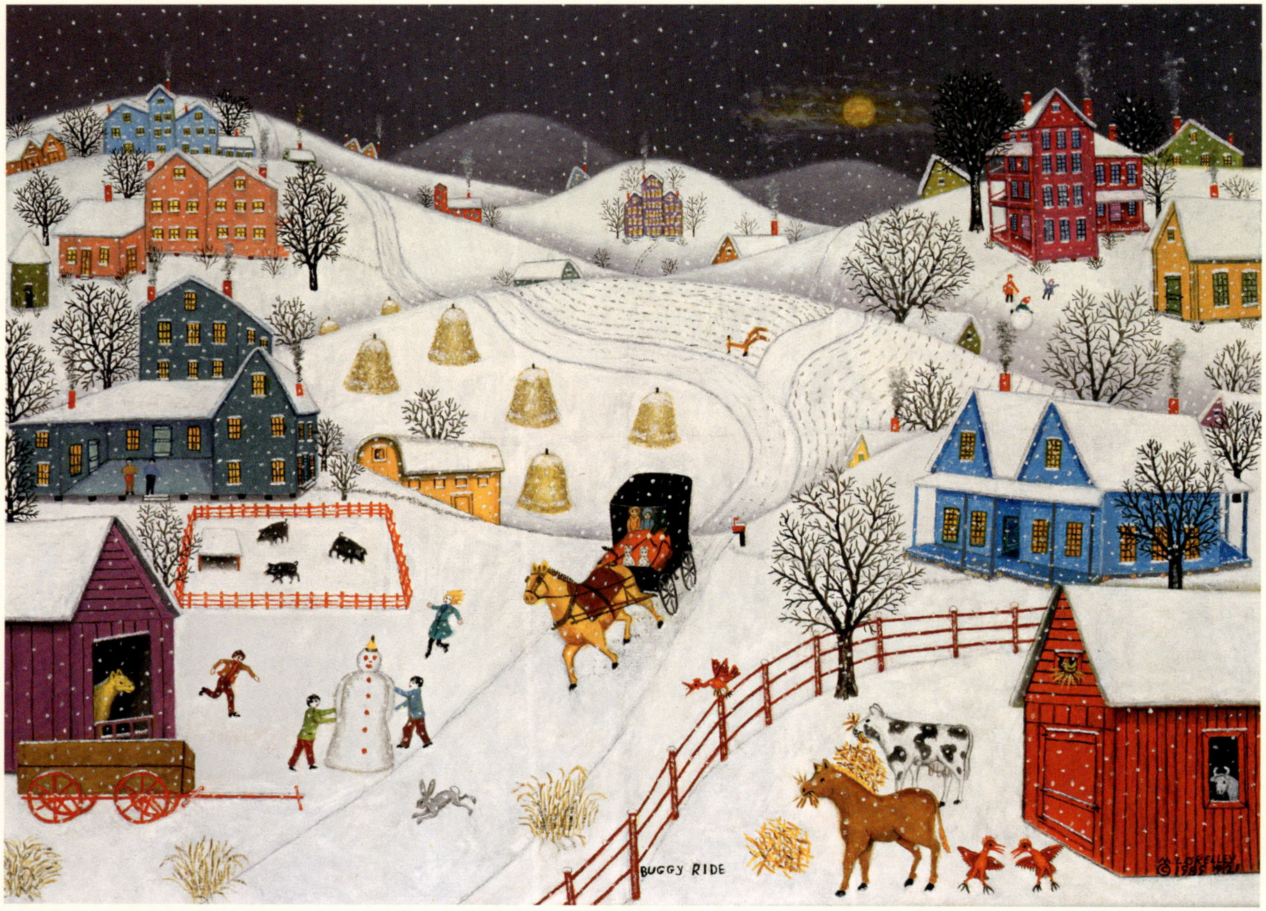

Buggy Ride is a painting in a series of twenty-four that Mattie Lou O'Kelley created to illustrate the children's book *Moving to Town*. The somewhat autobiographical story, which O'Kelley wrote, tells the tale of a family who moves from the country to the big city. The big city has lots of new things, but it isn't home so they end up returning to the country. This painting is near the end of the story and shows the family back home enjoying winter on the farm. In her attention to detail and use of vibrant colors, O'Kelley captures the peacefulness of a winter evening and the sense of community of a small rural town. There is also a hint of whimsy in the children building a snowman and the hens facing off in the yard.

O'Kelley grew up on a farm in rural Georgia in the early part of the twentieth century. In later years, after her siblings moved away and her parents died, O'Kelley, then nearly sixty years old, was left on her own. She decided to take up painting. She bought the necessary supplies and taught herself. Her memories of the farm and childhood with her three sisters and four brothers are the subjects of many of her paintings. For over twenty years, she created her art and received recognition for her work, which today is exhibited in various museums. The Abby Aldrich Rockefeller Folk Art Museum is fortunate to have received a gift of all twenty-four paintings from the *Moving* series.

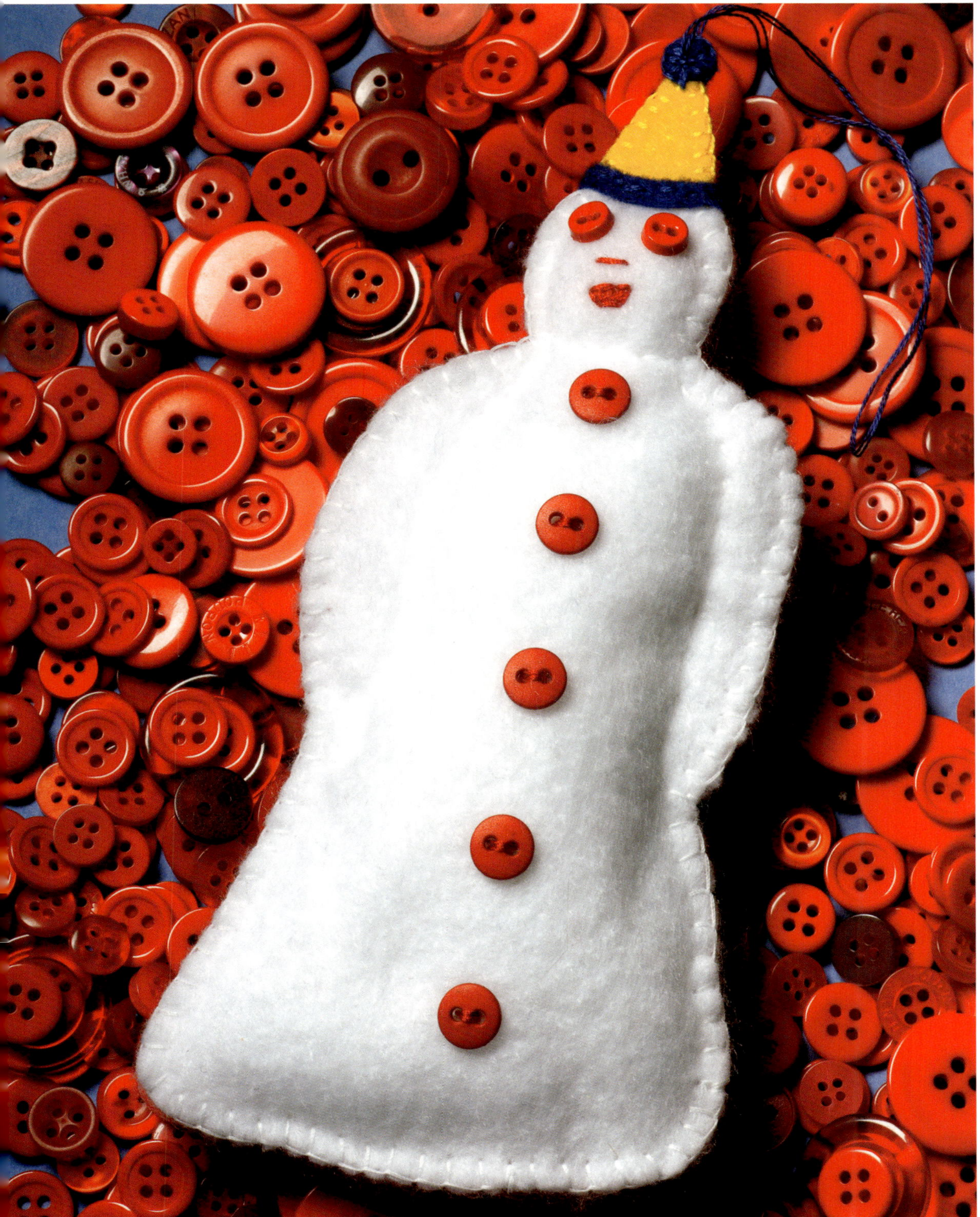

Felt Snowman

THE WHIMSICAL WHITE SNOWMAN, A QUINTESSENTIAL WINTER SIGHT, SEEMS PERFECT HANGING ON A GREEN TREE. IT BRINGS THE WONDER AND JOY OF THE WINTER SEASON INDOORS.

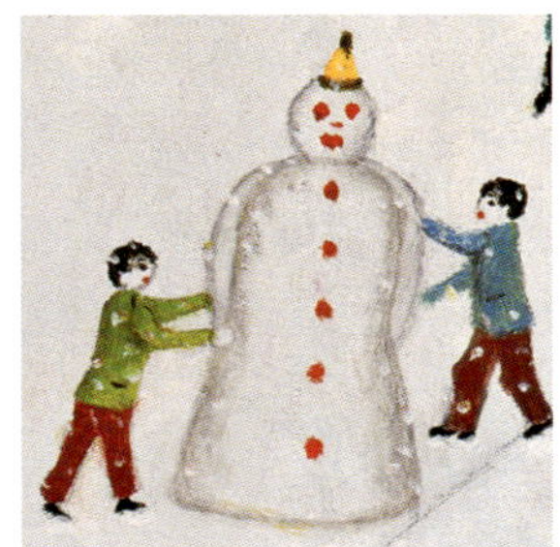

WHAT YOU NEED:

Body, hat, brim, and bob templates (page 128)
White, yellow, and blue felt
Matching floss
Scissors
Two 1/2-inch red buttons
Five 3/4-inch red buttons
Matching floss
Needle
Stuffing

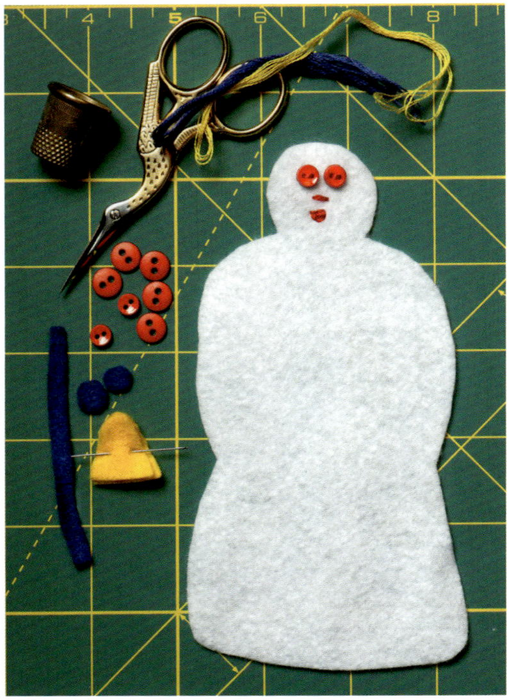

INSTRUCTIONS:

Using the templates, cut two bodies from the white felt, two hats from the yellow felt, and two brims and two bobs from the blue felt.

Before stitching together, create the face of the snowman: Use the red floss to stitch on the two ½-inch buttons as eyes. Use a straight stitch for the nose. Use a satin stitch to create the mouth. Outline the mouth using a running stitch. Dress up the snowman with the five ¾-inch buttons. Center the buttons down the front and stitch on with the red floss.

Lay the decorated body piece on top of the other body piece. Leaving an opening for stuffing, use white floss to blanket-stitch the two parts together. (We used red floss to make the stitches stand out in the instruction photo.) Stuff; then stitch closed.

Referring back to the template as a guide, add arms and neck using a running stitch.

To add the hat, place one of the yellow hat pieces on each side of the snowman's head. At the brim, stitch through all the layers with yellow floss to hold the hat in place. Continue to stitch around the outer edge of the hat using the blanket stitch. Next, place the blue brim pieces on the front and back of the base of the hat. Stitch through all layers with blue floss using the running stitch. At the top of the hat, place the two blue bobs on the front and back and stitch through all layers with blue floss using the blanket stitch.

To make a hanger, sew through the bob of the hat with blue floss, and tie off at the desired length for hanging.

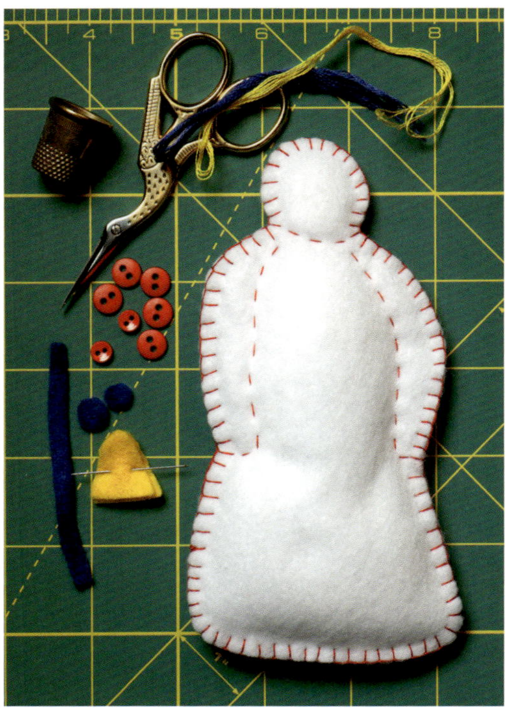

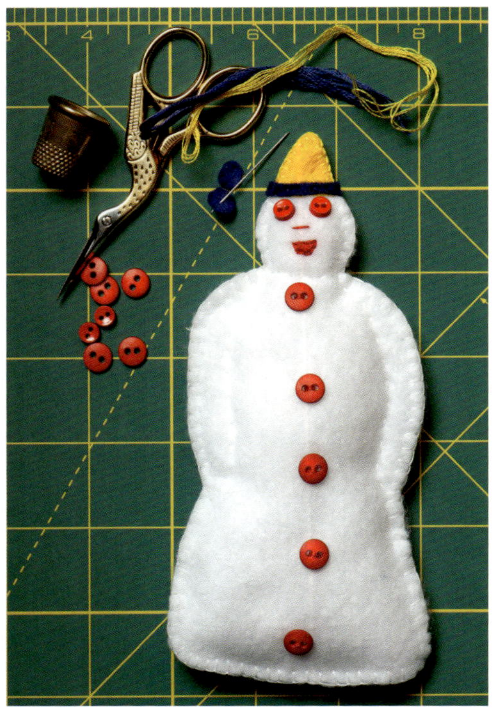

IDEAS: FOR DIFFERENT LOOKS, USE A VARIETY OF COLORED BUTTONS AND CHANGE THE COLORS OF THE HAT.

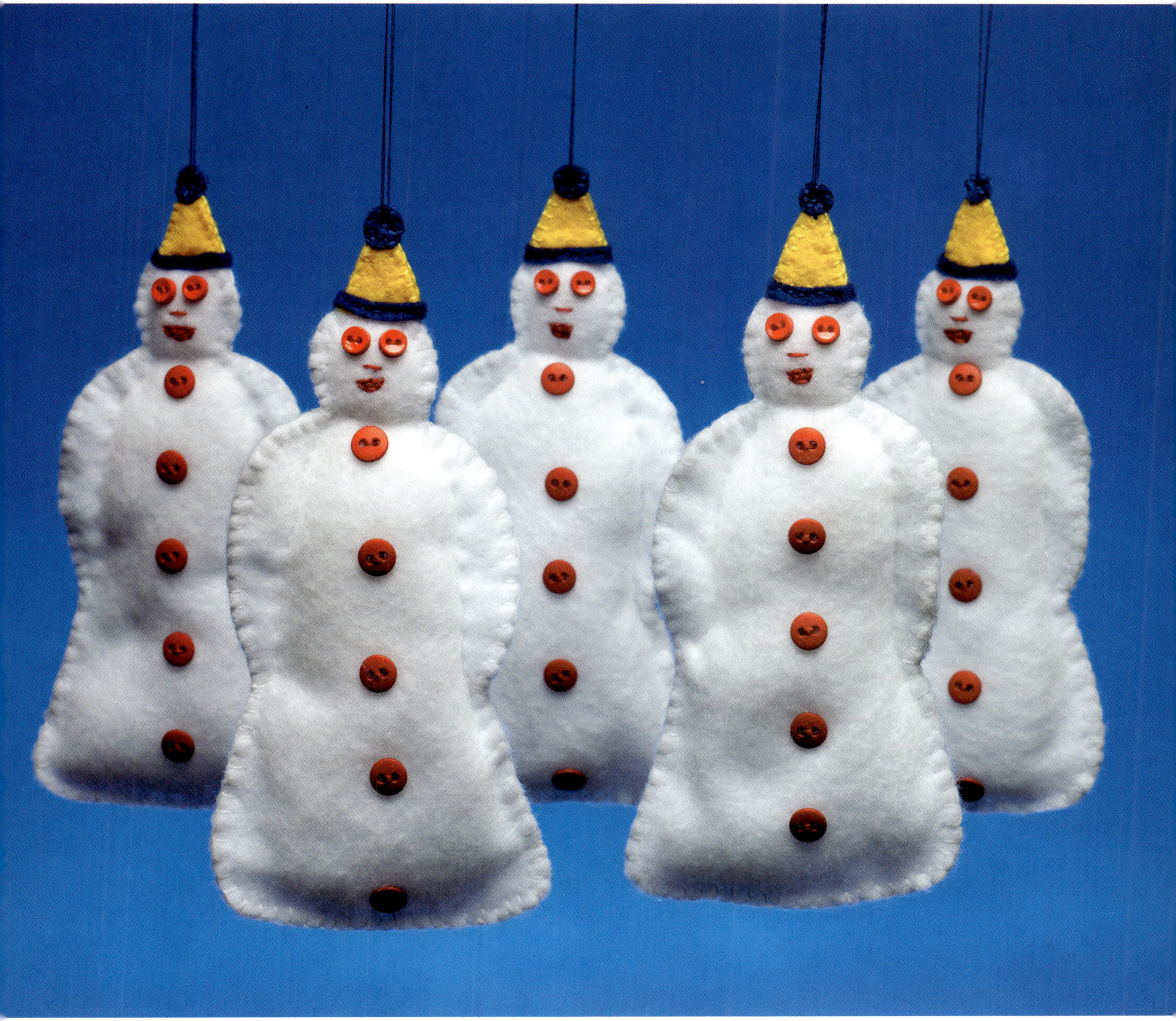

BIRTH AND BAPTISMAL CERTIFICATE OF ELIAS HAMMAN

the Strasburg Artist, Shenandoah Valley, Virginia, possibly 1806, watercolor, gouache, and ink on paper, 15" x 12 5/8", 1981.305.1

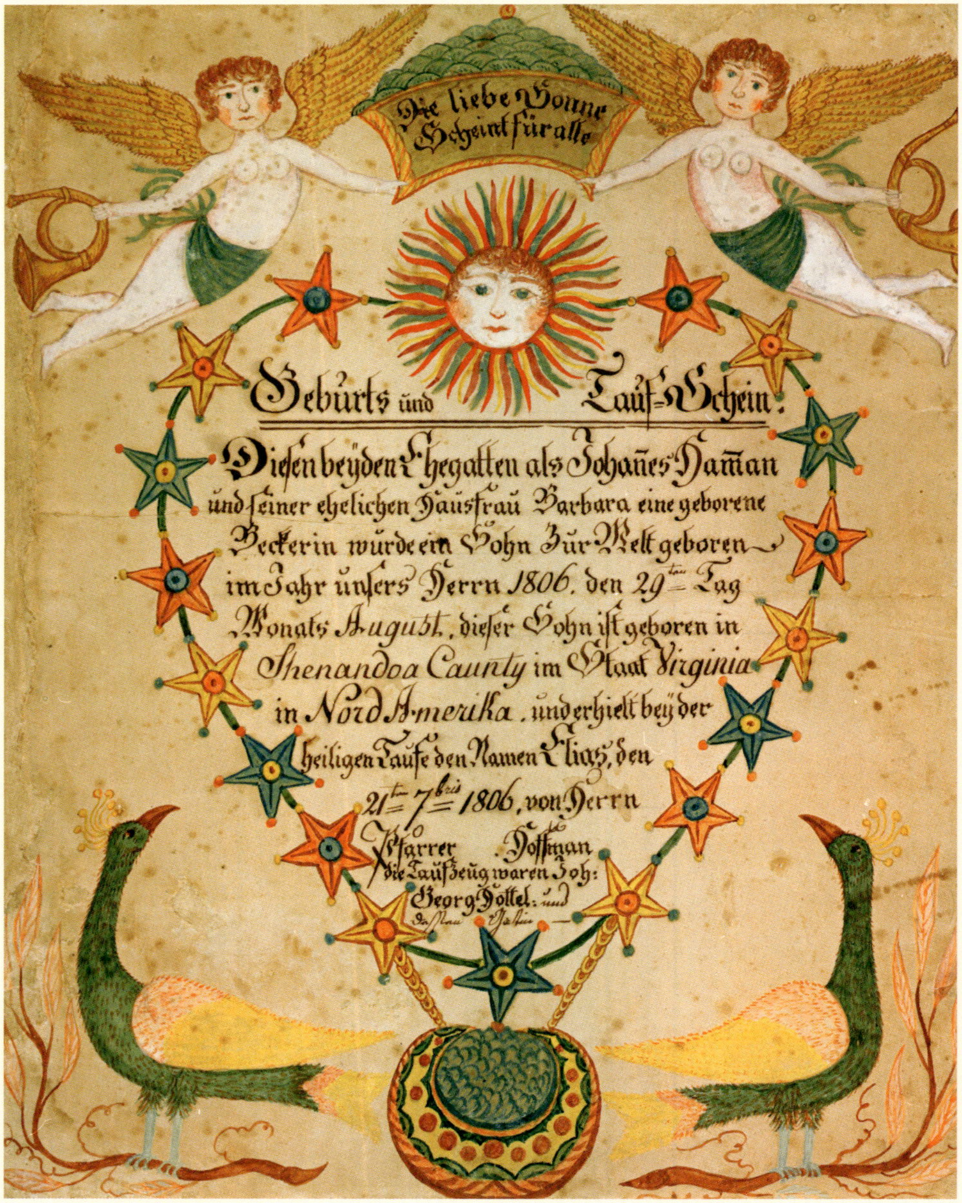

The practice of creating hand-drawn and hand-lettered certificates was common from the mid-eighteenth century through the mid-nineteenth century in the Pennsylvania German settlements. The illustrated documents are generically referred to as frakturs after the German script that has a distinctive "broken" style. In addition to the writing, the certificates feature standard design elements, like birds, stars, angels, and flowers, appearing in innumerable variations. The term *fraktur* also refers to drawings that did not include writing but were made in the same style. Many of the pieces were created by schoolteachers or ministers or the amateur artist or schoolboy. The documents were treasured family records. Some were hung on the walls; others have been found pasted to the interiors of chests.

The unidentified artist of this piece is known today as the Strasburg Artist. His distinctive style has identified him as the maker of other similar pieces. The detailed lettering, seen on this and many frakturs, was taught in the Strasburg German School in Shenandoah County, Virginia. The cultural influence of the Pennsylvania Germans reached other states as immigrants settled these areas. The Strasburg Artist made this certificate for Elias Hamman. The wording above the sun translates as "The dear sun shines for all." The rest of the text provides the names of Elias's parents and details of his birth and baptism.

Color, motifs, and composition make this fraktur an appealing piece. At first, the angels stood out as an inspiring element, but, once this project was done, it was hard to ignore the charm of the sun and the possibilities of the stars, so we did three projects from this one piece.

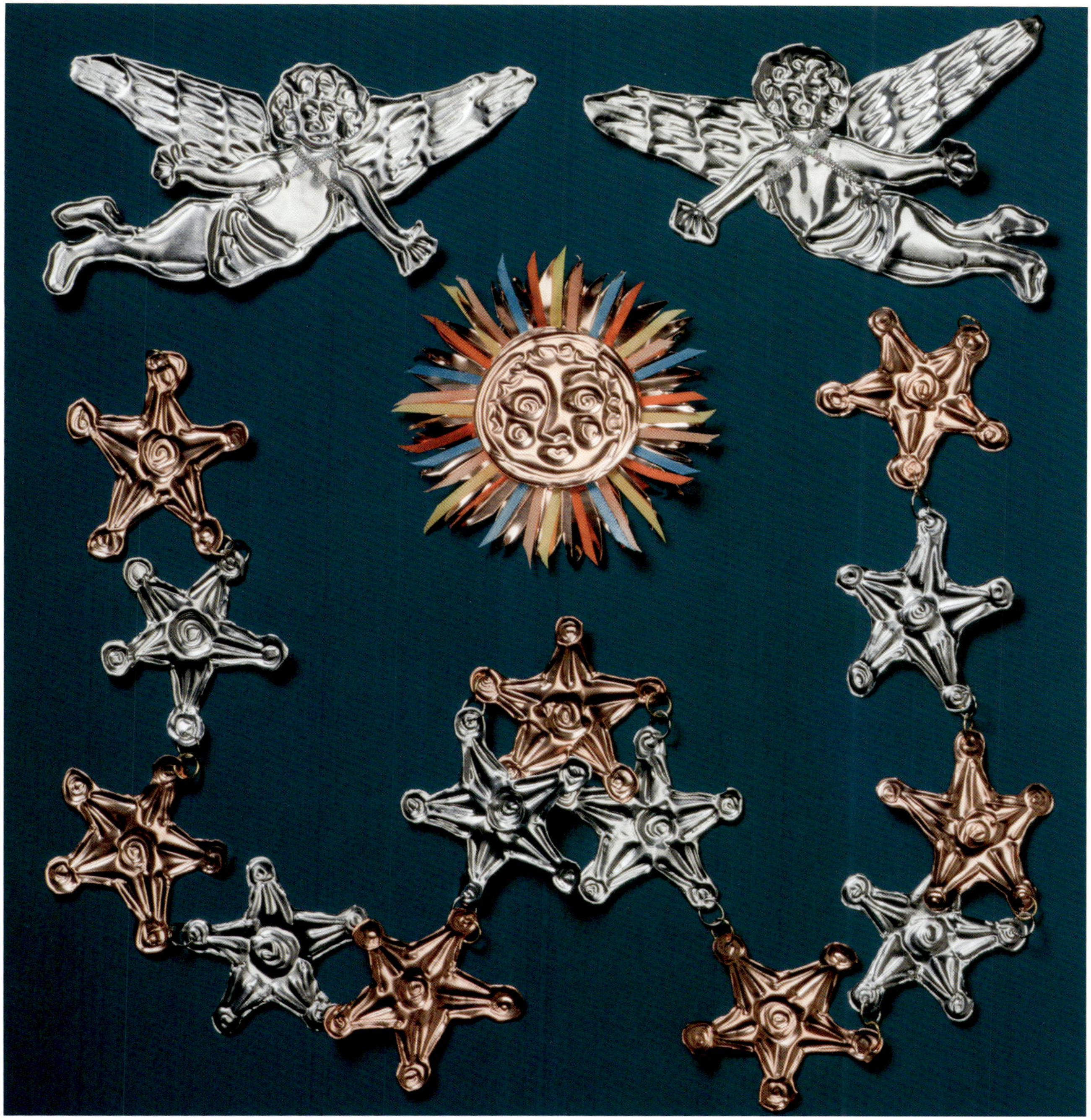

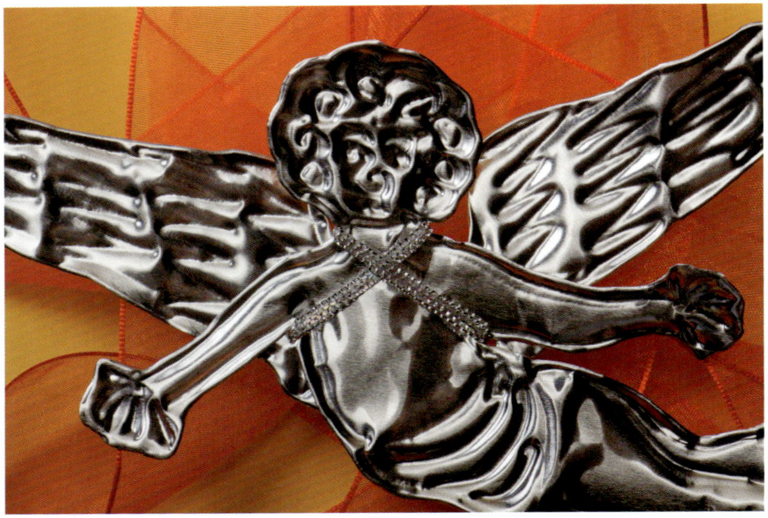

Aluminum Angel

WHAT YOU NEED:

Angel and wings templates (page 139)

Clear tape

36-gauge aluminum tooling foil

Piece of felt

Stylus (such as an old ballpoint pen or sharpened dowel)

Embroidery scissors

Awl or pushpin

1/8-inch silver ribbon, 13 inches long

White quilting thread

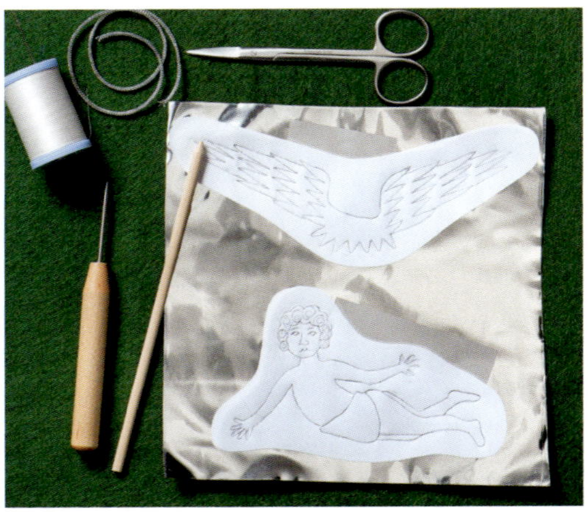

INSTRUCTIONS:

Tape the angel template to the tooling foil and place on the felt. The felt will protect your work surface and allow the stylus to create a deep impression into the foil. Trace the angel template, including all of the decorative details, with the stylus with even pressure. Remove the template. If necessary, go over the image more firmly with the stylus. Repeat the process with the wings template.

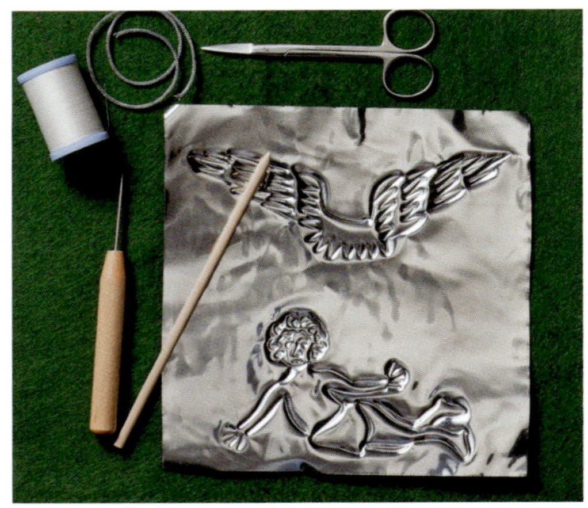

Cut out the foil angel and wings leaving a 1/8-inch margin on the outside of the drawn lines.

Place the wings on the felt and lay the angel on the wings; both pieces should be facing right side up. Position the angel so that the neck aligns with the curve between the wings. Using the awl or pushpin, poke a hole into the wings under each armpit. Remove the angel from the wings and make the hole a bit bigger if necessary. Be careful not to rip the foil. Place the angel back on the wings.

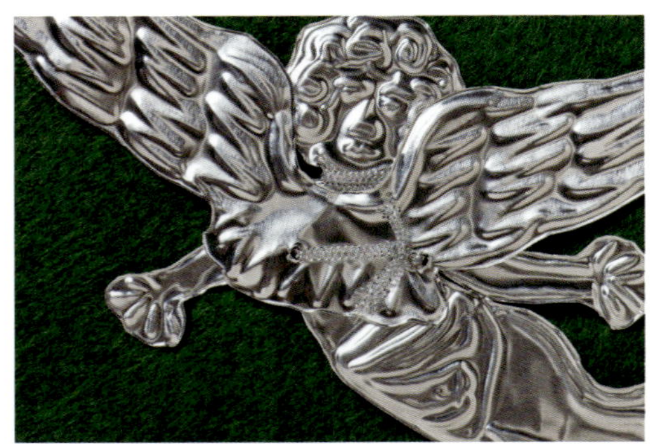

To attach the wings, place the center of the ribbon at the back of the angel's neck. Bring the ribbon ends forward and crisscross the ribbon across the angel's chest. Insert the ends of the ribbon into the corresponding holes in the wings and tie the ends together into a knot at the back. If desired, trim the edges of the ribbon.

To create a hanger, sew quilting thread onto the ribbon at the angel's neck, cut to desired length, and tie off.

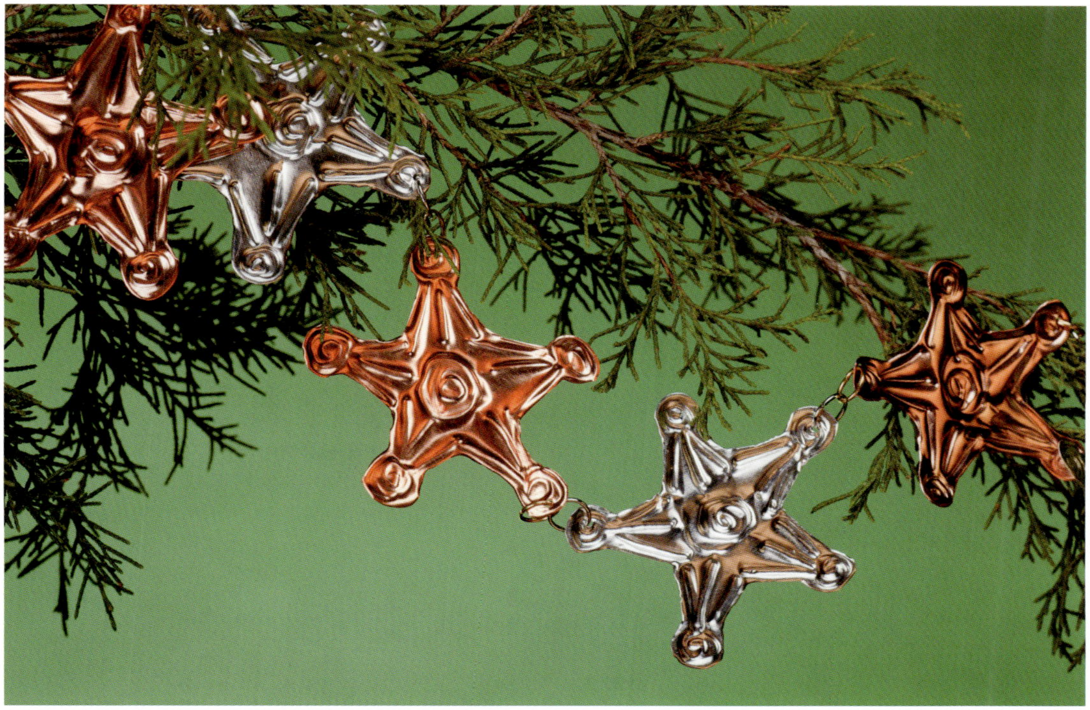

WHAT YOU NEED:

- Star template (page 140)
- Clear tape
- 36-gauge aluminum and copper tooling foil
- Piece of felt
- Stylus (such as an old ballpoint pen or sharpened dowel)
- Embroidery scissors
- 1/8-inch hole punch
- Pliers or bent needle-nose pliers
- Jump rings in silver and gold tones, 9 mm
- 1/4-inch ribbon, 24 inches long

Aluminum and Copper Star Garland

INSTRUCTIONS:

Tape the star template to either the aluminum or copper tooling foil and place on the felt. The felt will protect your work surface and allow the stylus to create a deep impression into the foil. Trace the star template, including all of the decorative details, with the stylus with even pressure. Remove the template. If necessary, go over the image more firmly with the stylus. Repeat the process to create a total of six aluminum stars and six copper stars.

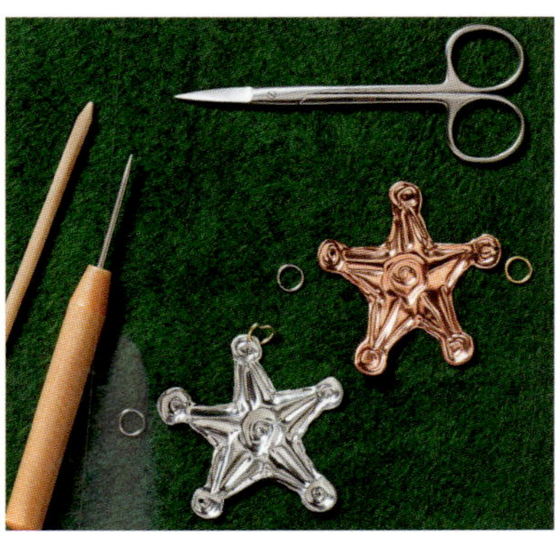

Cut out the foil stars leaving a 1/8-inch margin on the outside of the drawn lines.

Using the 1/8-inch hole punch, punch a hole in one point of the star and another hole in one of the points across from it. Using the pliers, attach a silver jump ring to each hole in each aluminum star and a gold jump ring to each hole in each copper star. Attach the gold and silver jump rings to each other to "string" the garland.

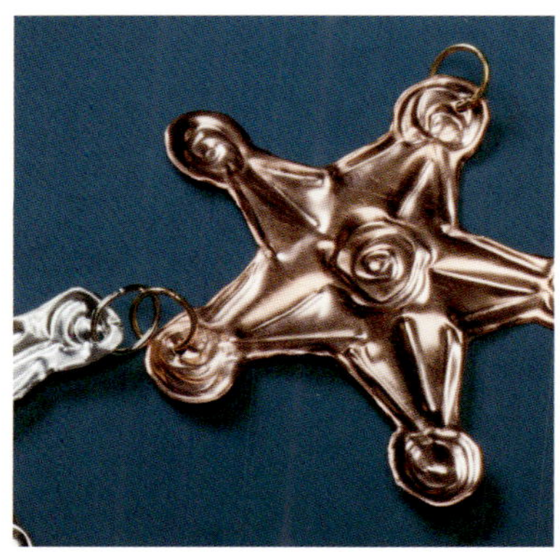

To create hangers, cut two 12-inch pieces of ribbon and attach one to each end of your garland of stars through the jump rings.

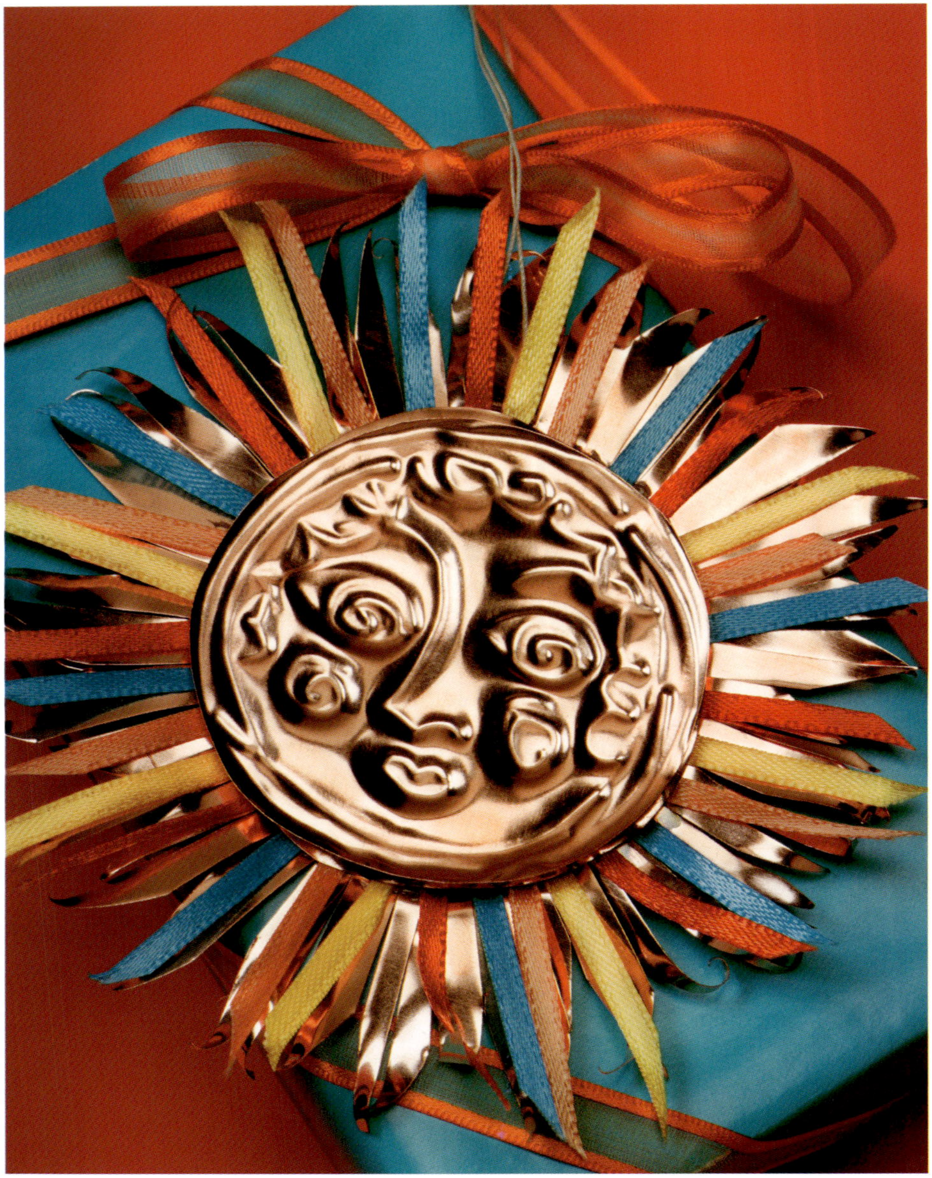

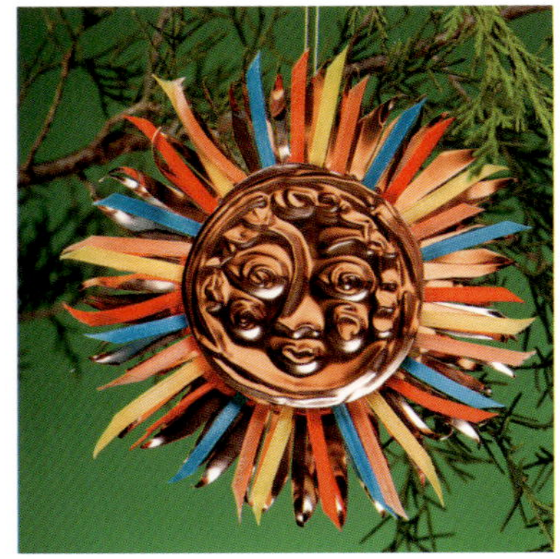

Copper Sun

WHAT YOU NEED:

Sun interior, sun face, and sun back templates (page 140)

Clear tape

36-gauge copper tooling foil

Piece of felt

Stylus (such as an old ballpoint pen or sharpened dowel)

Awl or pushpin

Embroidery scissors

Needle

White quilting thread

1/8-inch hole punch

1/8-inch ribbon, about 30 inches each: orange, peach, gold, and turquoise

Thick and tacky glue

INSTRUCTIONS:

Tape the sun interior template to the tooling foil and place on the felt. The felt will protect your work surface and allow the stylus to create a deep impression into the foil. Trace the sun interior template, including all of the decorative details, with the stylus with even pressure. Use the awl or pushpin to gently mark all thirty-two dots around the sun interior. There is no need to poke the holes too deeply; you will punch the holes in a later step. Remove the template. If necessary, go over the image more firmly with the stylus. Repeat the process with the sun face and sun back templates. Note that these two templates do not require the use of the awl or pushpin.

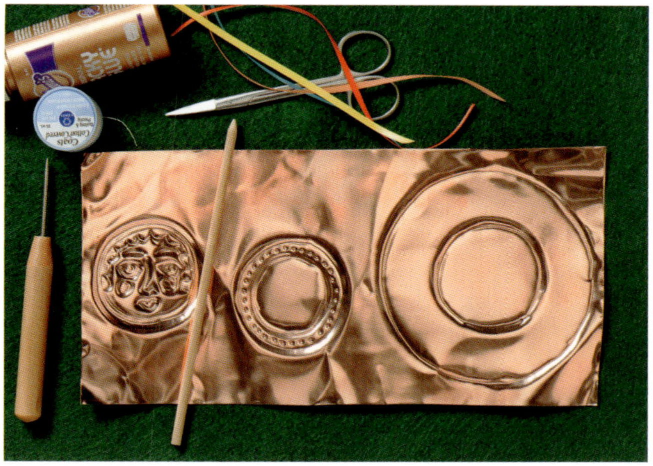

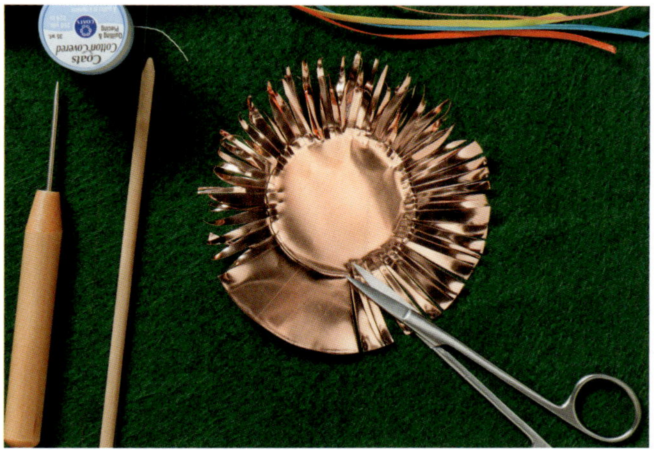

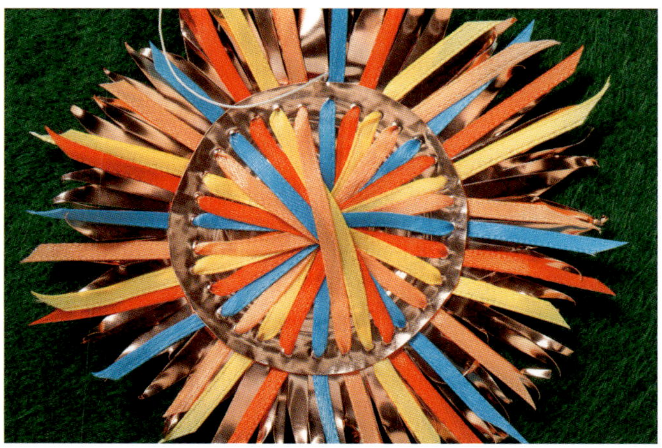

Cut out all three foil sun components leaving a 1/8-inch margin on the outside of the drawn lines.

Create the sun's rays by snipping 1/8-inch fringe around the edge of the sun back. Cut from the edge to the center. Snips do not need to be exact. Next, snip a point at the end of each piece of fringe. Again, these do not need to be exact. Be careful of the snipped points: they can be sharp.

To create a hanger, use the awl or pushpin to poke a hole at the top of the sun back, inside the fringe. Using the needle, pass the quilting thread through the hole and tie off at the desired length for hanging.

To make the sun interior, use a 1/8-inch hole punch to punch all thirty-two dots around the sun interior edge following the impressions you made with the awl or pushpin. Cut sixteen pieces of ribbon, four each of orange, peach, gold, and turquoise, in 7-inch lengths. Cut a deep point at the end of each ribbon to make it easier to thread the ribbon through the holes. Begin by threading one end of an orange ribbon into the first hole; count around to the seventeenth hole and thread through the opposite end. Use a peach ribbon next to the orange; cross over the orange and thread through the opposite end. Continue with the gold and turquoise ribbons. Repeat the sequence until all thirty-two holes have been filled. Pull the ribbons as necessary to make them relatively even. Do not snip the ribbons yet.

Place the sun interior copper side up and the sun back onto your work surface. Place a line of thick and tacky glue around the edge of the sun interior directly onto the ribbon; flip the sun interior and glue it to the sun back. You should be looking at the crisscrossed circle of ribbon once glued. Trim the ribbon to the same length as the rays of the sun back, cutting points at the ends, and then glue the sun face to the top.

IDEAS: CREATE THESE PROJECTS IN DIFFERENT FOIL COLORS OR COMBINE FOILS IN THE SAME PROJECT. THE ANGEL'S WINGS COULD BE A DIFFERENT COLOR THAN THE BODY. OR YOU COULD ADD PAPER. THE ANGELS LOOK NICE WITH BRIGHT WHITE WINGS AND A SILVER BODY, OR YOU COULD DRAW THE SUN FACE ON PAPER GIVING IT MORE COLOR AND DETAIL.

THE BARRETT SISTERS

Joseph H. Davis (1811–1865), New Hampshire, 1837, watercolor, ink, and pencil on wove paper, 7" x 8 7/8", gift of Juli Grainger, 2008.300.3

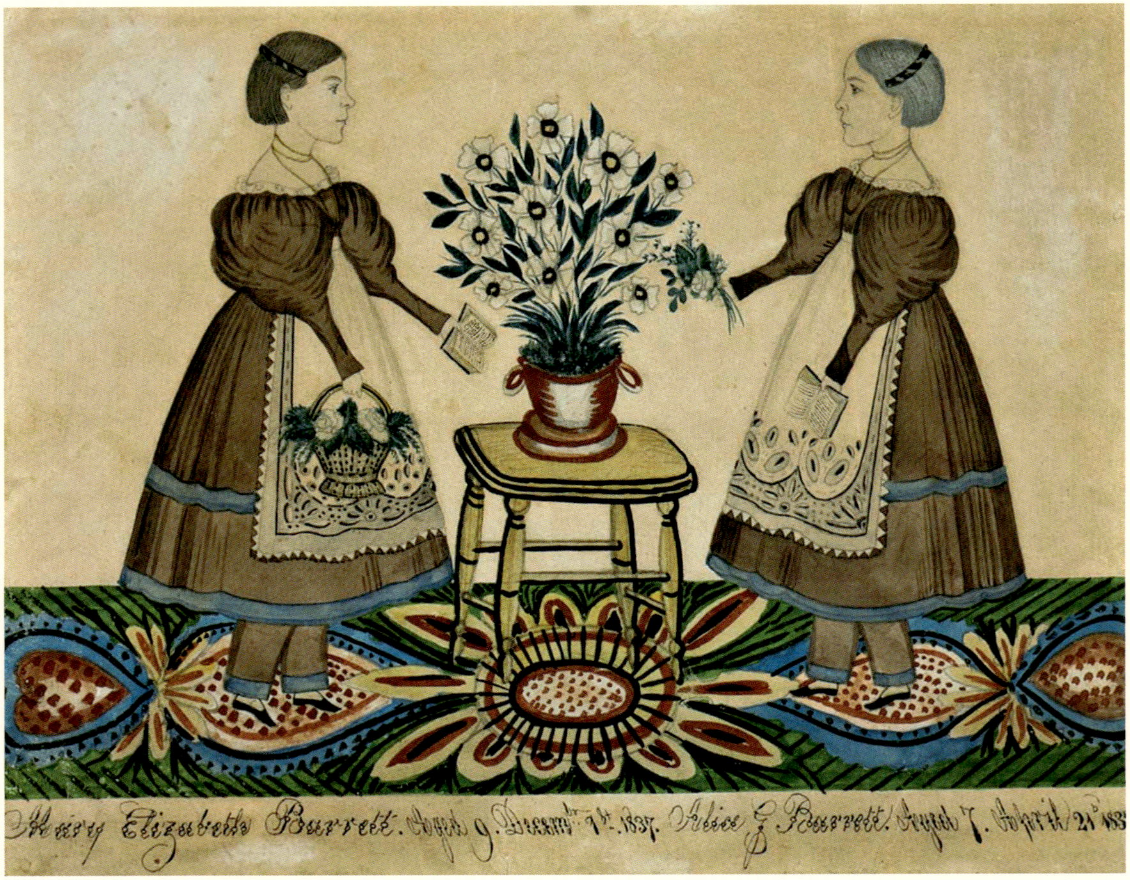

This charming double portrait of the sisters Mary Elizabeth and Alice G. is typical of the work of Joseph H. Davis. He often incorporated into his portraits wonderful details of nineteenth-century homes, including colorful, patterned floors and typical period furnishings. The furnishings, such as popular grain-painted pieces, are often as exuberant as the floors. Even with the startling details of the backgrounds, the watercolors portray the sitters as comfortable in their surroundings. The images of the two Barrett sisters are as arresting as the details of their aprons and the floor.

In this portrait, the girls flank a simple painted stool with a large bouquet of flowers. They stand on a highly decorative floor. The artist may have been representing a stenciled treatment, carpet, or painted floorcloth. The patterns may have actually existed, since these types of floor treatments were common in the period, or they may have come from the artist's imagination. Whatever the source, they make a very decorative stage for the artist's composition.

Although over a hundred examples of the artist's work survive (eight of which are owned by the Folk Art Museum), little is known about the artist himself. He inscribed one portrait with his name and the modifier "Left Hand Painter." He worked in the area around the Maine and New Hampshire border. He typically inscribed his watercolors with information about the sitters. In this instance, he provided the girls' names and ages, nine and seven, but, with their birthdays, he included the year in which the watercolor was created rather than the years in which the girls were born.

Punch-Needle Heart

DAVIS'S ATTENTION TO DETAIL HAD US LOOKING AT ALL ASPECTS OF HIS WORK FROM THE LOVELY FLOWERS TO THE DETAILS IN THE GIRLS' APRONS. IT WAS THE FLOOR, THOUGH, THAT CAUGHT OUR FANCY AND INSPIRED THE DESIGN FOR THIS PROJECT.

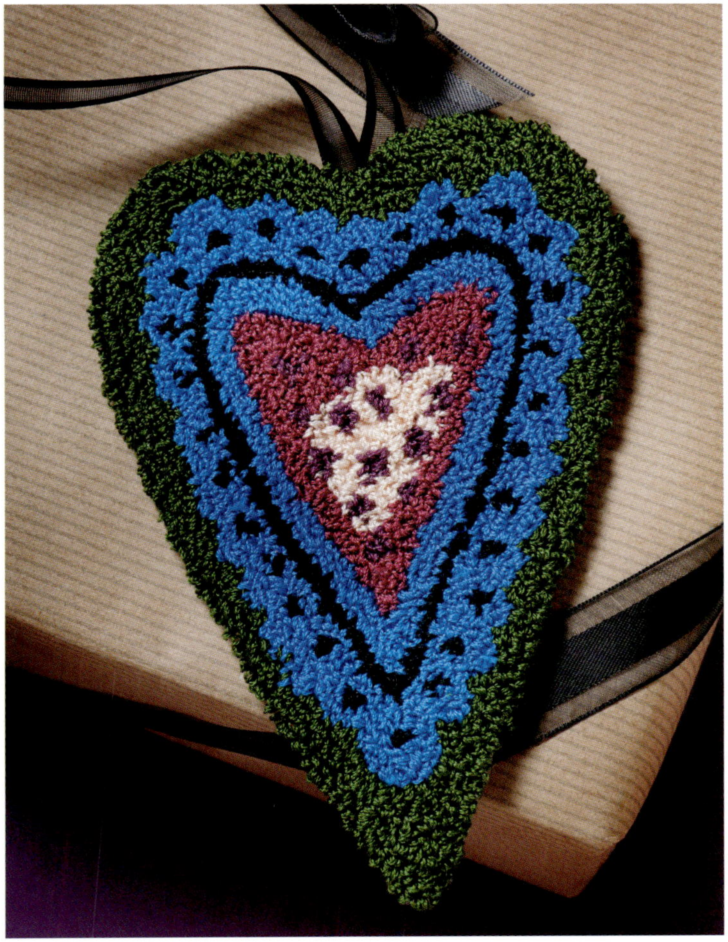

WHAT YOU NEED:

Heart template (page 135)
Tracing paper
Iron-on transfer pencil
Ecru weaver's cloth, 10 x 10 inches
Iron
Ironing board
6 3/4-inch interlocking hoop
3-strand punch needle
Punch-needle threader
Floss in the following DMC colors: 310, 995, 3345, 3803, 3834, 3866
Embroidery scissors
Matching felt
3/8-inch matching ribbon, 10 inches long

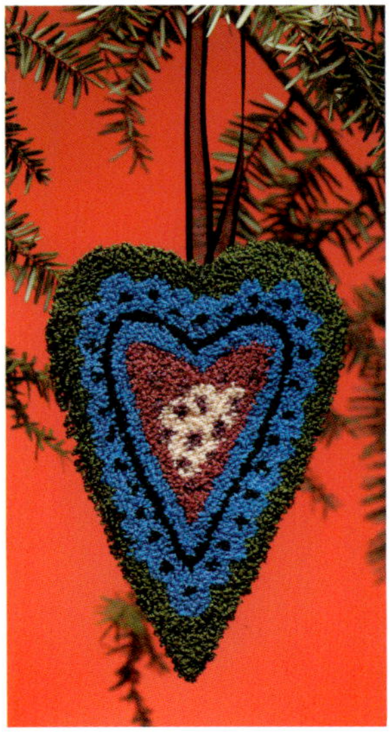

INSTRUCTIONS:

Trace the heart template onto the tracing paper using the iron-on transfer pencil. Following the manufacturer's instructions for the transfer pencil, iron the transfer onto the center of the weaver's cloth. Place the cloth into the hoop, centering the heart design.

Thread the punch needle with three strands of floss, and punch the design following the colors in the image. When the picture is complete, trim the thread from the back of the design.

Cut out the picture, leaving 1/2-inch fabric border all the way around. Make small cuts into the unworked fabric border, particularly at the curves, so that the fabric will lie flat when you fold it back. Fold the border toward the back and carefully iron so that it lies flat.

Using the heart template, cut out a felt heart. Stitch the felt to the back side of the fabric using a blind stitch. Before sewing up the top, form a loop with the ribbon and lay the ends of the ribbon on the back. Catch the ribbon in the stitches as you finish sewing up the top.

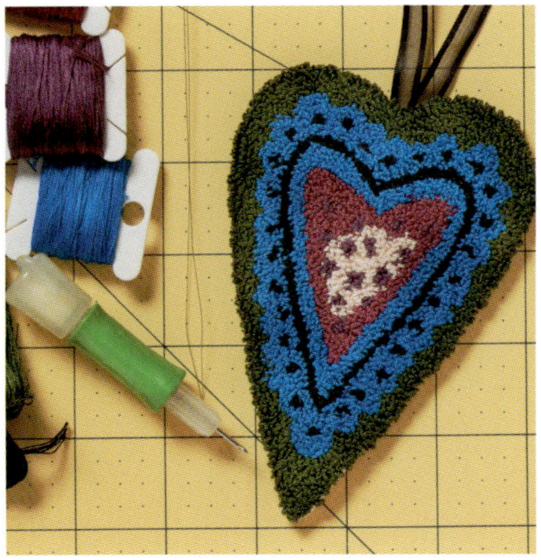

IDEA: MAKE THIS INTO A PINCUSHION BY CHOOSING A COORDINATING FABRIC AND STUFFING FIRMLY.

CRIB QUILT

attributed to Alma or Anna Richter, Sunman, Indiana, 1850–1860, cotton, 45" x 35", 1985.609.1

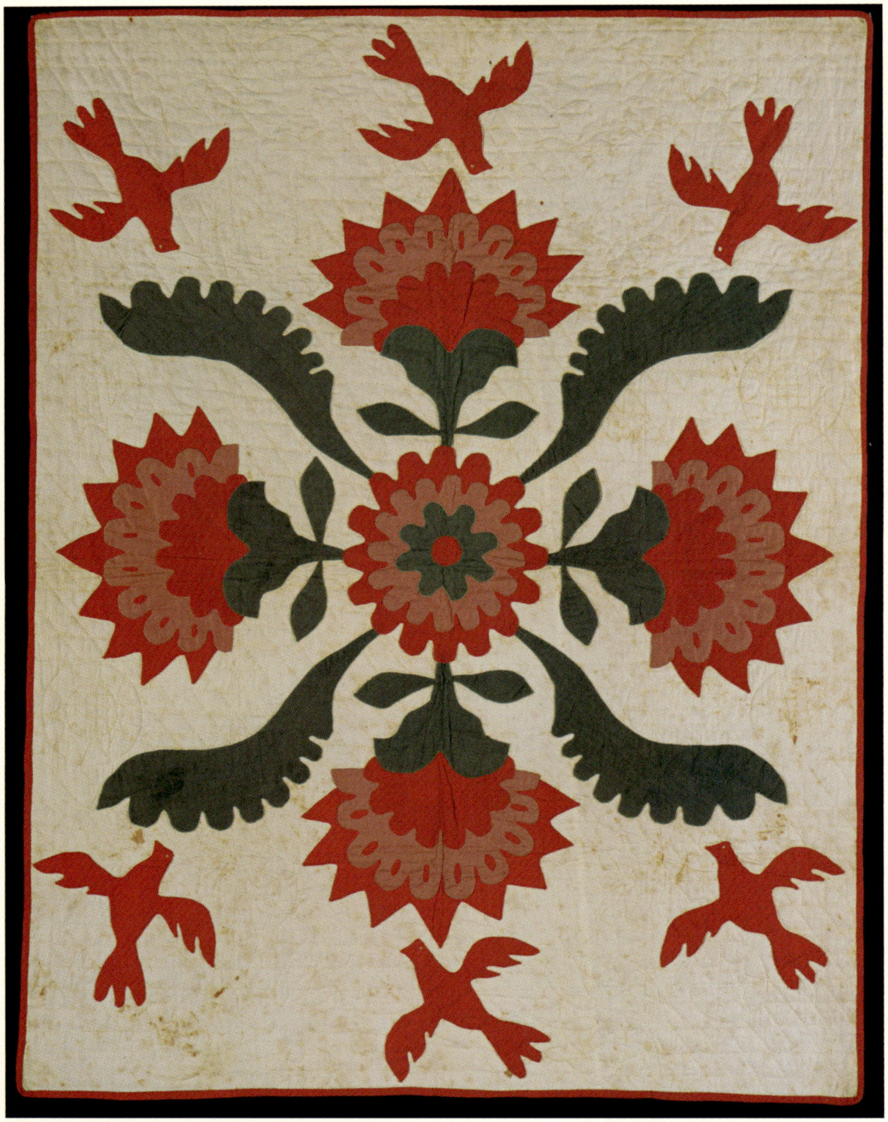

Intended as a crib quilt, this piece measures only 45 by 35 inches. The floral design, usually known as Tulip Cross, and the birds are characteristic of Pennsylvania German quilts. Each colored element was hand cut and appliquéd onto the background fabric. Since the possible maker lived in Indiana but was from a German family, she likely was familiar with the design tradition. The selection of color and pattern, although traditional, is nonetheless a personal choice made by the sewer.

When the Folk Art Museum acquired the quilt, family history noted that it had been made by Alma Richter. Over time, though, family history can get confused. Curators found that Alma Richter was not born until 1898, but the quilt was made in the 1850s. A little more research found that her German-born grandmother Anna Richter immigrated to America in 1841. Perhaps, then, Anna was the quilt maker and Alma the lucky baby who enjoyed being kept warm with it. Alma lived until 1984, and it was soon after that the museum acquired the quilt.

Paper Dove

WHILE THE STRONG TULIP CROSS DOMINATES THE QUILT, THE BIRDS CAUGHT OUR ATTENTION. THEY LOOK ELEGANT MADE FROM SNOWY WHITE PAPER WITH DELICATE PIERCED DECORATION.

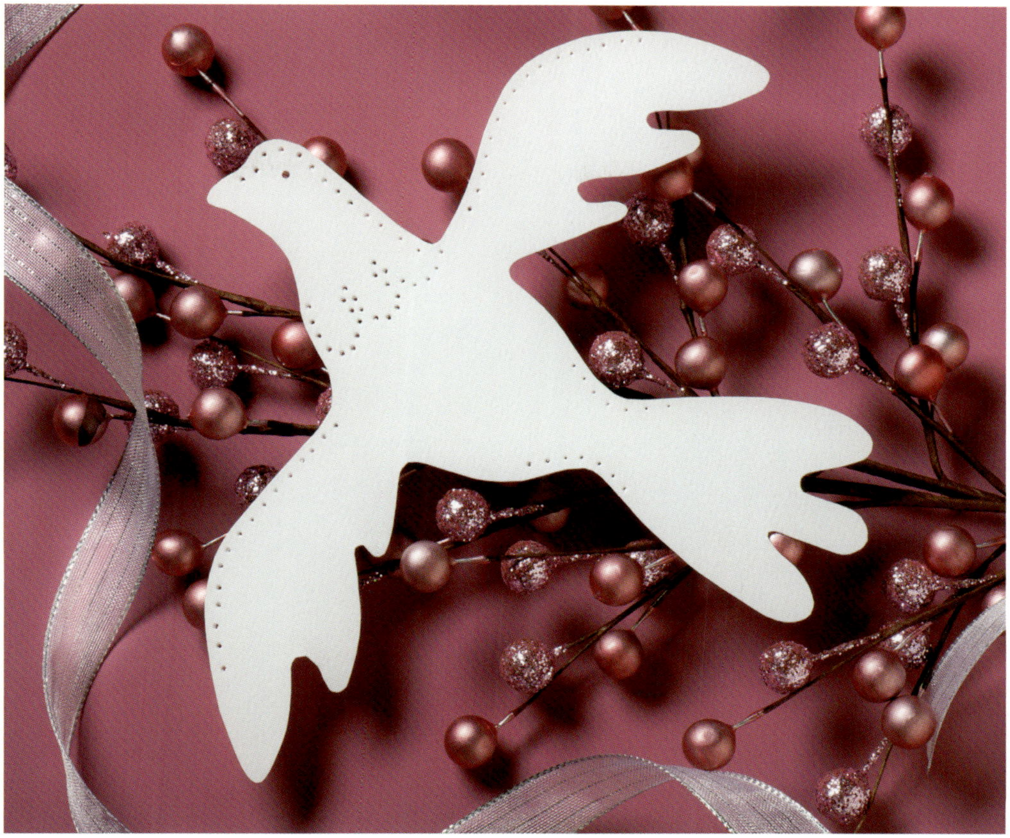

WHAT YOU NEED:

Dove template (page 136)
Cardboard (such as a cereal box)
Cutting mat (an extra layer of cardboard will also work)
Watercolor paper or card stock (any color)
Scissors
Awl or pushpin
1/8-inch hole punch
Needle
Clear thread

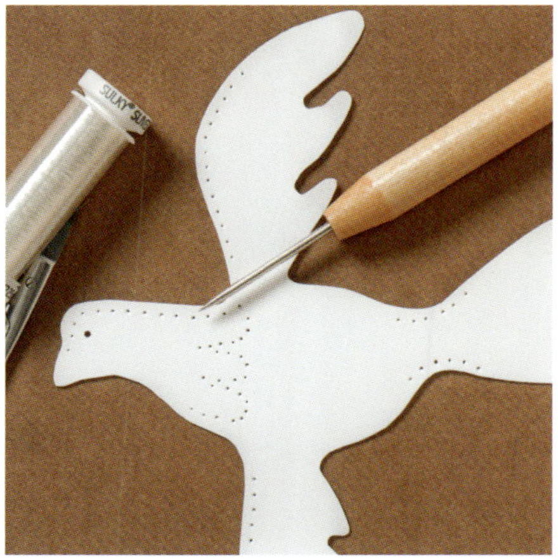

INSTRUCTIONS:

To prepare your work surface, lay a piece of cardboard down on top of the cutting mat.

Use the template to cut out a dove from the heavy paper.

Place the paper dove on the cardboard with the template lined up on top of it. Following the pattern on the template, carefully pierce the dove through both the template and paper using the awl or pushpin. Once the piercing is complete, carefully pull the template away from the paper dove.

Use the hole punch to create the eye.

To create the hanger, sew a length of clear thread through the top of the wing and tie off at desired length for hanging.

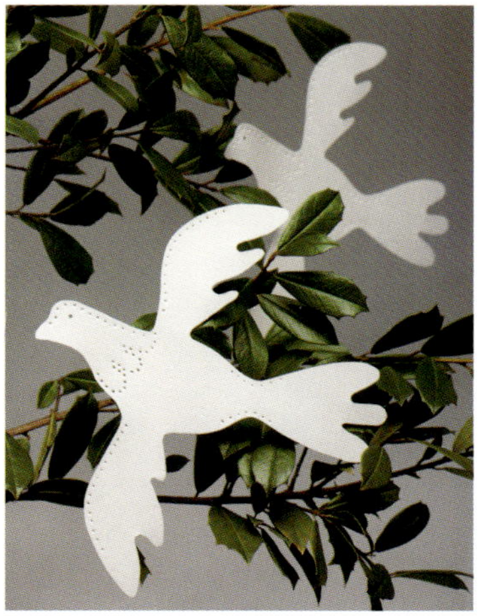

IDEAS: ALTHOUGH THE PAPER DOVE LOOKS GOOD SOLO, FOR A DIFFERENT LOOK CREATE A WHOLE FLOCK. THEY FLOAT GRACEFULLY ON THE TREE OR MAKE CHARMING GIFT TAGS FOR SPECIAL PACKAGES. TRY THEM IN DIFFERENT COLORS AND SIZES. FOR DIFFERENT SIZES, REDUCE OR INCREASE THE SIZE OF THE TEMPLATE ON A COPY MACHINE.

MT. HOOD AND MIRROR LAKE

Steve Harley (1863–1947), Oregon, 1927,
oil on canvas, 16 1/4" x 30 1/2", acquisition funded by
Dr. and Mrs. T. Marshall Hahn Jr., 2004.102.1

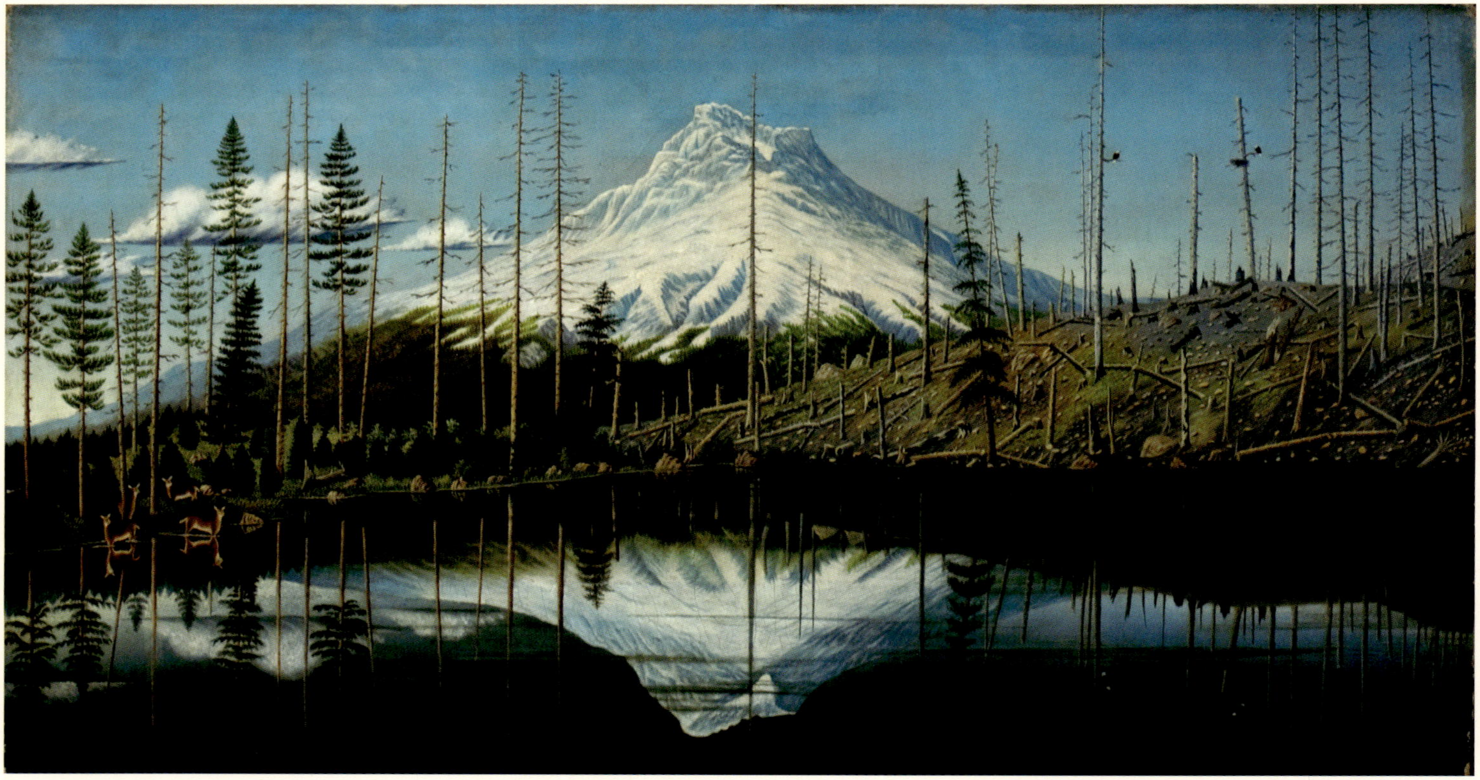

This painting of Mount Hood is the work of Steve Harley, a man inspired and awed by the splendor and strength of nature. He painted this scene while on a trip in Oregon in the late 1920s. Although he had experimented with a camera during his travels, he was not satisfied with the results. Instead, he chose to capture the scenery of the Pacific Northwest in paint. Four paintings from this trip survive, all of which are in the collection of the Folk Art Museum.

Harley's concern and delight in nature profoundly influenced his art. His paintings accurately depict the places he visited, but they also offer a very personal view. In this scene of Mount Hood and Mirror Lake, the stillness of the lake magnificently reflects the mountain dominating the scene. A fire-ravaged landscape on one side contrasts with the green, deer-inhabited forest on the opposite side. The artist effectively conveys his view of nature as beautiful, powerful, and a bit mysterious.

A Grand Rapids, Michigan, address on the back indicates that this painting traveled home with the artist. This raises the question of whether Harley completed his landscapes on-site or whether he returned to them once he was back home, adding finishing touches while working from sketches and memories.

Recycled-Plastic Landscape

To complement the painting that he and his wife had received directly from the artist, Donald Tonn made the frame around 1960 from wood reclaimed from old Wisconsin buildings, a fitting tribute to the artist's great respect for the environment. As a way to honor that spirit, we created our mini-landscapes out of recyclable materials.

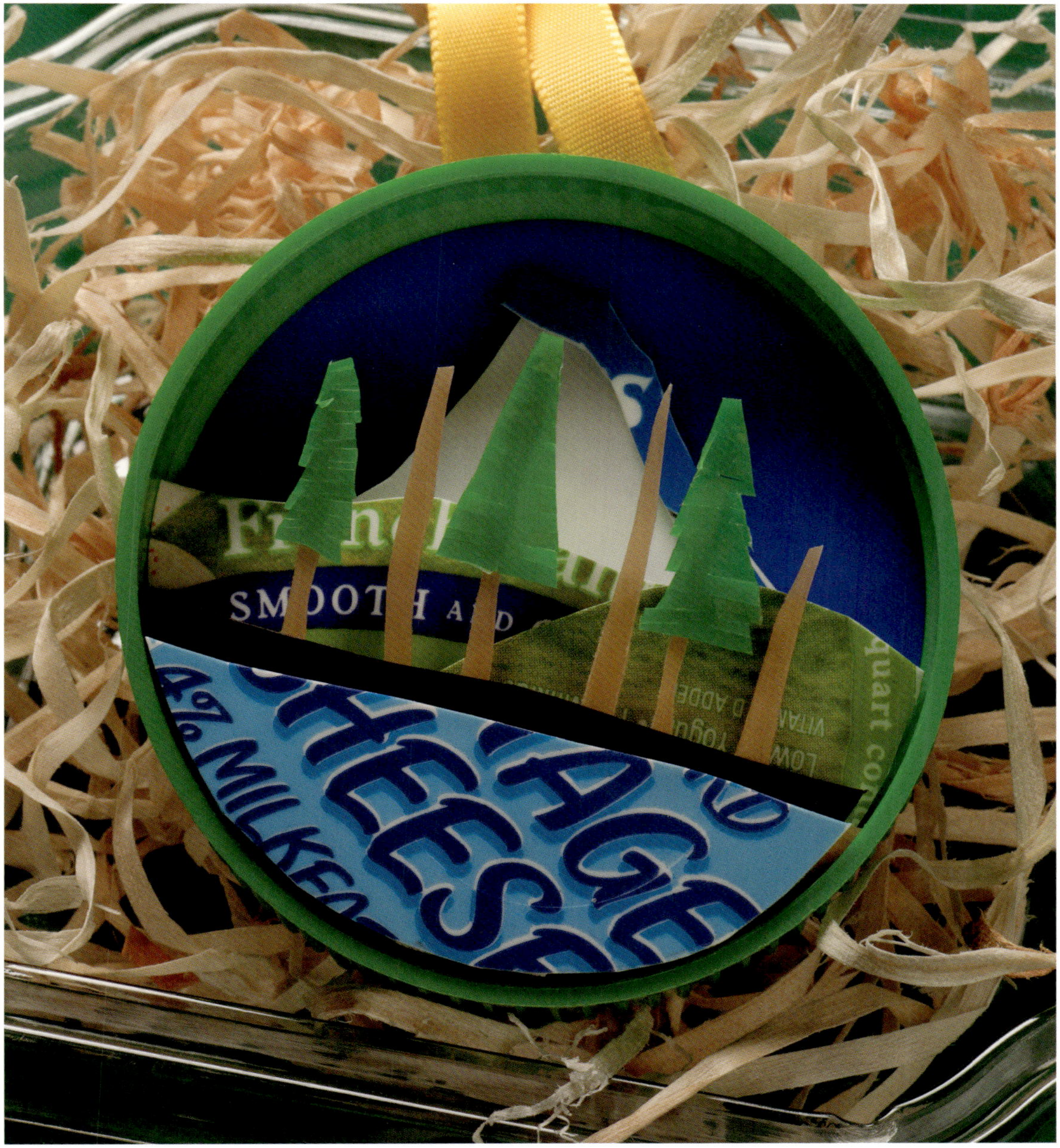

What You Need:

- Background, mountain, mountain edge, hill 1, hill 2, forest, forest edge, water, and tree templates (page 143)
- $2\frac{3}{4}$-inch-diameter plastic twist-off jar lid (peanut butter lids provide a nice deep base)
- Cardboard (such as a cereal box)
- Awl
- $\frac{1}{4}$-inch ribbon, 10 inches long
- Scissors
- Plastic lids: 2 blue, 1 white, 2 green, 1 brown, 1 black (the lids can be plain or printed)
- Mounting tape
- Thick and tacky glue

Note: These instructions were created using a $2\frac{3}{4}$-inch-diameter lid. If your lid is smaller or larger, adjust the sizes of your templates accordingly.

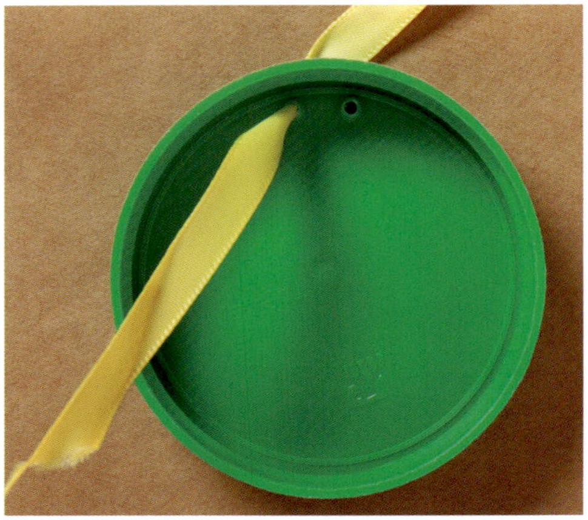

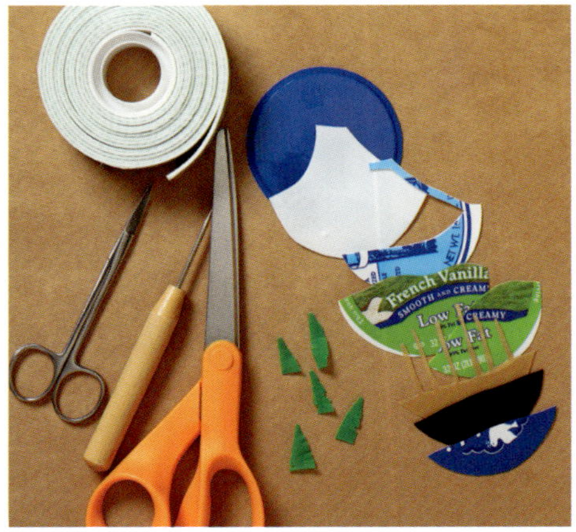

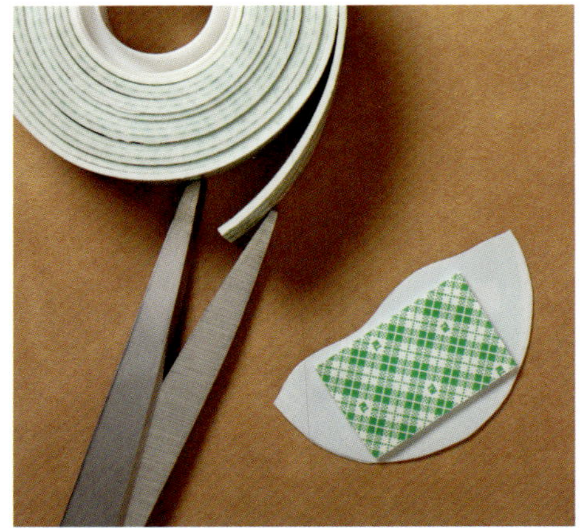

INSTRUCTIONS:

Create the hanger first: Place the $2\frac{3}{4}$-inch-diameter lid, top up, on the cardboard and a well-protected work surface. Use the awl to poke two holes, about $\frac{1}{2}$ inch apart, into the lid on the flat surface near the rim. Thread the ribbon through the holes so that both ends come out through the top of the lid and tie off at the desired length for hanging.

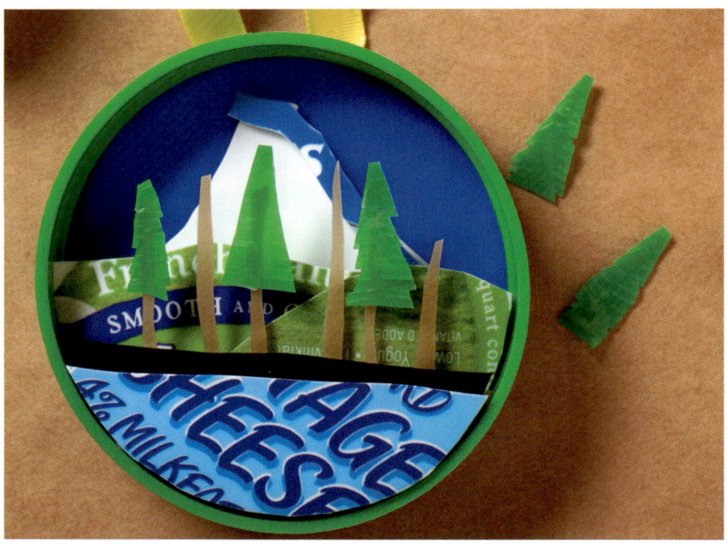

The three-dimensional effect of the landscape is created by cutting each element of the picture separately from the plastic lids and then layering them using the mounting tape. Using the templates, cut out all of the pieces:

Cut the background from a blue lid.

Cut the mountain from the white lid.

Cut the mountain edge from a blue lid.

Cut hill 1 and hill 2 from a green lid.

Cut the forest from the brown lid.

Cut the forest edge from the black lid.

Cut the water from a blue lid.

Cut five trees from a green lid. Feather snip the edges.

Before you mount the pieces in place, layer them in the order they were cut and make any changes to the scene now.

Place the $2\frac{3}{4}$-inch-diameter lid on your work surface with the ribbon hanger at the top. Place mounting tape on the back of the blue background and place it inside the lid. Continue in order with each piece. Always place the mounting tape on the piece to be mounted. Use the glue to add the trees once all the other pieces are mounted.

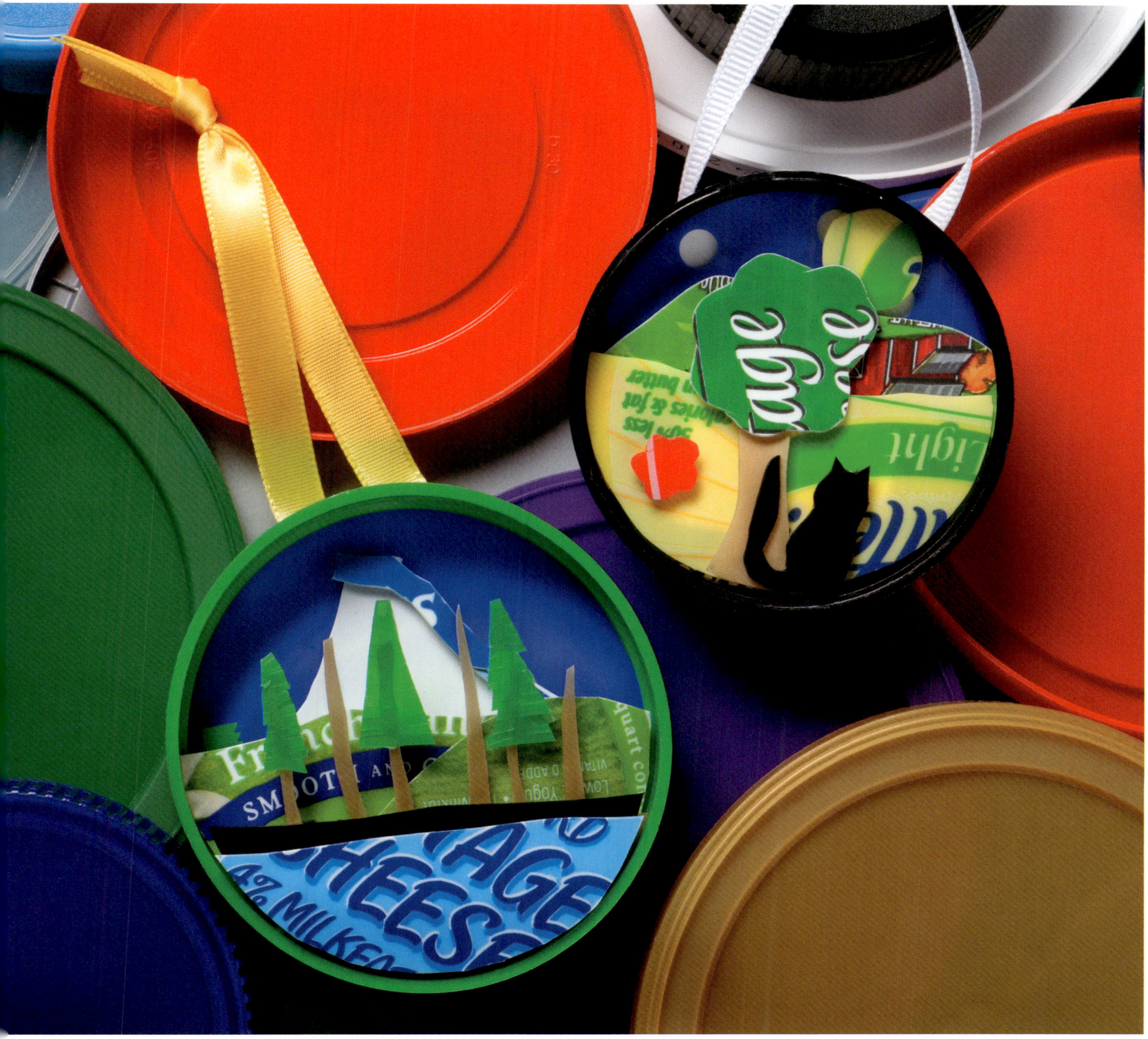

IDEAS: Create your own landscape. Will it be a farm yard or outer space? Will the setting be during the day or at night? Instead of an ornament, create a brooch or package tag.

BOOKMARK

southeastern Pennsylvania, ca. 1810,
watercolor and ink on laid paper, 4 1/8" x 2 3/4",
1963.305.1, 6

Small drawings, while perhaps more simplistic than larger pieces, have a charm of their own. Imagine opening a book and finding a hand-drawn piece of art holding your place. These bookmarks were small tokens given to loved ones and friends. In southeastern Pennsylvania, artistic traditions drew from the German roots of many of the inhabitants. The same color palette and motifs decorated not only bookmarks but also birth and baptismal certificates, marriage records, and religious texts created by professional record artists, many of whom also worked as schoolteachers, ministers, and professional painters. Some pieces were created by amateurs inspired by the tradition or by schoolchildren who created them as lessons in drawing and penmanship. The tulip in particular was a popular motif used in Pennsylvania German works.

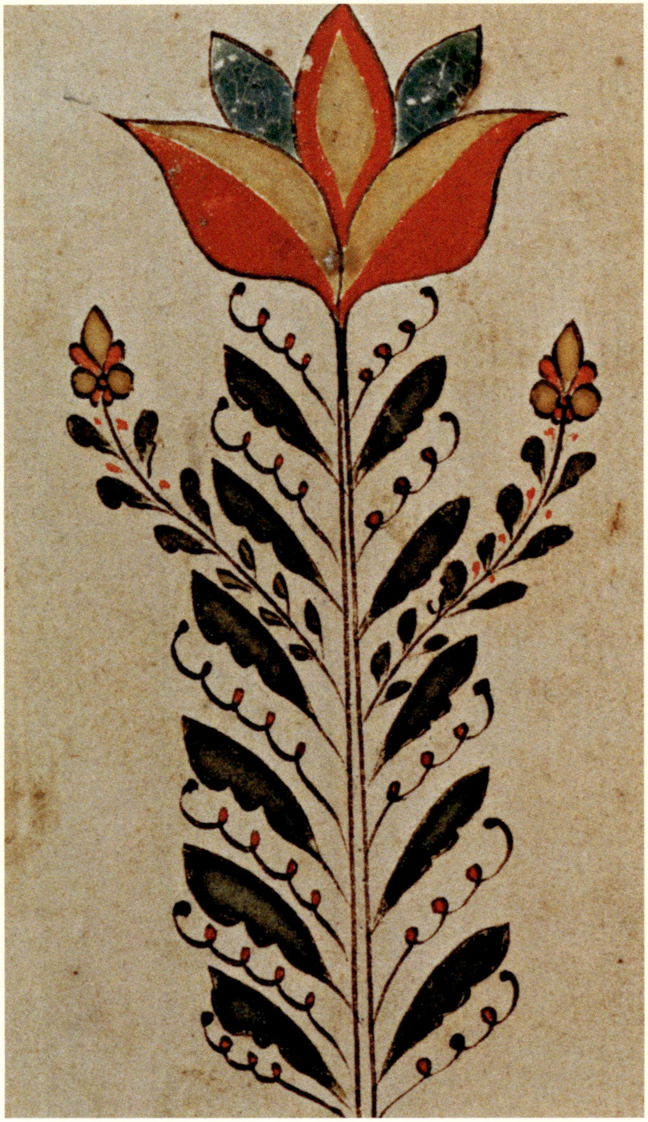

Cross-Stitch Tulip

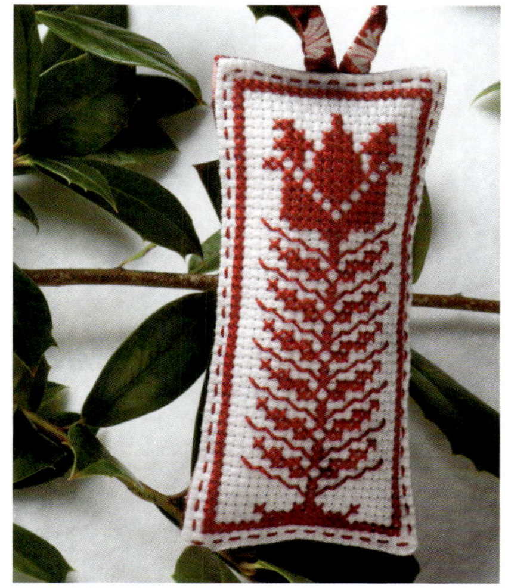

THESE SWEET CROSS-STITCHED ORNAMENTS LOOK GREAT INDIVIDUALLY, OR THEY COULD FILL AN ENTIRE TREE IN ANY COLOR COMBINATION YOU DESIRE.

WHAT YOU NEED:

Charted design

14-count white Aida cloth, $2^3/_4 \times 4^1/_2$ inches

Cross-stitch needle

Printed cotton fabric, 1 x 7 inches and $2^3/_4 \times 4^1/_2$ inches

Matching floss

Iron

Ironing board

Needle

Scissors

Pins

Stuffing

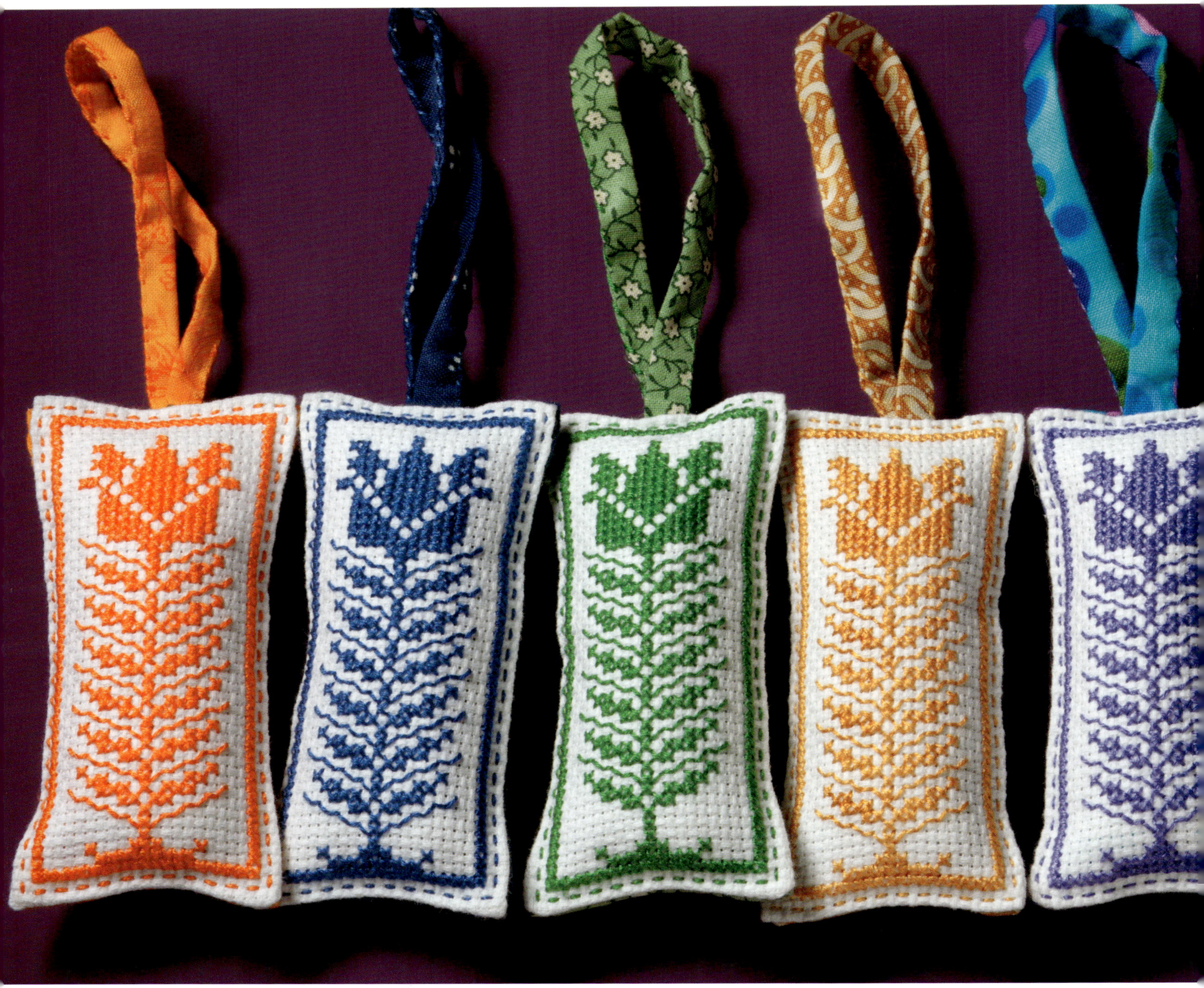

IDEA: MAKE THIS PROJECT INTO A BOOKMARK BY OMITTING THE STUFFING AND, INSTEAD OF THE LOOP, SEW A COLOR-COORDINATED RIBBON AT THE TOP.

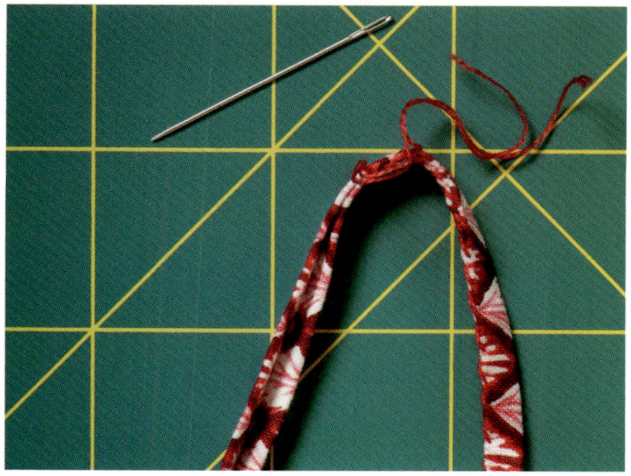

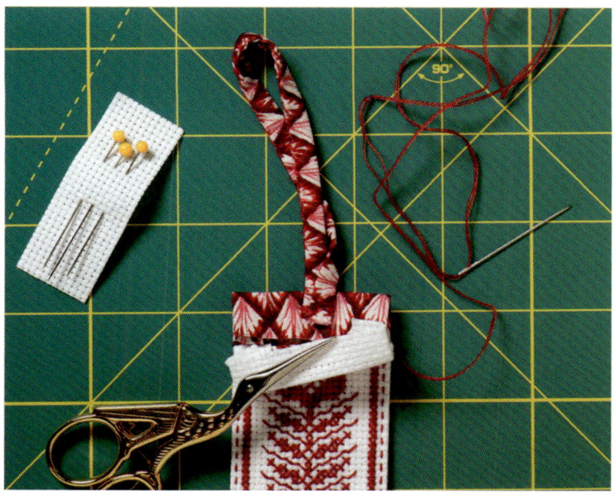

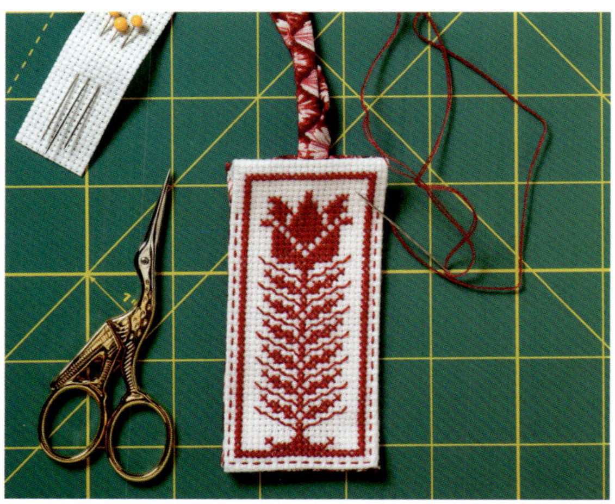

INSTRUCTIONS:

Referring to the charted design, create the cross-stitch on the Aida cloth. Start the stitches at the base of the stem and work the stem, leaves, flower, and border. Work the tendrils in backstitches. When the cross-stitching is complete, set it aside.

To make the hanger, take the 1 x 7–inch piece of cotton fabric and fold the long edges to the center keeping the right side of the fabric on the outside. Fold this in half and press in place with the iron. Whipstitch the folded edges together with the needle and floss. Bring the two ends together to form a loop and stitch to hold the loop shape. Set aside.

Remove the cross-stitched Aida cloth from the hoop and fold back the cloth 1/4 inch from the stitching on all four sides. Iron. Repeat the folding and ironing with the second piece of cotton fabric, folding the edges to the wrong side of the fabric. Place together the two folded pieces with wrong sides facing in. Line up all of the edges and pin. Stitch together using a running stitch, following the charted design. Leave the top open for stuffing and the hanger. Stuff to desired thickness. Set the fabric loop in the hole, and, using the running stitch again, close up the top catching the hanger as you do.

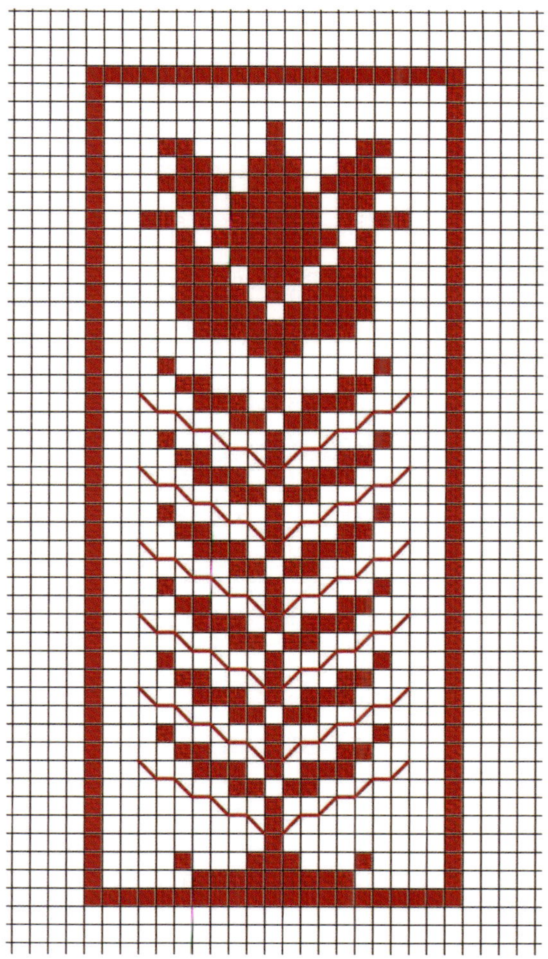

PRINCE

Irwin Weil (1887–1979), Coopersburg, Pennsylvania, 1930–1935, wood and paint, 16" x 17 1/8" x 5 1/2", 1981.701.1

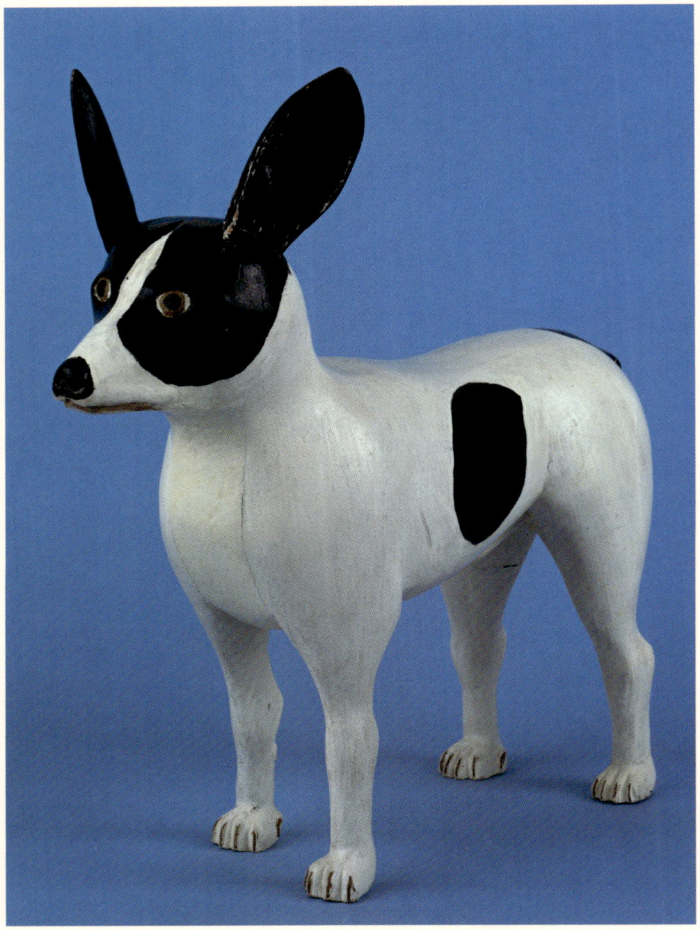

Although we think of portraits as paintings referring to people, this animal sculpture is also a portrait. Prince, a much-loved fox terrier, lived in Coopersburg, Pennsylvania, for seven years until his untimely death in a road accident. He was the pet of Russell, Alvin, and Harold Weil. The boys remembered Prince as a "good mouser." The boys' father, Irwin, carved the life-size sculpture soon after the tragedy. He painted the markings to match those of the real dog. The boys fondly remembered the wooden dog set out on the front porch. The sculpture was so realistic that it actually kept traveling salesmen from approaching the front door. Irwin Weil continued to carve and created many garden ornaments, including characters from fairy tales.

Prince came to the Folk Art Collection soon after the artist's death. He is an excellent example of the personal nature of folk art. The carver clearly knew and cared for his subject. The curators were so taken with him that we created an exhibition and storybook based on him. In the exhibition, we encourage guests to follow Prince on his adventure and at the end draw their own piece of art.

Felt Dog

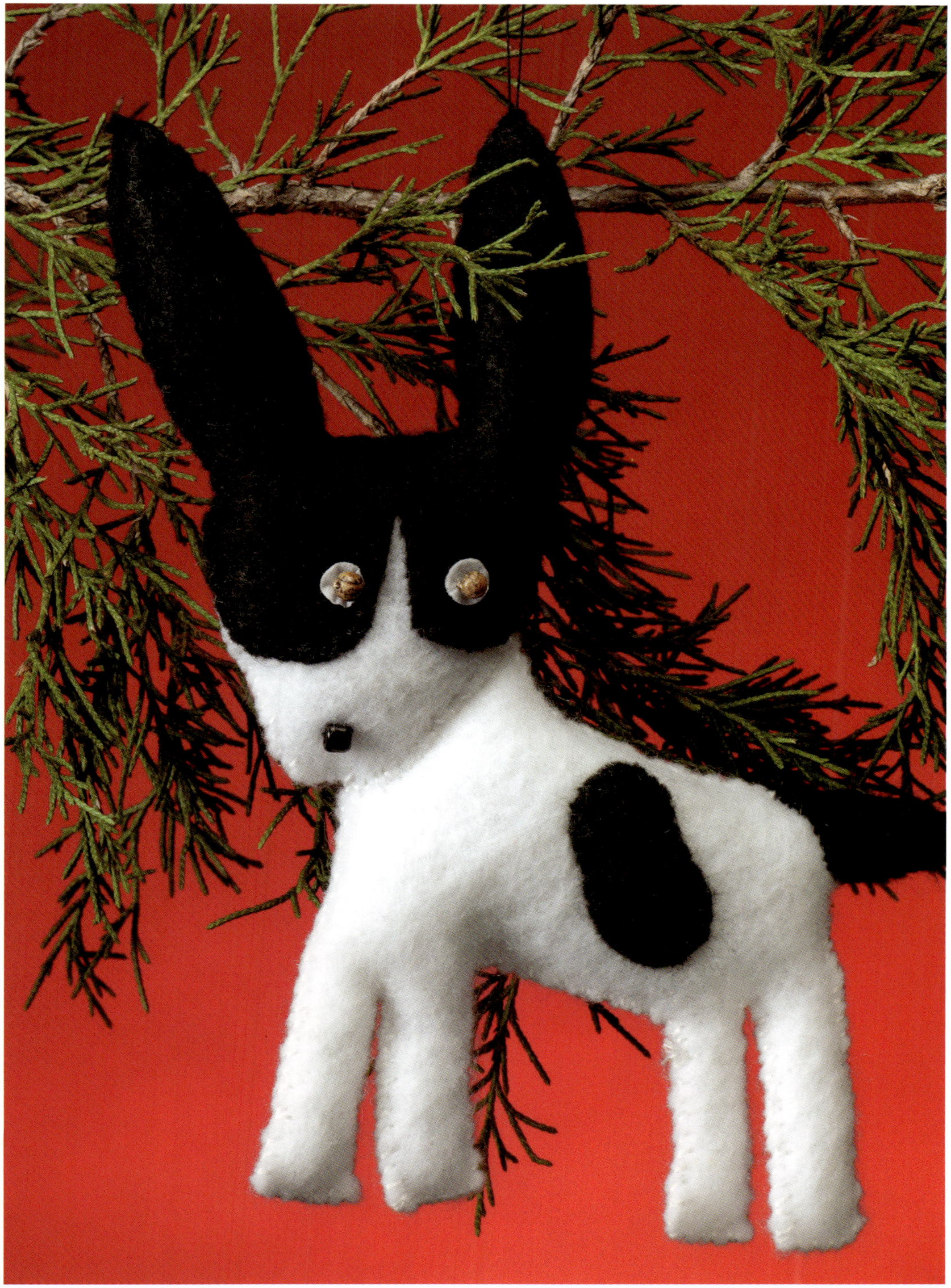

ONE OF THE DRAWINGS POSTED ON THE BOARD IN THE EXHIBIT WAS A CHILD'S DRAWING OF PRINCE. WE WERE SO INSPIRED BY HER INTERPRETATION THAT WE USED IT AS THE BASIS FOR THIS ORNAMENT.

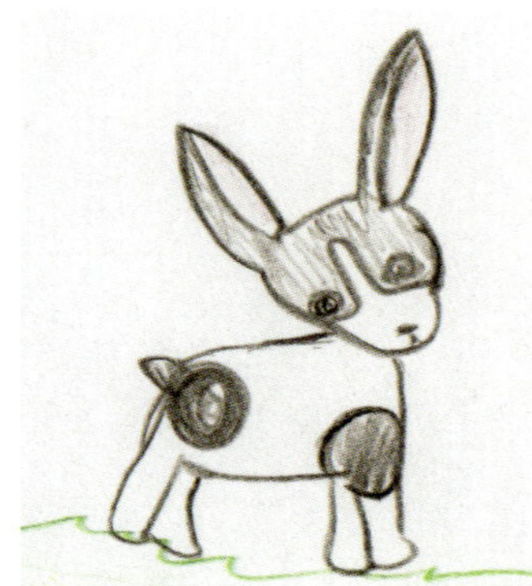

WHAT YOU NEED:

Body, spots, tail, head, ears/mask front, and ears/mask back templates (page 129)

Scissors

Black and white felt

Matching floss

Needle

Stuffing

Pins

White heavy interfacing

Cardboard (such as a cereal box)

1/4-inch hole punch

Two brown beads, 4 mm

Matching floss

One black glass bead, size E

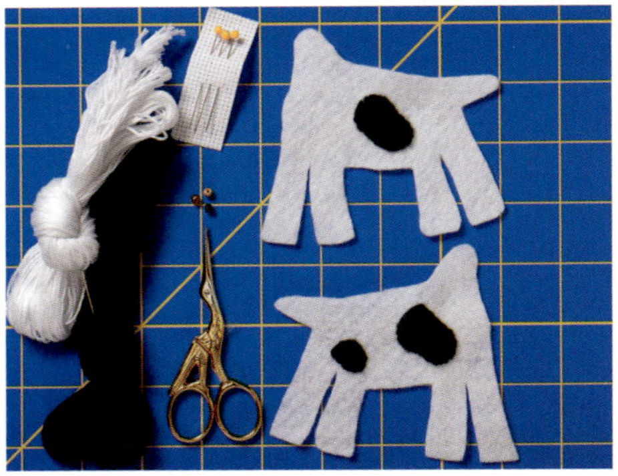

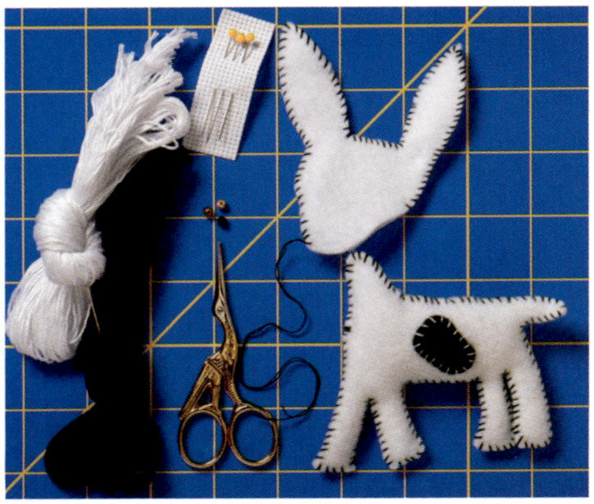

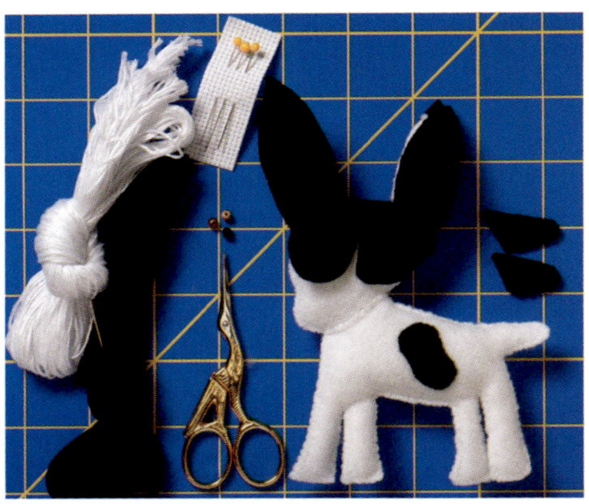

IDEA: LOOKING FOR A QUICK PROJECT? CREATE PRINCE FROM PAPER. YOU COULD GLUE HIM ONTO COLORED PAPER AND MAKE A GREETING CARD FOR A DOG-LOVING FRIEND.

INSTRUCTIONS:

This project is made in two pieces: the body and the head. Start by making the body. Use the templates to cut out two white felt bodies, three black felt spots, and two black felt tails.

Following the placement shown in the instruction photo, place the spots on the body pieces and sew on with black floss using a blind stitch. Align the body pieces with wrong sides together. Using white floss, begin whipstitching at the neck in the direction of the legs. (We used black floss to make the stitches stand out in the instruction photo.) Sew around the legs and tail. As you get past the tail and onto the back, loosely stuff the legs and tail and some of the body. Continue sewing along the back toward the neck. Add any final stuffing and then stitch closed.

To make the head, use the templates to cut out two white felt heads, one black felt ears/mask front, and one black felt ears/mask back. Place the head pieces with wrong sides together. Whipstitch using white floss leaving the neck open. Loosely stuff. Place the neck of the body into the neck of the head and stitch together with white floss using a blind stitch. Pin the ears/mask pieces in place on the front and back of the white head. With black floss, whipstitch the ears together and blind stitch around the mask as you stitch the black mask to the white head. To ensure that the white felt does not appear in between the black with the whipstitch, do not stitch through the white but rather stitch over it.

Pin the black tail pieces onto the tail of the white body. With black floss, whipstitch the tail together. Again be careful not to catch the white felt in the stitching.

To make the eyes, sandwich the interfacing in between two pieces of the cardboard and punch two circles. The cardboard helps hold the interfacing to ensure that you get a perfect circle with the hole punch. Discard the cardboard circles, and lay the interfacing circles onto the head following the placement shown in the instruction photo. Using the brown floss, stitch the brown beads to the center of the interfacing circles as you stitch the interfacing to the felt head to create the eyes. Be careful to take your needle through only the first layer of felt so that your stitches do not show on the back.

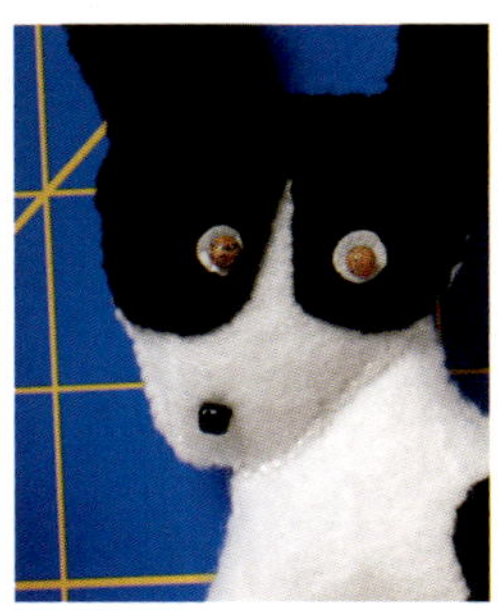

Stitch on the black bead for a nose. Again take the needle through only the one layer of felt.

Using the needle, thread a piece of black floss through the top of the left ear and knot to create a hanger.

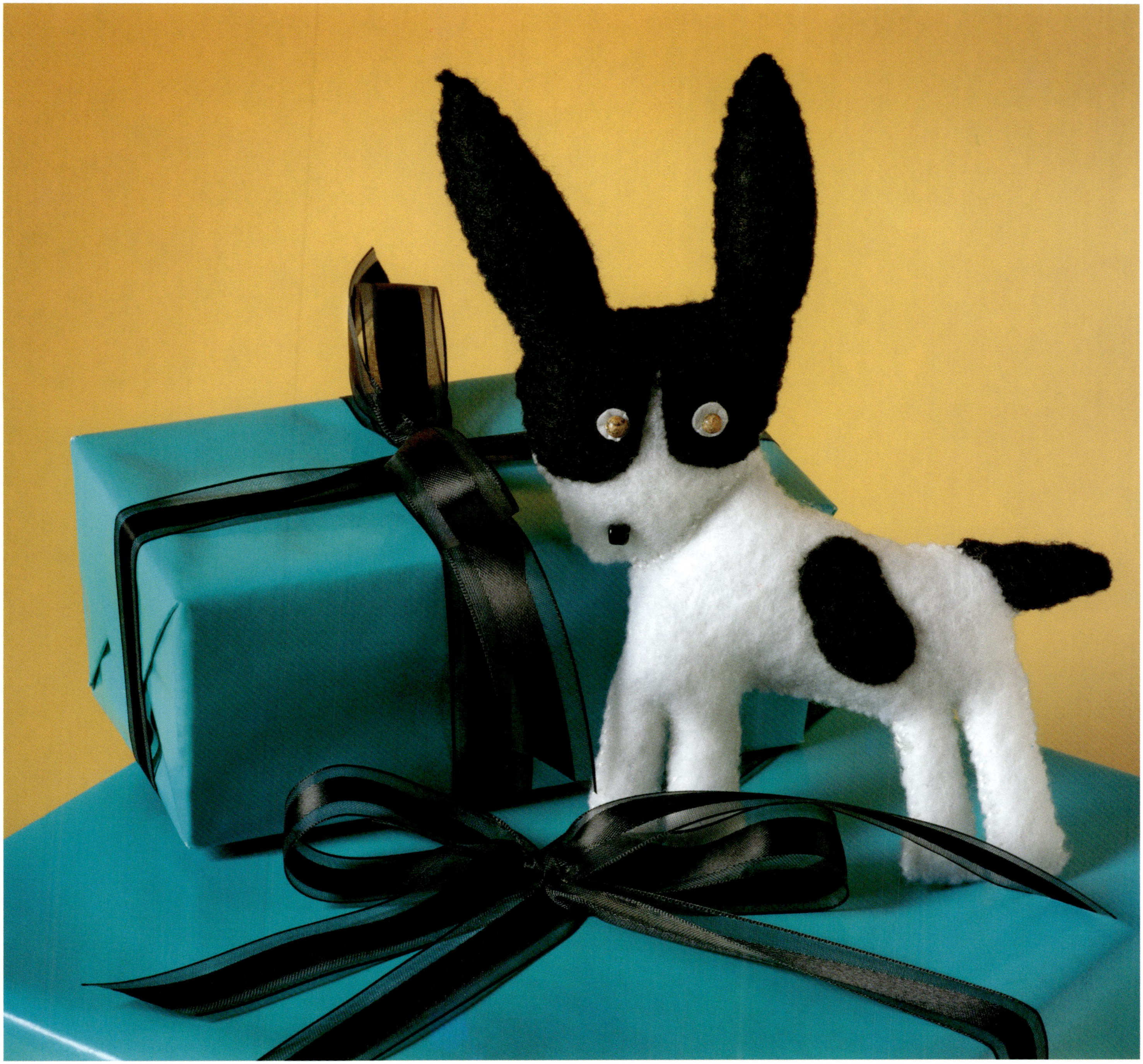

BUTTERFLY WEATHER VANE

attributed to L. W. Cushing & Sons, Waltham, Massachusetts, 1872–1900, copper, copper alloy, lead, paint, and gilding, $18^{1}/_{2}$" x 17" x $^{1}/_{2}$", 1962.800.2

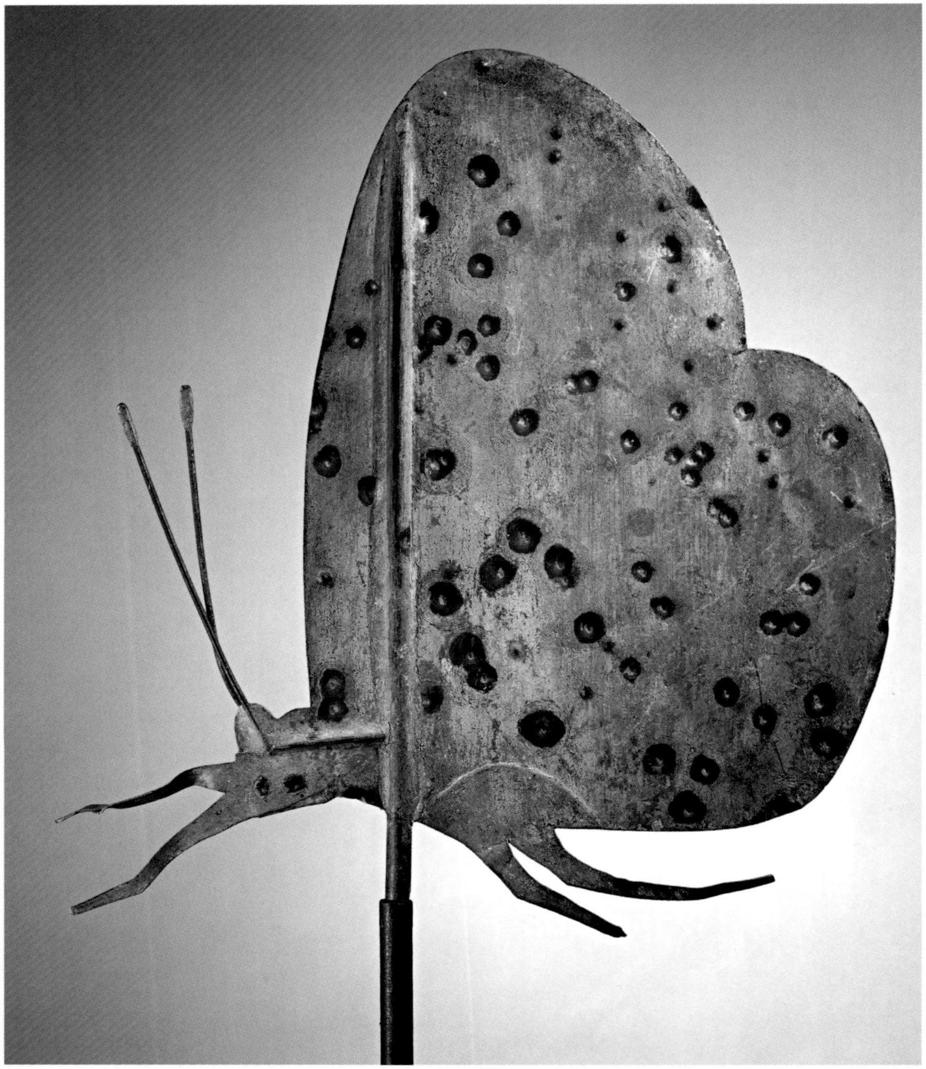

Viewing this butterfly today, it appears to have an interesting spotted design, but we must jump back over one hundred years to when it was new to appreciate what it was meant to look like. The "spots" are actually bullet holes garnered over the years. Both young and old shooters enjoyed taking shots at weather vanes to test their aim as well as watch the vanes spin. When this butterfly first went on top of a building, it shone with a bright gilt surface on smooth wings. It had a clean, uninterrupted look. The gilding eventually wore off, and a coat of yellow paint was applied as a cheaper alternative to regilding.

Horses, Indians, birds, fish, and deer were all very popular weather vane designs. Insects held not the same appeal if the low number of surviving examples is any indication. This butterfly is attributed to the Massachusetts company of L. W. Cushing & Sons; an illustration in its 1883 catalog is almost identical to this example.

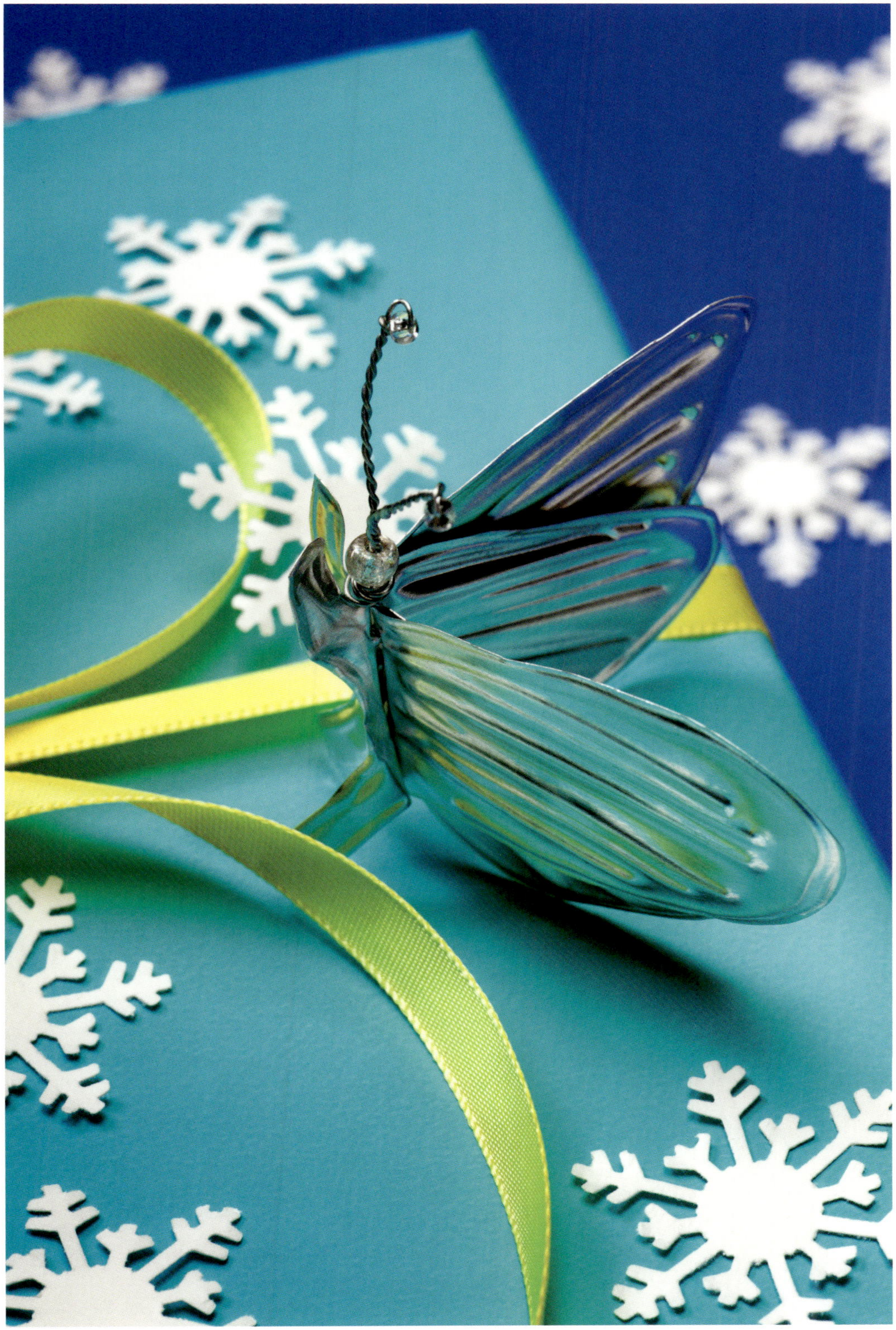

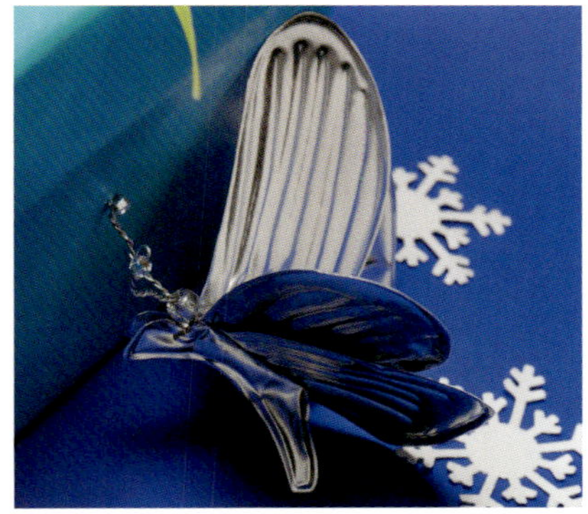

Aluminum Butterfly

DESPITE THE FLATNESS OF THE WEATHER VANE, THE BUTTERFLY LOOKS READY TO TAKE FLIGHT. OUR MINIATURE VERSION GIVES THE INSECT A FULL SET OF WINGS SO THAT IT CAN NESTLE ANYWHERE IN THE TREE.

WHAT YOU NEED:

Body, large wings, and small wings templates (page 141)

Clear tape

36-gauge aluminum tooling foil

Piece of felt

Stylus (such as an old ballpoint pen or sharpened dowel)

Embroidery scissors

Binder clip

Awl or pushpin

26-gauge wire, 24 inches long

One silver bead, 4 mm

Ruler

Two silver beads, 10/0

Pliers

INSTRUCTIONS:

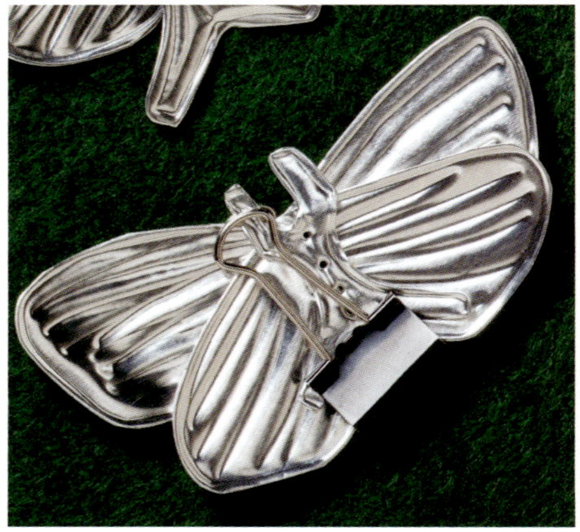

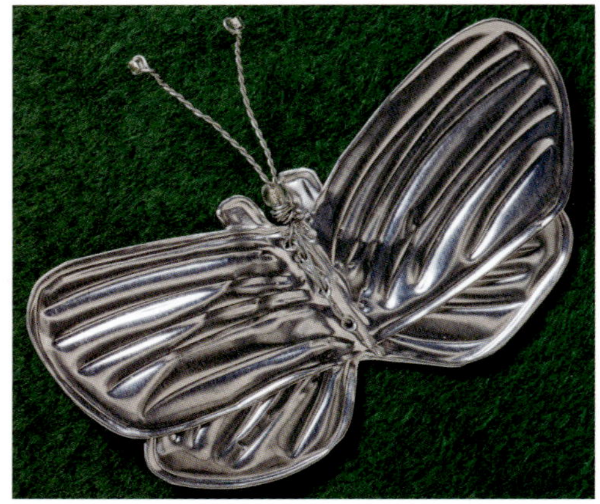

Tape the body template to the tooling foil and place on the felt. The felt will protect your work surface and allow the stylus to create a deep impression into the foil. Trace the template, including all of the decorative details, with the stylus with even pressure. Remove the template. If necessary, go over the image more firmly with the stylus. Repeat the process with the large wings and the small wings templates.

Cut out the foil body, large wings, and small wings leaving a 1/8-inch margin on the outside of the drawn lines.

Place the large wings on the felt and layer with the small wings and then the body, all with right sides down. Match up the center lines of all pieces and make sure they are evenly aligned at the base. Use the binder clip to hold the pieces in place. Turn the clipped pieces over (right side up), and, using the awl or push pin, poke four holes down the center seam of the butterfly making sure to penetrate all three layers. Be careful not to rip the foil.

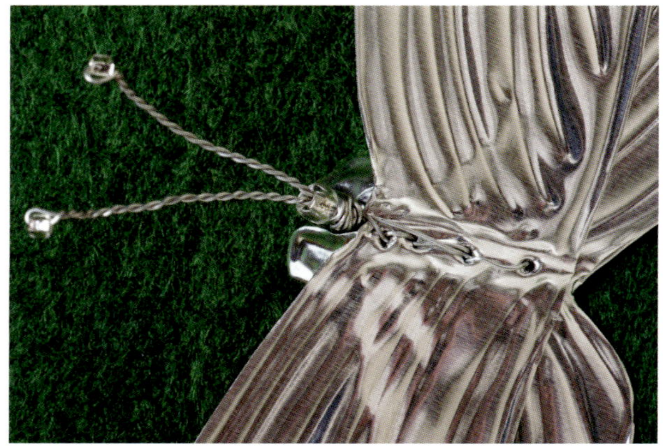

Fold the wire in half, and thread one end of it through the bottom hole in the butterfly. Continue threading both ends of the wire through the holes to the top of the butterfly alternating the direction of each end. Once past the first hole, each end goes through each hole. You are basically doing a running stitch with the wires through the three layers of the butterfly. The bend in the middle of the wire should end up secure in the first hole.

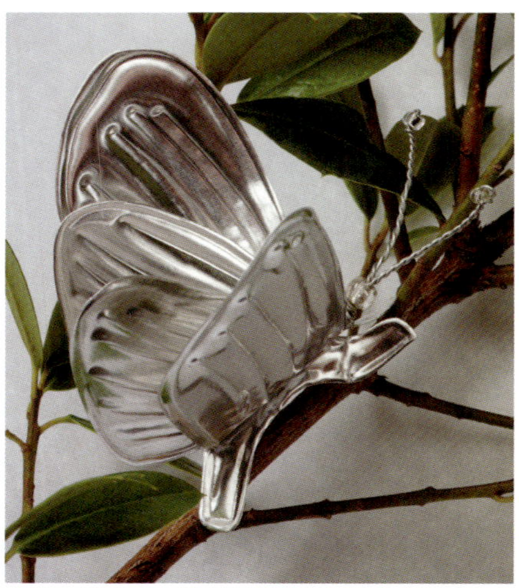

Once both ends of the wire are completely through the holes, thread the 4 mm silver bead onto both ends to create the head. To form two antennae, separate the wires, measure 1 1/4 inches away from the head, and create a bend in each wire. Thread a 10/0 silver bead onto each wire, placing it at the bend. Return the wires through the 4 mm bead. With the pliers, carefully grasp one of the antennae and twist the wire until the bead at the end of the antenna is secure. Repeat with the second antenna. To secure the loose wire ends, wrap them around the wire below the 4 mm bead.

Rather than hanging it, nestle the butterfly into the branches of your tree.

IDEA: THESE BUTTERFLIES WOULD BE SUPER CUTE MADE FROM VARIOUS SCRAPBOOK PAPERS.

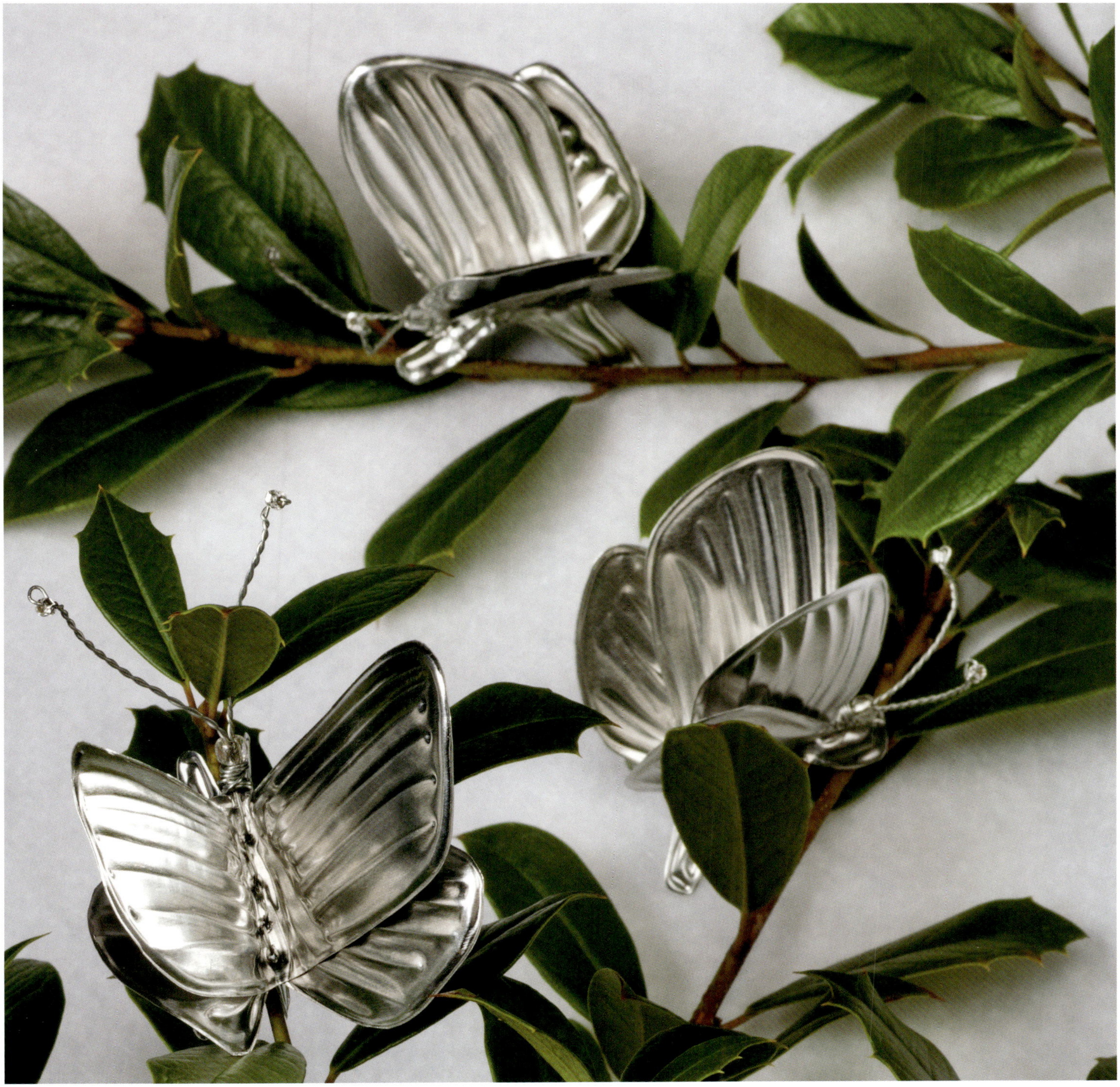

CUTWORK PICTURE

Martha Ann Honeywell (ca. 1787–after 1848), America, probably 1830–1848, paper, thread, and ink, $8\frac{3}{4}$" diameter, gift of Ted and Betty Stvan, 2008.306.2

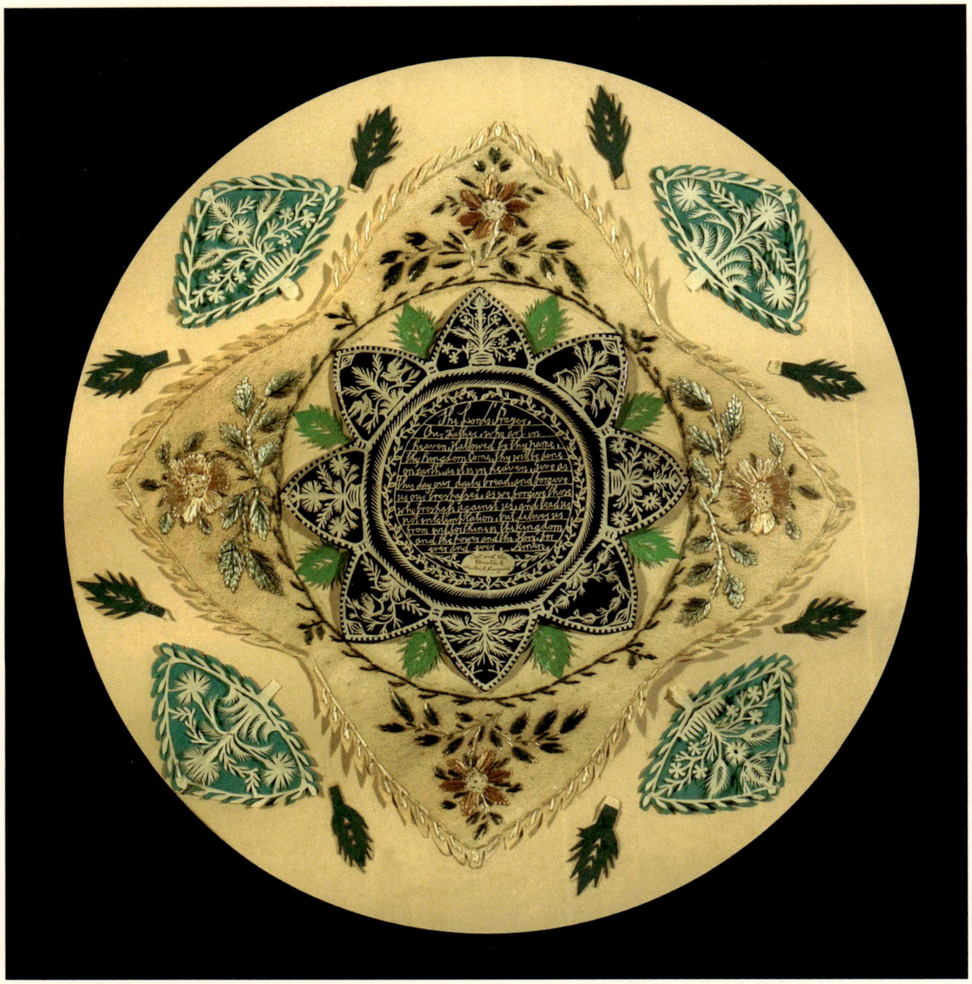

Look closely at this piece. There is a combination of detailed embroidery and intricate paper cutting. The center circle contains the words for the Lord's Prayer meticulously cut out. It might surprise you to know that the nineteenth-century creator of this piece, Martha Ann Honeywell, was born without arms and yet made a living with her paper cutting and talent with a needle.

In a time when many women stayed home and maintained the household, Honeywell traveled widely in eastern and midwestern America and in Europe demonstrating her skills and selling her work. Newspaper notices and broadsides advertised the events. She amazed audiences by holding "a common pair of Scissors" in her mouth. She also used her toes (although she was born with only three toes on one foot). An advertisement in a Louisville paper in 1830 touted her accomplishments, including watch papers, flowers, landscapes, and "even the Lord's Prayer." Martha Ann Honeywell plied her skills with a talent and finesse that placed her in the top ranks of artists with or without physical challenges.

Scherenschnitte Birds

When you try this lovely cutting taken from one "petal" of Honeywell's picture, consider how she was able to accomplish the task working with just her mouth and toes.

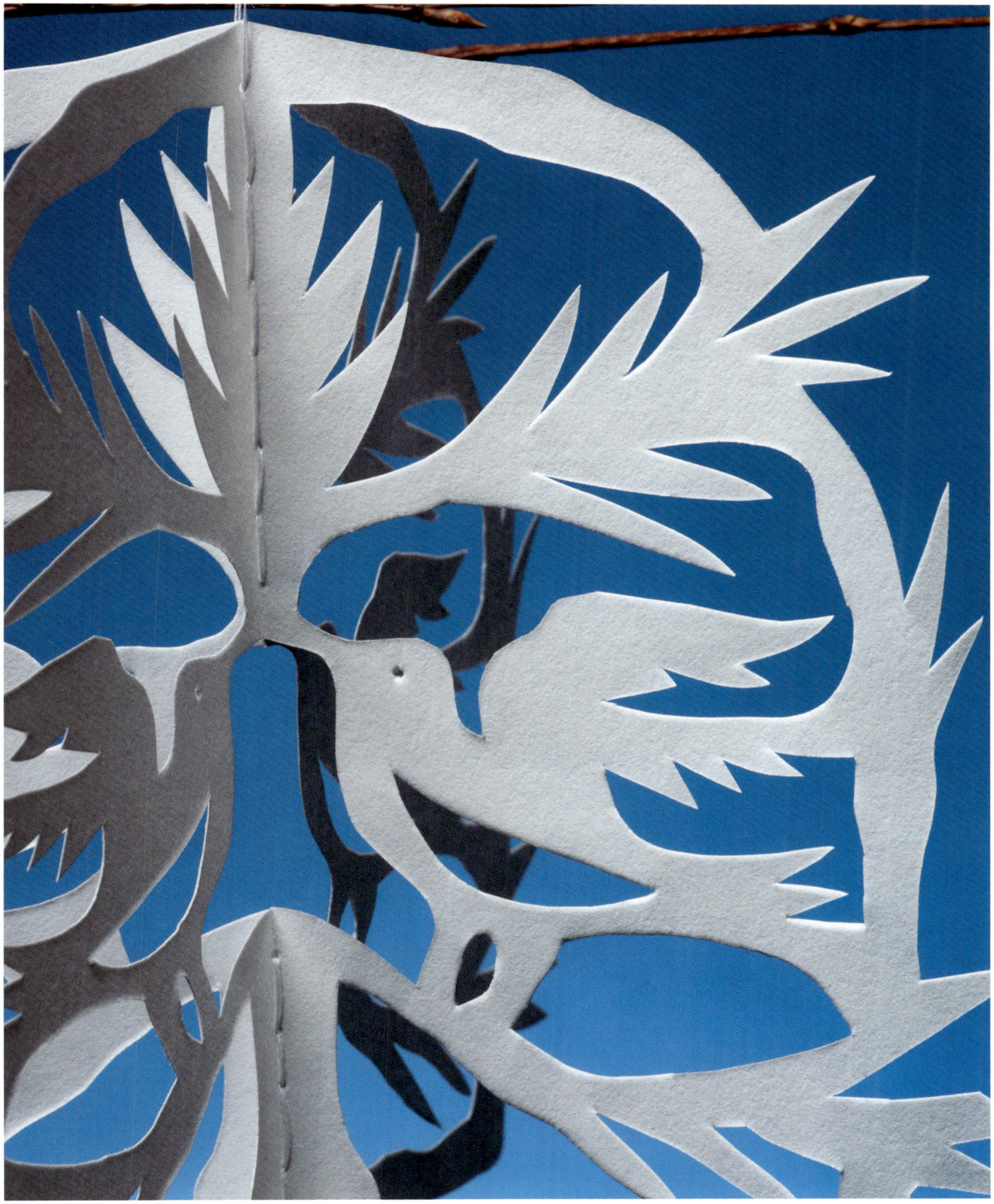

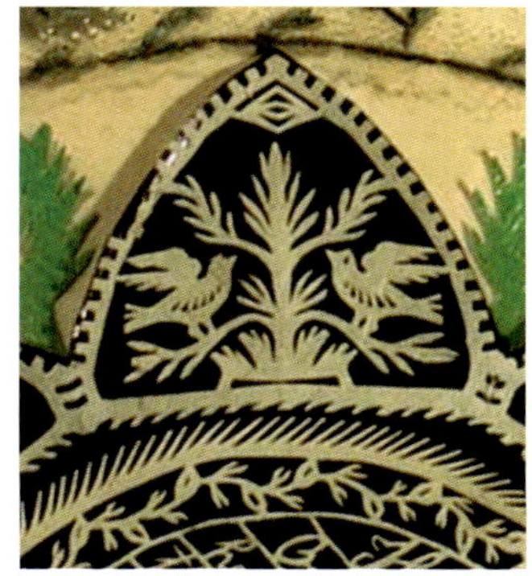

WHAT YOU NEED:

Bird in tree template (page 137)

Bird in tree cutting quide (page 137)

$8^1/2$ x 11–inch laid paper

Scherenschnitte scissors or embroidery scissors

Cardboard (such as a cereal box)

Needle

White quilting thread

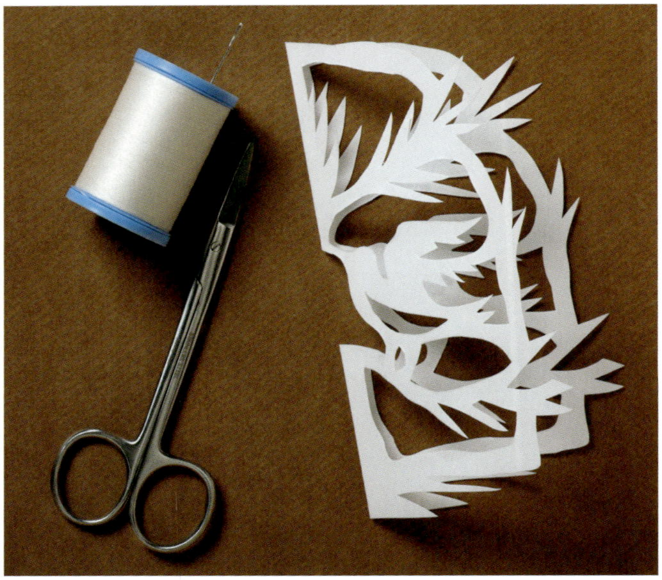

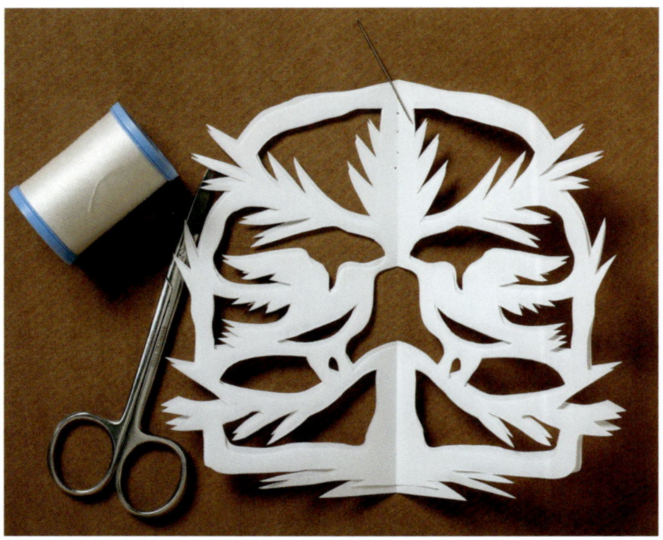

IDEA: Cut just one of the images out of white or colored paper and adhere to a larger piece of paper of contrasting color to create a custom greeting card.

INSTRUCTIONS:

Fold the paper in half the long way. Trace the template twice, placing the fold of the paper on the dotted line of the template each time. (You will have to open up the paper so that you can see through it to trace.) Cut apart the two traced pieces to make it easier to cut each separately.

Begin cutting. Cut each copy separately. The golden rule of cutting is to cut all of the interior elements first; then cut around the outer edge. Cutting from the bottom to the top of an image is recommended. To cut an interior section, carefully pierce the paper with the tip of your scissors. Then cut on the line. Refer to the cutting guide to remove all shaded areas from each image. Once all of the interior elements have been snipped away, cut around the outer edge.

To assemble the ornament, open both cut pieces and lay one inside the fold of the other. Lay them on the cardboard. Using the needle, pierce through both layers of the folds to create stitching holes down the entire length of the fold. It is easier to stitch the pieces together if the holes are pierced beforehand. With needle and thread, start sewing from the top down. Leave 4 inches of thread at the top. Sew through the holes to the beaks of the birds and then return back through the holes to the top. Measure out another 4 inches and then knot the two threads together to form the hanger. Stitch the bottom portion of the ornament in the same way, but weave in the ends of the thread as you sew.

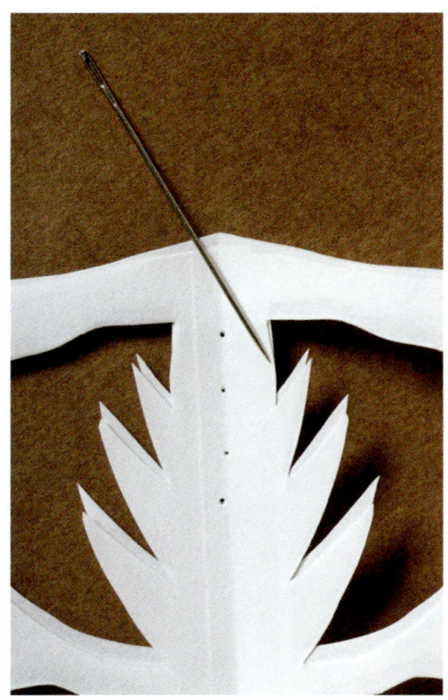

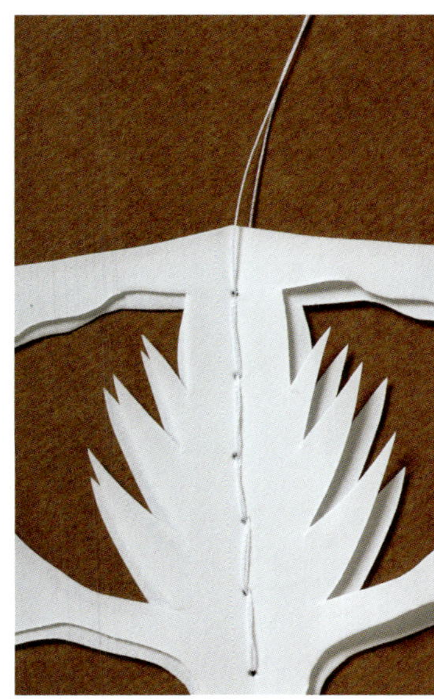

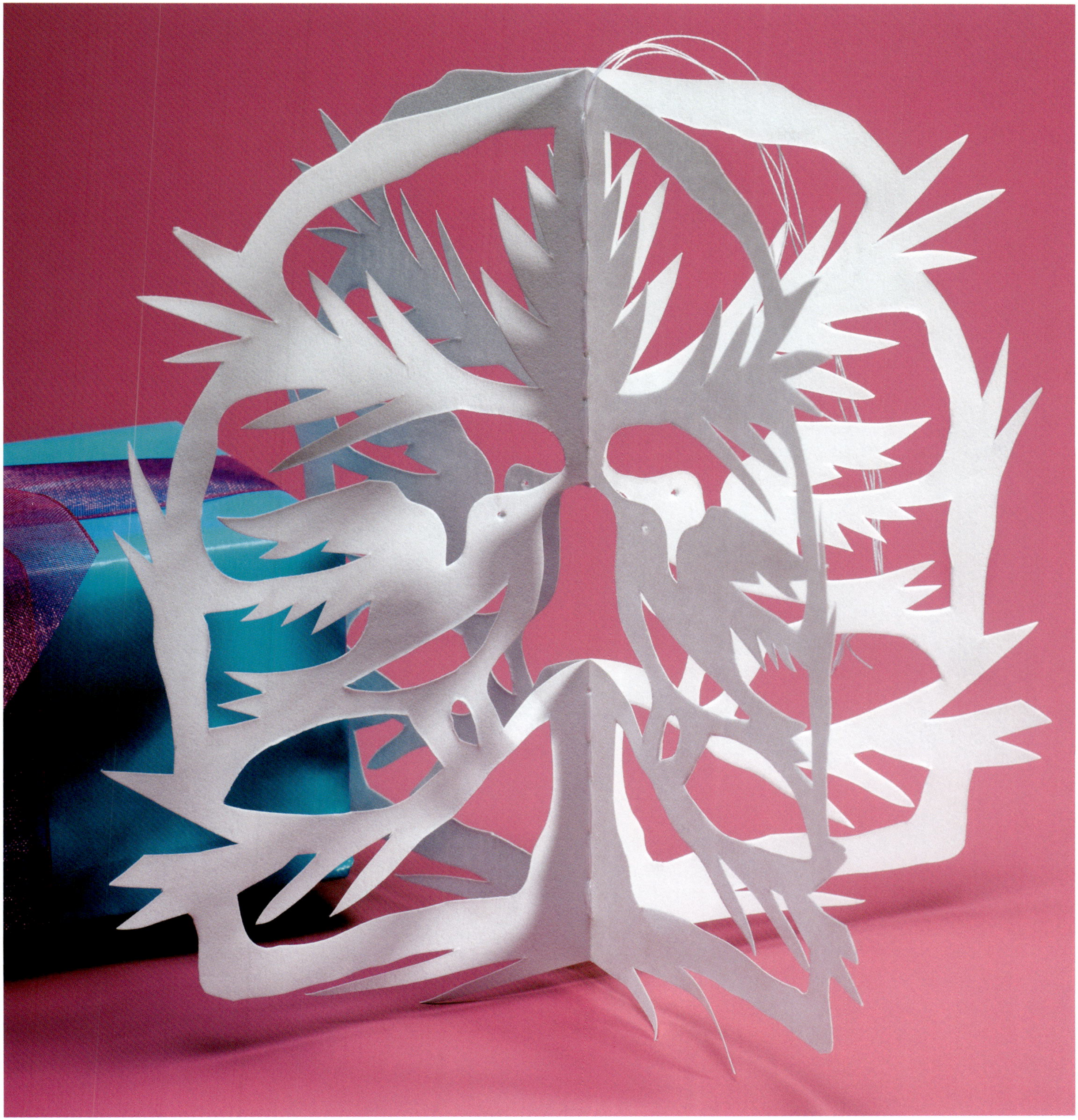

VIEW OF THE CASTLE OF MONTGOMERY

South Carolina, 1830–1840, oil on canvas, 36 1/8" x 54", gift of Mr. and Mrs. Thomas A. Moore, 1974.110.1

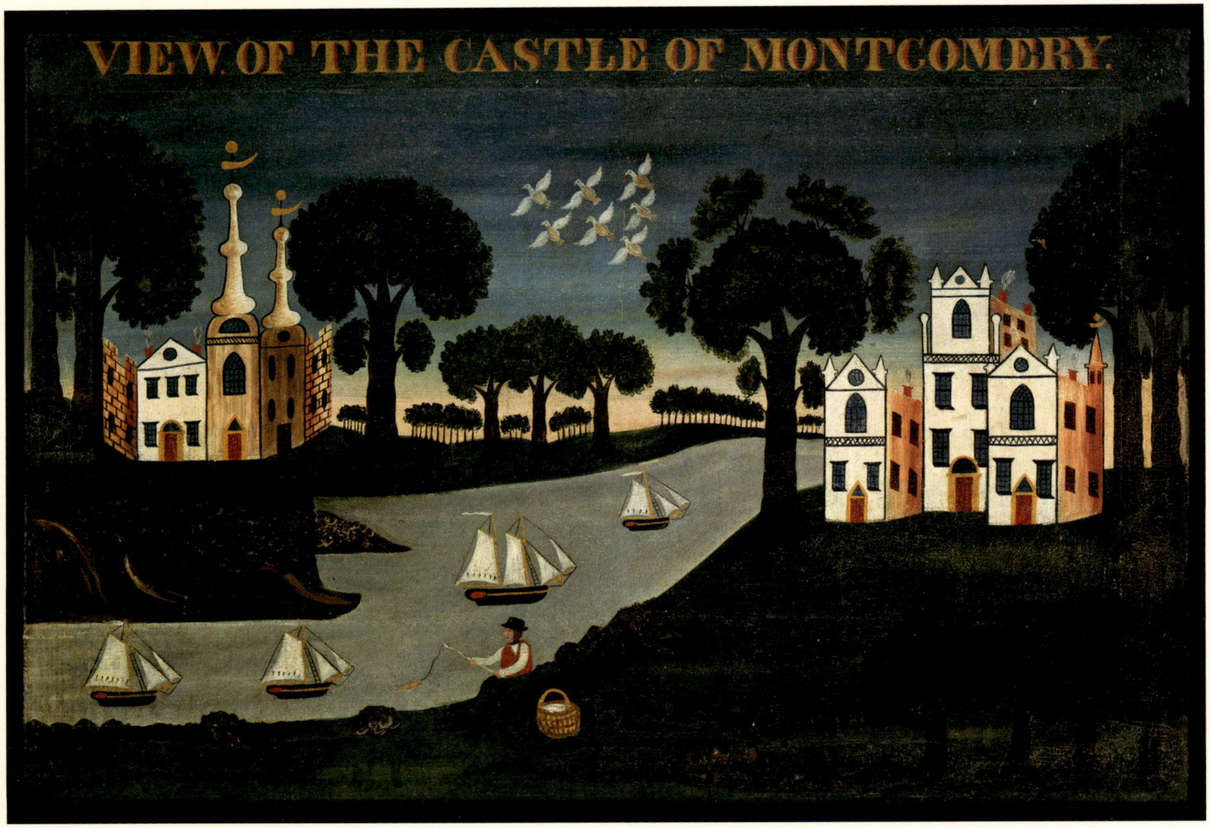

Fireplaces were the primary source of heat in eighteenth- and nineteenth-century homes. For probably half the year, the fireplace held a cheery fire to heat the room. But what about the other half of the year? The fireplace was still a focal point, but an empty one. To decorate the prominent feature, many people used fireboards, a painting on either a board or canvas set in front of the fireplace opening.

We are fortunate to know the history of this fireboard. Made specifically for the house Fredonia in Spartanburg County, South Carolina, it descended in the family until given to the Folk Art Museum. Fredonia was built in 1786, the land having been given free from father to son, hence the name. The fireboard was likely added in the 1830s when the owner at the time, Dr. Andrew Barry Moore, married Nancy Montgomery. A very similar fireboard was found in another house just seven miles away from Fredonia. The artist who created the pieces was probably local.

Landscapes and flower arrangements were particularly popular subjects for fireboards. Like many folk artists, the artist of this piece likely drew inspiration from a print source.

Punch-Needle Ship

SHIPS OF ALL KINDS WERE COMMON SIGHTS ON THE WATERWAYS OF AMERICA IN THE NINETEENTH CENTURY. WITH NO MODERN ROADWAYS, THE RIVERS ACTED AS THE HIGHWAYS FOR BOTH PASSENGER TRAVEL AND THE SHIPPING OF GOODS. IT SEEMS FITTING TO SHOWCASE A SHIP FROM THIS SCENE.

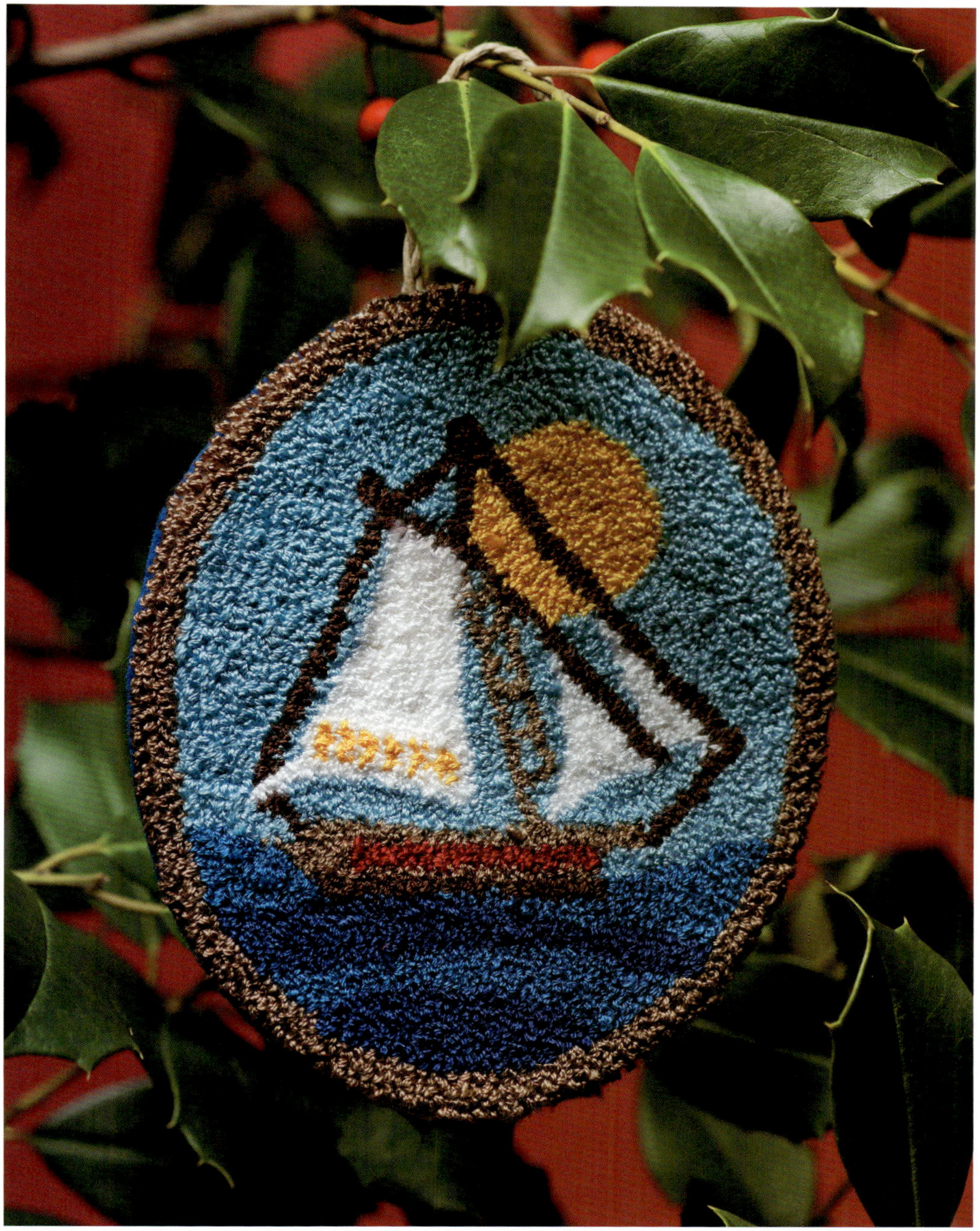

WHAT YOU NEED:

Ship template (page 135)
Tracing paper
Iron-on transfer pencil
Ecru weaver's cloth, 7 x 7 inches
Iron
Ironing board
4 3/4-inch interlocking hoop
3-strand punch needle
Punch-needle threader
Floss in the following DMC colors: 725, 803, 816, 838, 840, 3765, 3766, 5200
Embroidery scissors
Matching felt
48-pound hemp cord, 36 inches long

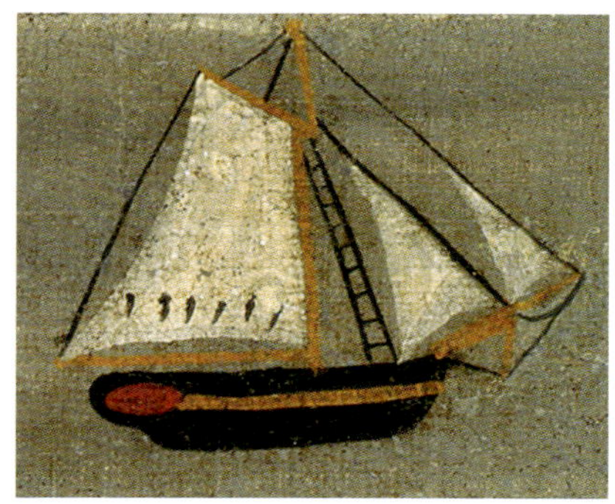

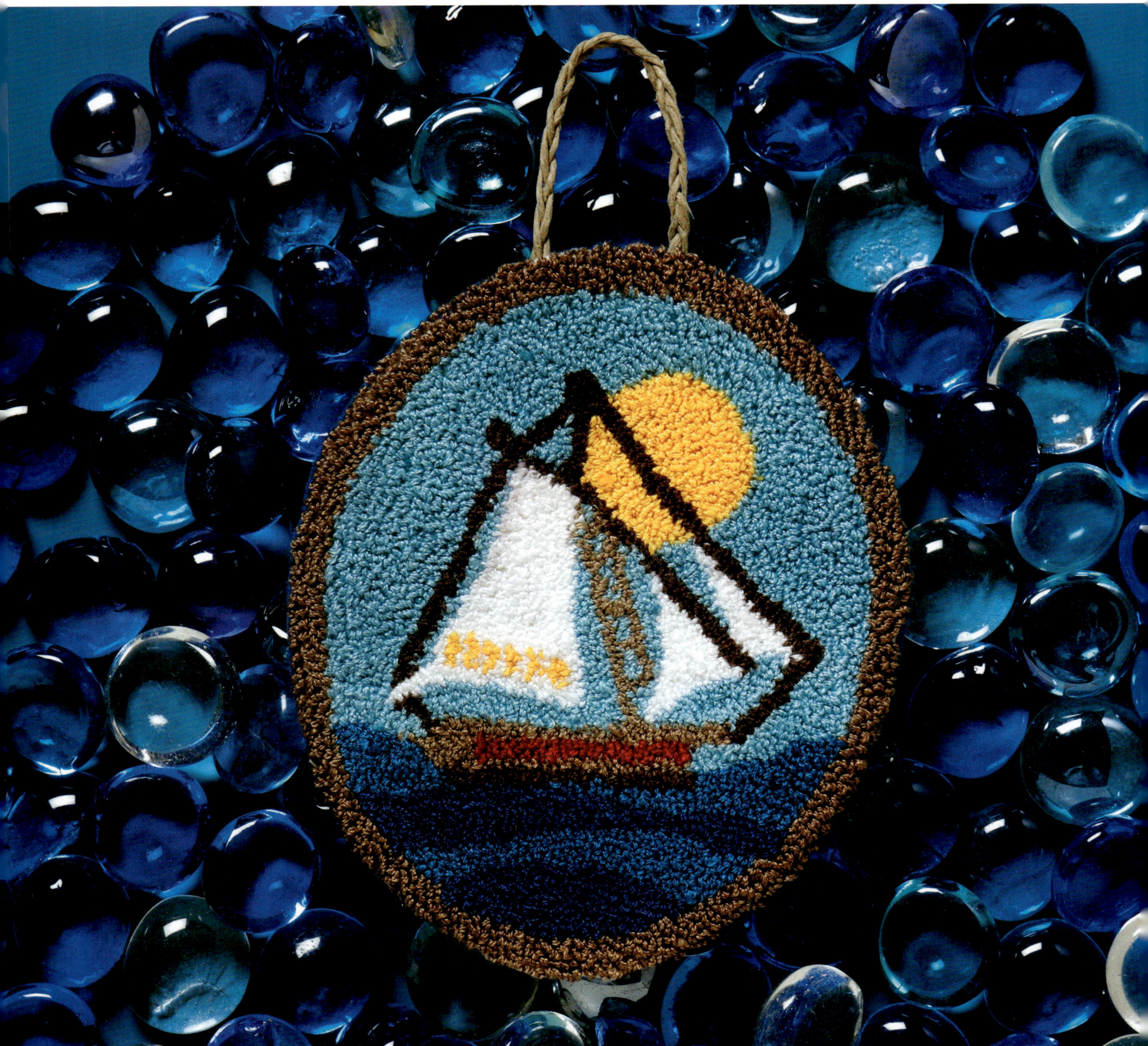

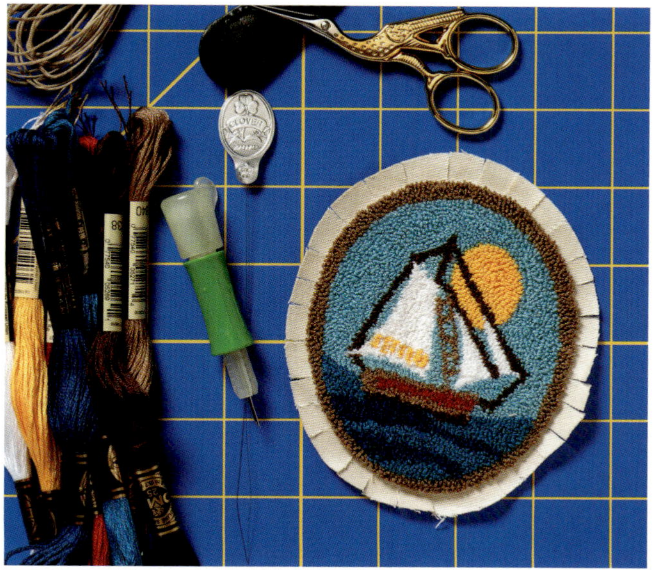 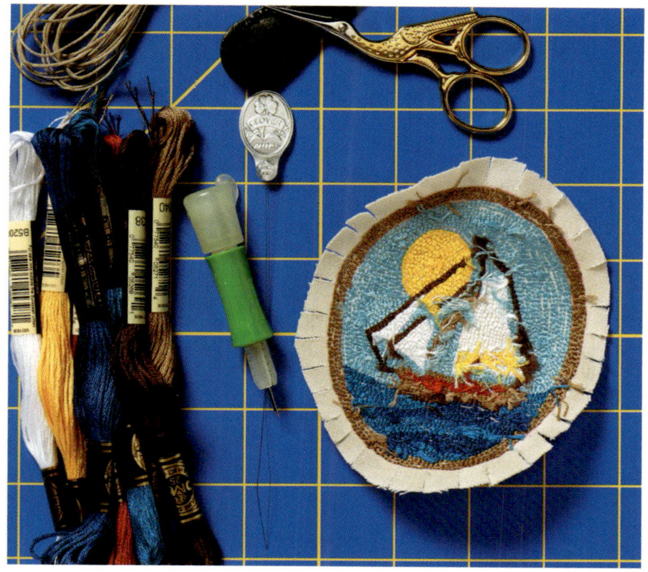

INSTRUCTIONS:

Trace the ship template onto the tracing paper using the iron-on transfer pencil. Following the manufacturer's instructions for the transfer pencil, iron the transfer onto the center of the weaver's cloth. Place the cloth into the hoop, centering the ship design.

Thread the punch needle with three strands of floss, and punch the design following the colors in the image. When the picture is complete, trim the thread from the back of the design.

Cut out the picture, leaving 1/2-inch fabric border all the way around. Make small cuts into the unworked fabric border all the way around so that it will lie flat when you fold it back. Fold the border toward the back and carefully iron so that it lies flat.

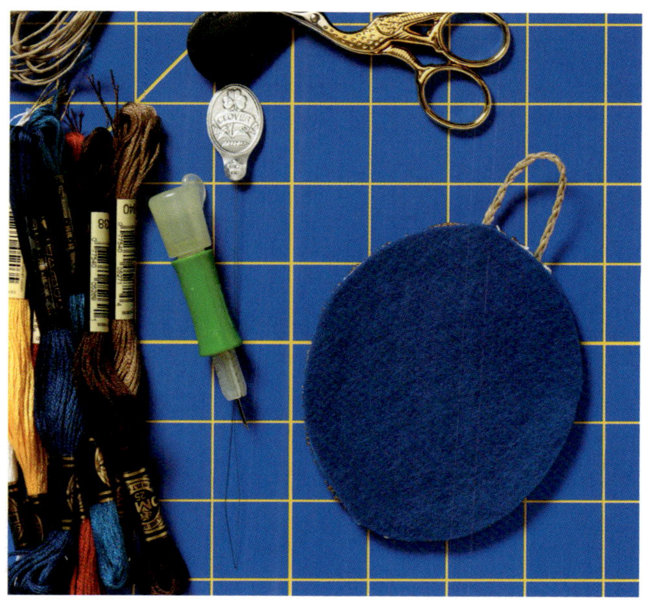

Using the ship template, cut out a felt circle. Stitch the felt to the back of the fabric using a blind stitch. Leave the top open for the cord hanger.

To make the hanger, cut three 12-inch lengths of hemp cord. Knot the three together at one end, braid, and tie off at the other end. Form a loop and place at the top back of the piece. Sew in place as you finish sewing the felt on.

IDEAS: This ornament would look fun hanging on a doorknob or in a window in a beach house.

MINERS' TRAIN

Jack Savitsky (1910–1991), Lansford, Pennsylvania, ca. 1970, oil enamels on plywood, 24 3/4" x 41 1/8", 1971.110.1

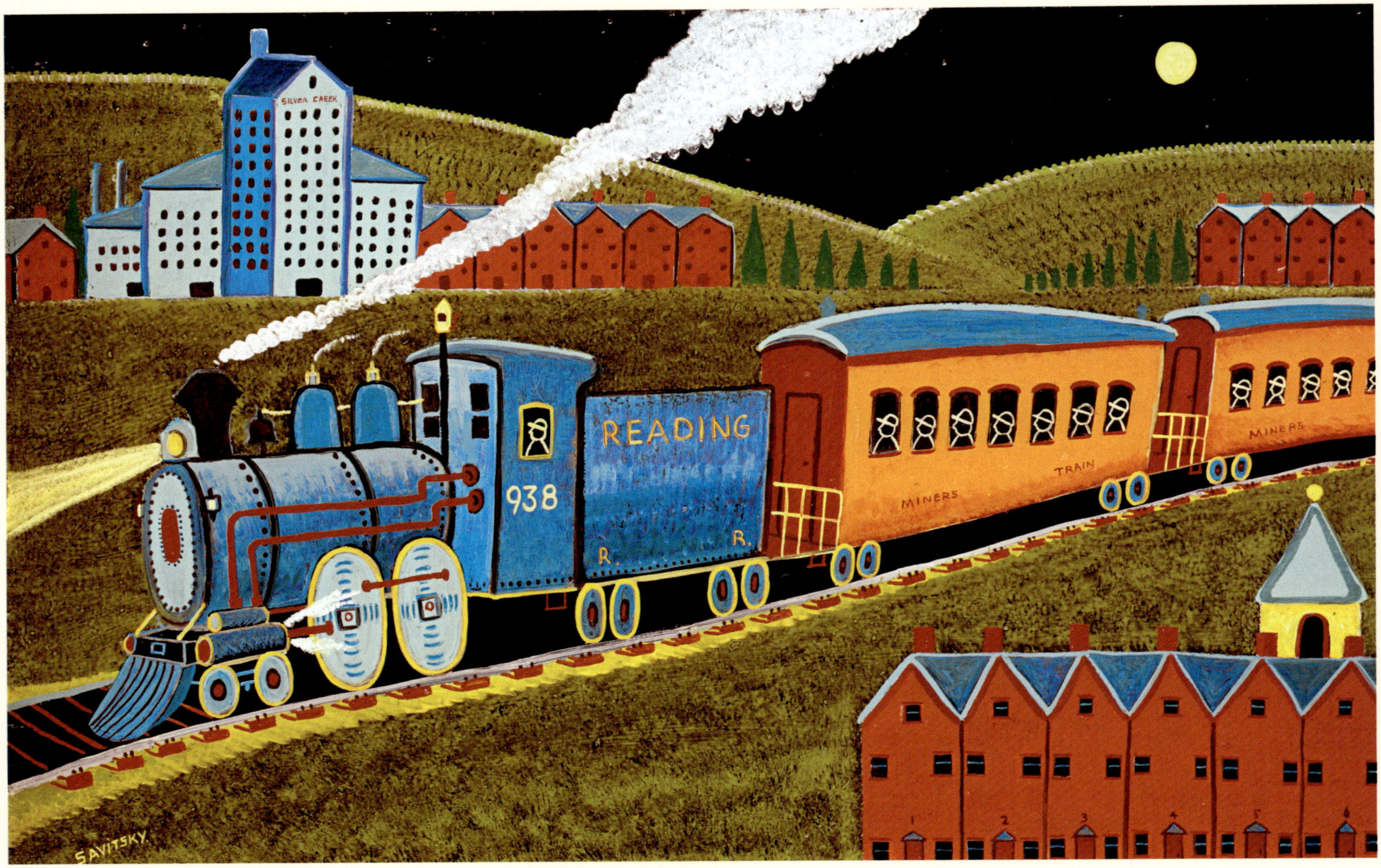

Jack Savitsky spent more than thirty-five years in the coal mines of Carbon County, Pennsylvania. This colorful, vivid image contrasts the realities the artist experienced. The train pictured here carried miners to their work sites. The bright orange look-alike houses are reminders of the company housing rented to the miners. The scene takes place at night when the miners must have been covered in coal dust and exhausted from a hard day in the mines. Yet the painting doesn't give away the hardships of a miner's life.

Once Savitsky retired from the mines in 1959, he took up painting at the encouragement of his son. Many of his works depicted what he knew—the life of a miner. Because of his years in the mines, he contracted black-lung disease. The oil paints he used aggravated his condition, so he changed to using colored pencils and markers. He would draw on almost anything from plywood to cracker boxes.

Wooden Train

IT IS HARD NOT TO BE ATTRACTED TO THE BRIGHT COLORS OF THIS SCENE. AND THE TRAIN ITSELF BROUGHT TO MIND A CLASSIC HOLIDAY TOY. THESE PAINTED WOODEN LOCOMOTIVES ADD CHEER TO ANY TREE.

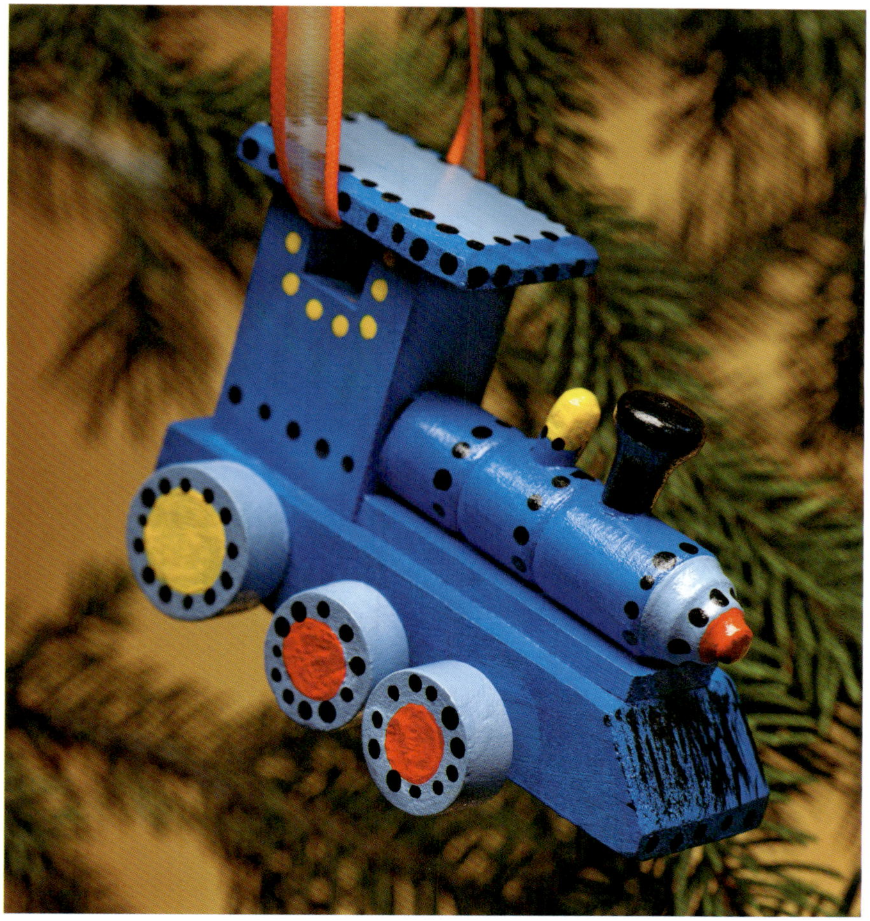

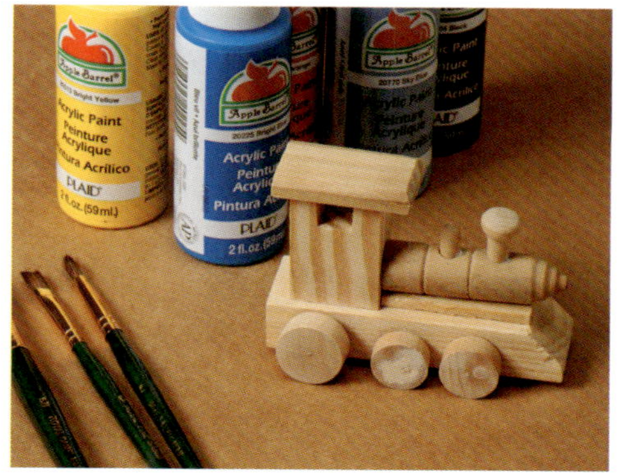

WHAT YOU NEED:

Unpainted wooden train engine

Acrylic paints in several colors (we used Apple Barrel colors bright blue, sky blue, orange, bright yellow, and black)

Paintbrushes

Clear acrylic coating spray or spray shellac

3/8-inch orange ribbon, 10 inches long

Note: There are a variety of unpainted wooden trains on the market; these painting instructions will work for all.

IDEA: PAINT THE TRAIN IN OTHER COLOR COMBINATIONS TO CREATE A HOLIDAY TRAIN IN RED, GREEN, AND WHITE OR MATCH THE COLORS OF A CHILD'S BEDROOM.

INSTRUCTIONS:

Paint the entire train engine in bright blue. As you paint, let each color dry completely before continuing with the next color.

Paint the wheels, the top of the roof, and the front of the train sky blue.

Paint the center of each wheel either orange or bright yellow.

Paint the front tip of the train orange.

Paint the tip of the pipe bright yellow, and paint bright yellow dots around the sides and bottom of the window.

Paint rows of black dots around the top and sides of the roof, each wheel, the yellow of the pipe, the circular body of the train, and the very front.

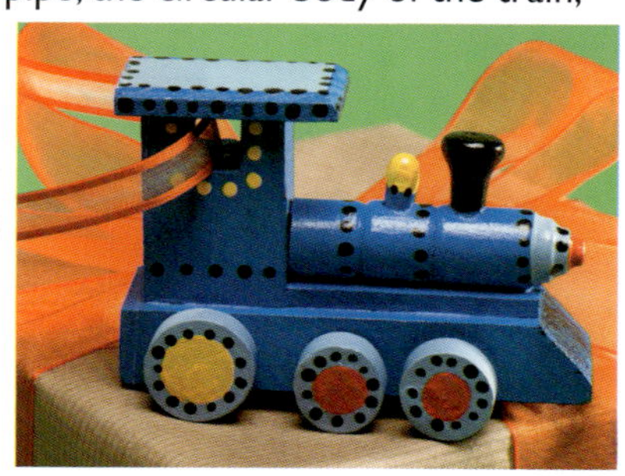

Finally, paint the smokestack black.

Allow to dry completely; then spray with clear acrylic coating or shellac.

Tie the ribbon through the window to hang.

PUTMAN FAMILY RECORD

John T. Adams, possibly New York, 1844,
watercolor and ink on wove paper,
20 1/4" x 14 7/8", 1957.305.1

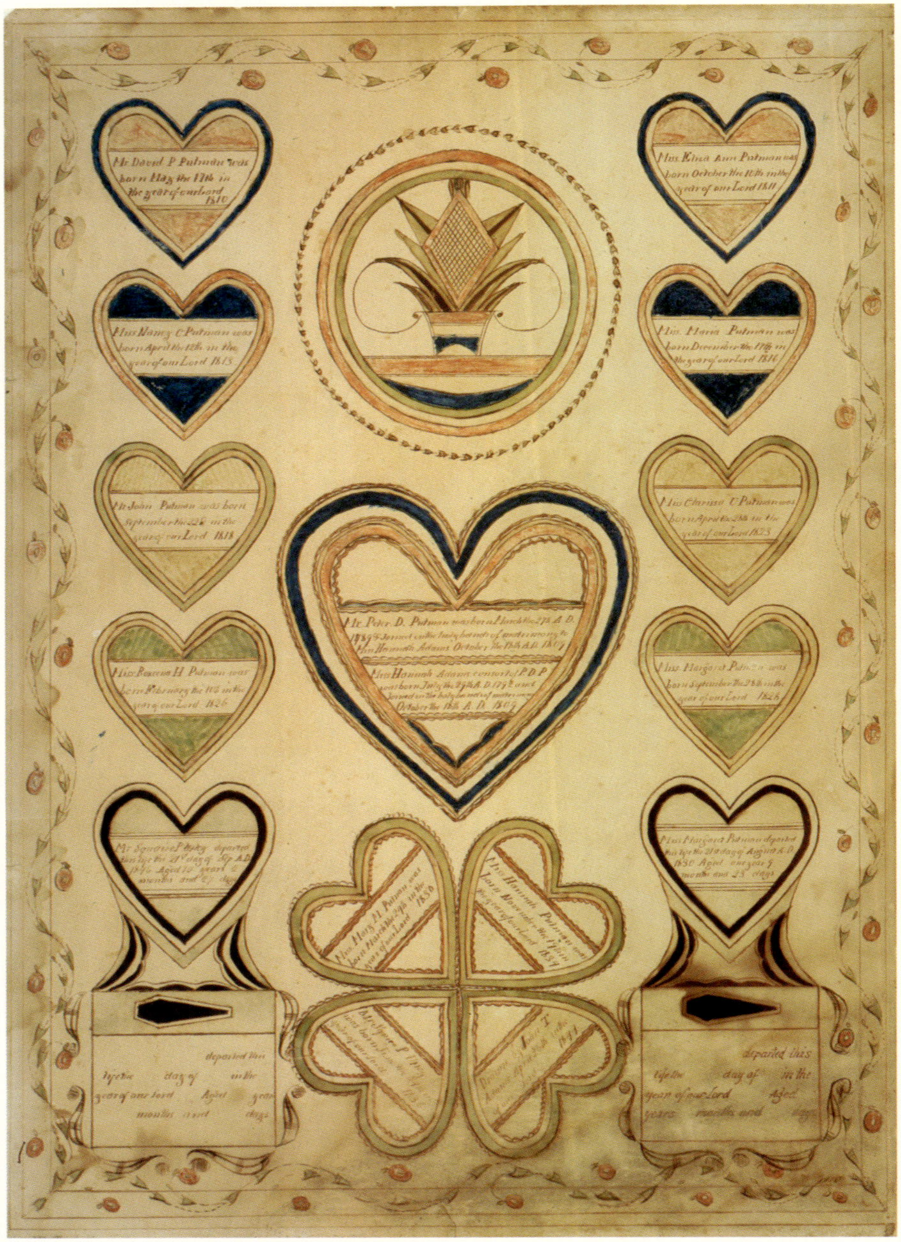

Documenting family ties gives a person a sense of belonging and a connection to loved ones. In the nineteenth century, young girls often recorded family member's births and deaths on samplers and mourning pictures. In areas of Pennsylvania, highly decorative frakturs, typically created by men, were reminders of births, baptisms, and marriages.

This heart-filled watercolor comes from a tradition of record keeping found in New England and New York. Each heart documents a different family member. Even though the information is straightforward, using the hearts to frame out the notices makes each record a loving memory of that person. The large central heart notes the birth dates and marriage of Peter D. Putman and Hannah Adams. The artist, John Adams, was likely related to Hannah Adams. The other hearts record the births of the couple's children. The first child was born in 1810 and the last in 1836. The bottom hearts, each of which flows into a rectangle with a coffin, document the sad loss of two of the children, one just over ten years old and the other not yet two. The boxes below these include incomplete text to allow for the documenting of two more deaths, a typical practice, but the blanks in the text were never filled in. One of the hearts in the cluster of four includes the artist's inscription, "Drawn by John T. Adams April 26th in the [year] of our Lord 1844." Although nothing more is known about the family or the artist, this wonderful document survived the generations to give us just a glimpse into the Putman family.

Recycled-Denim Heart

HOLIDAYS ARE A PERFECT TIME TO REMEMBER FAMILY AND FRIENDS. ADAMS'S CHARMING METHOD OF RECORD KEEPING INSPIRED THESE DENIM HEARTS. IF YOU CAN, USE THE CAST-OFF JEANS OF THE PERSON WHOSE NAME WILL GRACE THE HEART.

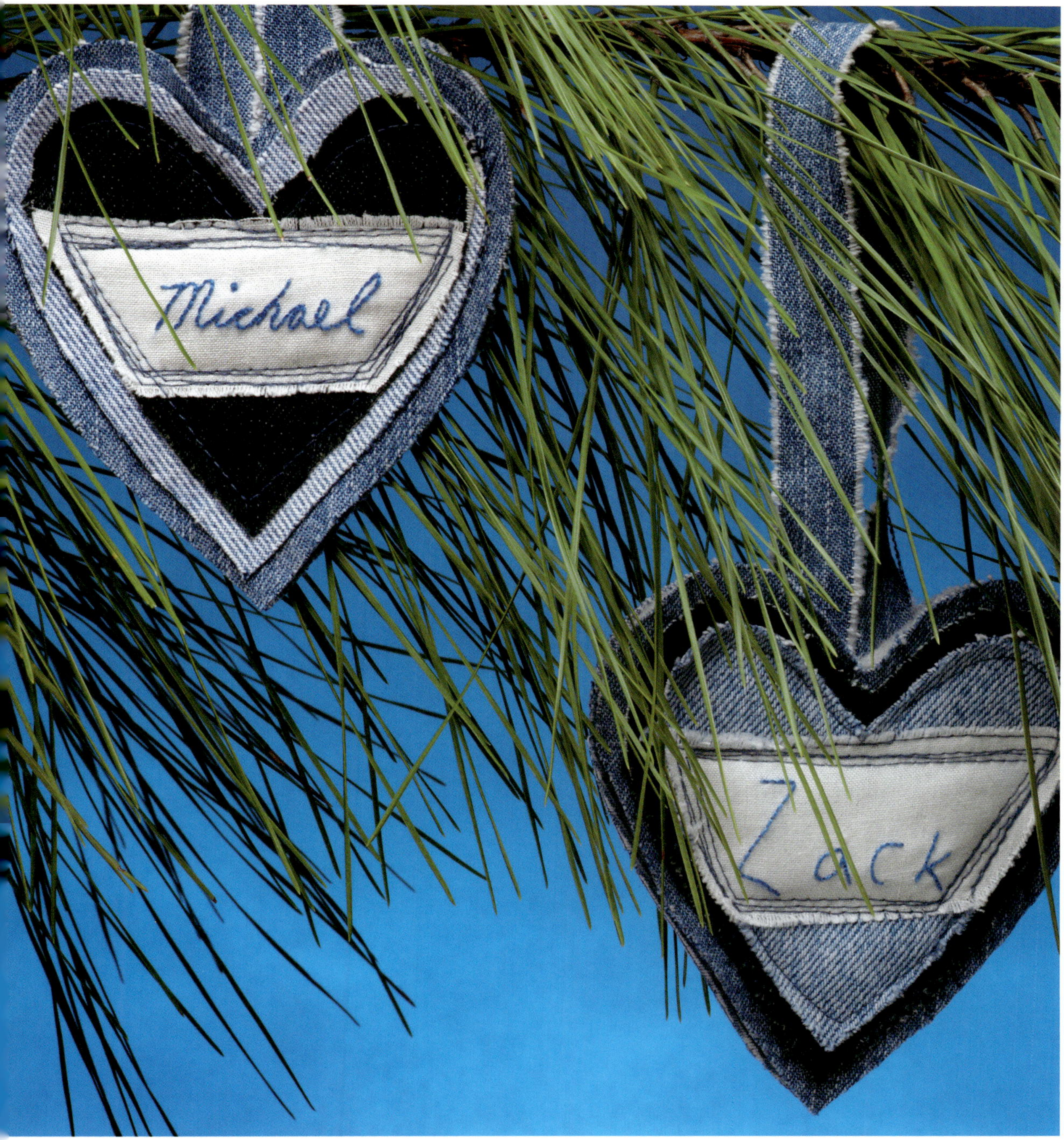

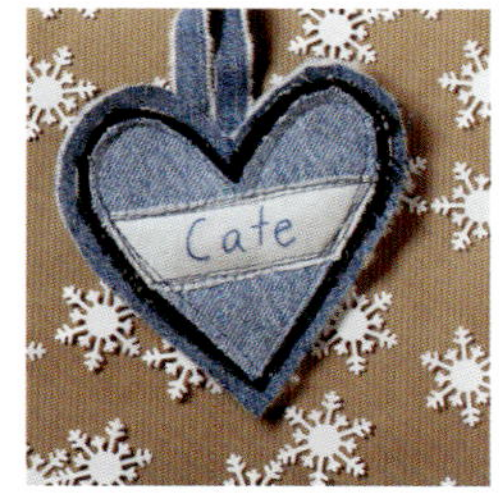

WHAT YOU NEED:

- Small, medium, and large hearts and nameplate templates (page 130)
- Old pair of denim jeans or scraps of denim
- Scissors
- Pins
- Old blanket or cotton quilt batting
- Old oxford shirt or scrap of white cotton or linen
- Fabric pen
- 6-inch embroidery hoop
- Needle
- Blue floss
- Sewing machine
- Denim needle
- Matching thread

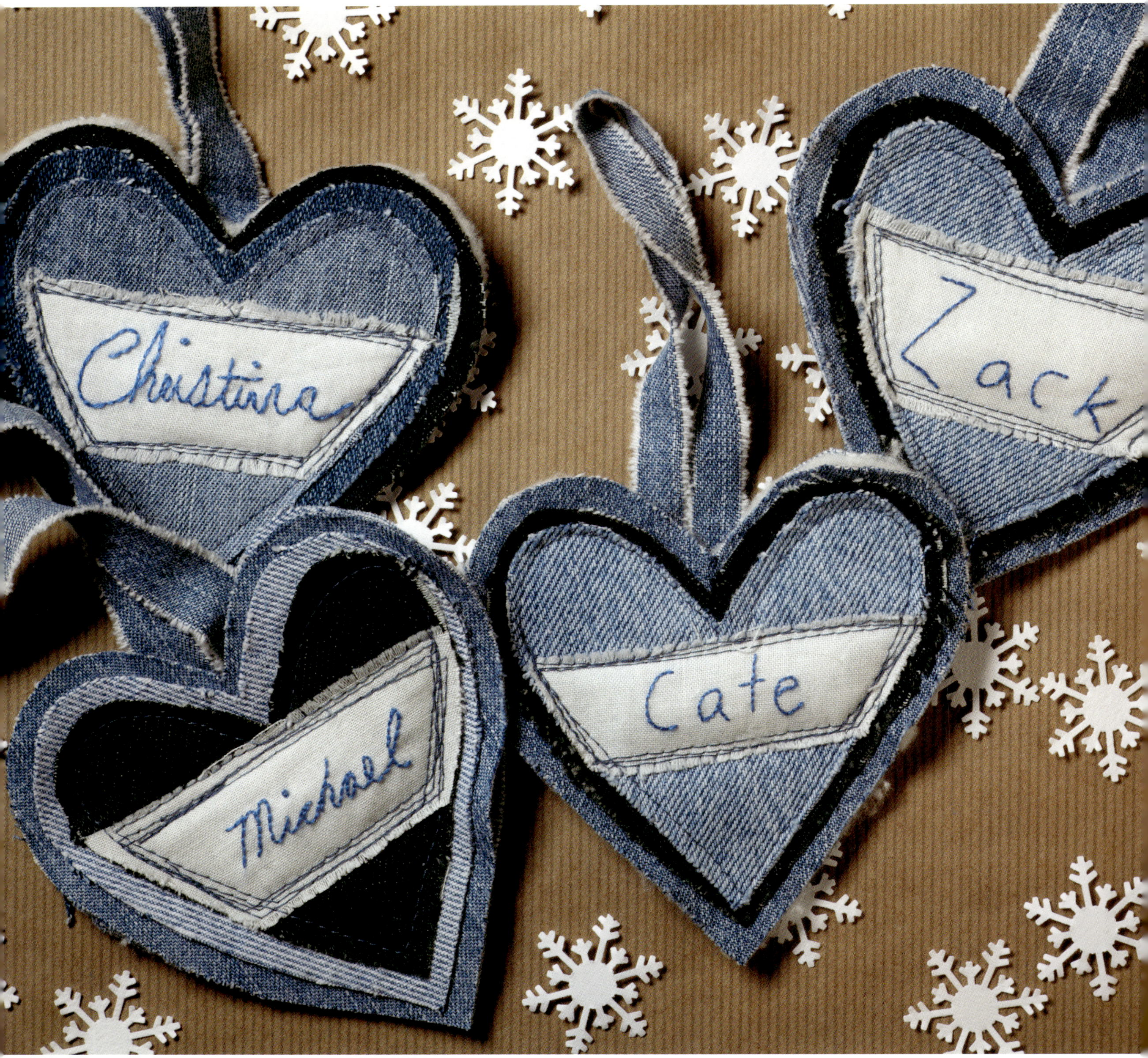
Christina
Zack
Michael
Cate

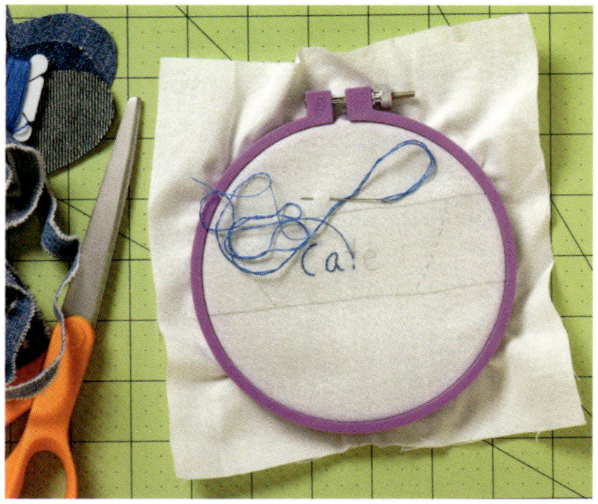

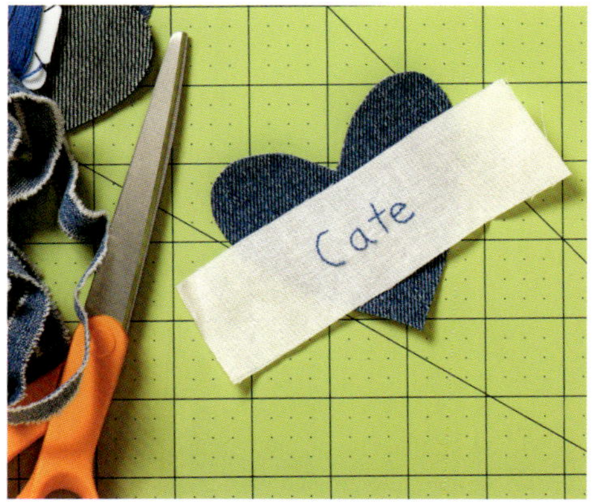

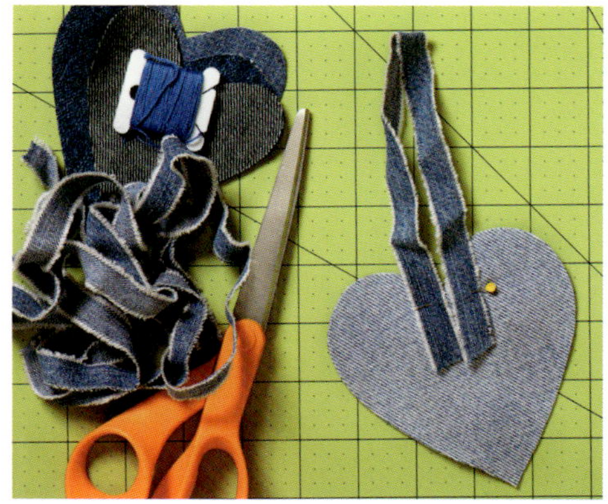

INSTRUCTIONS:

From the denim, select three areas that are different shades of blue. You can use the wrong side of the denim as one of the choices. Each area needs to be big enough to accommodate a heart template. Cut out one section from two of the colors and two sections from the third color. Fold each in half. Pin the heart templates onto the different colors of folded denim matching the dotted lines to the folds. You will need to use the large template twice. Cut out one small heart, one medium heart, and two large hearts. Also cut out one large heart from the blanket or batting.

Place the nameplate template on a piece of the oxford shirt. Using the fabric pen, trace the template. Then place the template beneath the fabric and with the fabric pen write a name in the center, using the dotted lines on the template as a guide. Place the fabric in an embroidery hoop, and, with the blue floss, stitch the name using a backstitch. When complete, remove the fabric from the hoop and cut out the nameplate. Pin the nameplate to the center of the small heart and trim the edges of the nameplate to align with the edges of the heart.

To make the hanger, rip a 12 x $^{3}/_{4}$–inch piece of denim, and pull out some threads to fray the edges.

Layer the pieces starting with the large heart right side down. Fold the denim strip in half and lay it so that the two ends reach to the center of the heart to ensure that the ends are held in place when you stitch the outline of the smallest heart. The loop is the hanger and should come out the top of the heart. Place the blanket heart on top of the strip. Place the other large heart right side up on top of the blanket heart, then the medium heart right side up centered on the large heart, and then the small heart with the nameplate centered on the medium heart. Carefully pin all the pieces in place.

Stitch through all layers using the sewing machine set to the longest stitch and equipped with a denim needle. Begin by stitching around the nameplate several times. Continue to stitch around each piece working your way out. You can also stitch by hand.

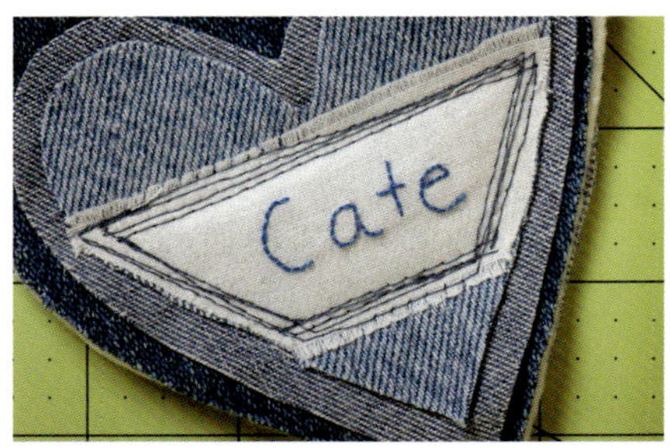

IDEAS: Send paper nameplates to your friends and family, and have them write their names on the papers and return them to you. Then trace each name onto the fabric and embroider to create a personal and unique family Christmas tree. You can also look for old family letters and trace the signatures of your ancestors and make a true family tree.

LEOPARD

probably America, 1870–1900, wood, paint, metal, and leather, 3 3/8" x 8" x 1 3/4", 1961.1200.65

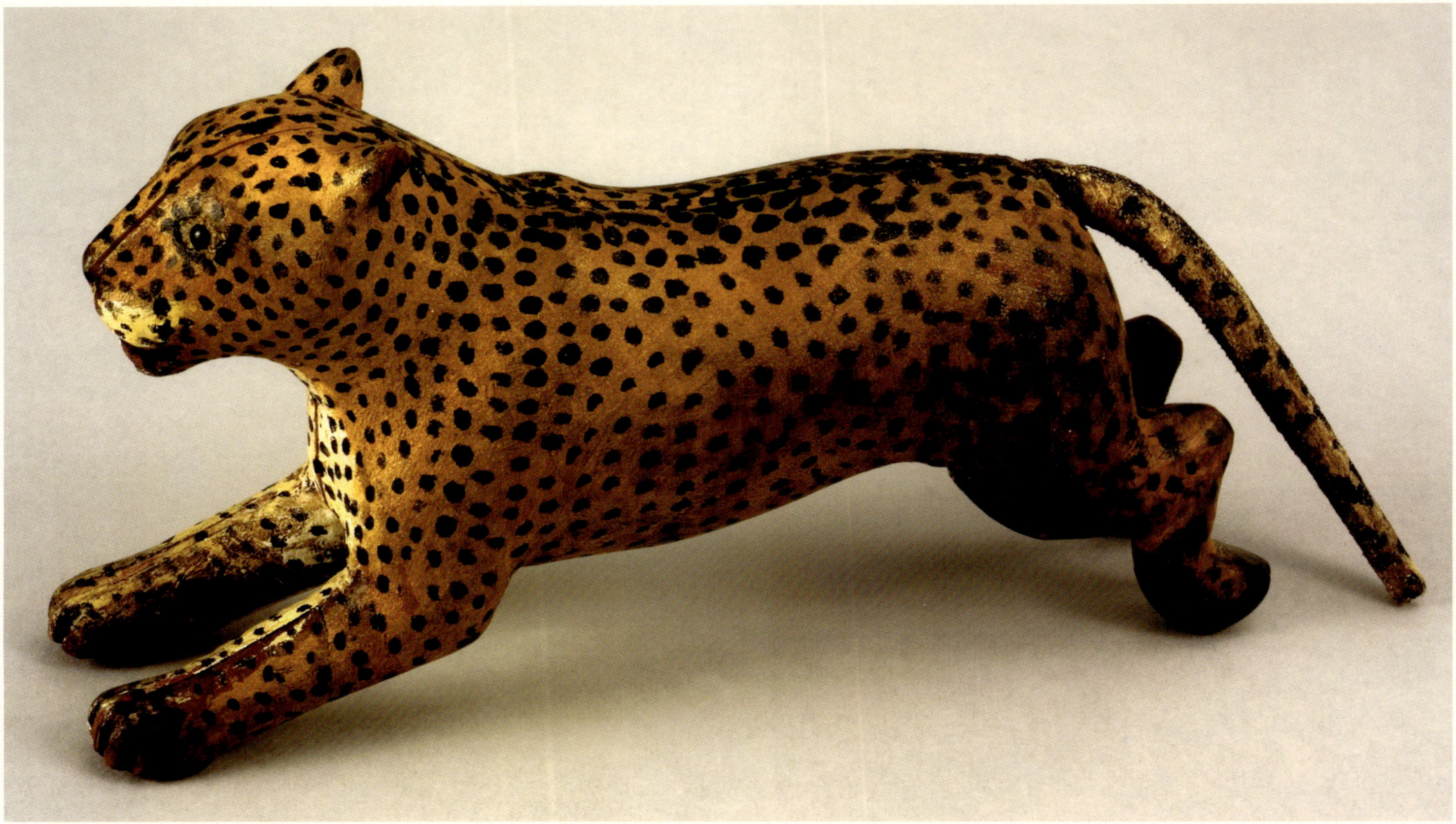

This engaging spotted feline looks almost as if it could jump right off the ground. It is less than 4 inches high, but the carver's attention to detail gives it a realistic appearance. Although the body is made of wood, the tail is leather, which perhaps explains how such a long, thin appendage could survive intact for over one hundred years. There is no history associated with this piece, so we don't know whether it was a toy or a sculpture meant only for decoration. Could a child given access to such a charming creature resist playing with it?

It is intriguing to consider what the maker used as a model. For the majority of the nineteenth century, people gained their knowledge of exotic animals from published prints and illustrated children's storybooks. The first zoo in America wasn't established until 1874 (in Philadelphia). As lifelike as this leopard is, might the carver have visited one of the early zoos? Or was it his talent that allowed him to create the piece from a two-dimensional illustration?

Needlepoint Leopard

AS CURATOR OF TOYS, JAN COULDN'T RESIST INCLUDING A PROJECT INSPIRED BY ONE OF HER FAVORITE PIECES IN THE TOY COLLECTION.

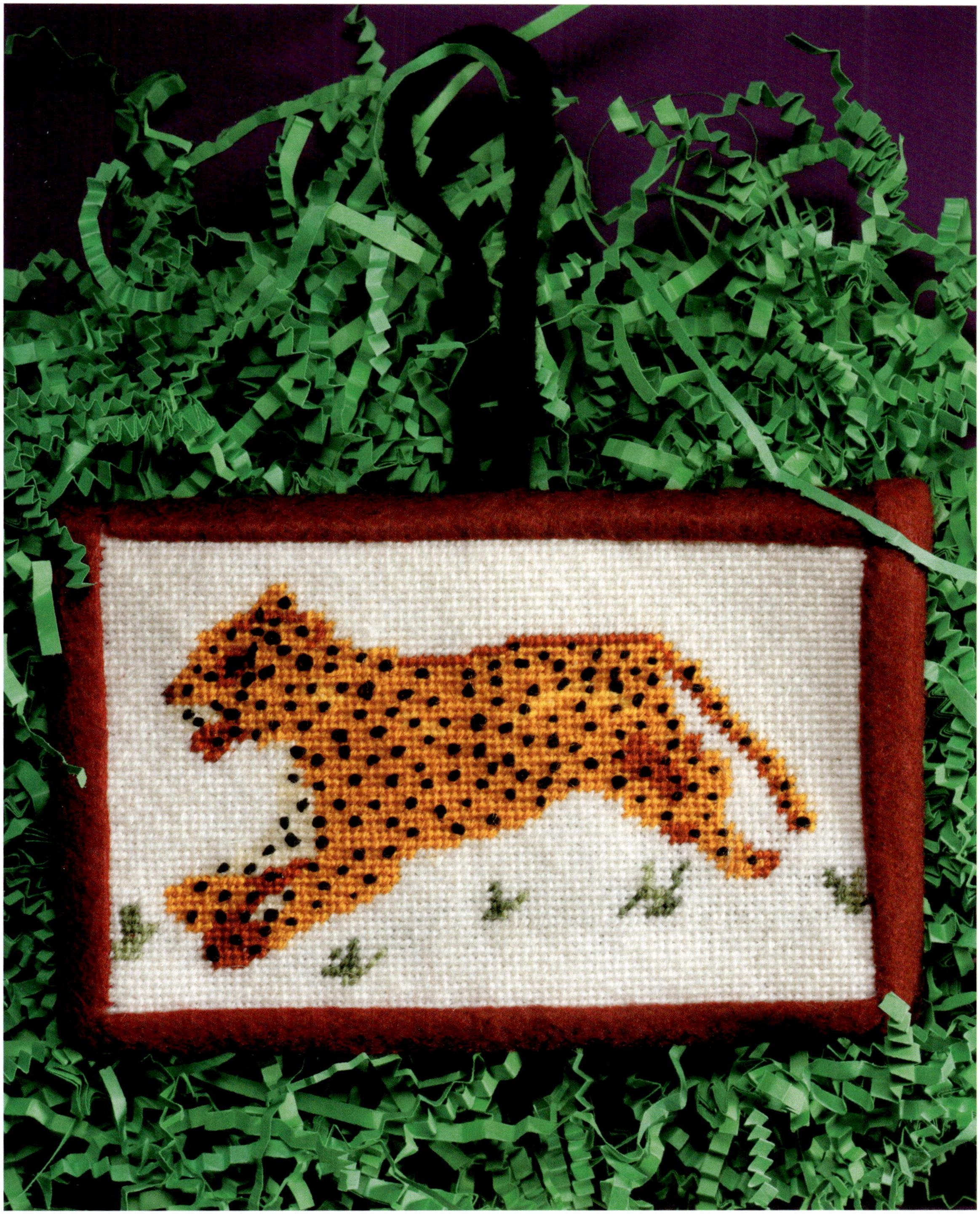

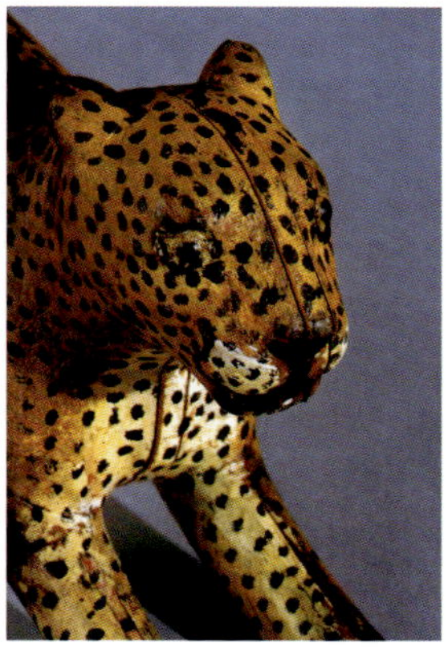

WHAT YOU NEED:

- Charted design
- 18-gauge canvas, 7 x 9 inches
- Masking tape
- Tapestry needle, #22
- Persian yarn: deep gold, light gold, very light yellow, rust red, and black
- Scissors
- Black floss
- Dark red felt
- Needle
- Matching thread
- Cord, 10 inches long

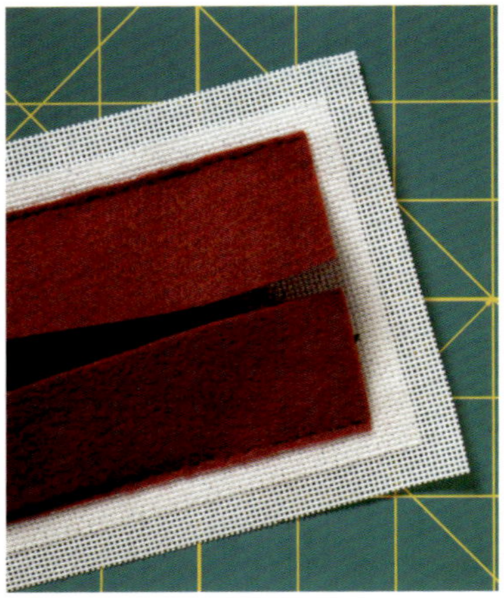

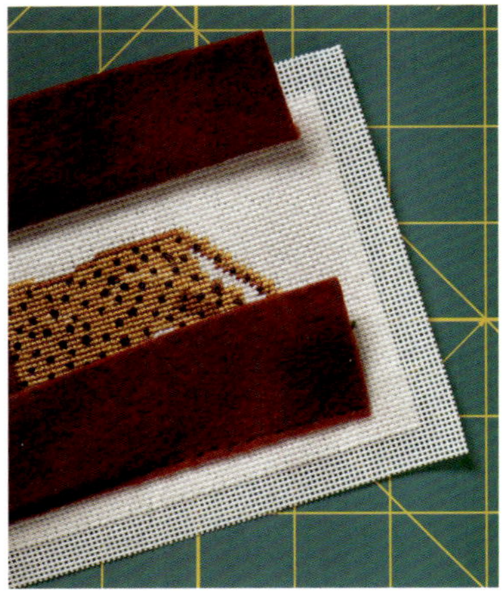

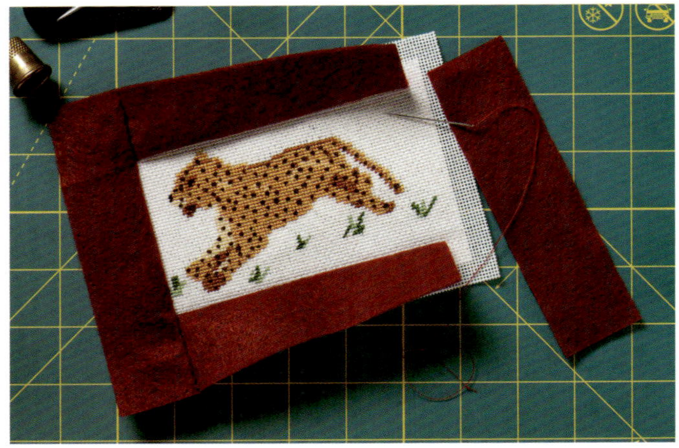

INSTRUCTIONS:

Prepare your canvas by placing masking tape along the four edges to keep it from unraveling as you work. Referring to the charted design, begin in the lower corner with the leopard's front paws. Work the entire figure and grass in tent stitch. Fill in the background with tent stitch.

To create the leopard's spots, thread the regular needle with three strands of the black floss. Decide where you would like the spots. Make a French knot for every spot. (See the stitch guide to see how to make a French knot.) Continue making knots until you have as many spots as you like.

Once the needlepoint is complete, trim the canvas leaving six empty holes from the stitched area on each of the four sides. Set aside.

Create a frame for the piece: Cut the following pieces from the felt: two strips $5 \times 1\frac{1}{2}$ inches, two strips $5\frac{1}{2} \times 1\frac{1}{2}$ inches, and one piece $5\frac{1}{4} \times 3\frac{3}{8}$ inches. Place the two 5-inch strips side by side, centered, on top of the needlepoint. Sew each strip to the canvas along the outside 5-inch edge with a running stitch. Bring the felt strips up and away from the stitched area. With the 5-inch strips pressed out, attach the $5\frac{1}{2}$-inch strips to the sides of the needlepoint in the same way. Line up each $5\frac{1}{2}$-inch strip with the ends of the 5-inch strips so that they span the length of the sides. As you attach each $5\frac{1}{2}$-inch strip, sew through the edge of the top felt strip, the canvas, and the edge of the other felt strip. Bring the $5\frac{1}{2}$-inch felt strips up and away from the stitched area.

Now fold the felt strips toward the back. Do the top and the bottom first and then the two sides. As you fold, the felt will form a slight curve due to the canvas seam underneath, forming a nice frame around the piece. You want about $\frac{1}{4}$ inch of felt to show from the front. Tack down the strips from the back to hold them in place. Take your needle through the felt and through the back of the tent stitches. Do not go through to the front of the needlepoint. You don't have to worry about even stitches; all of the stitching will be covered by the backing piece. After all fours sides are tacked down, slip stitch the rectangular piece of felt to the back of the ornament. Before you slip stitch across the top of the ornament, insert the cord for hanging into the center of the top and catch the cord with your stitches as you continue stitching.

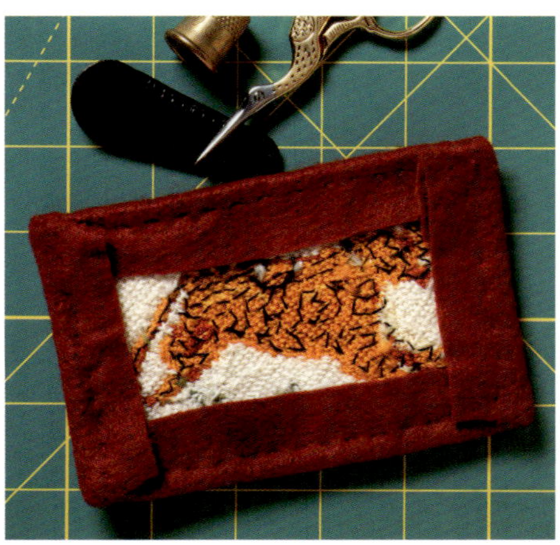

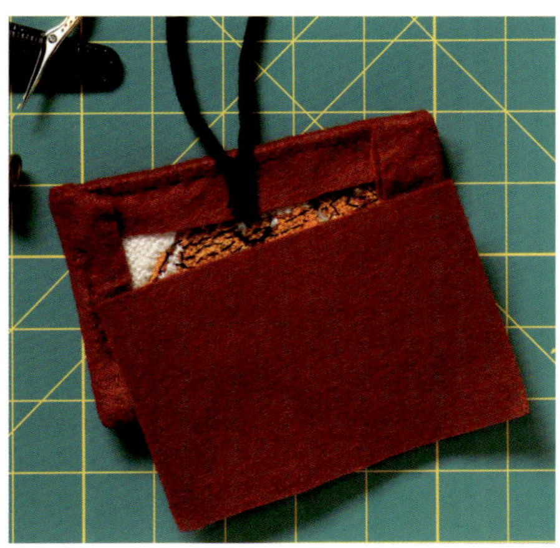

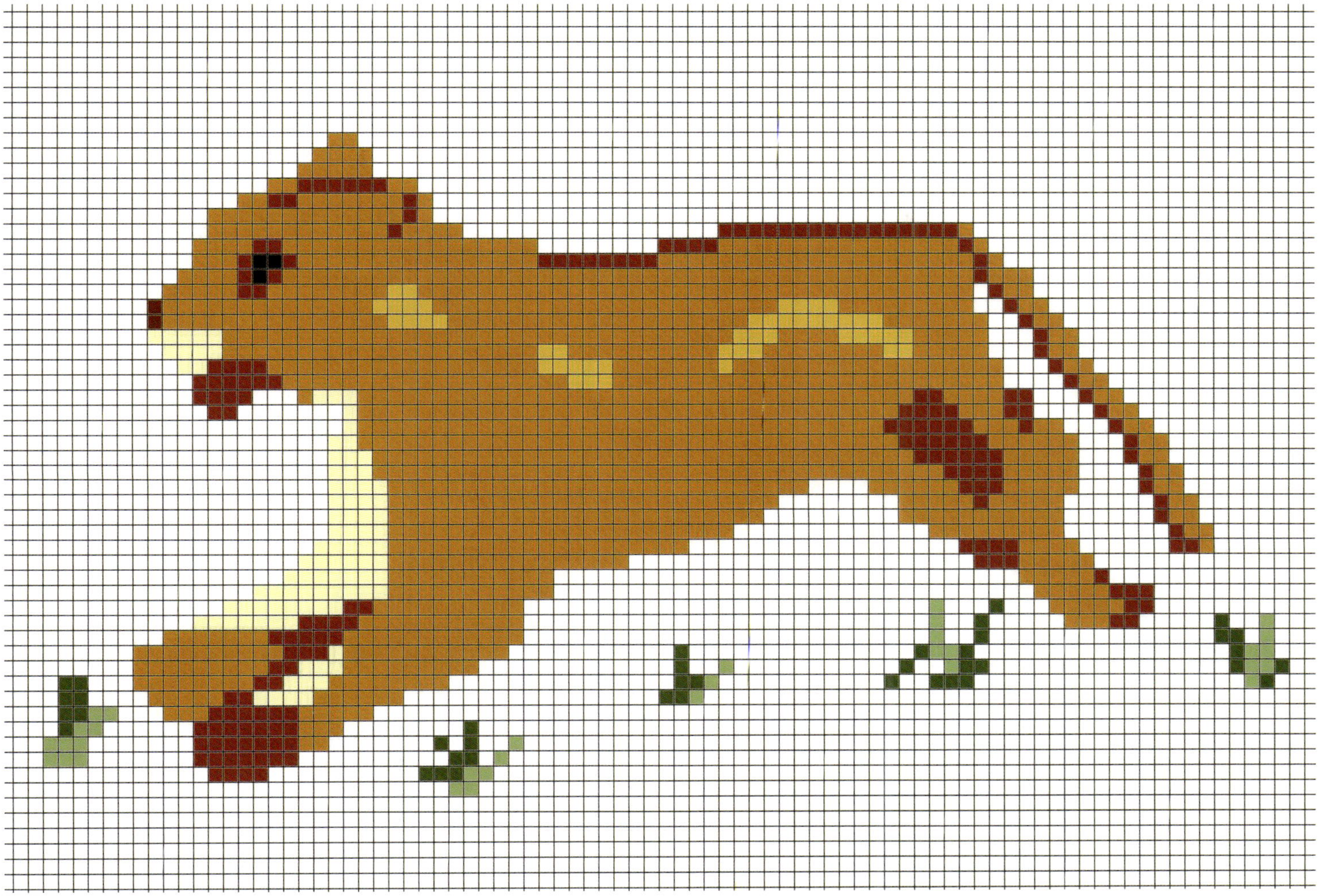

IDEA: For a fun, funky look, change out the colors of the leopard: maybe a pink leopard with green spots?

SAMPLER

Molly Coppuck, Burlington County, New Jersey, 1796,
silk embroidery threads on linen ground, 17" x 15 1/8",
gift of the estate of Ella Lodge Stackhouse Van Siclen (1896–1992)
by Mr. and Mrs. Garret T. Van Siclen, 1994.608.1

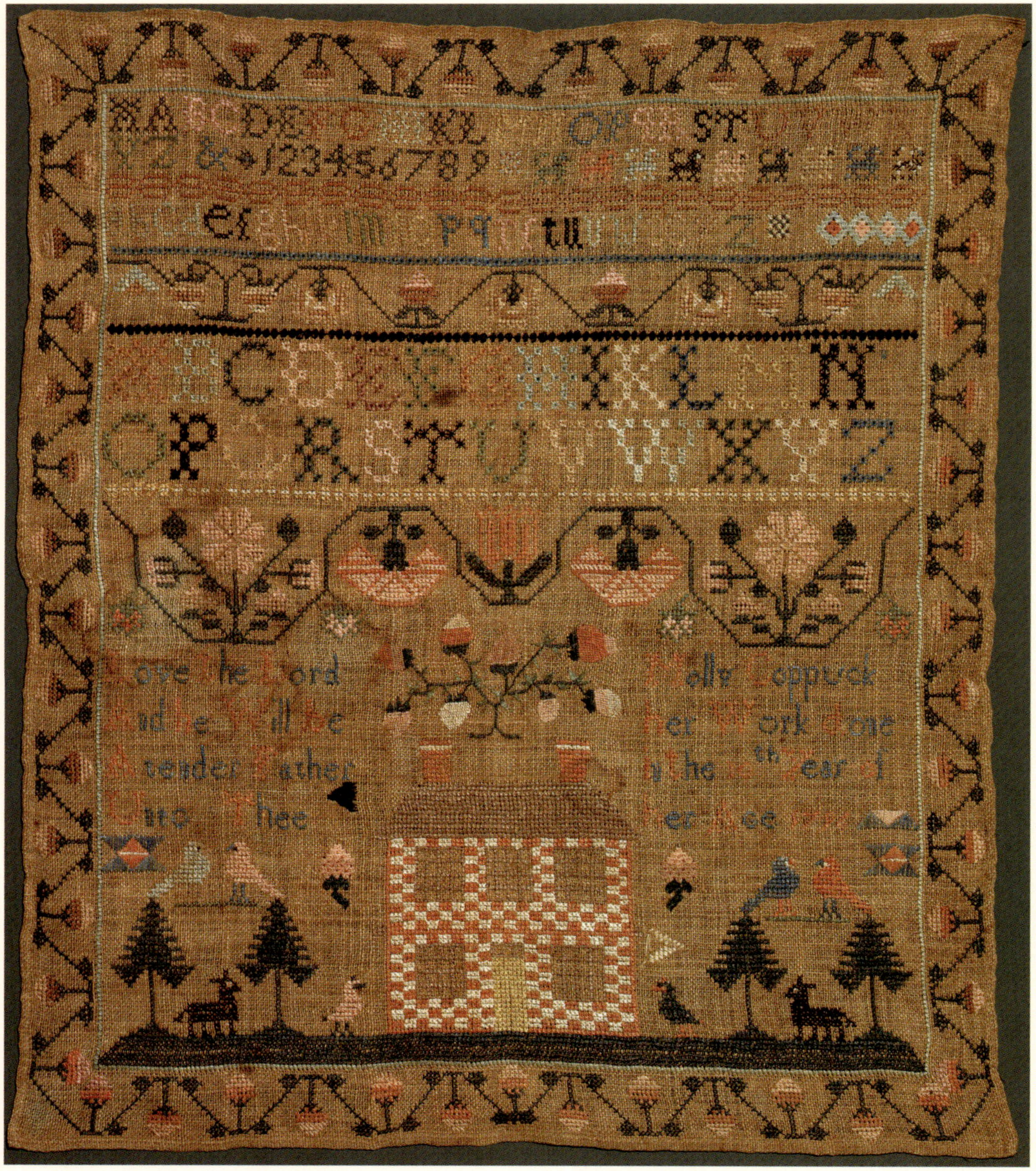

"Molly Coppuck her Work done in the 10th Year of her Age 1796": The young needleworker cross-stitched these words into her sampler as part of her overall design. The sampler is worked in cross- and eyelet stitches and features the alphabet as well as a decorative border and a lovely scene at the bottom. What were you doing at ten years of age? Not many of us today would have accomplished such a task. Girls were taught to sew at an early age. Some samplers indicate that their makers were as young as six or seven. While the final product was a piece worthy of hanging (and sometimes they did), it also demonstrated a skill with a needle and the successful preparation for larger sewing projects that would be a part of the girl's adult life. This sampler is almost identical to others worked in the New Jersey area. Some of these similar pieces list Sarah Shoemaker as the schoolmistress. It is likely that Molly also worked her piece under this teacher's supervision.

Cross-Stitch Tree Stocking

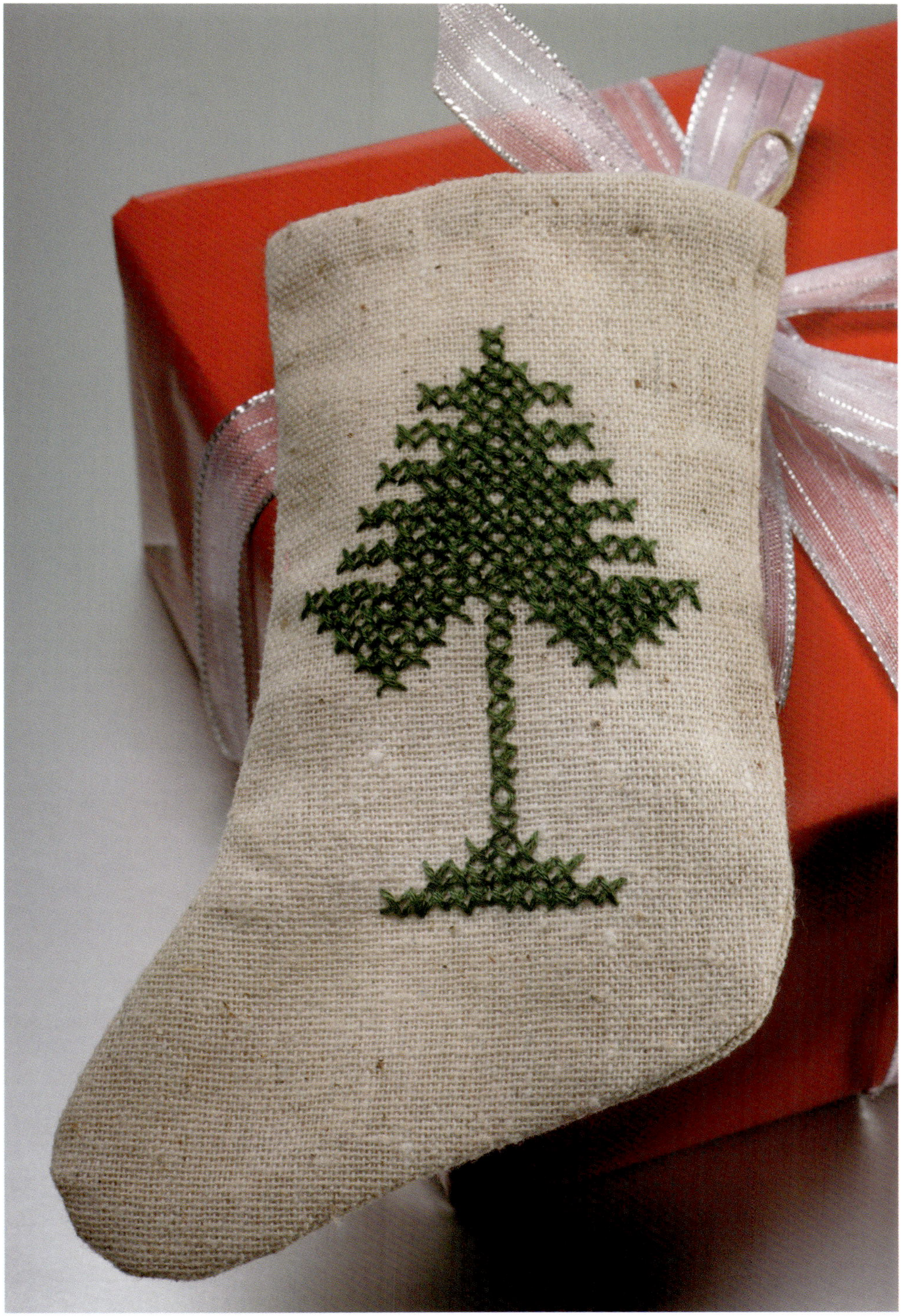

WHILE MANY OF THE MOTIFS IN MOLLY'S SAMPLER ARE ATTRACTIVE, THE TREES STAND OUT AS PERFECT FOR A HOLIDAY DESIGN.

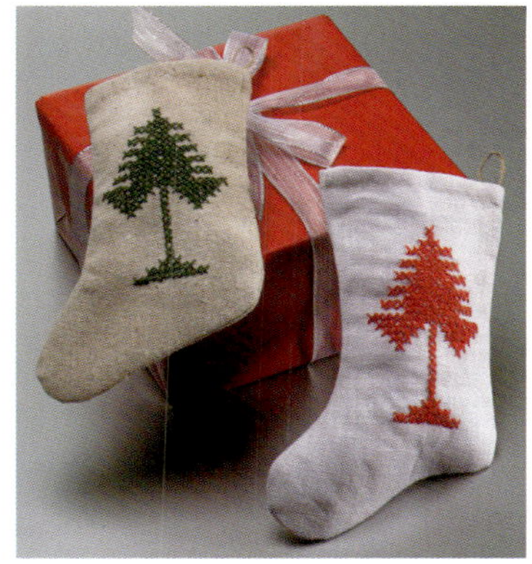

WHAT YOU NEED:

Stocking template (page 132)

Charted design

Two pieces of plain cotton, linen, or wool fabric, 9 x 9 inches

Dressmaker's carbon

Washable fabric pen

6-inch embroidery hoop

Pins

10-count waste canvas, 5 1/2 x 3 inches

Needle

Floss (any single color)

Sewing machine

Scissors

Iron

Ironing board

Twine, 6 inches long

Note: This project uses waste canvas to cross-stitch onto fabric. As with Aida cloth, you follow the grid to work your stitches on waste canvas.

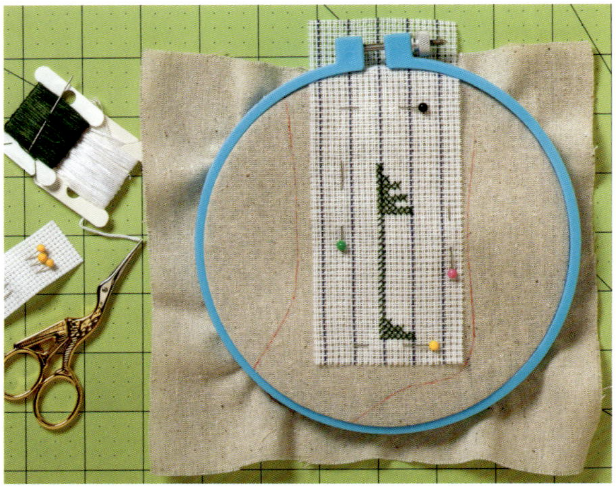

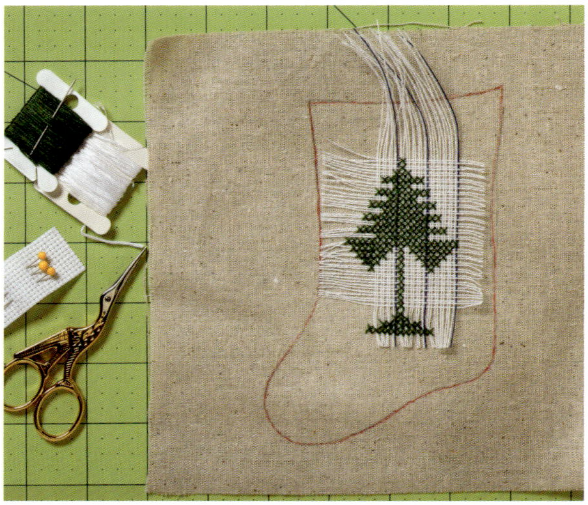

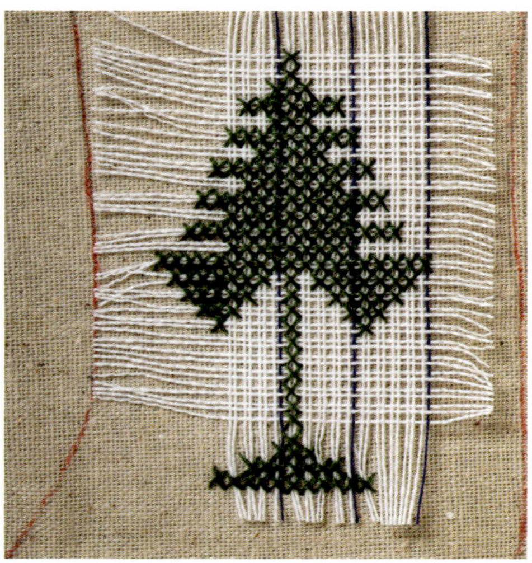

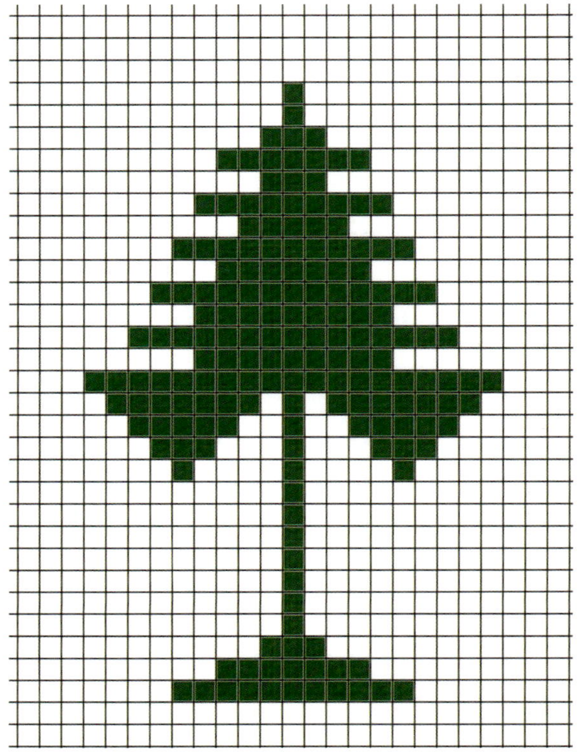

INSTRUCTIONS:
Trace the stocking template onto one piece of fabric using the dressmaker's carbon: Place the dressmaker's carbon, carbon side up, onto your work surface; lay the fabric right side up on top of the carbon; place the stocking template in the center of the fabric and trace with the fabric pen. As you trace the stocking onto the right side of the fabric, the carbon will make a stitching line on the back.

Place the fabric in the embroidery hoop, and pin the waste canvas to the fabric. Use the lines that you traced from the template onto the fabric to line up the waste canvas: Place the bottom edge of the waste canvas just below the horizontal line on the fabric; center the waste canvas left to right on the vertical line. Referring to the charted design, create the cross-stitch by stitching through both the waste canvas and the fabric together. Start stitching at the base of the tree, working up to the top.

Once the stitching is complete, remove the piece from the hoop and begin removing the waste canvas. Refer to the removal instructions on the waste canvas package. Tips: Begin by removing all waste canvas threads that do not hold cross-stitches. Carefully pull the longest threads first; then remove the shorter threads. If a thread breaks, use a pin to remove it. Iron the piece from the back side. Do not iron from the front over the cross-stitching.

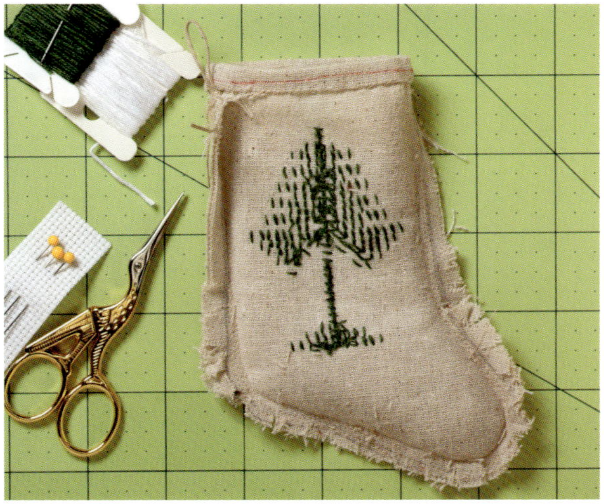

Pin together the fabric with the stitched tree and the remaining piece of fabric with right sides facing in. Machine stitch following the line made by the dressmaker's carbon. Do not stitch across the top. Cut around the stocking leaving a 1/4-inch seam allowance. Fold the top of the stocking to the inside 1/4 inch, and hem the top using a blind stitch. Snip curves, and then turn the stocking right side out. Iron the stocking from the back.

Fold the twine in half and stitch to the top of the stocking for hanging.

IDEA: LOOKING FOR AN ADVENT CALENDAR? STITCH TWENTY-FOUR OF THESE LITTLE STOCKINGS AND STRING THEM UP FOR TWENTY-FOUR DAYS OF HOLIDAY FUN. RATHER THAN A TREAT INSIDE EACH STOCKING, INCLUDE A SLIP OF COLORED PAPER WITH AN ACTIVITY OR A PARTICULAR TASK WRITTEN ON IT. DAY 1 PUT UP THE TREE, DAY 14 MAKE COOKIES, DAY 21 GO FOR A FAMILY DRIVE TO SEE THE HOLIDAY LIGHTS.

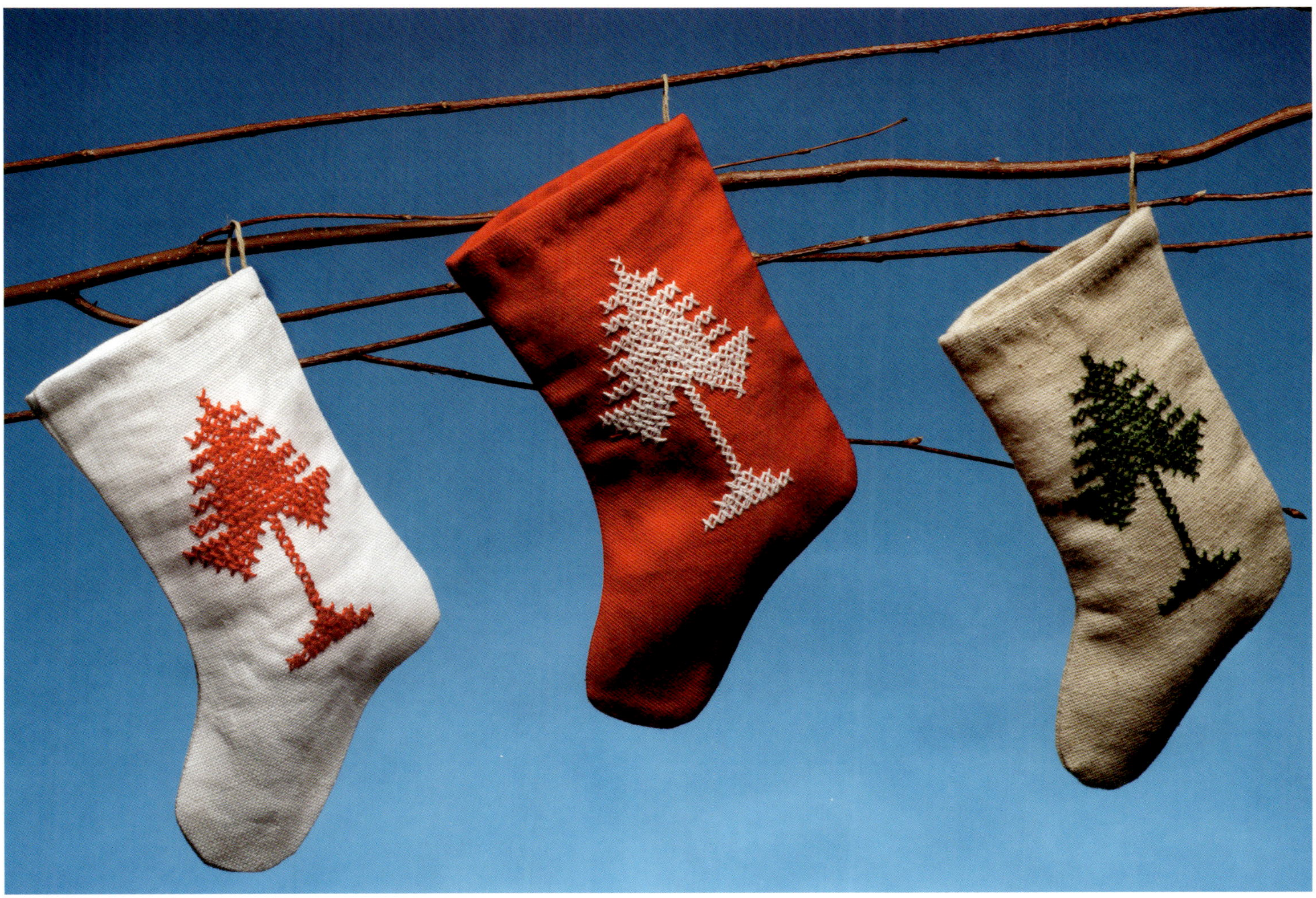

QUILT TOP

Sarah Elizabeth Haines Dunham and Theodore Runyon Dunham, New Jersey, ca. 1855, cotton, 84" x 77", gift of Mrs. John D. Green, 1972.609.3.

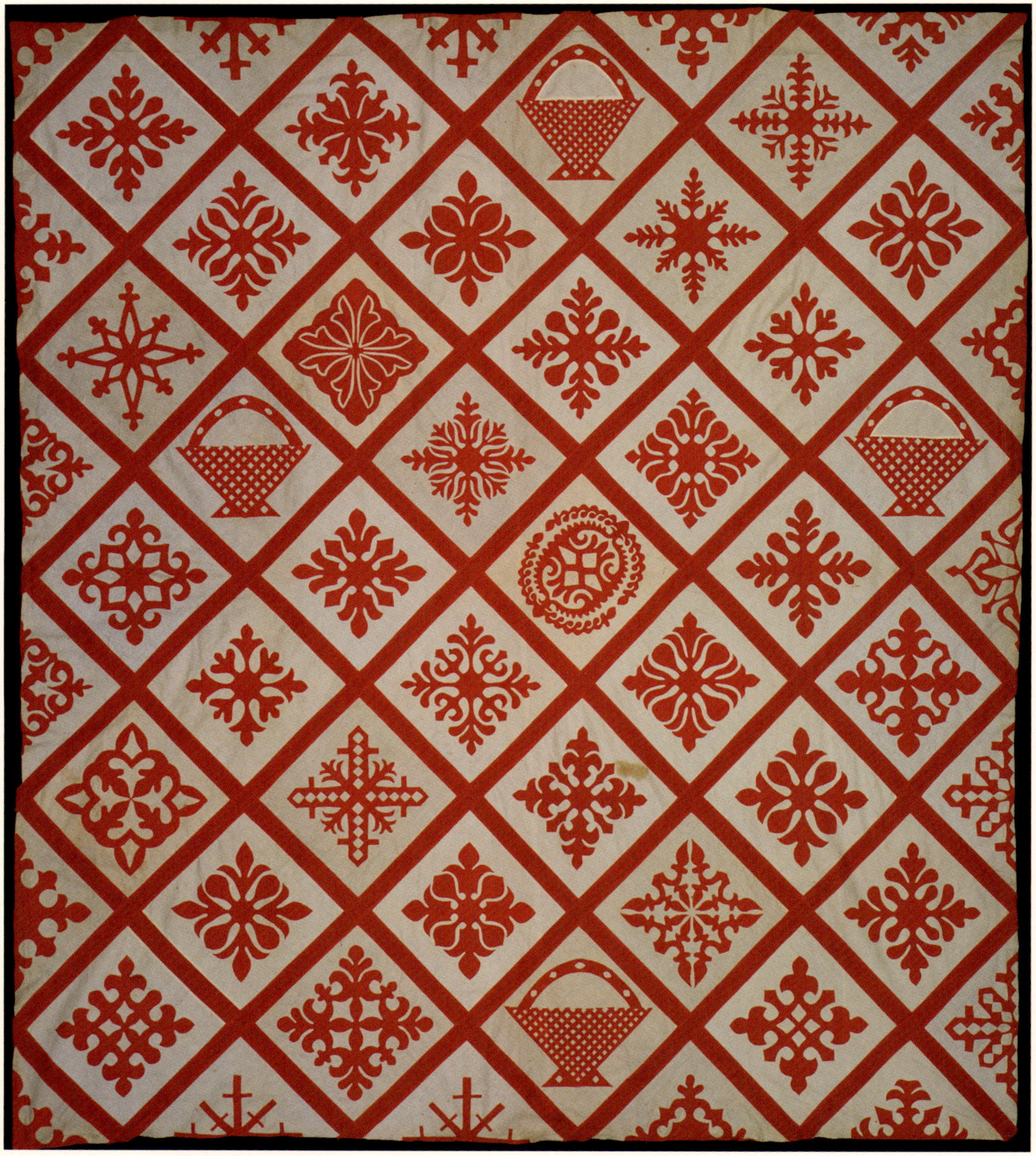

A quilt made by a husband and wife? This one was. According to family tradition, Theodore designed and cut the patterns for the appliqués; Sarah stitched them to the white background fabric. The quilt top was never attached to a backing or batting. It was kept in the family until Sarah and Theodore's great-granddaughter gave it to the Folk Art Museum.

The quilt's motifs, except for the baskets, are all based on twice-folded paper patterns. If you look carefully at each design, you can see that each one is made up of four equal parts. A piece of paper folded into fourths and cut, when unfolded, would create the complete design. The bright red patterns against the snowy white give the impression of a field of snowflakes. The Turkey red fabric did not fade or bleed when washed and gave rise to the popularity of red and white color schemes in the period between 1840 and 1925.

Recycled-Book Snowflake

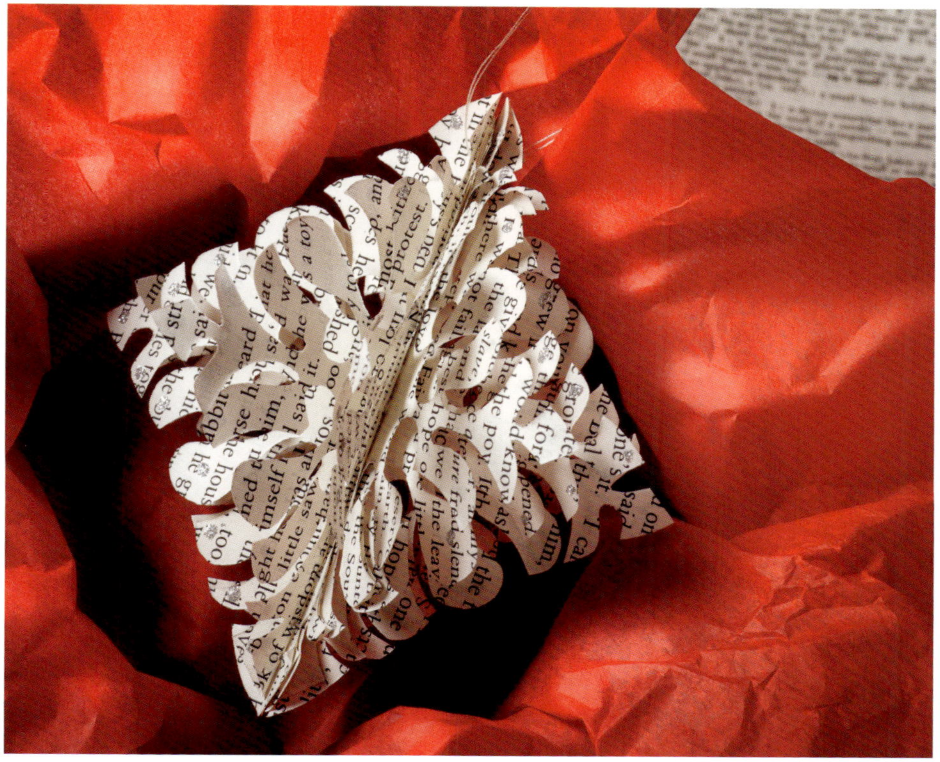

LOOKING AT THE RED AND WHITE COLOR SCHEME, WE COULDN'T HELP BUT THINK OF THE HOLIDAYS. WITH WINTER AND SNOW IN MIND, THE SYMMETRICAL PATTERNS STAND OUT AS SNOWFLAKES WITH NO TWO ALIKE. WE HAD A HARD TIME SELECTING JUST ONE.

WHAT YOU NEED:

Snowflake template (page 138)
Old hardcover book
Scissors
Pencil
Scherenschnitte or embroidery scissors
Newspaper
Glue pen
Glitter
Cardboard (such as a cereal box)
Binder clip
Needle
White or off-white thread

INSTRUCTIONS:

Deconstruct the book: Carefully pull off the hard covers and separate out the sets of pages. Cut the string that holds each set together, and then you can either carefully tear the pages along the fold or cut them apart. A hardcover book works best as the pages are usually a bit nicer and stronger than paperback book pages.

Take six pages from the book. Fold each page in half matching short ends. Place the dotted line of the template on the fold of the book page. Trace the template with the pencil. Using the scherenschnitte scissors, cut out. Repeat with each page.

Cover your work surface with the newspaper. Open each snowflake and place on the newspaper. Decorate the edges of each snowflake by adding glue with the glue pen and then sprinkling with glitter. Once dry, decorate the reverse side. Allow to dry.

To create the three-dimensional ornament, layer the snowflakes, making sure the folds and the edges line up and clip them together with the binder clip. Place the clipped snowflakes on the cardboard. In the fold, use the needle to pierce through the six layers to create about nine stitching holes. It is easier to stitch the snowflakes together when the holes have been pierced beforehand. Using a running stitch, sew the snowflakes together with the thread. Weave in the ends of the thread. Tie a loop of thread at the top for hanging. Remove the binder clip. Separate the pages so they are displayed evenly to give the ornament its fullness.

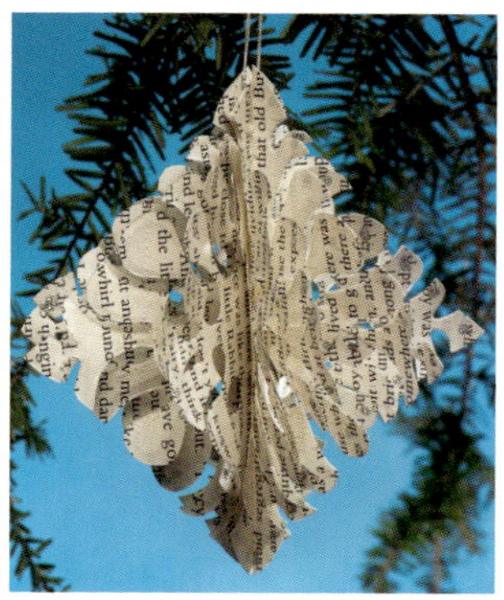

IDEAS: BY SUBTRACTING OR ADDING TO THE NUMBER OF LAYERS, YOU CAN CHANGE THE LOOK OF THE SNOWFLAKE. ALSO, YOU COULD ADD MORE GLITTER OR A VARIETY OF COLORED GLITTERS.

MRS. JOSIAH B. KEYLOR'S CAT

Pennsylvania, ca. 1885, oil on canvas, 17" x 14", bequest of Marion Day Beardsley, 1973.101.2

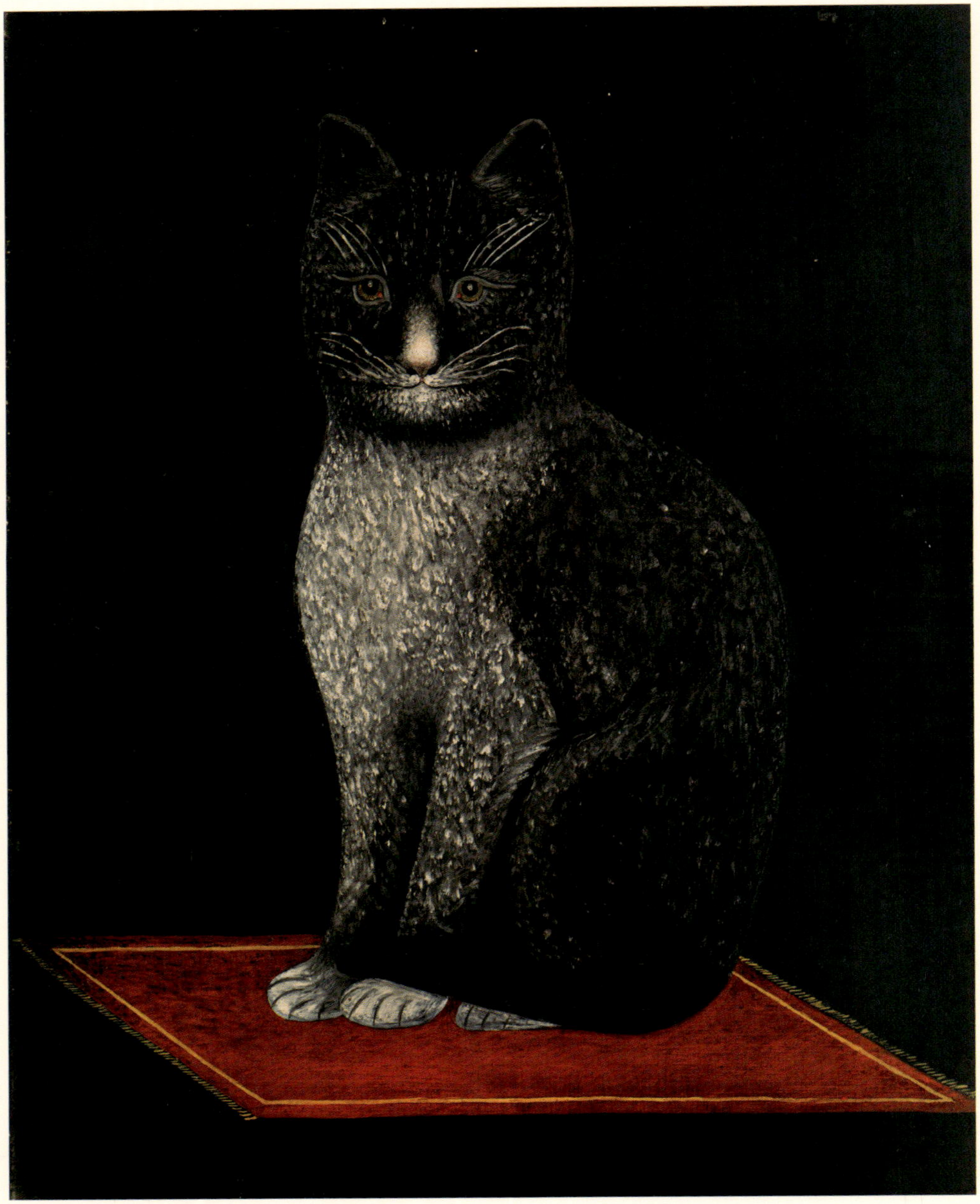

For many people, pets are as much a part of the family as any human member. It is not surprising that a devoted owner would want a remembrance of a cherished friend. This painting is not some generic representation of a feline. The cat has detailed markings and an expression that captures its character. The artist knew this cat. A label attached to the painting in 1969 notes, "This cat was owned by and, perhaps, painted by the first wife of Dr. Josiah B. Keylor, Cochranville, Pa. Marion Day, my wife, bought this picture from her cousin, Mrs. David Bair, nee Keylor, daughter of Dr. Keylor's second wife."

It is intriguing to think that perhaps Mrs. Keylor actually painted this charming picture and that the cat actually let her. The whole focus is on the cat with no extraneous details beyond the "flying carpet" on which the animal poses.

Embroidered Cat

BEING CAT PEOPLE, WE HAD TO INCLUDE AT LEAST ONE REPRESENTATION OF A FELINE FRIEND. THE FOLK ART MUSEUM HAS SEVERAL IMAGES, BUT MRS. KEYLOR'S CAT IS ONE OF OUR FAVORITES. DURING THE CREATION OF THIS BOOK, CHRISTINA'S ELDERLY CAT, PATTY, WAS A CONSTANT COMPANION AS CHRISTINA SEWED FOR HOURS AT HOME. SADLY, PATTY PASSED AWAY SOON AFTER. THIS CAT IS A FITTING TRIBUTE TO FAITHFUL PATTY.

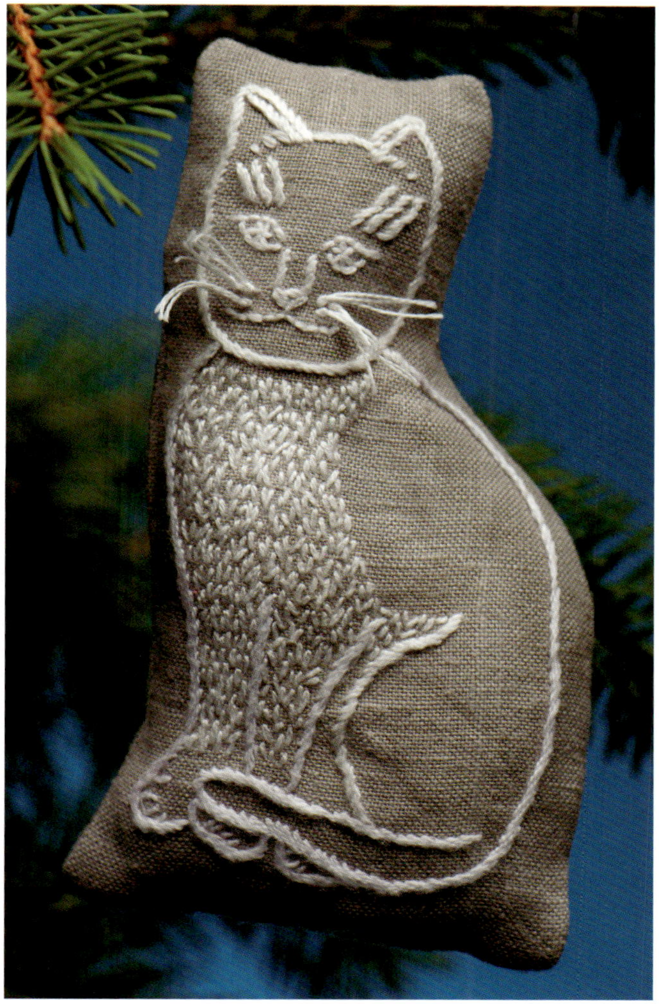

WHAT YOU NEED:

- Cat template (page 134)
- Tracing paper
- Iron-on transfer pencil
- Iron
- Ironing board
- Two pieces of linen or cotton fabric, 8 x 8 inches (any color except white)
- 6-inch embroidery hoop
- Embroidery needle
- White floss
- Fabric pen
- Pins
- Stuffing
- Ruler
- Scissors
- Clear thread

IDEA: MRS. KEYLOR'S CAT WOULD LOOK VERY SMART STITCHED IN HOT PINK ON WHITE OR WHITE ON GREEN OR PURPLE ON PINK. WHAT COLOR COMBINATION WILL YOU CHOOSE?

INSTRUCTIONS:

Trace the cat template onto the tracing paper with the iron-on transfer pencil. Following the manufacturer's instructions for the transfer pencil, iron the cat onto the center of one piece of the fabric.

Center the fabric in the embroidery hoop. Thread the needle with two strands of floss. Use a stem stitch to outline all the features of the cat except for the eyes, mouth, toes, base of the ears, and fur. For the eyes and mouth, use a backstitch; for the eyeballs, use a star stitch; for the toes and the base of the ears, use a running stitch. To create the fur effect on the cat's chest, randomly fill the chest with various running stitches but do not fill in completely.

Remove the embroidered piece from the hoop. On the back side of the fabric, draw a 1/2-inch seam allowance with the fabric pen.

Pin the second piece of fabric to the right side of the cat, and use a running stitch to sew around the cat following the seam allowance. Leave the bottom of the cat open for stuffing. Turn the piece right side out and loosely stuff. Stitch closed with a slip stitch.

To add the whiskers, thread a needle with a length of three strands of floss, and tie a knot about 2 inches from the end. Push the needle in at the right side of the cat's nose and out on the left side of the cat's nose. Pull the thread through until the knot reaches the fabric on the right side; then tie a knot close to the fabric on the left side and snip about 2 inches from the knot. Repeat twice. Snip whiskers to about 1/2 inch.

Add a loop of clear thread at the top the cat for hanging.

SPILL HOLDER

probably Pennsylvania, 1825–1850, tinplate, $10^{5}/_{8}$" x $5^{1}/_{8}$" x $3^{5}/_{8}$", acquisition funded by Mr. and Mrs. William T. Earls Sr., 1978.808.1

A very unremarkable, utilitarian object is transformed into a decorative accessory under the hand of a creative individual. This spill or splint holder hung near a fireplace to hold small pieces of rolled paper (spills) or wood (splints) that were used to start the fire. A mundane task but an excellent opportunity for embellishment. The fireplace was likely the center of family activity particularly in the winter when it was a welcome source of heat. The holder would be in plain sight, so making it pleasing to look at made sense. The designs were created with a punch. The pattern on the front was punched all the way through whereas that on the back was not. The variation gives dimension to the decoration. When the punched technique that went all the way through was used on tin lanterns, the light from a candle would shine through the holes projecting the pattern into the room.

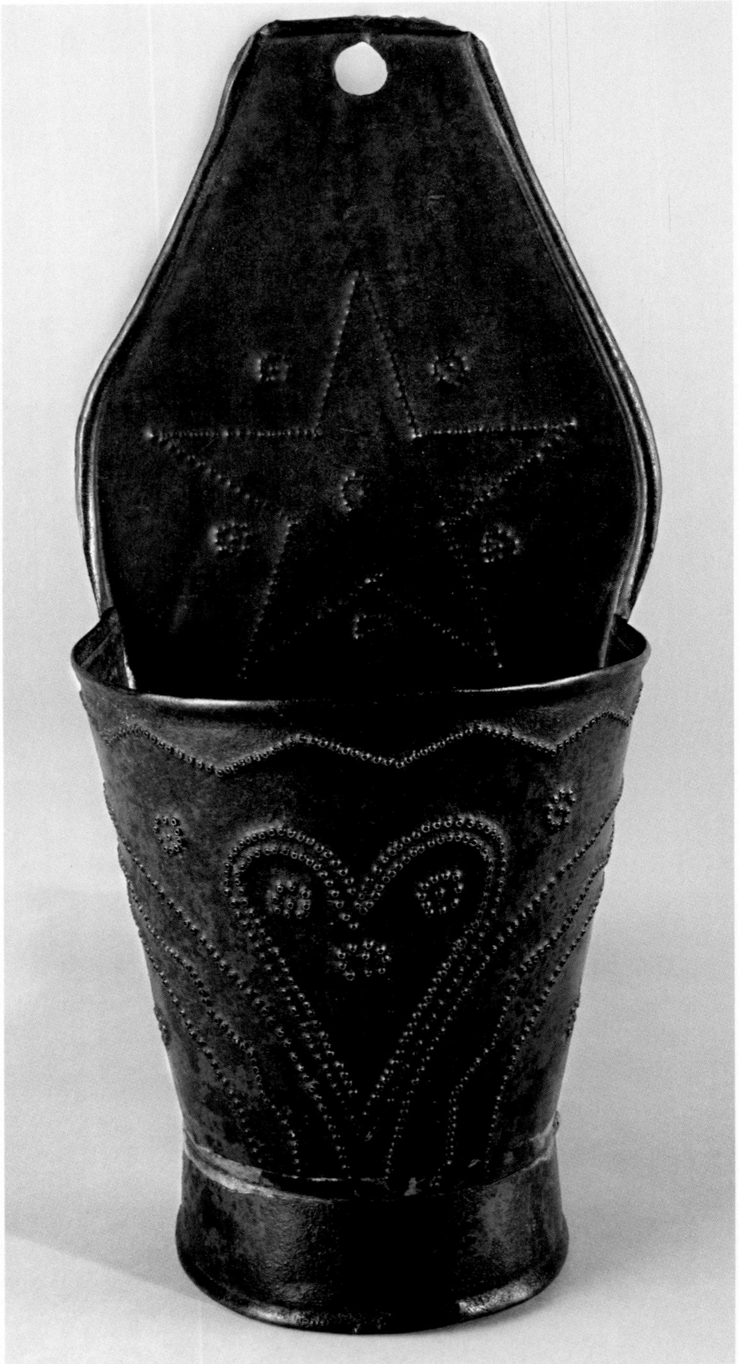

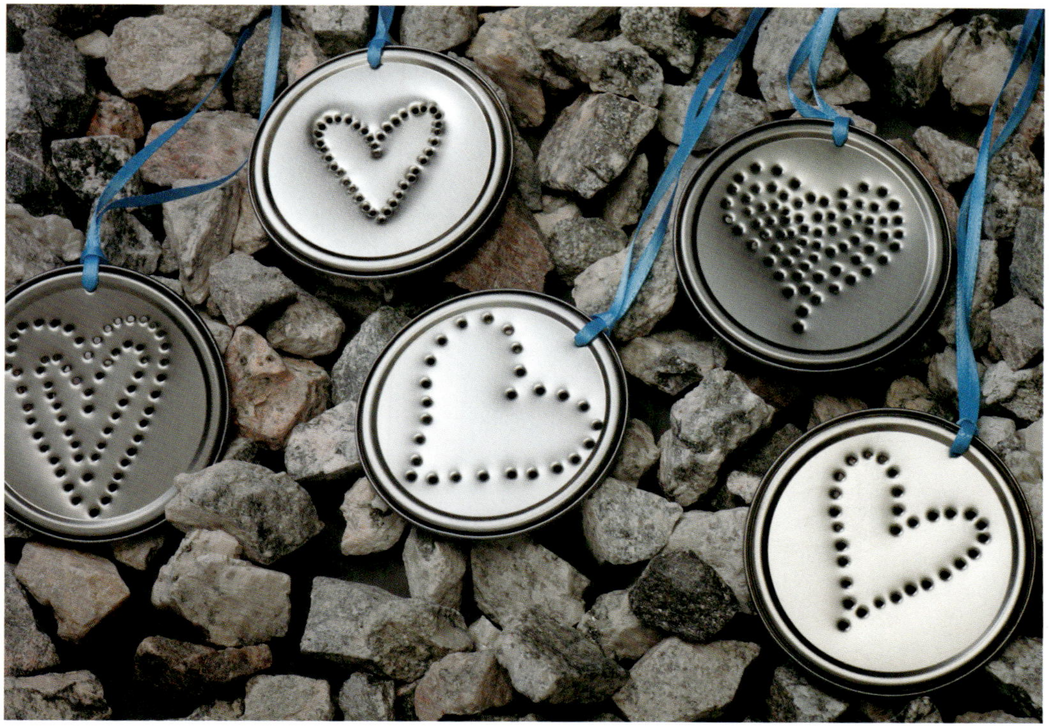

THE IDEA OF TAKING AN EVERYDAY OBJECT AND MAKING IT PRETTY INSPIRED US TO LOOK AROUND THE HOUSE FOR OUR MATERIAL FOR THIS PROJECT. YOU CAN GIVE A NEW PURPOSE AND LOOK TO A THROWAWAY MATERIAL.

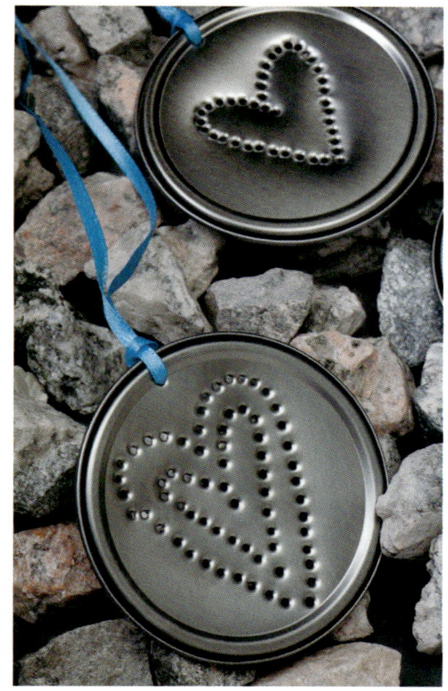

Recycled-Metal Heart

INSTRUCTIONS:

To prepare your work surface, lay a piece of cardboard down on top of the cutting mat.

Using the template as a guide, sketch the heart design onto the can lid with a pencil. Use the awl to carefully punch the design into the lid; don't push too hard and end up going through your mat.

Add a hole at the top with the awl for the ribbon. Fold the ribbon in half and insert the folded end through the hole from the front just far enough to make a loop. Thread the two ends through the loop and pull tight so the ribbon is held tight to the lid. Tie off the ends of the ribbon at the desired length for hanging.

IDEAS: COME UP WITH OTHER PATTERNS TO PUNCH: A STAR, A CANDY CANE, A TREE. ATTACH YOUR PUNCHED LIDS TO THE OUTSIDE OF A CLEAR GLASS CYLINDER WITH A CANDLE INSIDE SO THAT THE LIGHT WILL SHINE THROUGH THE PIERCED DESIGN.

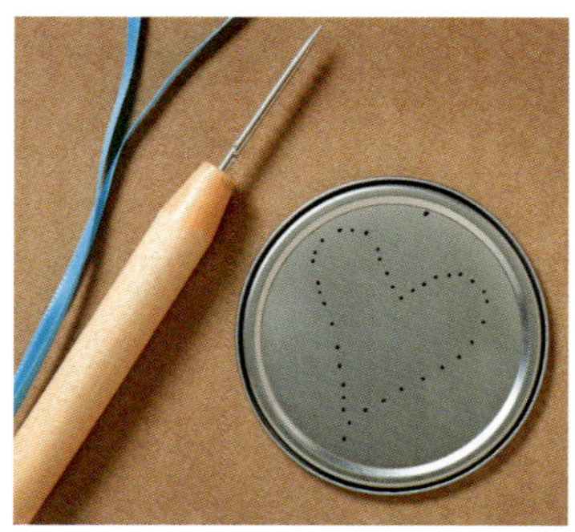

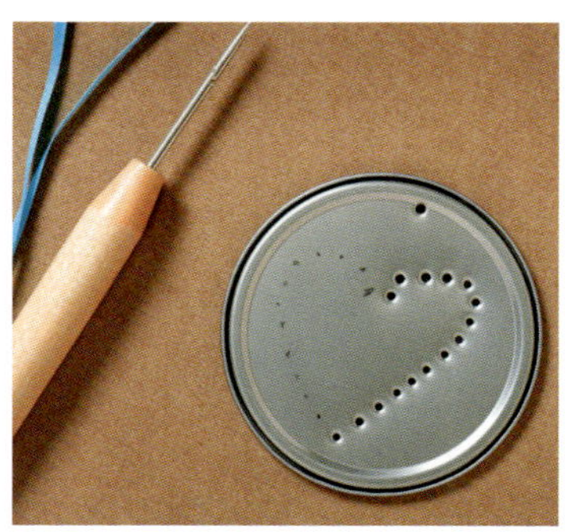

WHAT YOU NEED:

- Heart template (page 141)
- Cardboard (such as a cereal box)
- Cutting mat (an extra layer of cardboard will also work)
- Metal juice can lid
- Pencil
- Awl
- 1/8-inch ribbon, 15 inches long

MARY JANE SMITH

Joseph Whiting Stock (1815–1855), Springfield, Massachusetts, 1838, oil on canvas, 41 7/8" x 30 1/4", gift of Abby Aldrich Rockefeller, 1941.100.9

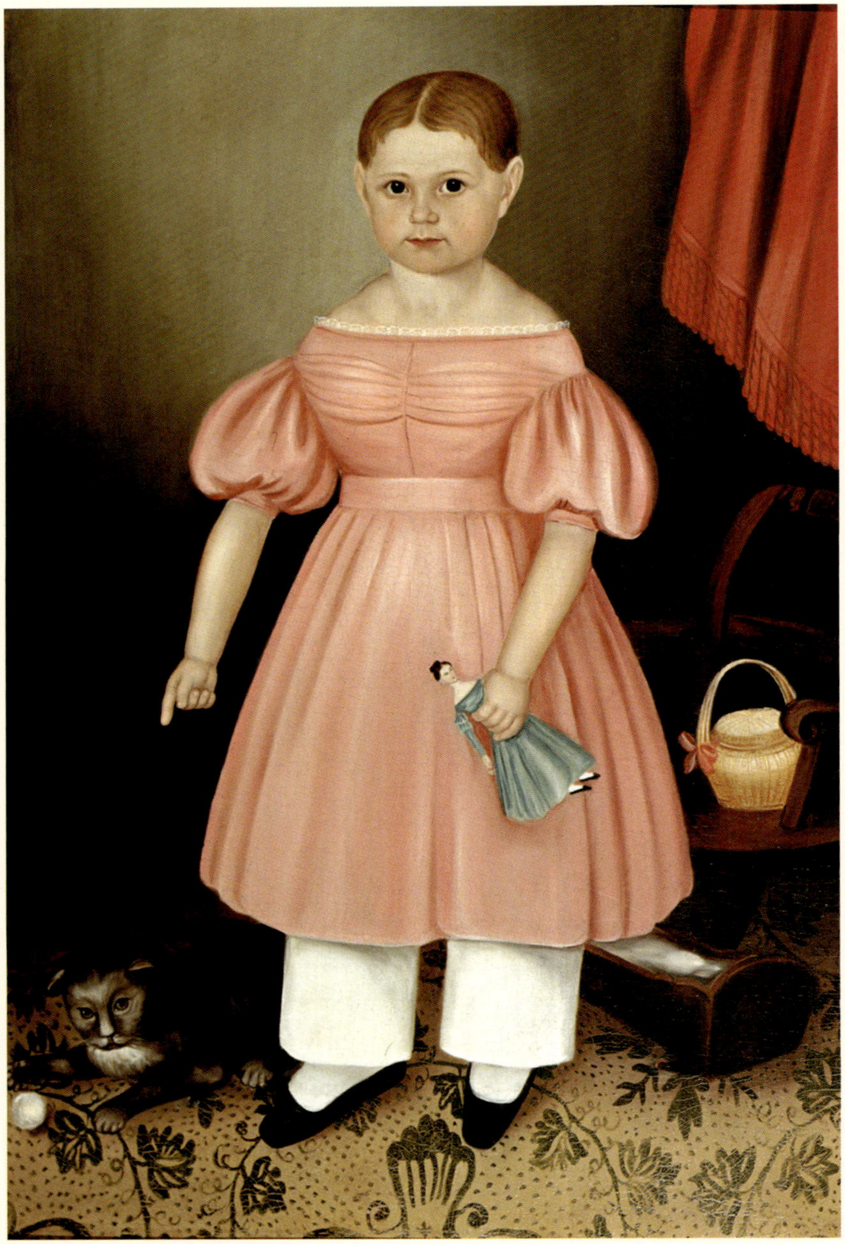

The youngsters portrayed in folk art portraits tend to have personality and appeal that resonate with today's viewers. Many portraits survive without the identification of the sitter or with a name that can't be traced. While these portraits still have the power to charm, it is exciting to view images of children who can be named and placed in context. Mary Jane is such a child. The companion portrait of her brother, William Howard, is owned by the Folk Art Museum as well. Both portraits were painted by the artist Joseph Whiting Stock in June 1838. At the time, Mary Jane was two years and four months old and her brother five years and seven months. What do you suppose the children thought about as their portraits were being completed? Given that it was June, would they much rather have been outdoors?

The children's parents, David and Harriet Smith of Springfield, Massachusetts, commissioned the almost life-size portraits from the artist at the cost of twelve dollars each. Stock often used props to indicate the interests and personalities of his subjects. In this case, Mary Jane clutches her doll and just behind her is the doll's cradle. With her other hand, she points down to the playful cat at her feet. As a toddler, no doubt Mary Jane enjoyed playing with both her cat and her doll.

Today we see Mary Jane as a pleasant two year old and hope that she grew up to have a good life. In reality, however, Mary Jane died at age eighteen from an illness she contracted while attending a Methodist revival. This knowledge makes the portrait all the more poignant. (Her brother grew up, had a successful carriage and stagecoach-making business, and lived to be seventy-nine.)

Fabric Doll

MARY JANE'S DOLL INSPIRED OUR FABRIC ORNAMENT. MADE IN GERMANY AND TYPICAL OF THIS PERIOD, THE DOLL HAD WOODEN ARMS AND LEGS, JOINTED SO SHE COULD BE DRESSED AND POSED. CLOTHES WERE OFTEN MADE BY A FAMILY MEMBER OR A YOUNG GIRL LEARNING TO SEW.

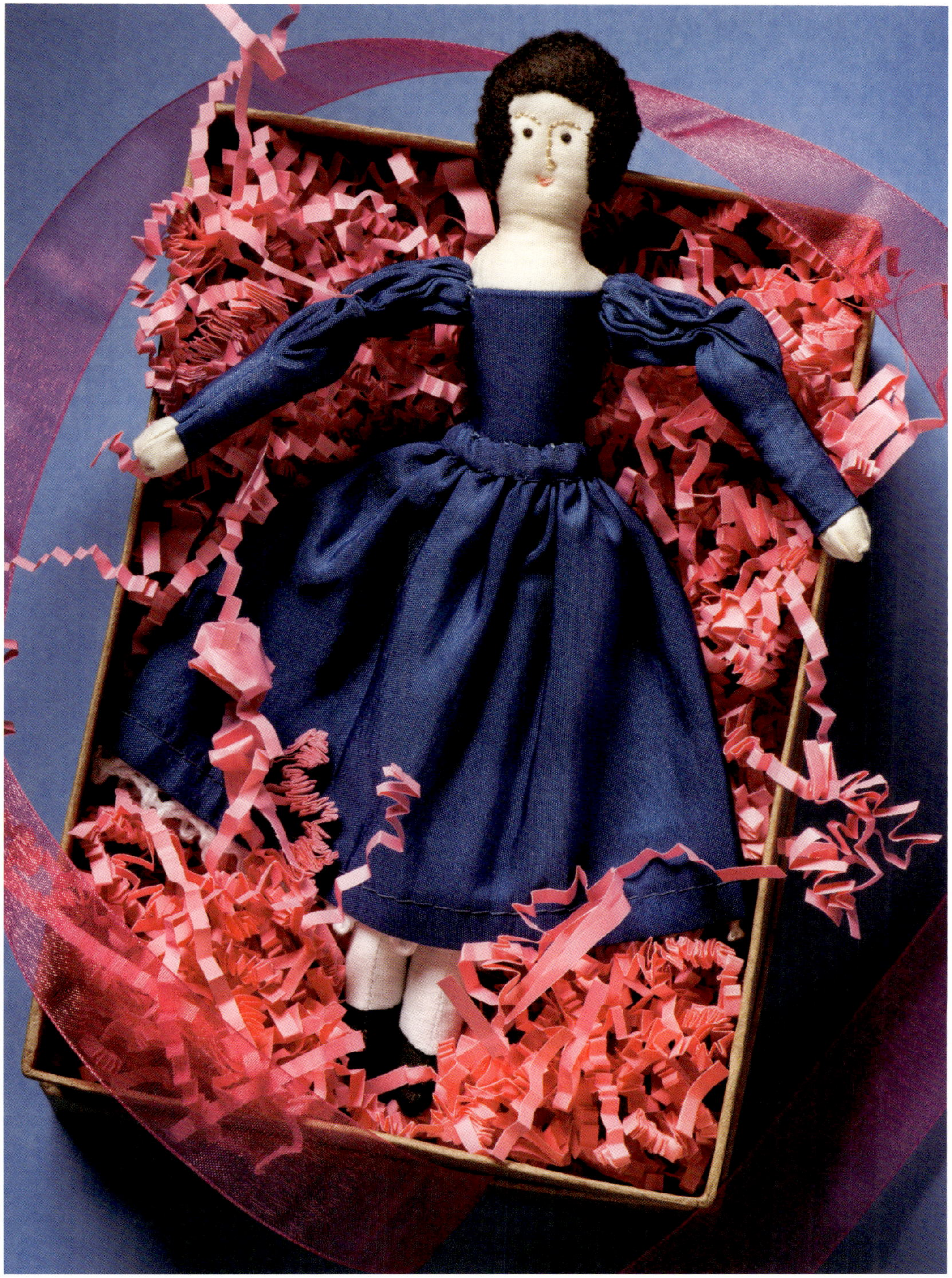

WHAT YOU NEED:

- Body, arm, leg, hair front, hair back, and bun templates (page 131)
- Natural muslin fabric, 3 x 9 inches
- Matching thread
- Blue taffeta fabric, 4 x 9 inches, 10 x $8^{1}/_{4}$ inches, and $^{1}/_{2}$ x $3^{1}/_{4}$ inches
- Matching thread
- Sewing machine
- Iron
- Ironing board
- Pins
- Scissors
- Disappearing-ink fabric pen
- White cotton fabric, 8 x 6 inches
- Matching thread
- Chopstick
- Stuffing
- Needle
- Cotton edging
- Black thread
- Black fabric marker
- Brown felt
- Matching floss
- Dark brown, light brown, and pink floss
- Pink pencil

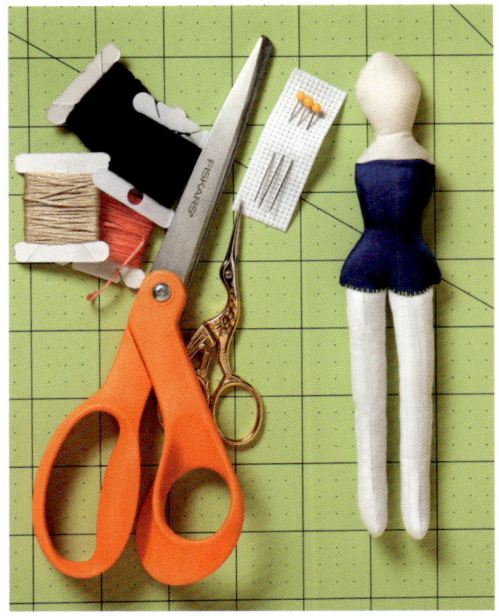

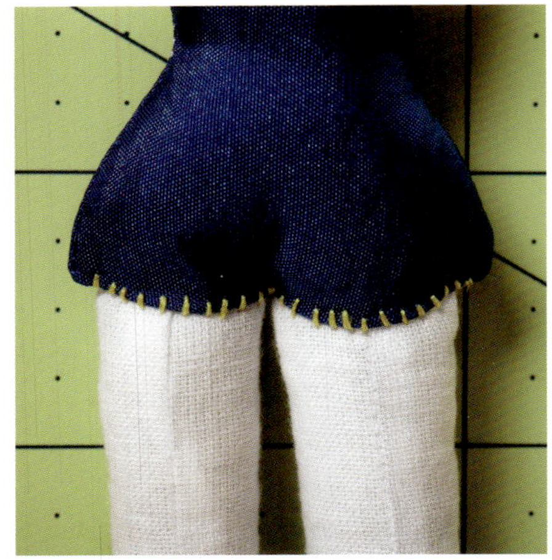

INSTRUCTIONS:

To make the body and the arms, place the muslin on top of the 4 x 9–inch piece of blue taffeta with right sides together. The taffeta will be slightly wider than the muslin. Using the sewing machine, stitch the two pieces of fabric together along one of the long sides. Then open up the sewn fabric and iron the edges of the seam toward the blue taffeta. Place the opened-out fabric on the table with the right side showing and with the muslin at the top. Take the left edge and fold it over to meet the right edge and smooth down. As you fold, carefully line up the seam and pin the fabric in place so that the seam remains lined up.

Using the disappearing-ink fabric pen, trace the body template once and the arm template twice onto the cloth, matching the solid lines on the templates to the seam where the muslin and taffeta meet. Machine stitch the body and the arms along the traced lines. Do not stitch the bottom of the body or the ends of the arms as these openings will be used for turning and stuffing. Cut out the body and the arms leaving a 1/8-inch seam allowance around each piece, and snip curves. Set aside.

To make the legs, fold the white cotton fabric in half so that the folded piece measures 6 x 4 inches, pin, and using the fabric pen trace the leg template twice onto the cloth. Machine stitch the legs along the traced lines, leaving the top unstitched for turning and stuffing. Cut out the legs leaving a 1/8-inch seam allowance around each piece, and snip curves. Set aside.

Flip the body, arms, and legs cloth right side out to prepare for stuffing. For this process, a chopstick is quite handy. Place the chopstick at the tip of the piece and carefully pull the fabric over the chopstick to turn the piece right side out. Repeat for all parts.

Gently stuff the body, turn the raw edges in, and whipstitch closed. Gently stuff legs, turn the raw edges in matching seams, and whipstitch closed. Stitch the legs to the body. (In the instruction photos, we often used floss of a contrasting color to make the stitches stand out. You should use matching floss.)

To finish the arms, make running stitches by hand 1/4 inch from the end of the muslin, turn the raw edge in, and gather. Tack the thread in place; this will form the hands. Create the sleeves by stitching three rows of running stitches on the taffeta section as indicated on the template. Before gathering each sleeve, stuff the arm from the hand up to the first row of gathers. The gathers will create the fullness in the rest of the arm. Now, gather each row, and tack the thread into place. When gathering the top row, turn the raw edge in, and stitch closed. Stitch the arms to the body.

Make the skirt using the 10 x 8¼–inch piece of blue taffeta. Fold the taffeta in half, matching the short sides, and machine stitch the edges together with a ¼-inch seam allowance. Press open the

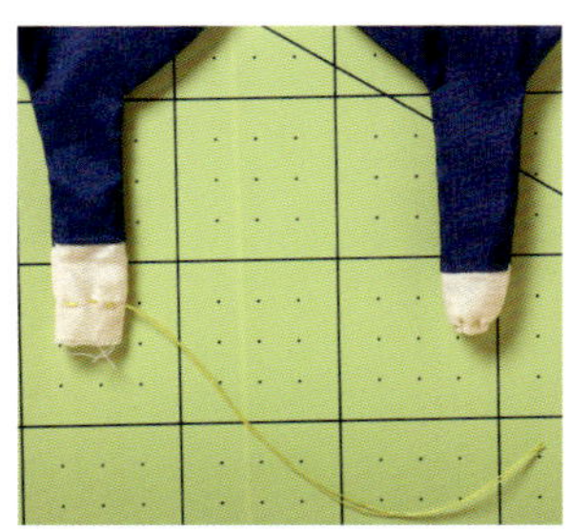

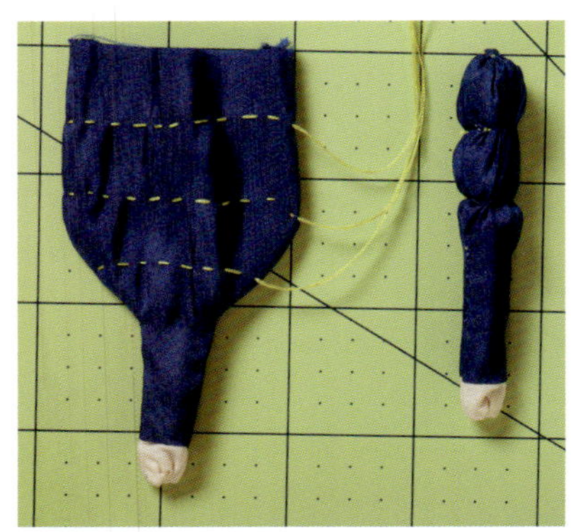

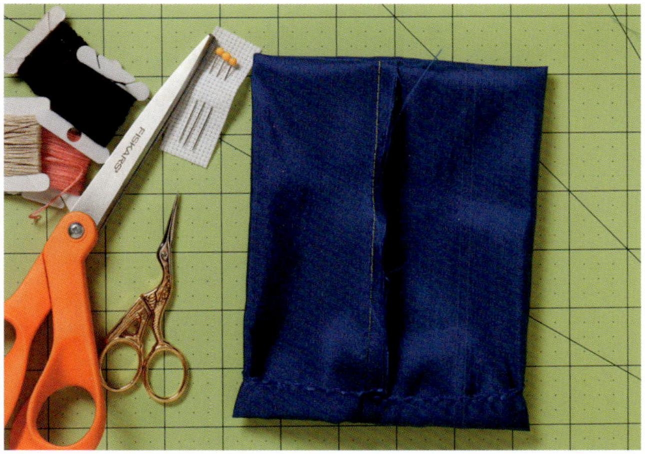

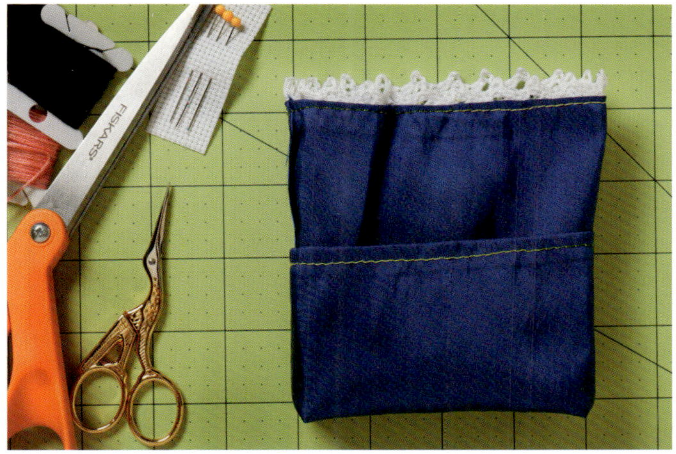

seam. You now have a tube of fabric. Fold one raw edge of the tube toward the inside of the tube (which is the right side of the fabric) and machine hem. Fold the other raw edge of the tube in the opposite direction toward the outside of the tube and machine hem. By hand or using the sewing machine, attach the cotton edging to the first hemmed edge, placing it on the inside of the tube. Take the tube in your hands holding the second hemmed edge up. Begin folding it down onto itself toward the cotton edging. Leave just a little bit of the cotton edging showing. Flatten the now doubled piece and iron. Both hems should now be facing in.

To pleat the skirt, start by machine stitching two rows of wide stitches, about 1/16 inch apart, around the folded edge of the skirt. Be sure to leave some extra thread as it comes off the machine so that you can pull it into gathers. Slide the skirt onto the doll, and

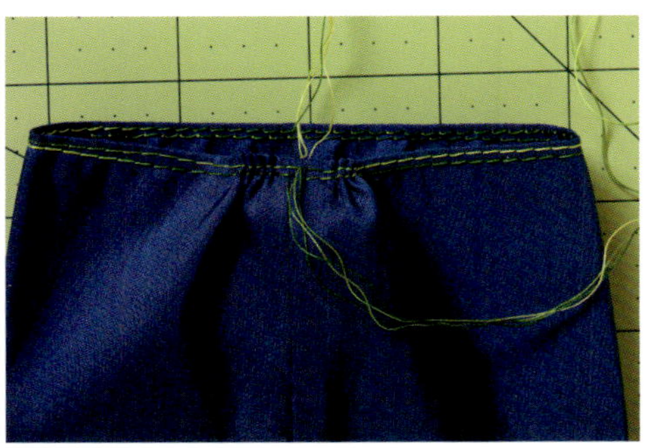

gather the two rows of stitches tightly by pulling the loose threads. When the skirt is tight to the body, knot the pulled threads to hold the gathers in place. To finish off, take the remaining thin piece of blue taffeta, fold the raw edges of the long sides under, and, using a blind stitch, attach this belt at the top edge to the body and at the bottom edge to the top of the skirt covering the gathers. Fold the raw edges in at the back and stitch closed.

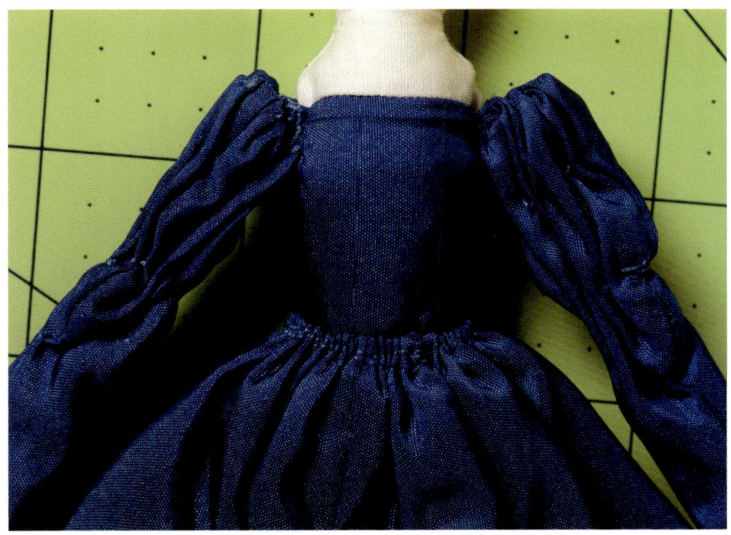

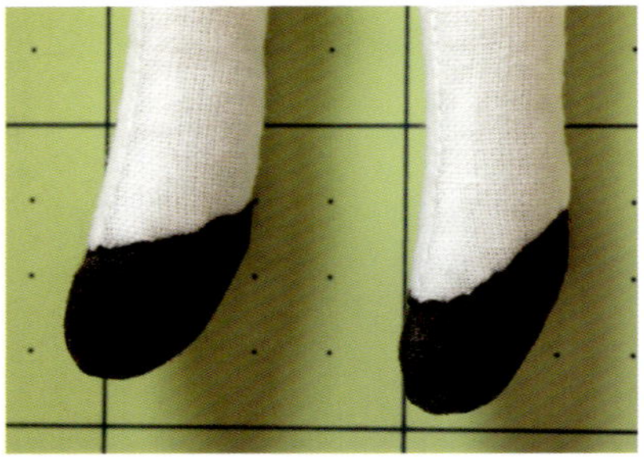

With black thread, outline shoes onto the legs; then color in with the black fabric marker.

Using the templates, cut out a hair front, a hair back, and a bun from the brown felt. Stitch the hair front to the doll's head using matching floss and a blind stitch. Before attaching the back hair, create the face. Using dark brown floss, make a French knot for each eye. Using light brown floss, make backstitches for the brows and nose. Using pink floss, make three small stitches for the mouth. Use the colored pencil to add pink to the cheeks. Now, using matching floss, stitch the back hair to the head, which will cover the knots from the face stitching. To create the bun, make a running stitch around the edge of the felt bun piece, draw to close loosely, tack to head, and end the stitches in the center of the bun to create an indentation.

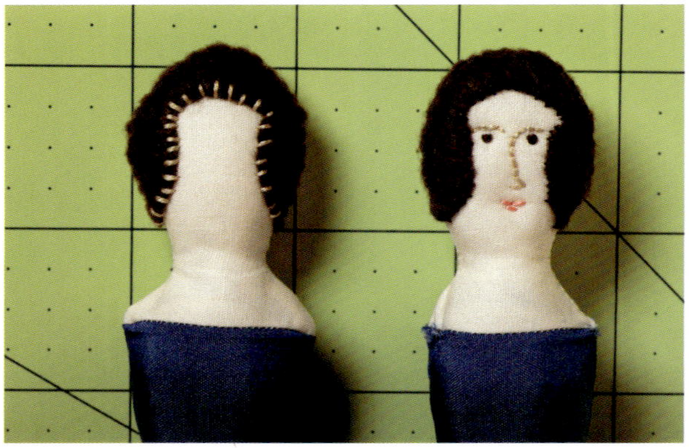

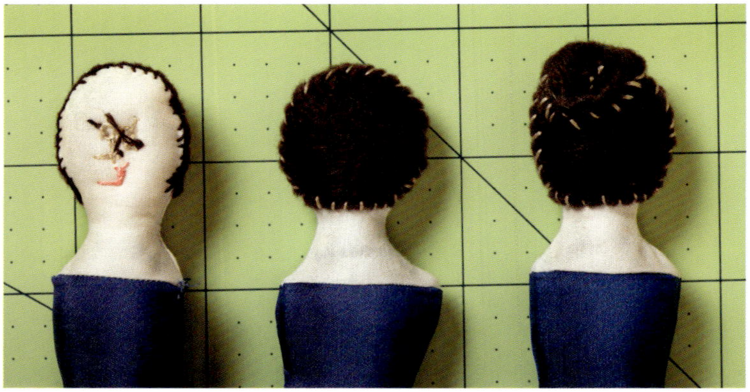

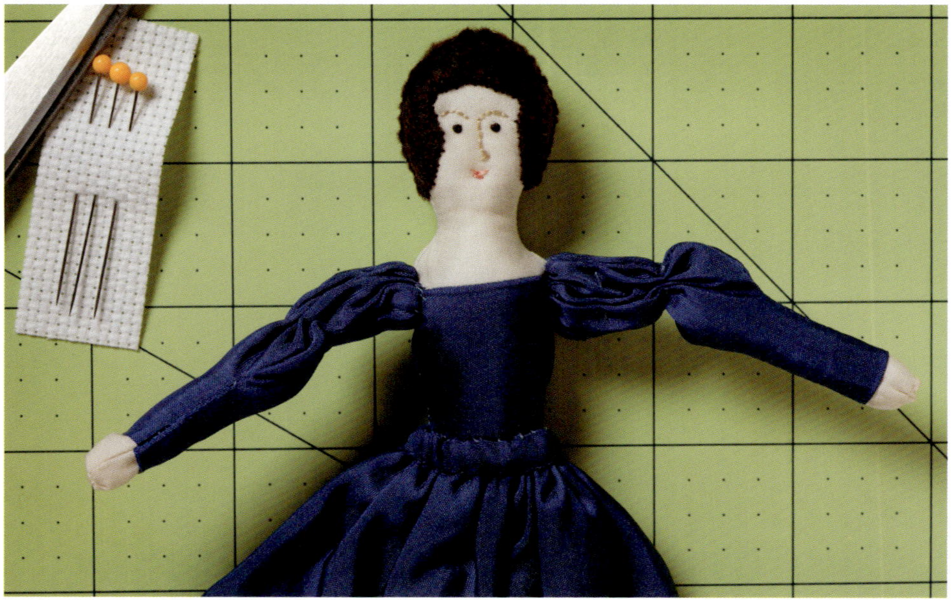

IDEAS: CHANGE OUT THE COLOR OF HER DRESS, HER HAIR, OR HER EYES. PERHAPS MATCH THE FEATURES OF A LITTLE GIRL IN YOUR FAMILY. IF YOU ARE FEELING ADVENTUROUS, TRY MAKING THE GOWN OF WHITE OR GOLD, ADD WINGS, AND CREATE AN ANGEL FOR THE TREE.

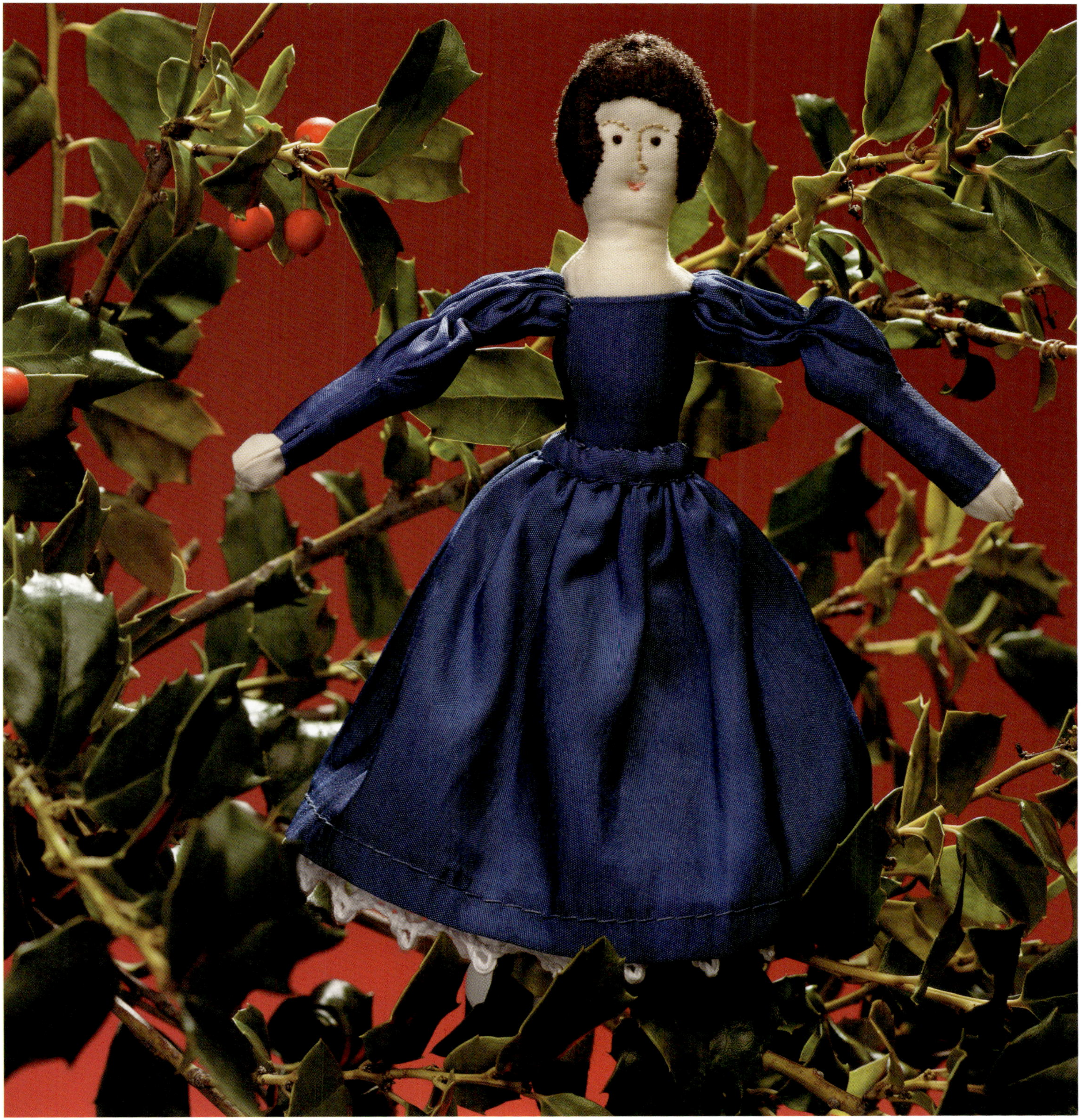

CHEST

Lehigh County, Pennsylvania, 1769, tulip poplar, iron, brass, and paint, 29 1/8" x 50 3/4" x 22 3/4", 1972.2000.5

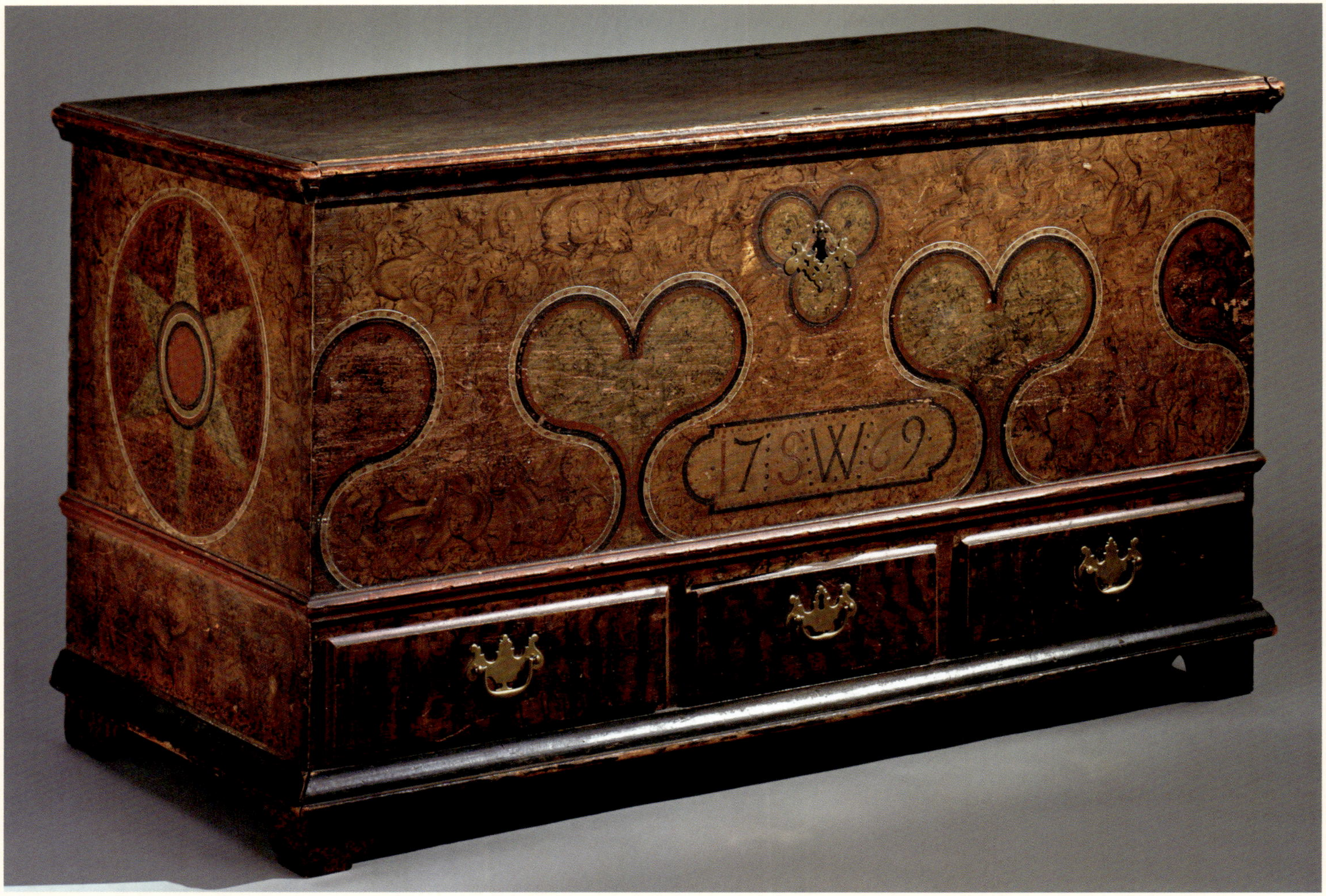

What today we might call a blanket chest was a common form of storage furniture in the eighteenth century. The chests were used to store clothing as well as household textiles. The hinged lid of this chest opens to reveal a large space with a till on one side. There are three drawers just above the base of the piece. The large board construction offers a large expanse of wood that could be embellished. This chest is made of tulip poplar, a secondary wood that was often disguised with paint. Painted chests like this one were often found in American homes of German settlers and their descendants. The motifs often symbolized love, marriage, life, and religion. Since this chest is dated 1769 and carries the initials "S W," it is possible that it was made to commemorate a birth or marriage. The open-ended heart design is one that is also found on frakturs, another Pennsylvania German tradition.

Four Hearts Needlepoint

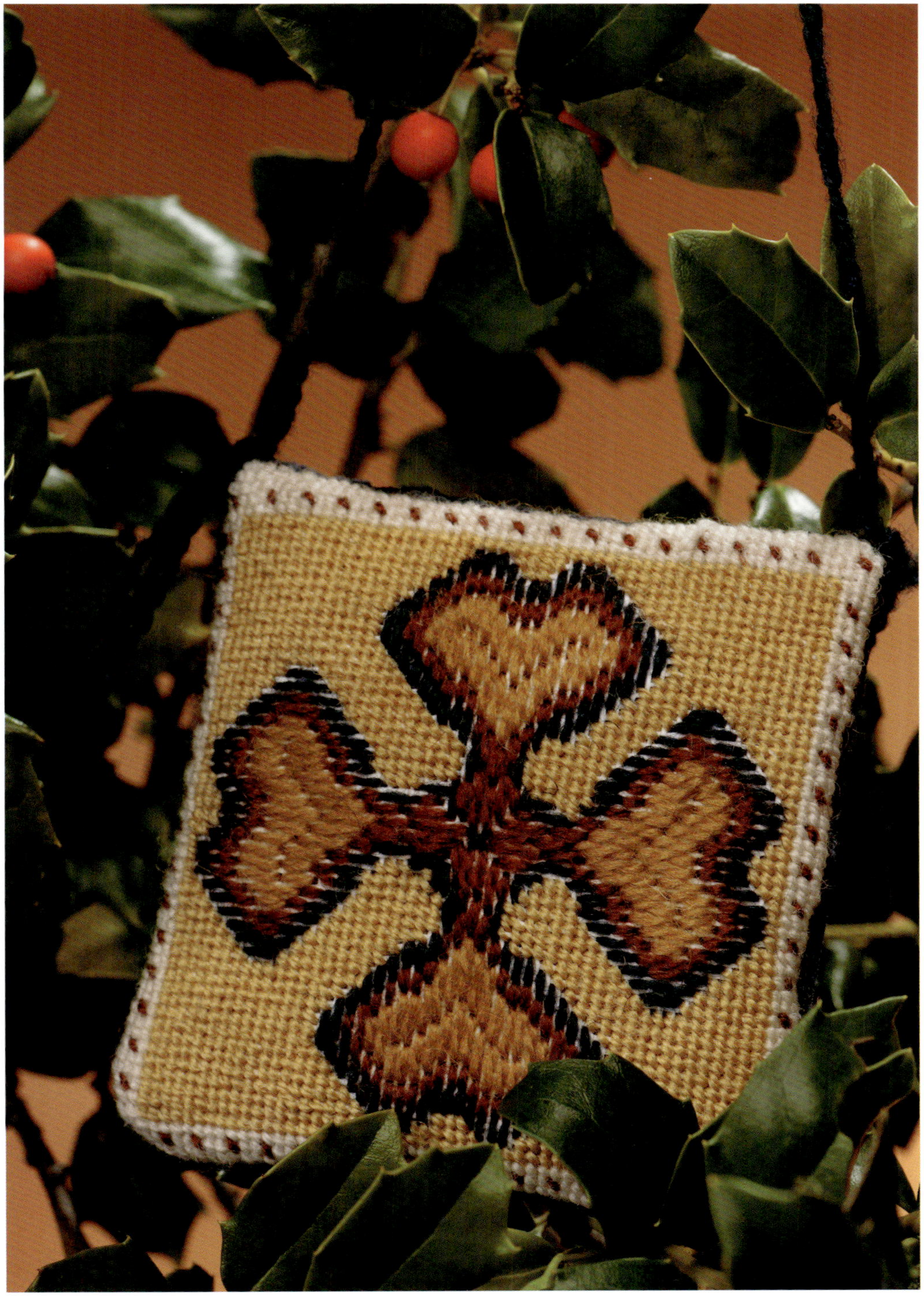

THE DECORATIVE NATURE OF THE CHEST INSPIRED US TO THINK ABOUT THE ELEMENTS OF THE DESIGN IN A CREATIVE WAY. WE CHOSE COLORS THAT COMPLEMENTED THE ORIGINAL PIECE, BUT ANY COMBINATION OF COLORS WILL DO.

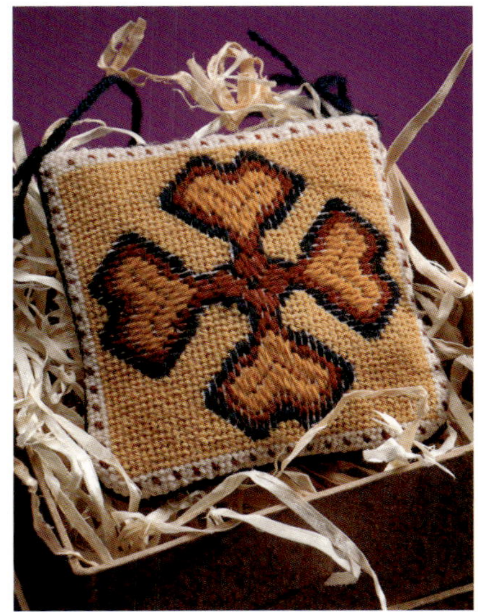

WHAT YOU NEED:

Charted design
18-gauge canvas, 7 x 7 inches
Masking tape
Tapestry needle, #22
Persian yarn: deep gold (two shades), dark blue, rust red, and beige
Scissors
Upholstery fabric, 5 x 5 inches
Pins
Needle
Matching thread
Stuffing

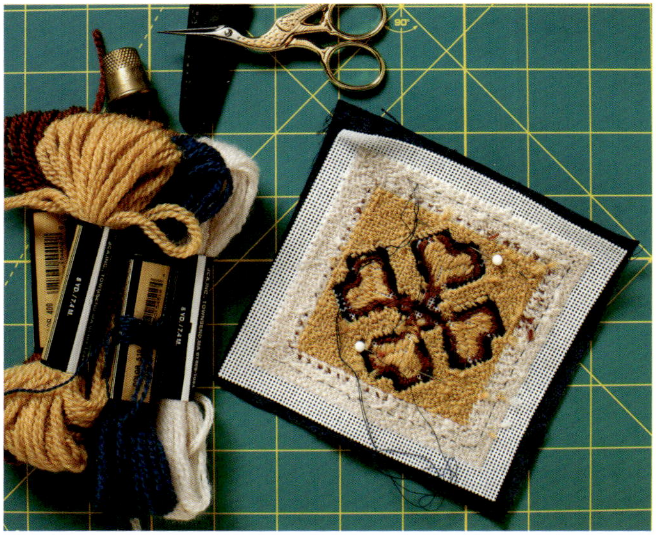

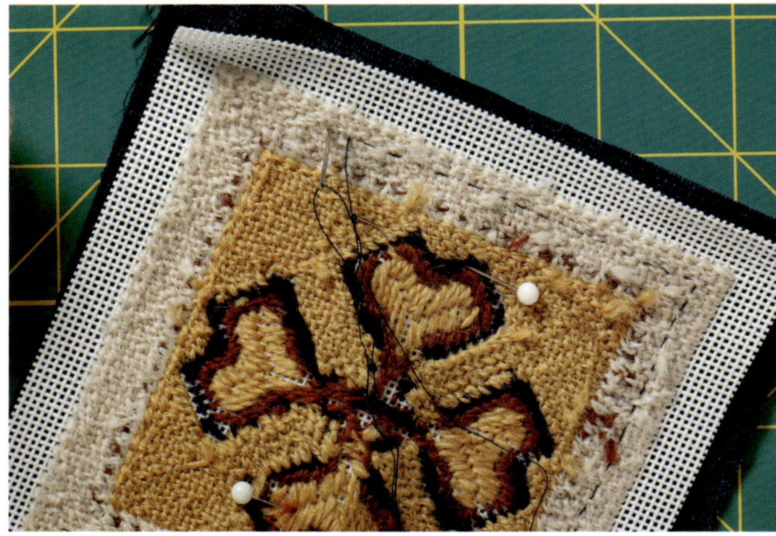

INSTRUCTIONS:

Prepare your canvas by placing masking tape along the four edges to keep it from unraveling as you work.

This ornament is worked in two different needlepoint stitches. The heart design is done in bargello, and the background and border in tent stitch. Complete the bargello work first, and then fill in the rest. Begin stitching the top heart following the charted design. Each stitch is worked straight up and down going over the number of holes as indicated on the chart. Turn the canvas so that you can work each heart with vertical stitches; always keep the element you are working on at the top.

Once the four hearts are worked, fill in the rest of the canvas with the tent stitch, all worked in the same direction. Do the background first and then follow the chart for the border design. The two outer rows will be worked in as part of the seam.

Once the needlepoint is complete, trim the canvas leaving six empty holes from the stitched area on each of the four sides.

The upholstery fabric will form the backing. Lay the fabric right side up. Lay the needlepoint face down on the fabric, and pin to hold in place. Using needle and thread, stitch the two pieces together from the canvas side so that you can keep a straight line by following the row in the canvas. Sew along the fourth row from the edge of the tent stitch. Sew three sides. Turn the ornament right side out. Add a little stuffing, just enough to give it body. Fold in the canvas and fabric edges, and slip stitch closed.

For the hanger, cut a 16-inch piece of dark blue yarn. Separate the three strands. Knot the three strands together about 1 inch from the ends. Braid the three strands; it will help to have someone hold the knotted end or to weight it. When you get about 1 1/2 inches from the other end, tie the three strands into another knot. Trim the ends if needed. Attach the hanger to the ornament by sewing the knots to any adjacent corners.

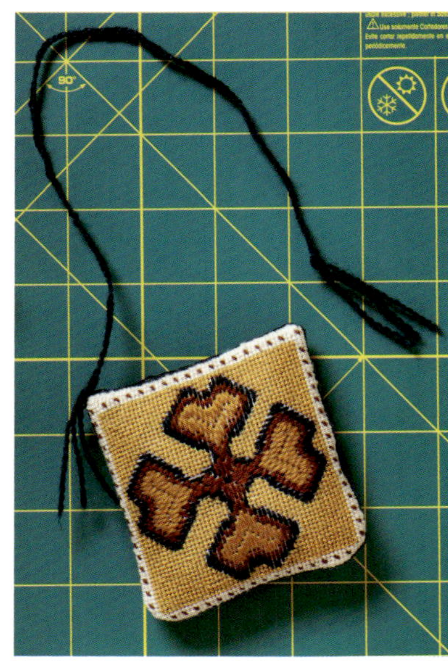

IDEA: THIS PIECE COULD ALSO BE USED AS A PIN CUSHION IF YOU STUFF IT HEAVILY AND FORGO THE HANGER.

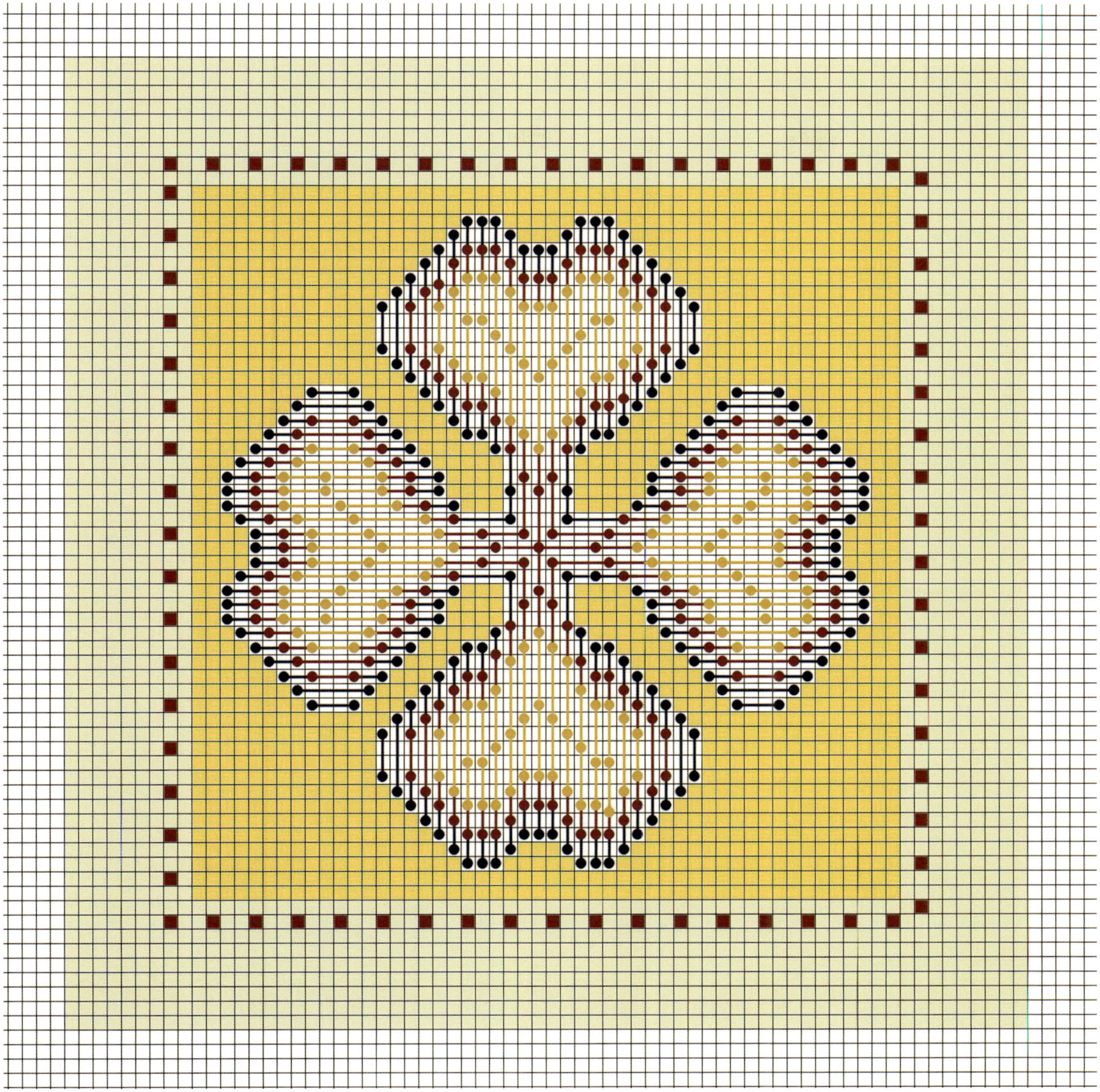

BALTIMORE ALBUM QUILT

Sarah Anne Whittington Lankford Miles (1830–1898) and possibly Mary Evans (1829–1916), Baltimore, Maryland, 1847–1853, cotton with wool and cotton or silk embroidery, ink, and metal and glass beads, 99" x 84", gift of Marsha C. Scott, 1979.609.14

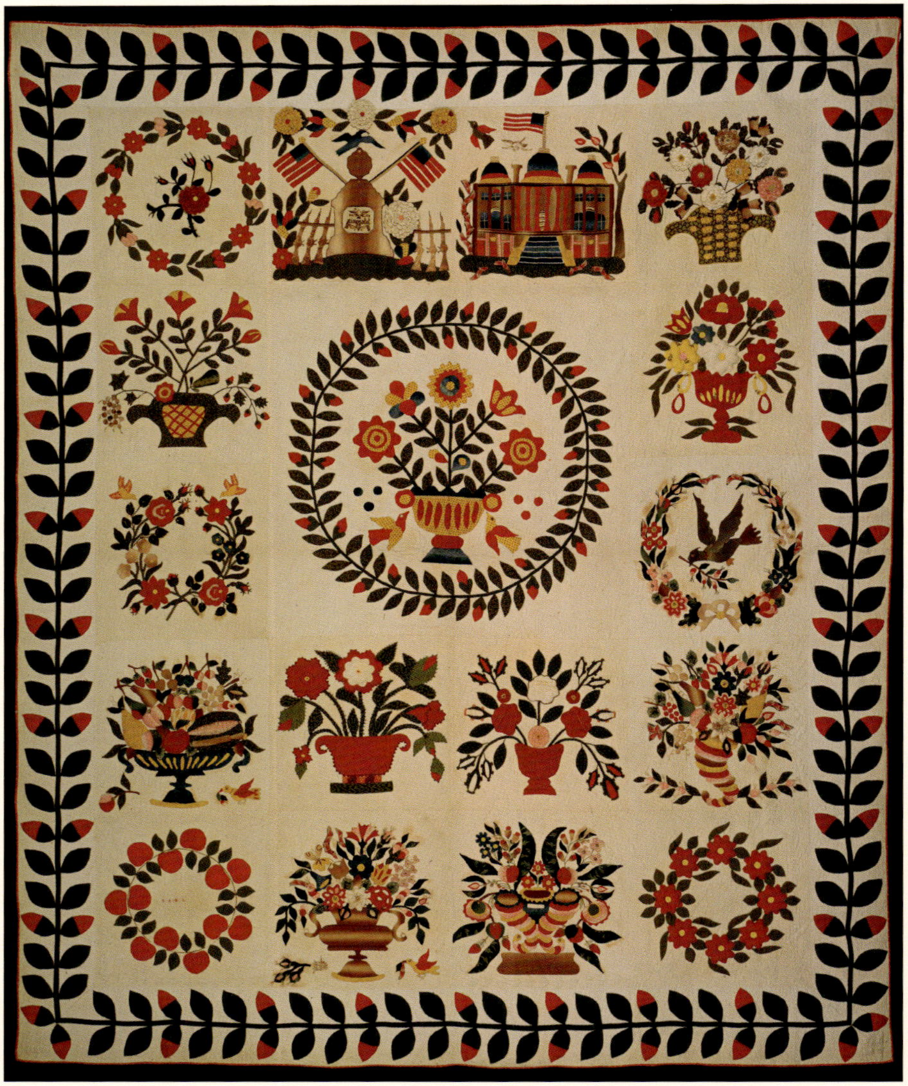

This appliquéd quilt is typical of a group of quilts commonly referred to as Baltimore Album quilts. They were most popular in the 1840s and 1850s. At that time, Baltimore was one of the most prosperous and largest cities in the United States. Some of the quilted squares in the Baltimore Album quilts were created by professionals.

It is believed that Henry Smith Lankford purchased the squares in this quilt from the Order of the Masons, into which he was initiated in 1850. The more detailed squares may have been made by Mary Evans, a professional Baltimore quilter. Sarah Anne Whittington Lankford, Henry's sister, assembled the squares and quilted the entire piece. The quilting stitches are about thirteen stitches to the inch. Not all of the squares are sewn with the same level of skill, and it is possible that Sarah Anne created some of the simpler squares and the border. She cross-stitched her initials into the middle of the apple wreath at the lower left. Sarah had an older sister, Julia, who, if still living at home, might have also contributed to the quilt. The piece descended in the family until it was given to the museum.

The two top center squares stand out from the other floral squares. The one to the right is the U. S. Capitol in Washington, D. C. The other monument, less well-known, is a tribute to Major Samuel Ringgold, a Maryland soldier who was killed in the first engagement of the Mexican War of 1846–1848. As a local man, he became an instant hero, and a few other quilts from this period also honor his memory.

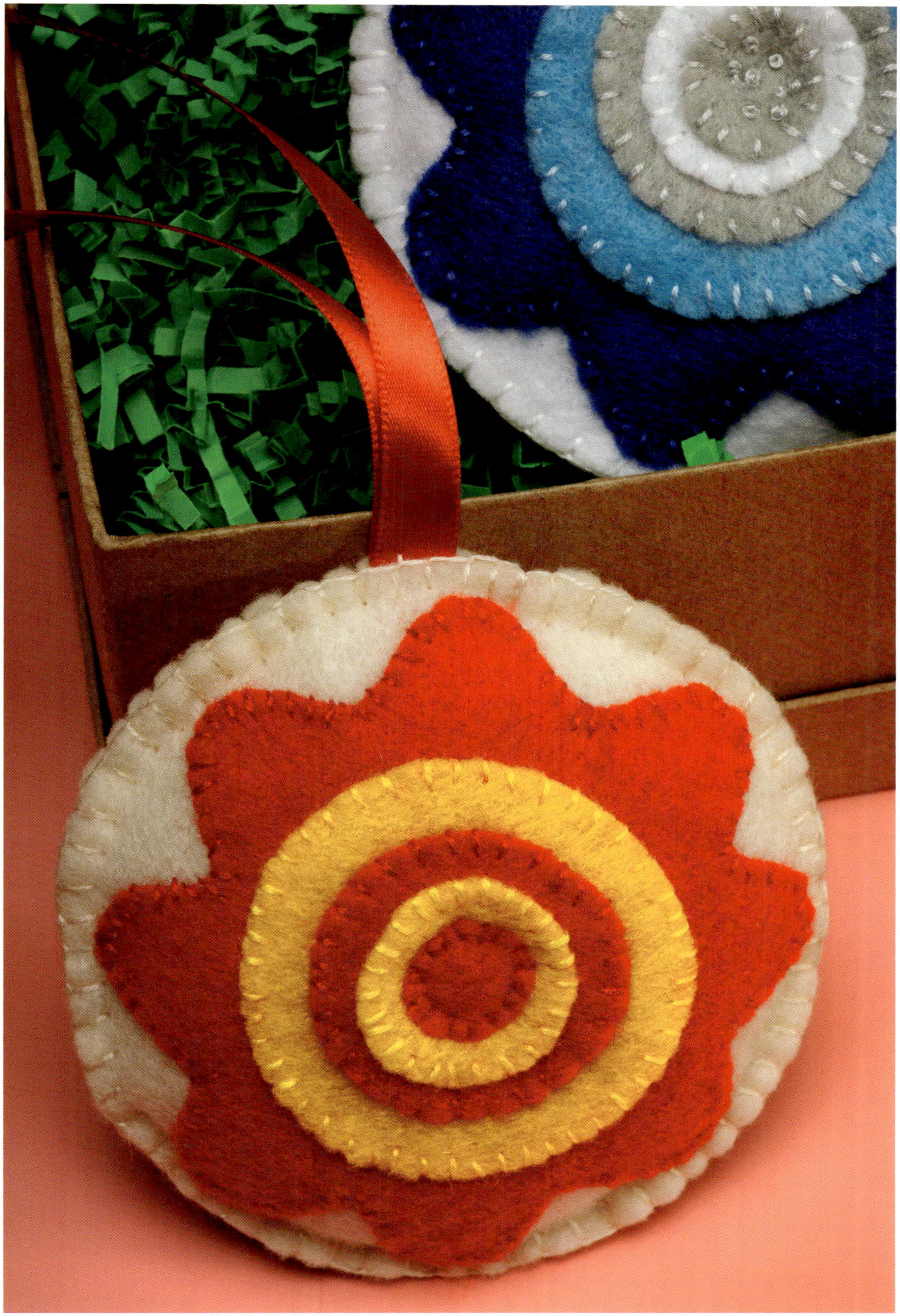

Layered Felt Flower

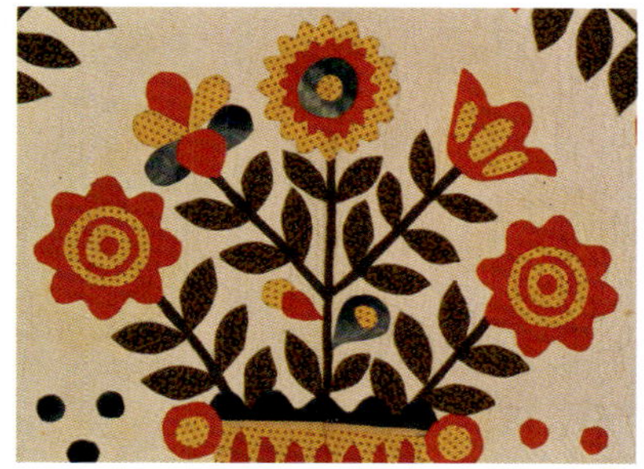

THE EDGES OF THE APPLIQUÉD PIECES ON THE QUILT WERE TURNED UNDER AND SECURED WITH OVERCAST STITCHES, BUT SOME, HAVING EXPOSED RAW EDGES, WERE SECURED WITH BLANKET OR BUTTONHOLE STITCHING. THE FLORAL DESIGNS ALONG WITH THE APPLIQUÉ TECHNIQUE OFFERED US A CHANCE TO PLAY WITH COLOR AND LAYERING TO CREATE OUR OWN FLOWERS.

WHAT YOU NEED:

- Circles 1–5 and flower templates (page 130)
- Scissors
- Red, yellow, and cream felt
- Matching floss
- Embroidery needle
- Stuffing
- 1/2-inch ribbon in coordinating color, 12 inches long

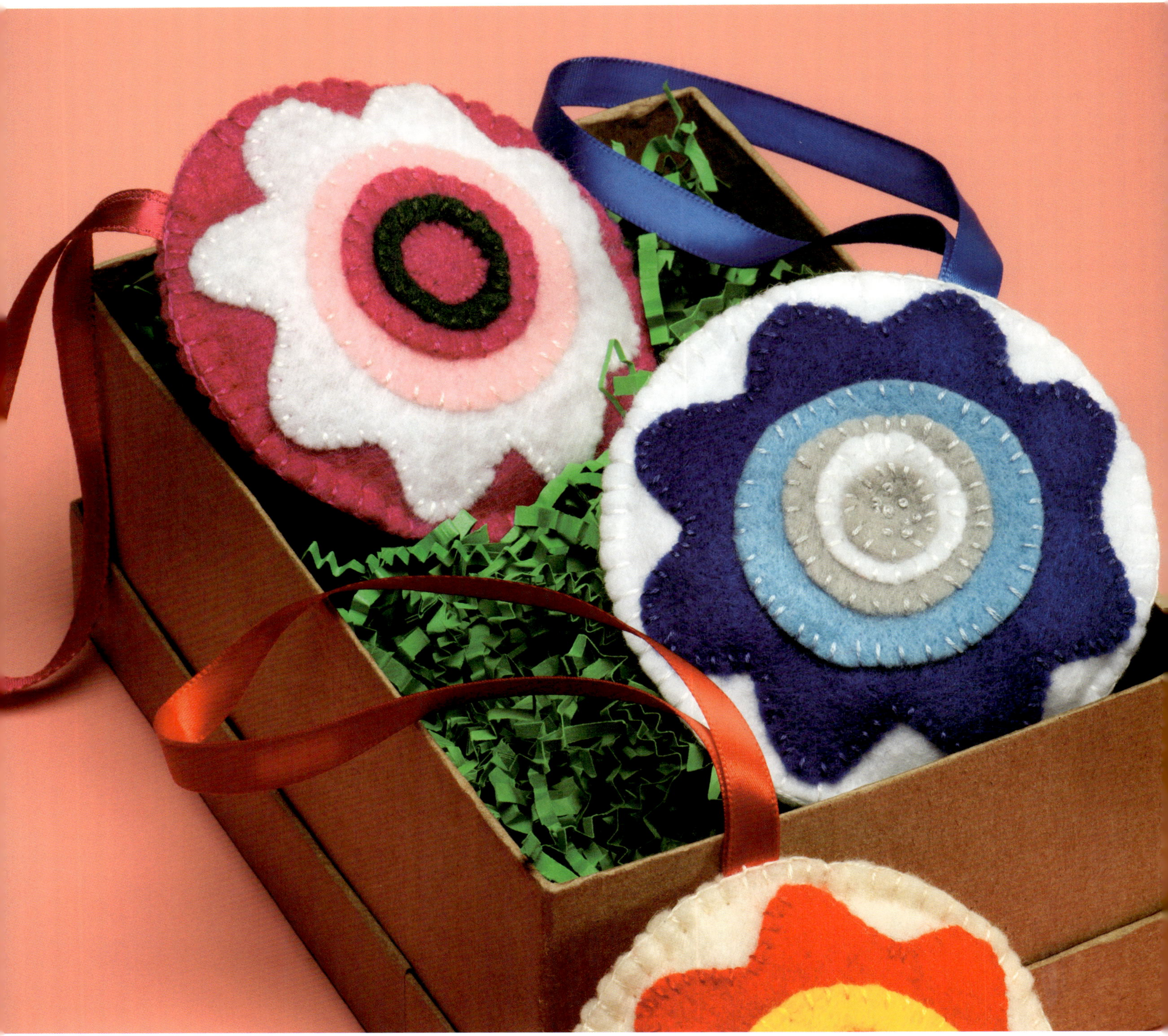

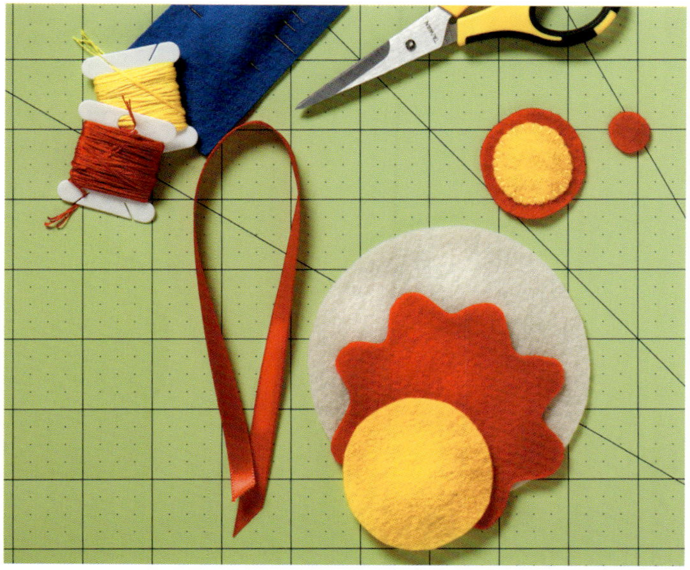

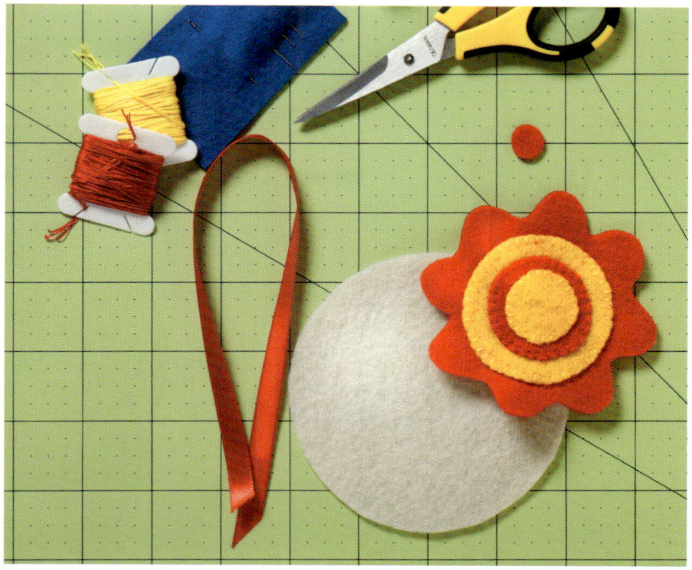

INSTRUCTIONS:

Using the templates, cut out two of each piece in the color of felt indicated: circles 1 and 3 in red, circles 2 and 4 in yellow, circle 5 in cream, and flower in red.

Using one of each piece, stitch the flower together in the following sequence using a blind stitch: stitch yellow circle 2 to red circle 3, stitch red circle 3 to yellow circle 4, stitch yellow circle 4 to flower, and stitch flower to cream circle 5. Stitch red circle 1 to yellow circle 2 through all the layers of felt. If you like, you can add a few French knots in the center to resemble seeds. Repeat for a second layered flower.

Align the two flowers with cream circle 5 to cream circle 5 wrong sides together. Stitch together using a blanket stitch. Leaving 1/2 inch open, loosely stuff.

To create the hanger, fold the ribbon in half, place the ends inside the 1/2-inch opening, and stitch through the ribbon to hold in place as you sew up the opening.

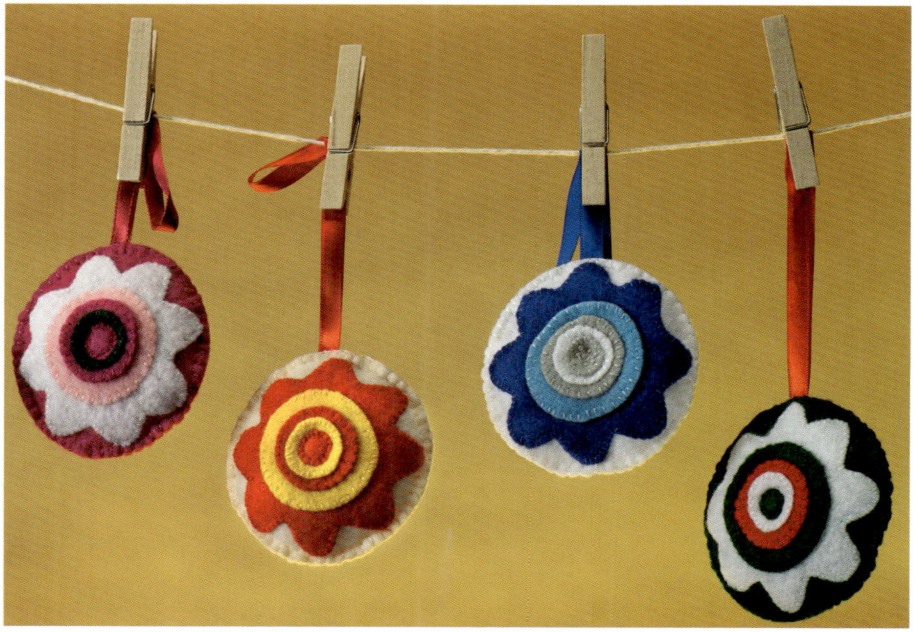

IDEAS: CHOOSE DIFFERENT PALETTES OF YOUR FAVORITE COLORS. ATTACH THEM TO WIRES AND MAKE A UNIQUE BOUQUET.

MEMORY POT

possibly Virginia, ca. 1910, tinplate covered in putty and encrusted with various personal memorabilia made of several materials, 11 1/2" x 7" x 6", gift of Benjamin and Virginia Brinn in memory of his parents, Frank and Marion Brinn, and his sister, Barbara Brinn Sawyer, 1999.801.1

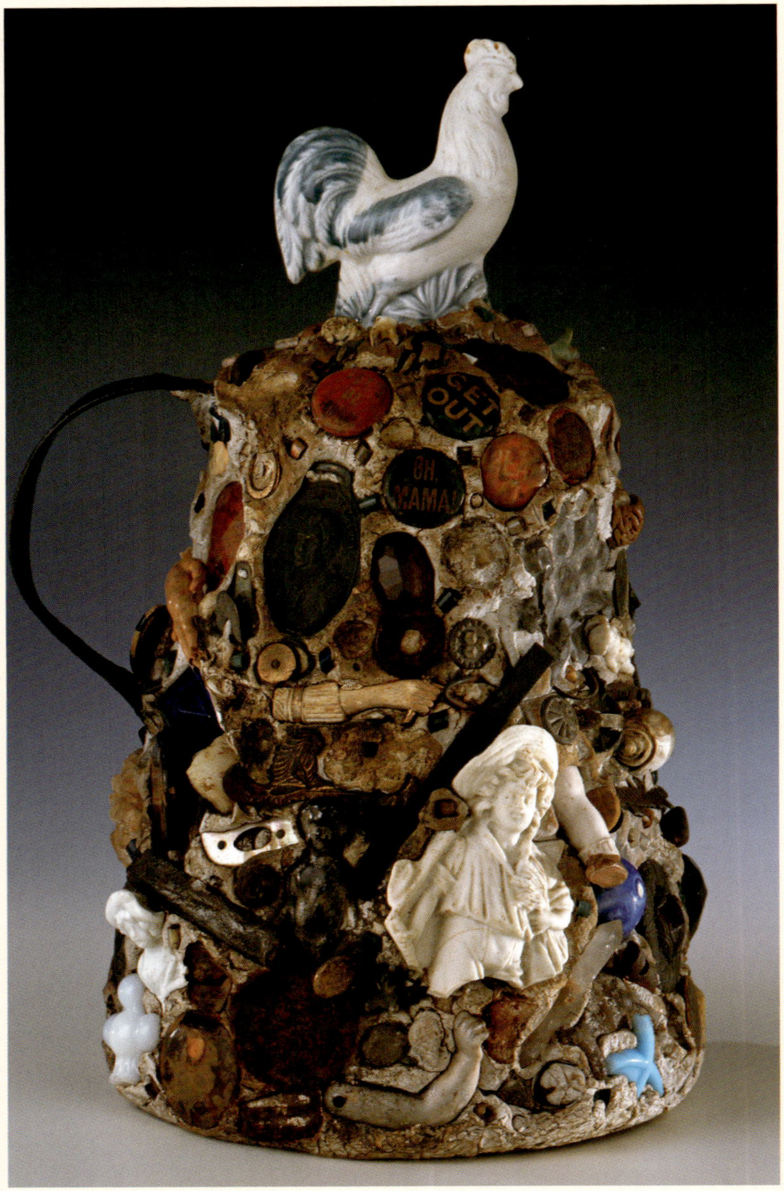

Each little item encrusted on this pot has a story to tell. Overall, it is a collection of memories for the person who created it. The maker started with a tin coffeepot, covered it in putty, and then impressed mementos that include pins, trinkets, seashells, jewelry, and bits of things. Although this is a personal piece, the concept was popular in the late nineteenth and early twentieth centuries, and many such three-dimensional memory pieces exist.

No one really knows if memory pieces had a purpose. Some believe they were made as memorials to loved ones. Other scholars think that they were specific to the African-American community and placed on burial sites. Still others suggest that these pieces were made as a kind of hobby or craft, a kind of three-dimensional scrapbook.

Looking more closely at this piece, some items suggest specific interests about the unidentified maker. There is a 1905 political button with "Willard for Governor" under the spout. Was the person interested in politics? The SPCA button suggests an animal lover. The thimble near the spout could imply a sewer or could be a cherished reminder of a family member who sewed. Maybe the person was an avid reader. Near the bottom is a button about a "Woggle Bug." L. Frank Baum, author of *The Wizard of Oz*, wrote *The Woggle-Bug Book* in 1905. There are shells, buttons, and broken bits of things. What meaning did each of these have for the maker?

Recycled-Paper Memory Ball

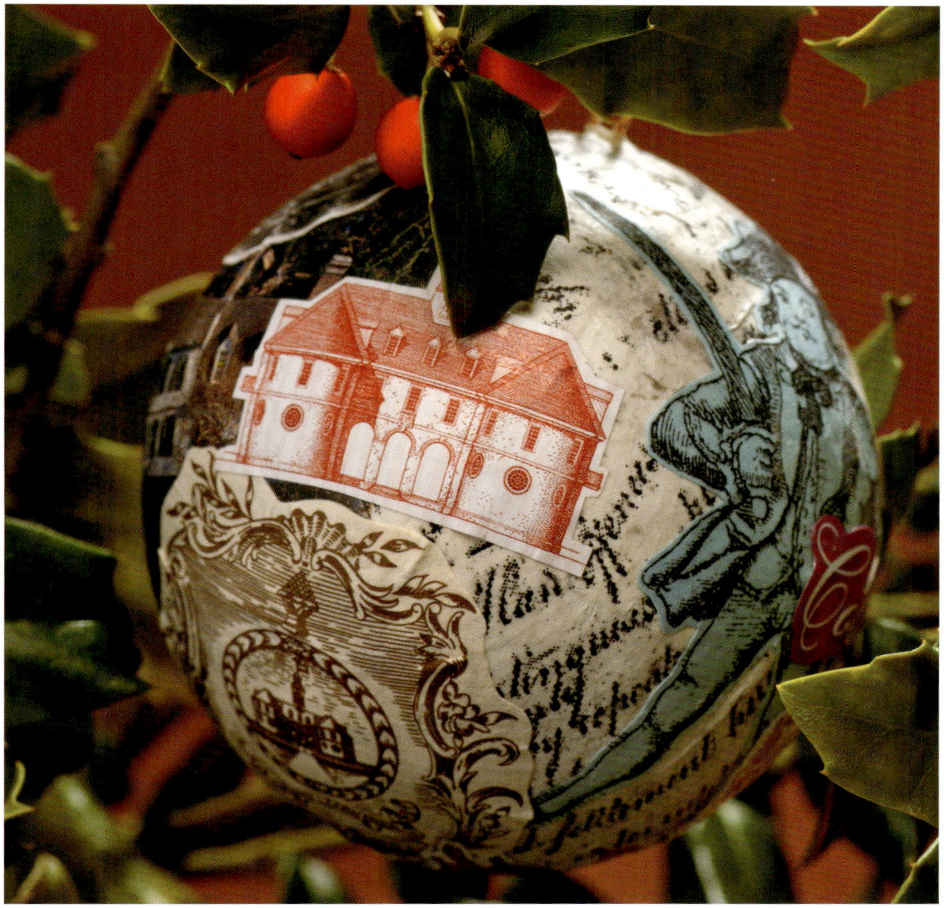

SAVING MEMORIES CAN TAKE ANY SHAPE AND BE MADE FROM ANY TYPE OF MATERIAL. COMMEMORATE AN EVENT IN YOUR LIFE WITH SAVED PAPER ITEMS AND A BIT OF GLUE.

WHAT YOU NEED:

Brochures from a trip or event
Scissors
School glue
Paper-mache ball
Spray shellac
Ribbon or raffia

INSTRUCTIONS:

Cut out from the brochures specific images and words that you might want to display prominently on the memory ball. Put these aside for now. When making your choices, think about how they will appear together on the ball. You can create scenes, frame out images, or place in random designs.

Tear some or all of the remaining brochures into pieces and strips no larger than 1 inch wide. The length can vary. Glue the strips onto the paper-mache ball. You may wish to cover the entire ball or leave some of the background visible. Be sure all paper is completely glued down. Allow the glue to dry.

Decide how you would like to display the pieces that you cut out earlier and glue these to the ball. Again, be sure each piece is completely glued down. Let the ball dry overnight.

Following the manufacturer's instructions on the can, spray the ball with shellac and allow to dry.

Tie the ribbon or raffia around the hanger at the point where it attaches to the ball. A touch of glue can be used to hold it in place.

IDEA: CREATE A MEMORY BALL TO COMMEMORATE EACH VACATION YOU TAKE WITH YOUR FAMILY. AT HOLIDAY TIME, YOU CAN REMINISCE WITH FRIENDS AND FAMILY ABOUT THE GREAT TIMES.

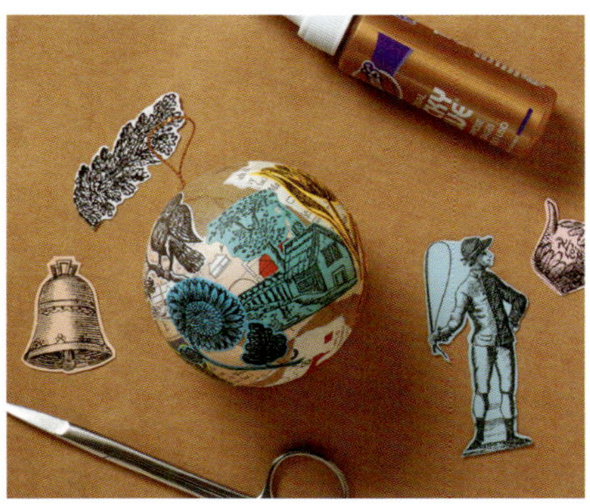

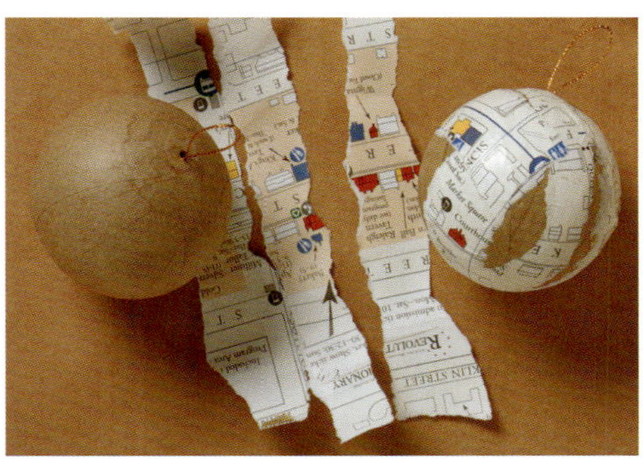

PORTRAIT OF TWO CHILDREN

attributed to Joseph Badger (1708–1765), probably Boston, Massachusetts, ca. 1760, oil on canvas, 41 1/8" x 49 3/4", 1957.100.15

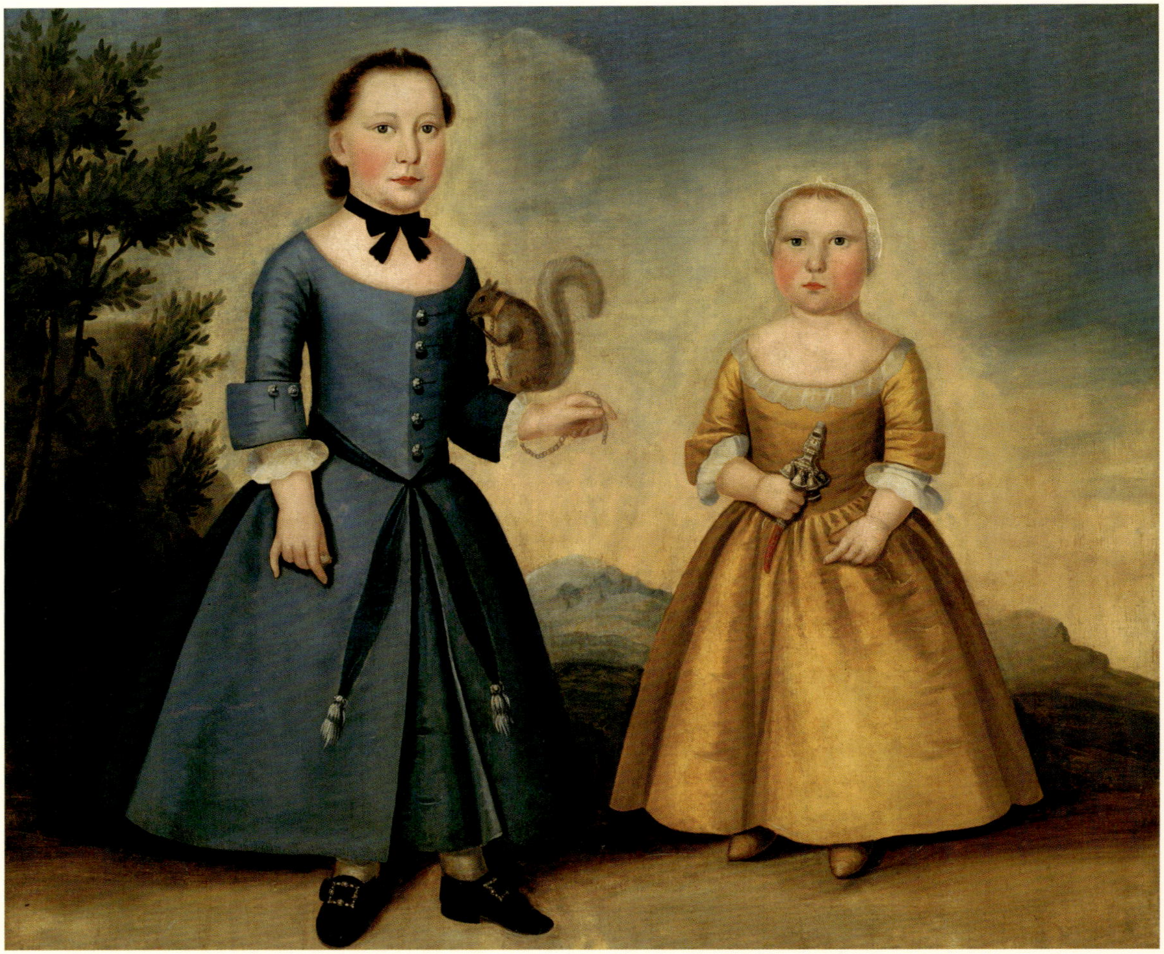

The two children in this wonderful portrait are likely brother and sister. It is possible that they are the children of a couple who lived north of Boston in the mid-eighteenth century. The older child, who may appear to be a girl because of the dress, is a boy. Boys in this period were clothed similarly to young girls until they reached the age of six or seven. The fact that the child is holding his pet squirrel is an indication of gender. The younger sister grasps a typical rattle of the period that was made with coral at one end and a silver whistle with bells at the other. Coral was thought to be good for teething.

The artist, Joseph Badger, was born in Charlestown, Massachusetts, and later moved to Boston where he remained for the rest of his life. He listed his career as glazier and house painter but created portraits as a sideline. During his career, he painted some eighty portraits though, as far as is known, he had no formal training. Living in Boston, he had access to other artists and their work, which may have encouraged his abilities.

Cross-Stitch Squirrel

We couldn't resist the squirrel in this picture. To modern eyes, it may seem a little strange to see a squirrel wearing a gold collar attached to a chain, but, in the eighteenth century, these small creatures were kept as pets.

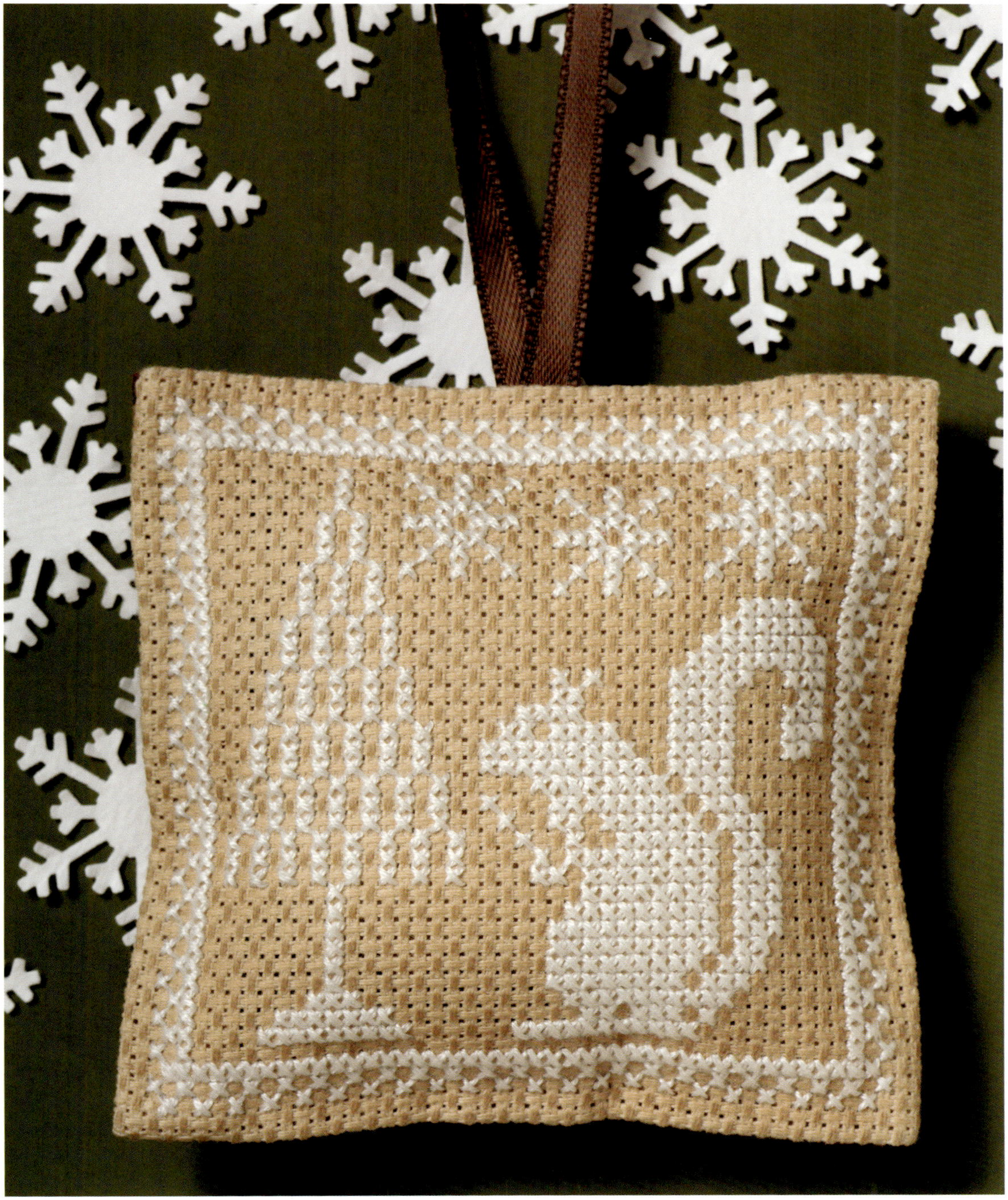

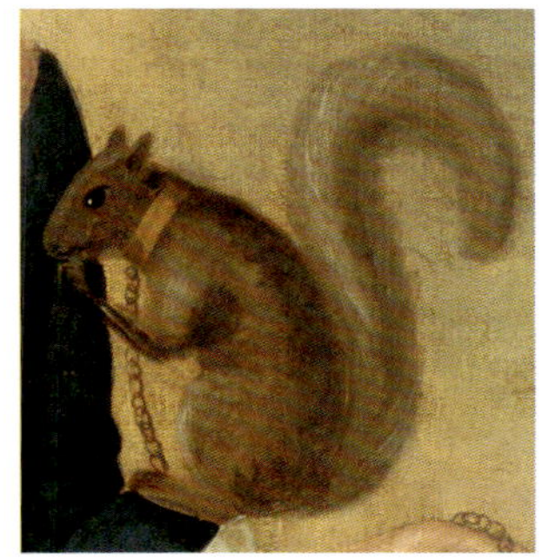

WHAT YOU NEED:

- Charted design
- 14-count beige Aida cloth, 4 x 4 inches
- Cross-stitch needle
- White floss
- Scissors
- Iron
- Ironing board
- Matching printed cotton fabric, 4 x 4 inches
- Pins
- Needle
- Stuffing
- Thin brown ribbon, 10 inches long

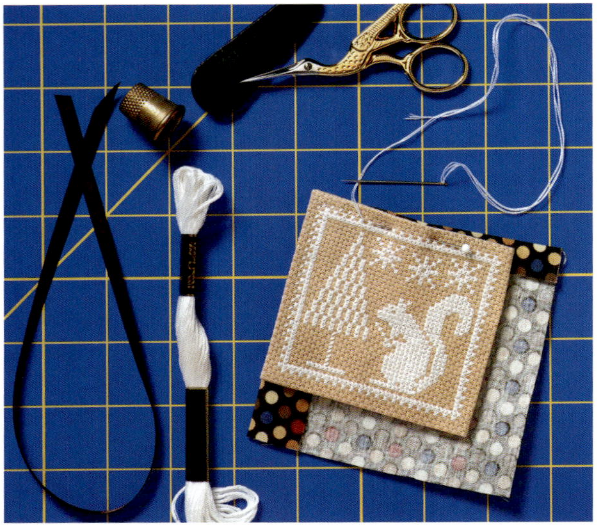

INSTRUCTIONS:

Referring to the charted design, create the cross-stitch on the Aida cloth. Start the stitches at the center of the sampler and work your way to the outside edges. Do not work the outermost border of cross-stitches; these will be used to finish the project.

Once the stitching is complete, fold back the cross-stitched Aida cloth 1/4 inch from the stitching on all four sides. Iron. Repeat the folding and ironing with the cotton fabric, folding the edges to the wrong side of the fabric. Place together the two folded pieces with wrong sides facing in. Line up all of the edges and pin. Stitch the pieces together following the cross-stitch border design on the chart. Start at the upper left, and work down and around the piece leaving the top for last. Before closing, lightly stuff. For the hanger, fold the ribbon in half, and place the edges in the opening. Cross-stitch the top closed catching the ribbon in the stitches as you do.

IDEAS: Try switching out the color of Aida cloth to a deep blue or any color you desire. Make one into a greeting card by taking heavy paper and cutting a square opening for the piece to show through and backing it with another piece of heavy paper.

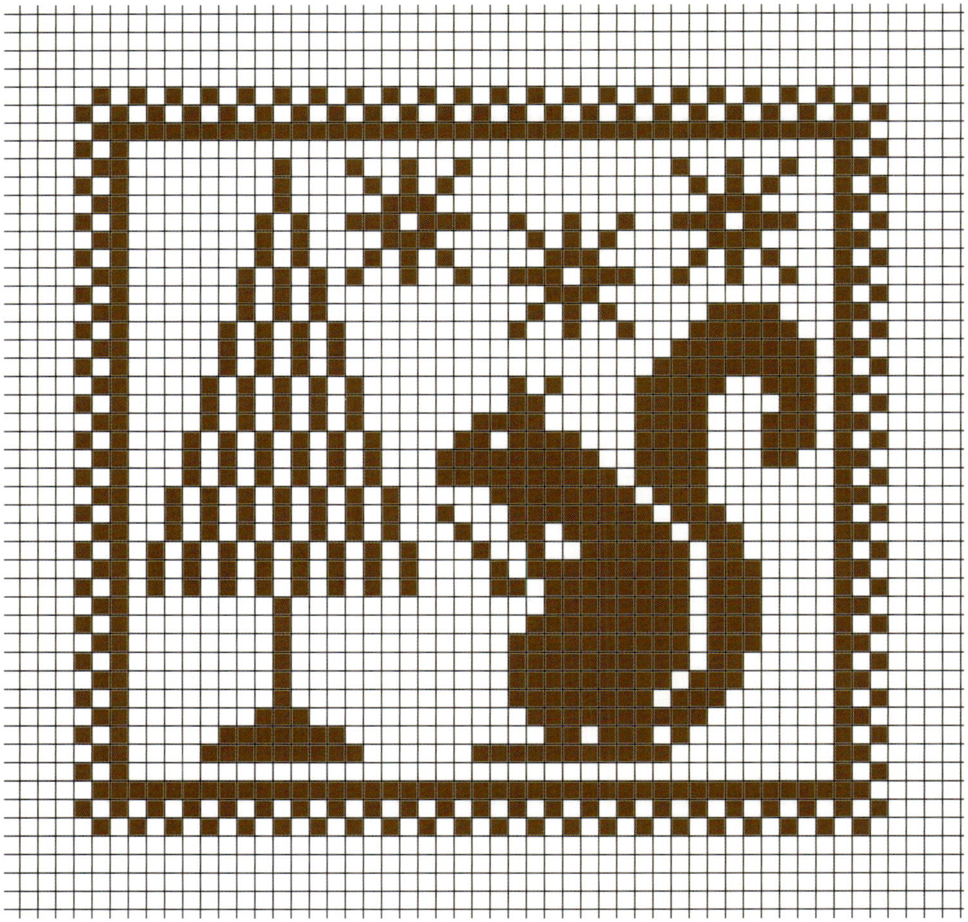

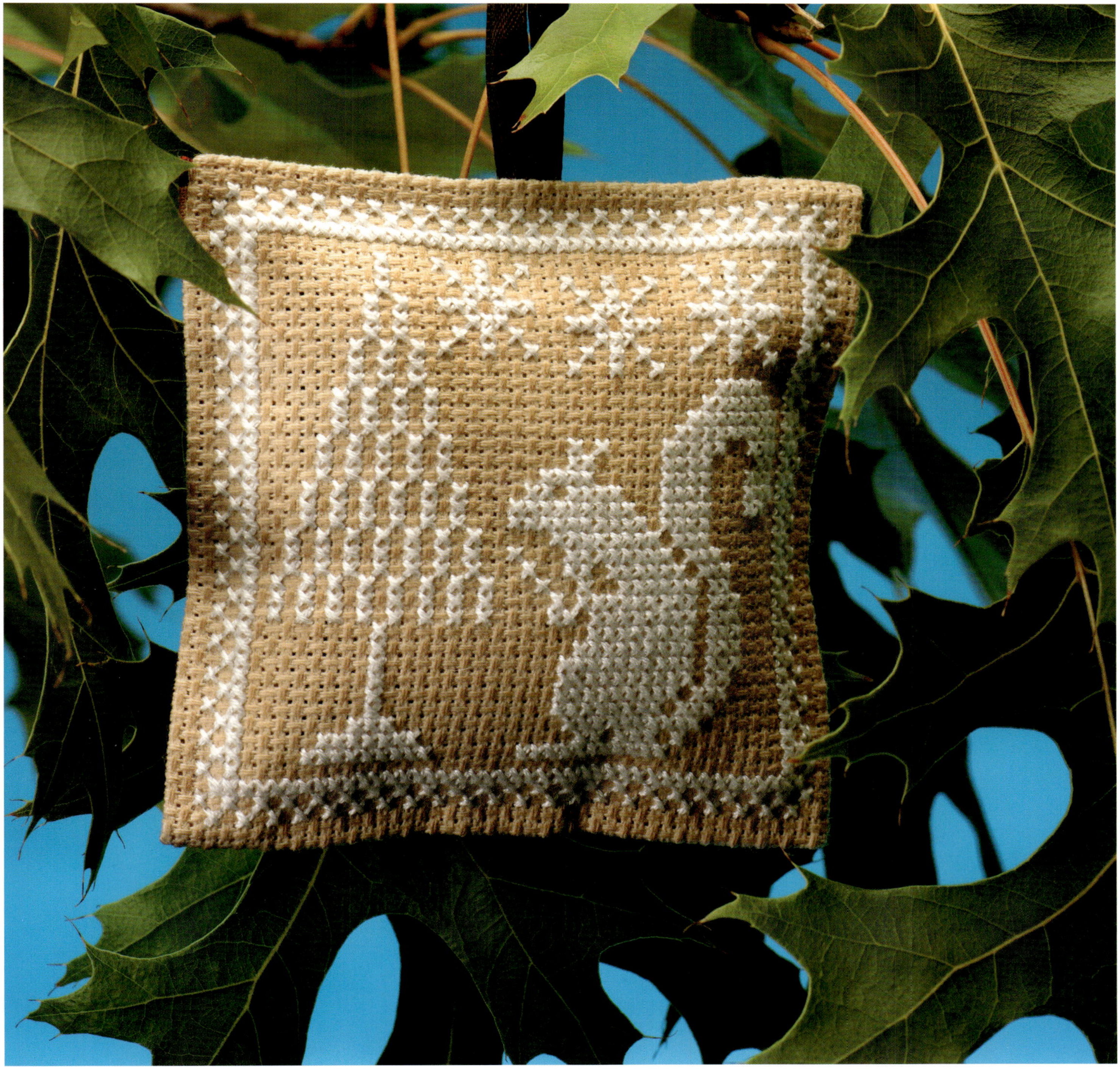

QUILT

Clarissa Dodge Marschalk, possibly New York, 1845–1855, plain and printed cottons with chintz border, 100 1/4" x 98 3/4", gift of Robert W. Pitt, 1972.609.1

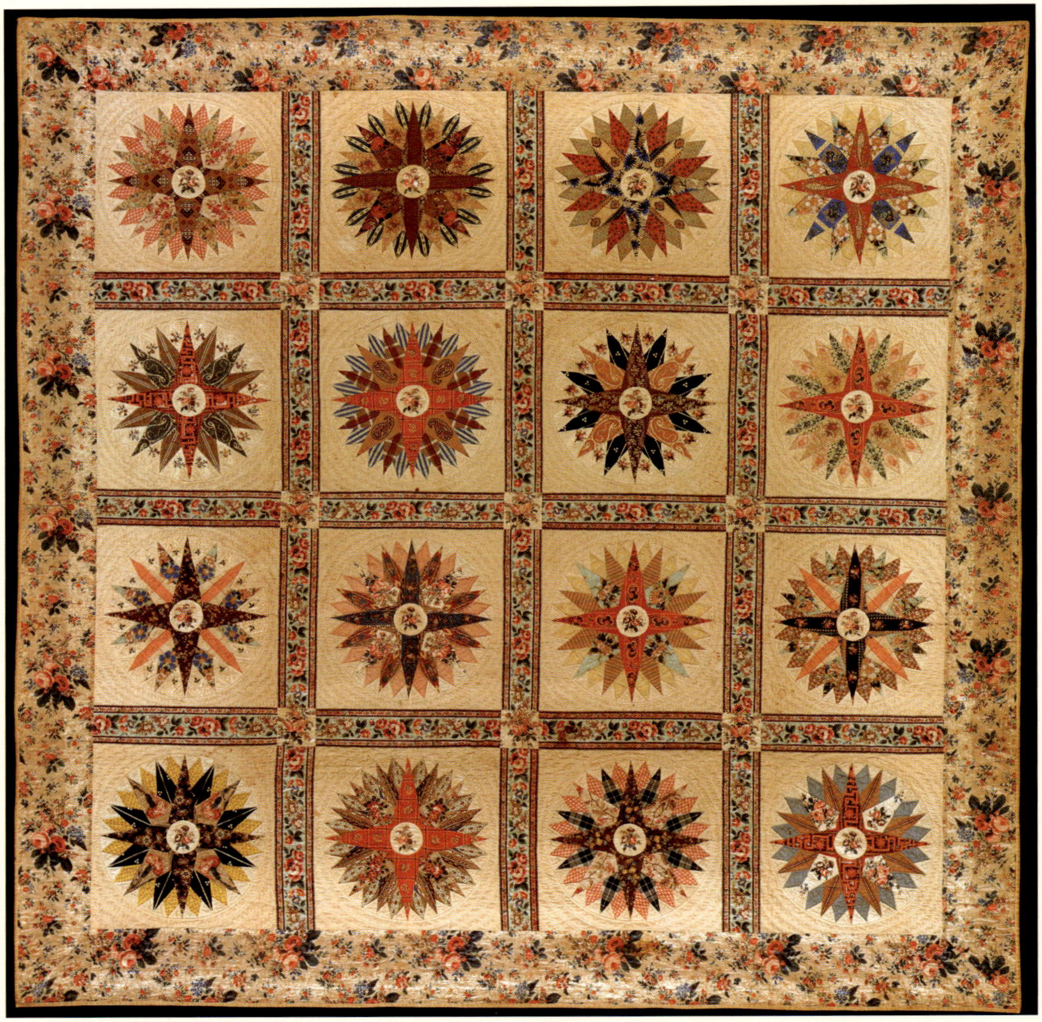

This quilt is almost square, measuring 100 by almost 99 inches. The design is Mariner's Compass. Each star or compass features the requisite thirty-two points as found on the nautical instrument from which the quilt pattern's name derives. Although the individual stars are all different, the overall quilt has a pleasing and harmonious quality. The quilter had an expert eye for selecting and combining colors and patterns. The borders are appliquéd. Many of the fabrics feature roses, which provide a unifying theme. Care was taken when cutting out the smaller pieces so that the roses serve as the central design on each compass. The piece was hand quilted using twelve stitches per inch in circles, diamonds, and outlining.

The quilt came to the museum with a small calling card pinned to it: "Mrs. Louise Marschalk Chapman." On the reverse is an ink inscription: "Designed and made one hundred years ago by Clarissa Dodge Marschalk and left to Louise Marschalk Chapman."

Today we admire the handiwork of women from the past. Skillfully pieced quilts and elegant embroidery are evidence of time spent with a needle and thread. But what about the tools needed to accomplish such projects? There were, of course, fabrics, needles, and threads but also patterns. Patterns could be written instructions and drawings found in ladies' magazines or actual templates made of sturdy materials that could be purchased. A sewing box in the museum's collection includes two tinplate patterns among its contents. Being made of metal, they could be used over and over again. Although the patterns resemble shapes used in quilting, they were used for another needlecraft called *plush work*. The sewer placed the pattern on fabric and stitched wool yarn over the metal template and through the fabric. Once the stitches completely covered the pattern, the wool threads were cut and the pattern removed, leaving raised threads in a flower or star design.

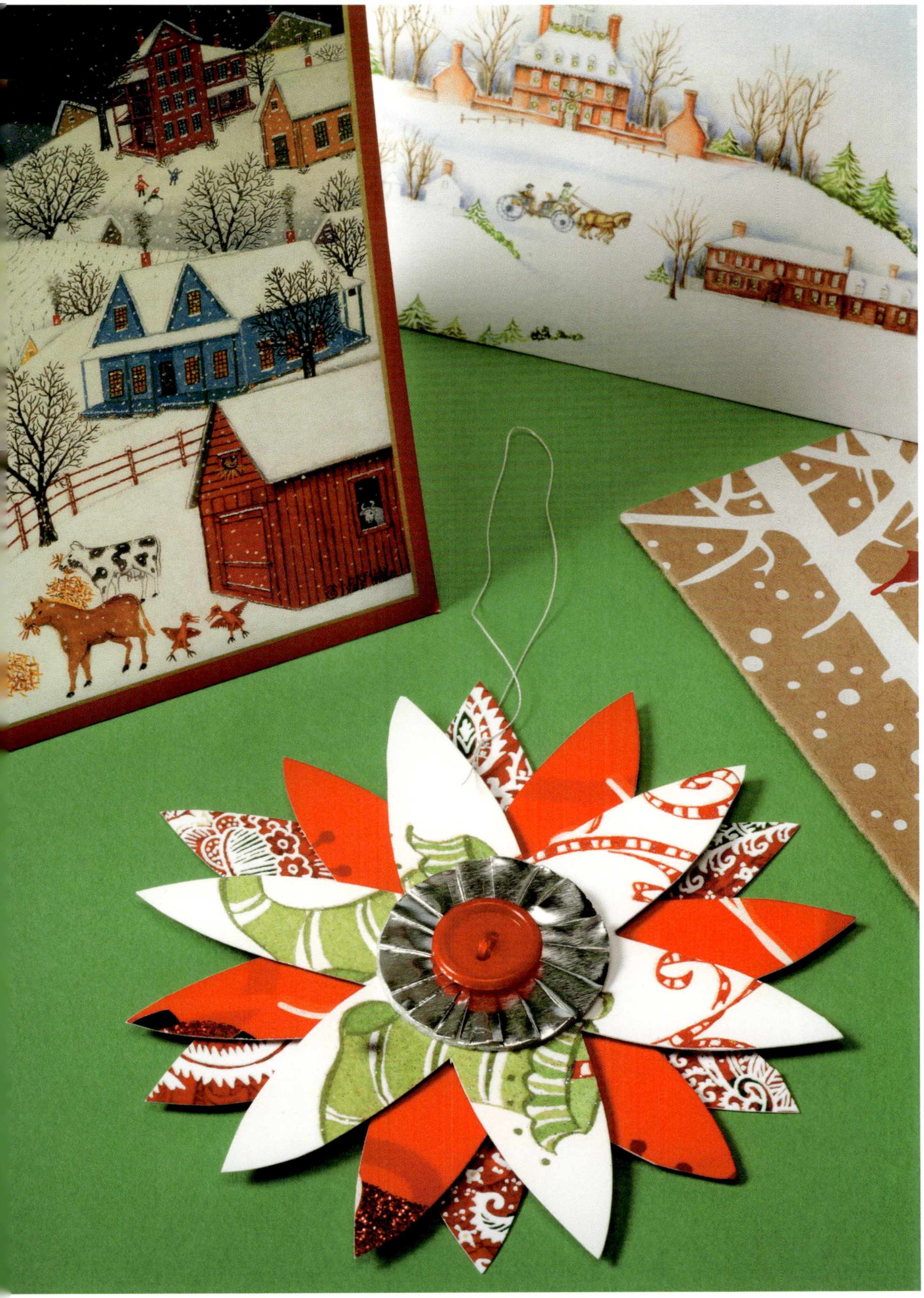

Recycled-Card Star

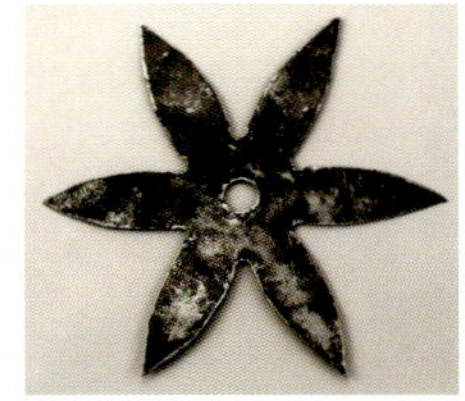

MARSCHALK'S QUILT SERVED AS INSPIRATION FOR THIS PROJECT; THE METAL COMPASS PATTERN FROM THE SEWING BOX PROVIDES THE SHAPE. NOW IT'S YOUR TURN TO USE YOUR EXPERT EYE TO SELECT PATTERN AND COLOR TO CREATE THIS "GREEN" ORNAMENT.

WHAT YOU NEED:

Star and circle templates (page 138)
Pencil
Scissors
Used greeting cards
Styrofoam tray or plate
1 1/4-inch hole punch (optional)
Aluminum pie pan
Button
Needle
Coordinating floss
White quilting thread
School glue (optional)
Mounting tape (optional)

INSTRUCTIONS:

Using the star template, cut out three stars from the greeting cards. Think about color combinations when placing the template. Using the circle template, cut out three foam circles from the foam tray. Alternatively, you can use a 1 1/4-inch hole punch to cut the circles; the punch is especially handy if you are planning to make several stars. Using the circle template, cut out a circle from the aluminum pie pan.

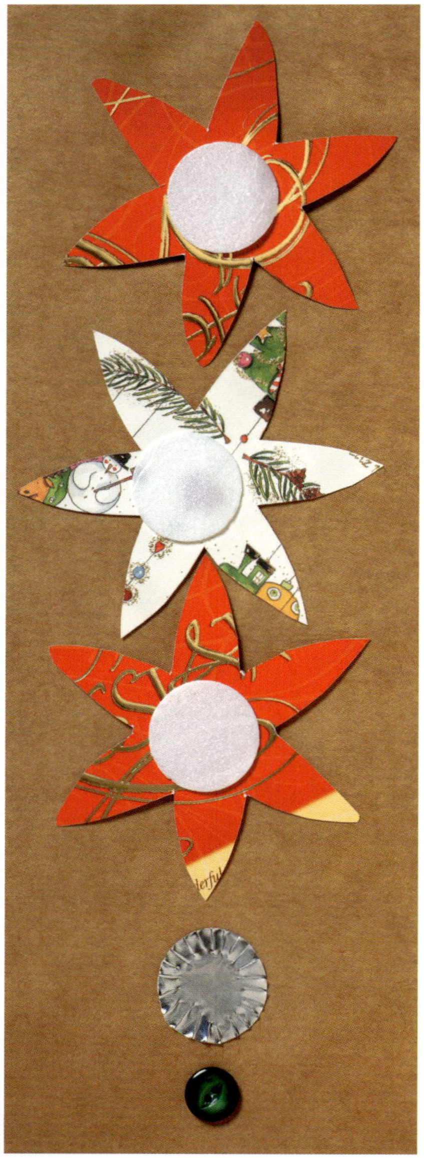

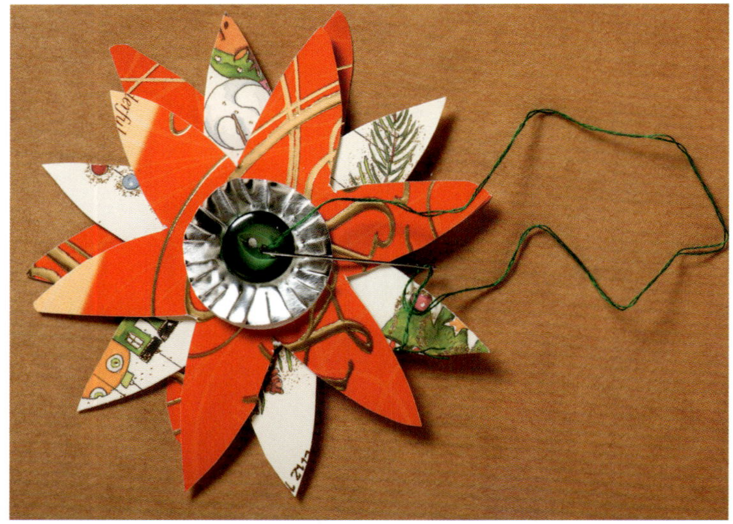

To create the star: Layer star, foam circle, star, foam circle, star, foam circle, foil circle, and button. Stagger the arms of the stars. Stitch together using the needle and floss through the holes of the button.

To create a hanger, insert a needle with quilting thread into the tip of one arm, and tie off at the desired length for hanging.

Note: You may wish to use a dab of glue between each layer to hold the layers in place while you stitch. To ditch the stitching altogether, glue or use mounting tape throughout.

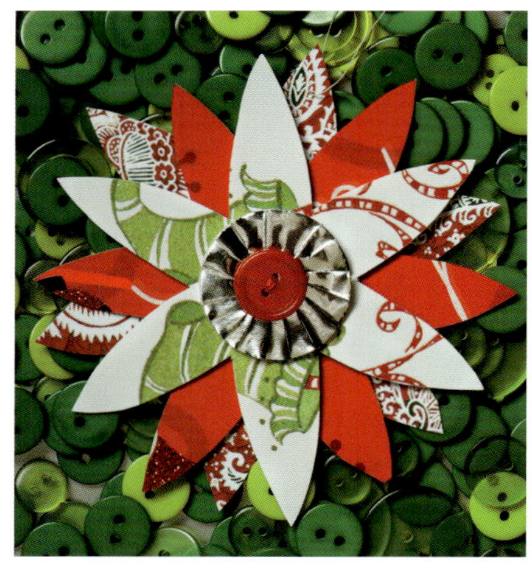

IDEAS: THESE STARS LOOK ESPECIALLY GOOD WHEN THERE ARE SEVERAL TOGETHER. GATHER SOME FRIENDS AND HAVE AN AFTERNOON OF CUTTING AND CREATING. BE SURE EVERYONE BRINGS OLD GREETING CARDS. THE STARS COULD ALSO BE USED TO DECORATE PACKAGES.

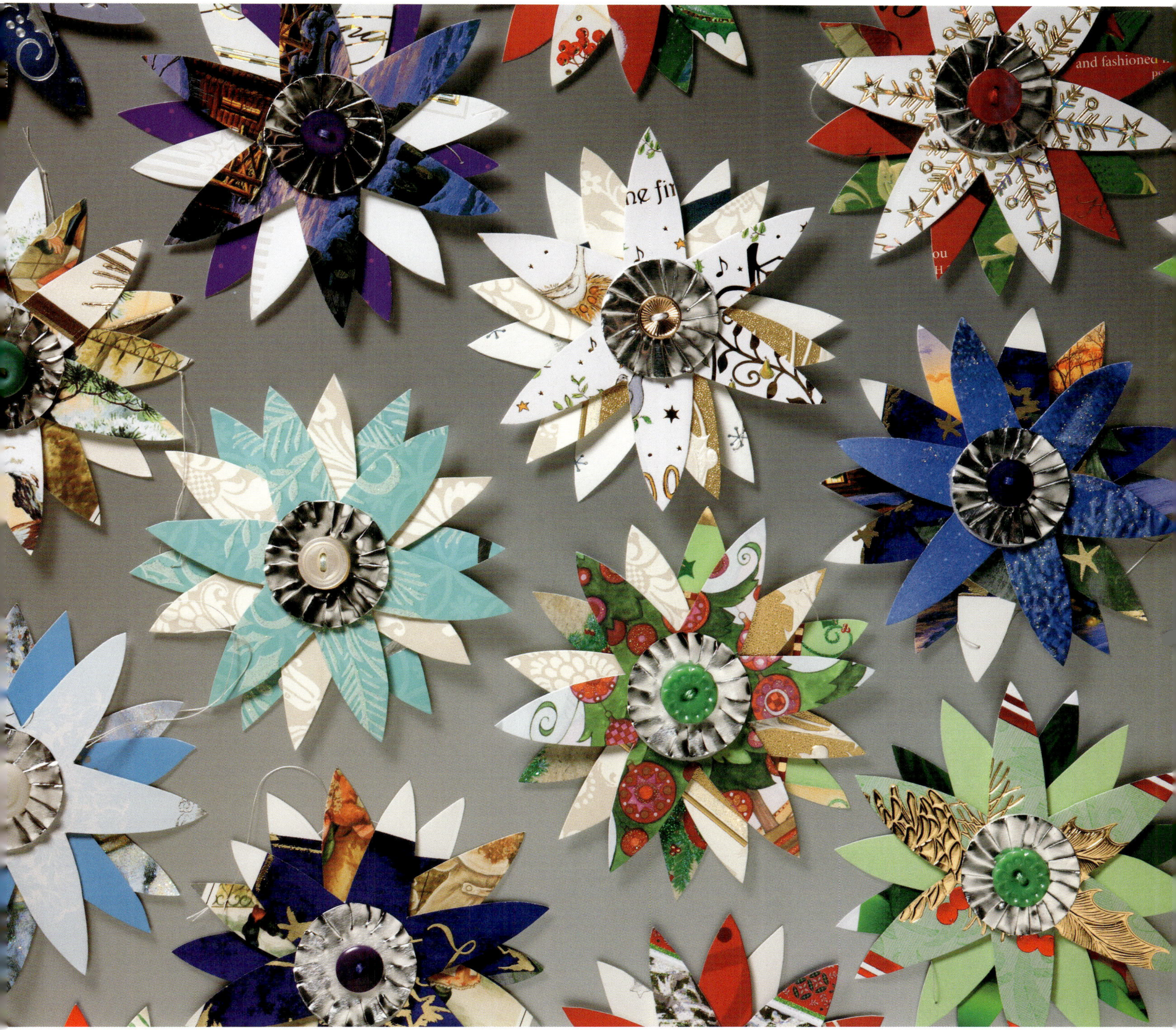
and fashioned

FISH BOTTLE

Rudolph Christ (1759–1833), Moravian Pottery, Salem, North Carolina, ca. 1825, lead-glazed earthenware, 2 3/4" x 4 1/2" x 1", gift of Mr. Frank P. Dickinson, 1978.900.2

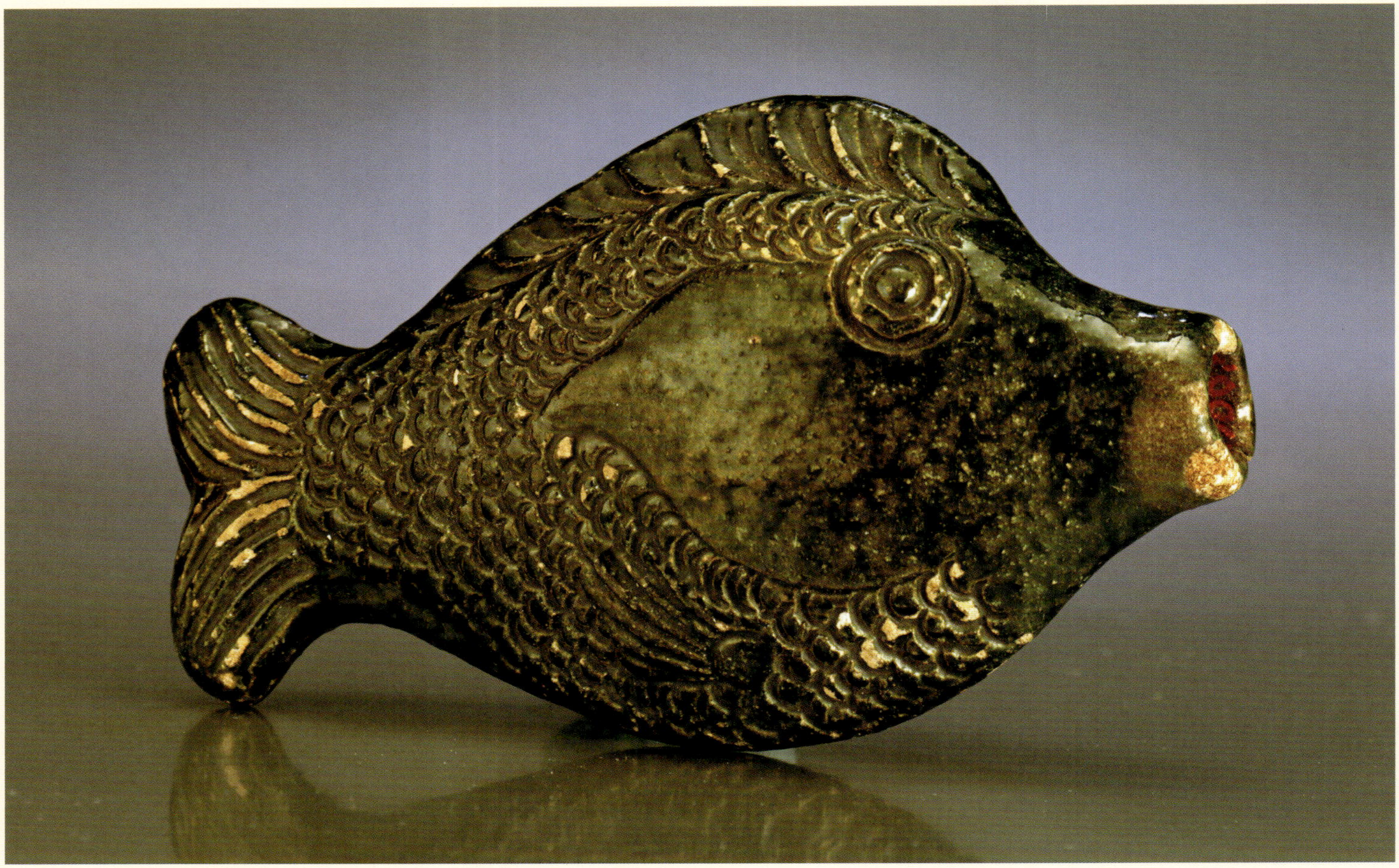

The rich green color of this two-sided fish bottle attracts the eye. A closer look reveals the details of fins, gills, scales, and eyes, giving it a realistic appearance. This bottle is just one example of the many animal-figured ceramics made in Salem, North Carolina, in the early nineteenth century.

At the beginning of the century, the Moravian master potter Rudolph Christ began producing press-molded ceramics in many shapes including squirrels, turtles, owls, bears, and fish. The plaster mold carried the details of the figure so that a good impression was left in the clay that was pressed onto it. The use of molds also meant that the potters could produce their wares in greater numbers. Although Salem was a small town in the southern backcountry, these popular wares were sold not only locally but in the surrounding states. The fish in particular came in four sizes. This fish bottle, at 4½ inches tip to tail, was the second smallest and sold for nine pence in 1819. The open mouth serves as the opening to the bottle. Given that the inside is not glazed, the fish likely carried nonliquid items like spices. The contents would have been kept secure with a cork.

Aluminum Fish

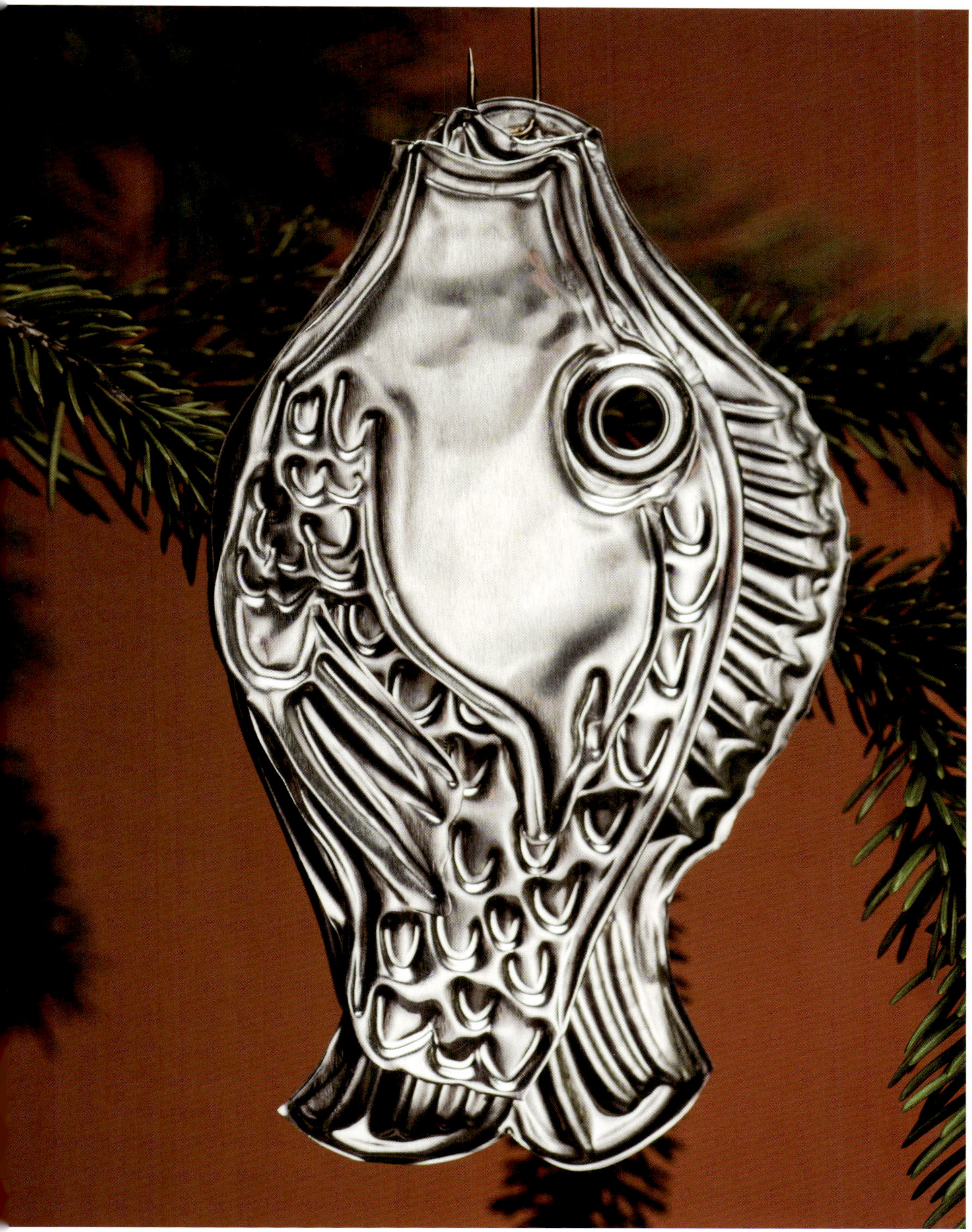

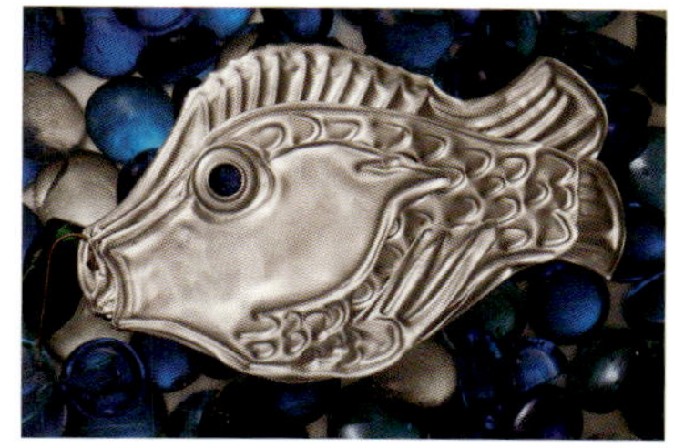

THE IMPRESSED DETAIL ON THE BODY OF THE BOTTLE FISH GIVES IT A LIFELIKE QUALITY. THE FOIL WE USED FOR THIS PROJECT MIMICS THAT IMPRESSED DETAIL.

WHAT YOU NEED:

- Body, eye piece 1, eye piece 2, scale piece 1, and scale piece 2 templates (page 142)
- Clear tape
- 36-gauge aluminum tooling foil
- Piece of felt
- Stylus (such as an old ballpoint pen or sharpened dowel)
- Embroidery scissors
- Binder clip
- ¼-inch hole punch
- Grommet tool
- ¼-inch grommet
- Fishhook, size 4, pre-tied with monofilament

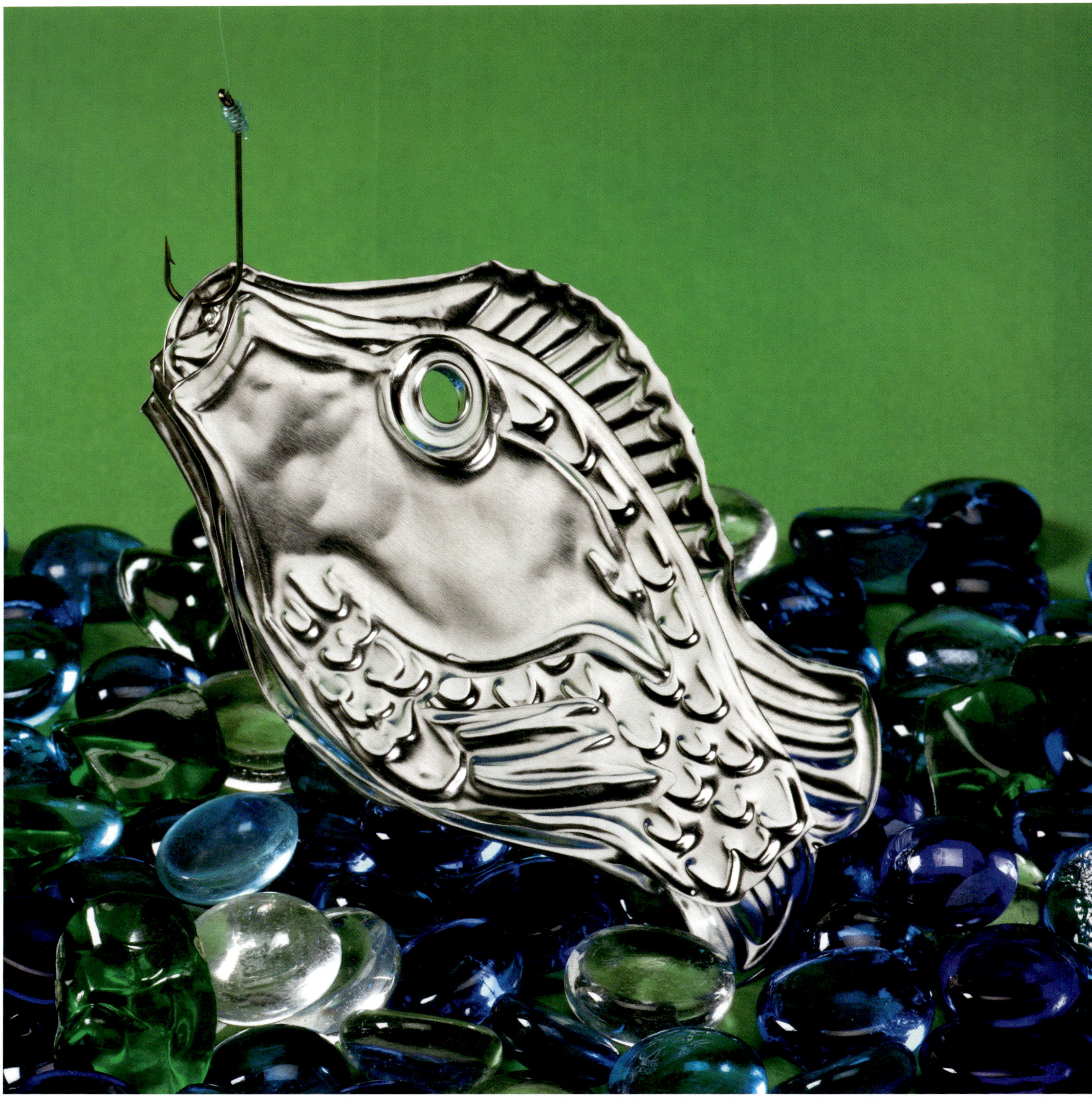

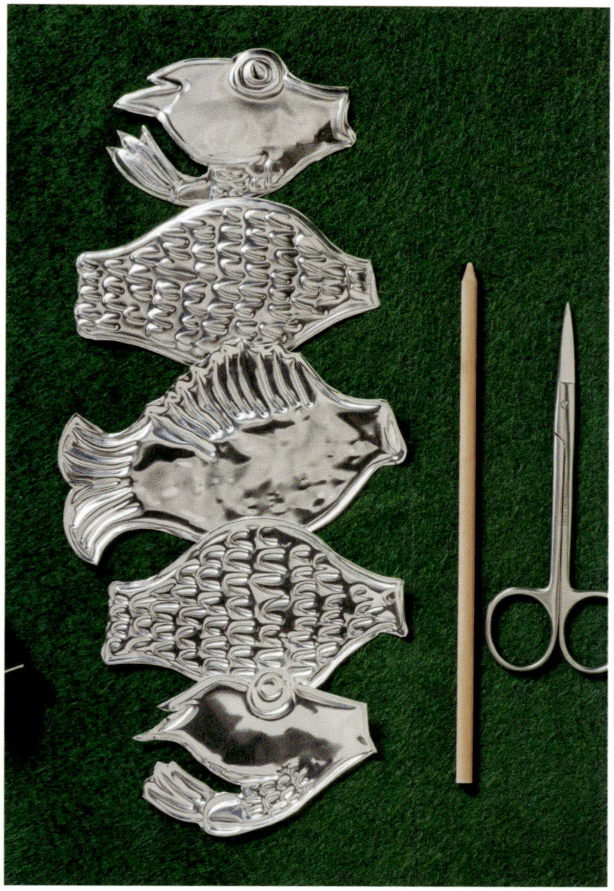

INSTRUCTIONS:

Tape one of the five fish templates to the tooling foil and place on the felt. The felt will protect your work surface and allow the stylus to create a deep impression into the foil. Trace the template, including all of the decorative details, with the stylus with even pressure. Remove the template. If necessary, go over the image more firmly with the stylus. Repeat the process with each of the other four templates.

Cut out the five foil fish pieces leaving a 1/8-inch margin on the outside of the drawn lines.

Layer the five fish pieces in the following order: eye piece 1 right side down, scale piece 1 right side down, body piece right side up, scale piece 2 right side up, eye piece 2 right side up. Line up the corresponding pieces, that is, the eye pieces and the scale pieces; use the binder clip to hold the pieces in place. Punch the eye with the hole punch. Following the instructions with the grommet tool, place a 1/4-inch grommet in the eye hole. The grommet will hold the layers together. Remove the binder clip.

To create a hanger, put the fishhook through the pre-tied loop at the end to create a larger loop to hang over a tree branch. With the sharp end of the fishhook, make a small hole at the mouth of the fish and hook it through.

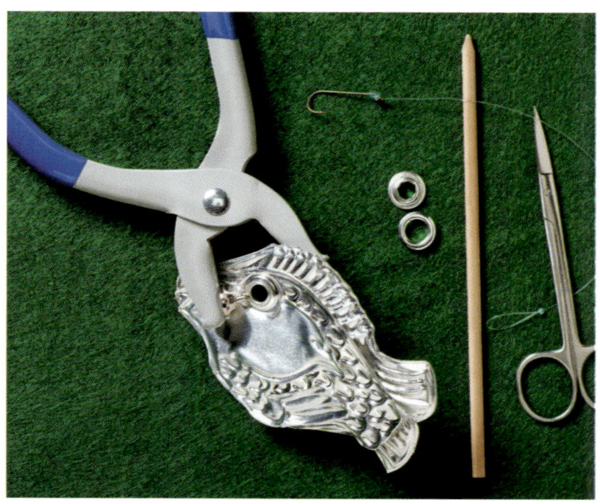

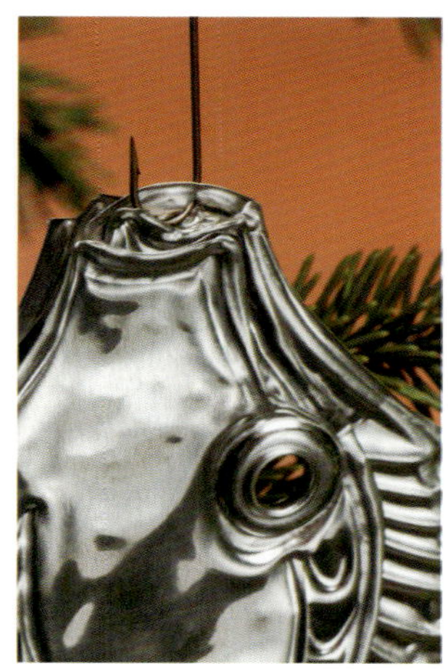

IDEAS: EXPERIMENT WITH COMBINING DIFFERENT COLORED FOILS, PAPER AND FOIL, FABRIC AND PAPER, ETC.

BASKET OF FRUIT

Mary Bradley, Lee, Massachusetts, ca. 1825, paint on velvet, 13 1/2" x 16 1/2", 1958.403.1

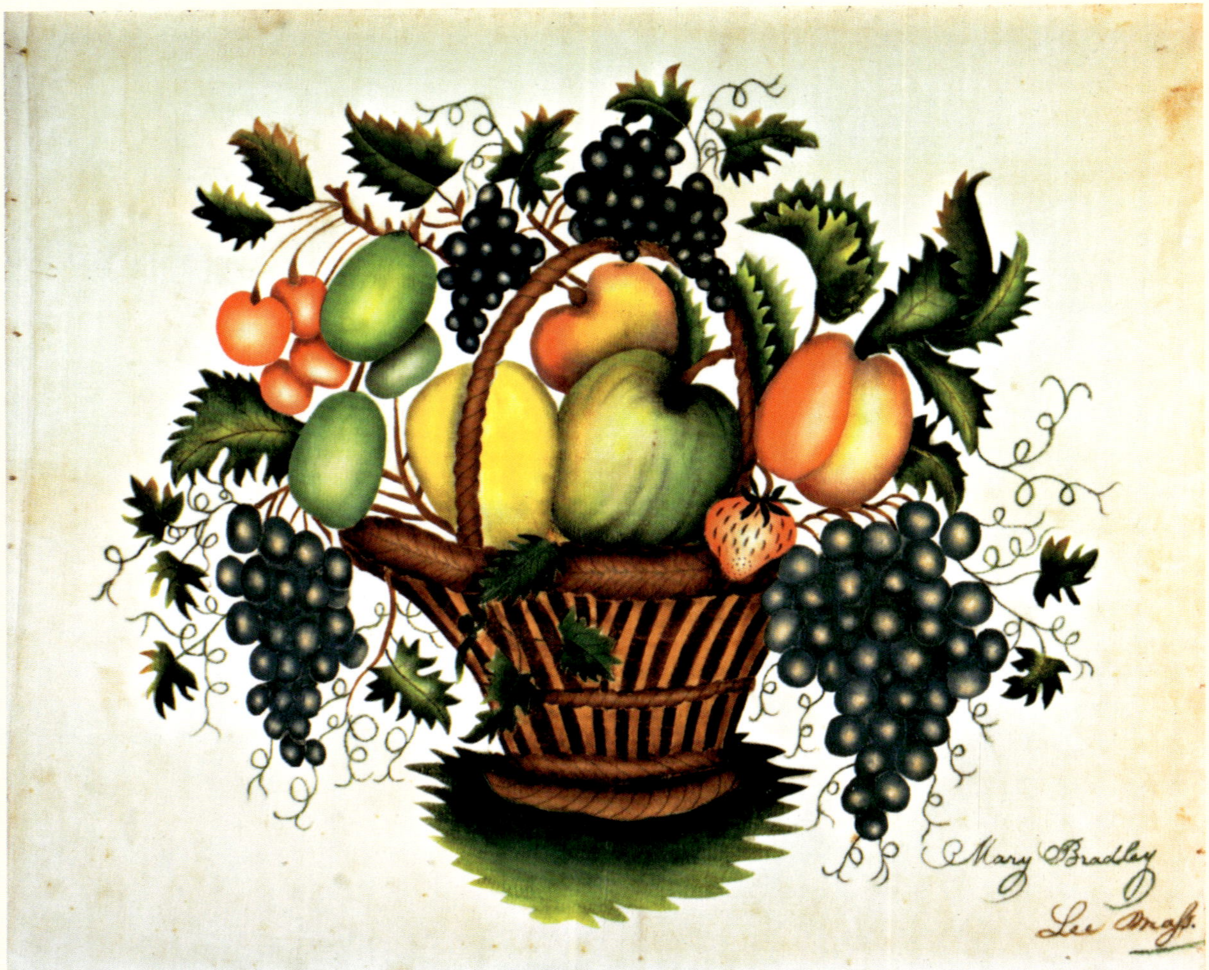

Theorem, or stencil, painting was particularly popular among women in America about 1820 to 1840. Some works were done on paper; others, like this one, were done on velvet. Although stencils would seemingly denote a certain similarity among pieces, the way the artist chose to position and color them could make all the difference.

Mary Bradley piled her fruit into a basket. She paid particular attention to shading in the leaves and fruit. The basket and fruit outlines are crisp and have made a slight depression in the velvet. Bradley probably used a pointed tool to create this effect. The curly vines and her nicely crafted signature show that she was also experienced with a pen.

The inscription with her signature and location gives us hints about the artist, but records show two Mary Bradleys in Lee, Massachusetts, born within a year of each other in the early nineteenth century. Either girl might have created this piece. Whichever, she certainly had an eye for composition and color.

Punch-Needle Basket of Fruit

SINCE GIRLS WERE TAUGHT SKILLS WITH THE BRUSH AND THE NEEDLE IN THE NINETEENTH CENTURY, WE THOUGHT IT WOULD BE INTERESTING TO GO FROM BRUSH TO NEEDLE BY TRANSLATING MARY BRADLEY'S PAINTED THEOREM INTO A NEEDLEWORK ORNAMENT.

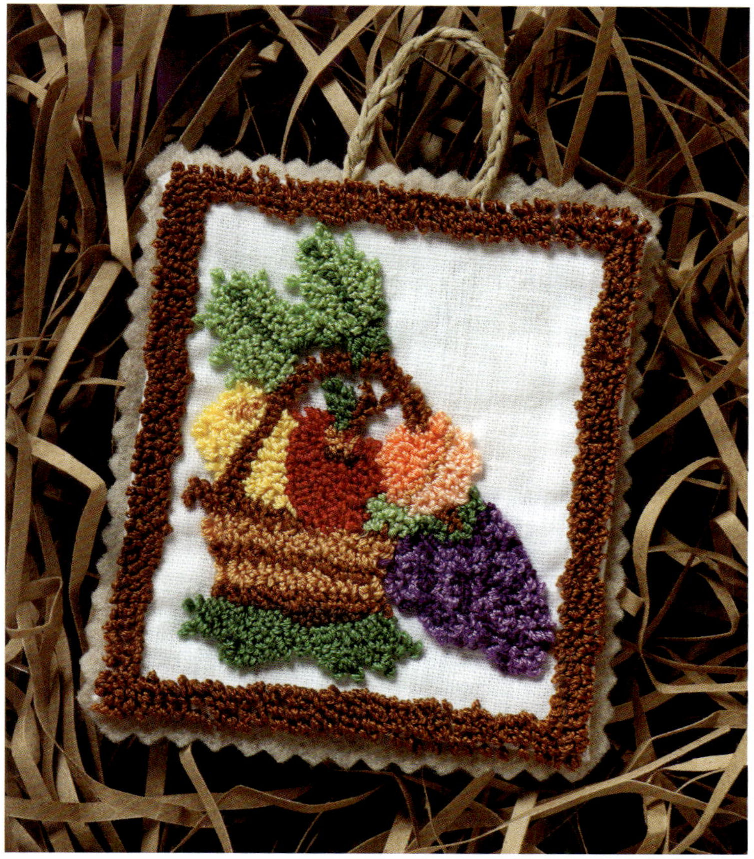

WHAT YOU NEED:

- Basket of fruit template (page 134)
- Tracing paper
- Iron-on transfer pencil
- Ecru weaver's cloth, 7 x 7 inches
- Iron
- Ironing board
- 4 3/4-inch interlocking hoop
- 3-strand punch needle
- Punch-needle threader
- Floss in the following DMC colors: 208, 352, 353, 367, 368, 433, 436, 550, 816, 838
- Embroidery scissors
- Matching felt
- 48-pound hemp cord, 36 inches long

INSTRUCTIONS:

Trace the basket of fruit template onto the tracing paper using the iron-on transfer pencil. Following the manufacturer's instructions for the transfer pencil, iron the transfer onto the center of the weaver's cloth. Place the cloth into the hoop, centering the basket of fruit.

Thread the punch needle with three strands of floss, and punch the design following the colors in the image. When the picture is complete, trim the thread from the back of the design.

Cut out the picture, leaving a 1/2-inch fabric border all the way around. Make small cuts into the unworked fabric border, particularly at the corners, so that the fabric will lie flat when you fold it back. Fold the border toward the back and carefully iron so that it lies flat.

Using the template, cut out a felt square. Stitch the felt to the back of the fabric using a blind stitch. Leave the top open for the cord hanger.

To make the hanger, cut three 12-inch lengths of hemp cord. Knot the three together at one end, braid, and tie off at the other end. Form a loop and place at the top back of the piece. Sew in place as you finish sewing the felt on.

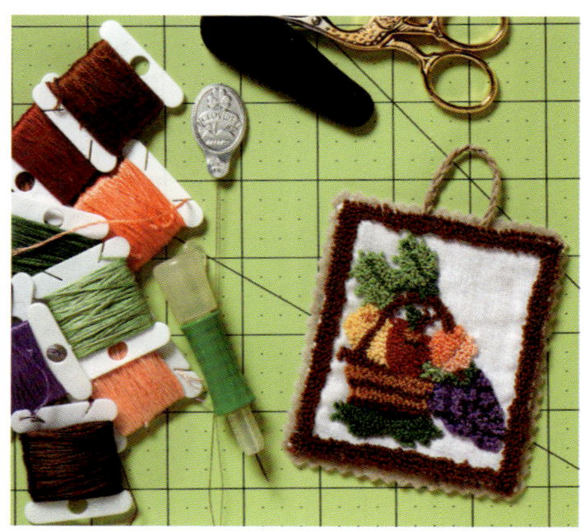

IDEA: INSTEAD OF ATTACHING A CORD FOR HANGING, ATTACH A PIN BACK SO THAT YOU CAN WEAR IT AS A BROOCH.

COVERLET

Harry Tyler (1801–1858), Jefferson County, New York, 1839, wool and cotton, 89" x 80 1/2", gift of Lucretia Irene Elderkin, 1978.609.10

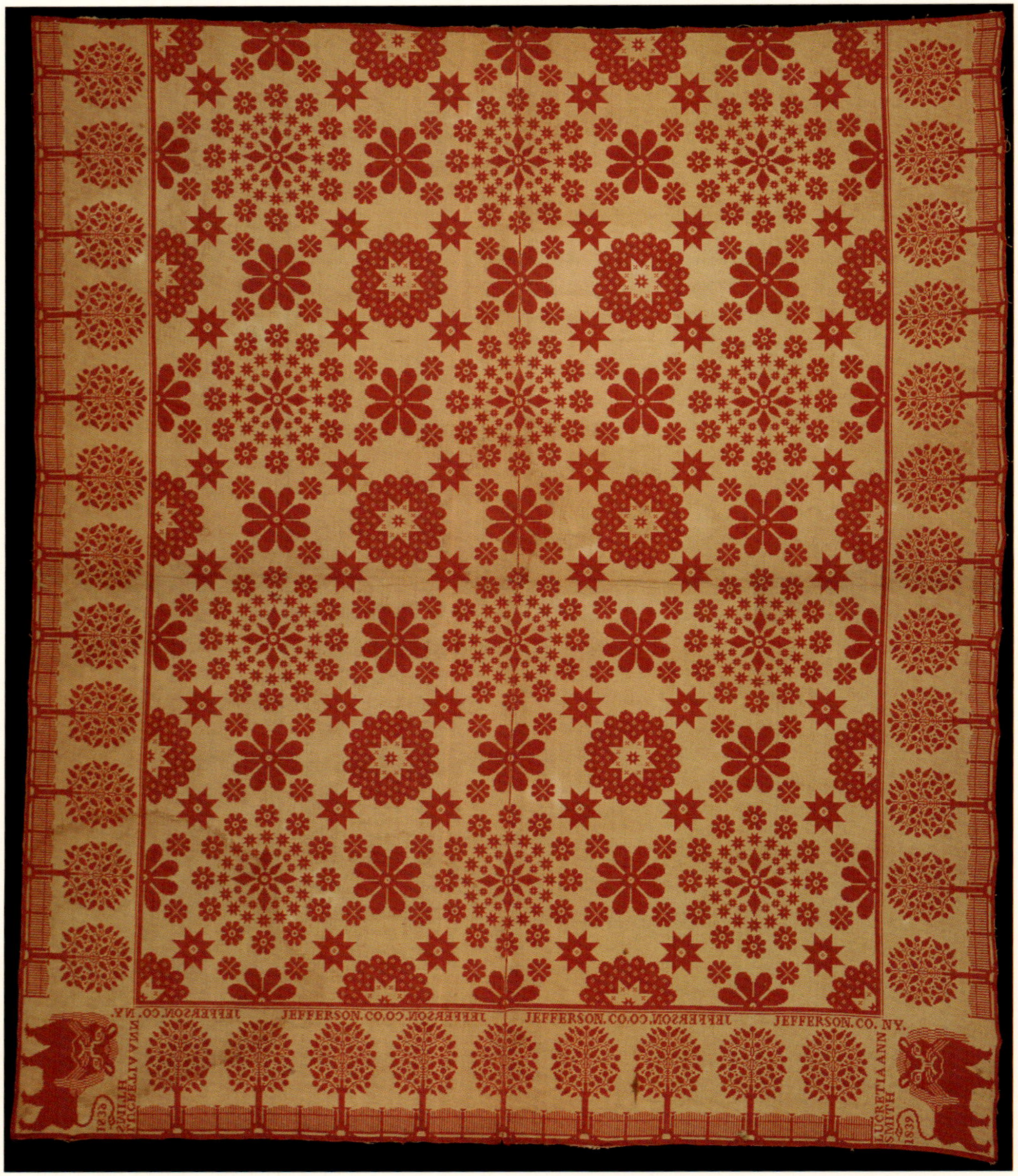

At first glance, you might not notice that this woven coverlet contains evidence of its origins. Worked into the design above the trees in the bottom border are the names of the county and state where it was made. In the two corner blocks by the imposing lions is "Lucretia Ann Smith 1839," the name of the client and the date she commissioned the coverlet. The corners of many coverlets served as signature blocks that might include the name of the maker or client, a date, and/or a place.

Although there were women weavers, many professional weavers were men. Harry Tyler, the weaver of this coverlet, made many such pieces and is now recognized for his distinctive lions as well as motifs such as the trees and picket fences combined with lacy medallions and stars in the center field. That isn't to say that Tyler was the only weaver using these details, but his combinations and style stand out.

This coverlet was woven on a loom in two pieces because looms were limited in the width they could produce, though length was not restricted. It was woven in a double-weave structure and seamed up the center. The pattern was woven with the intent to seam, indicated by the matching up along the center seam.

THE MOTIFS OF THIS COVERLET OFFER MUCH INSPIRATION, BUT WE CHOSE TO PICK OUT THE SMALL EIGHT-POINTED STARS TO CREATE A LOVELY GARLAND. WE MADE THE STARS A SOLID RED THREADED ON RED FLOSS, BUT YOU CAN SELECT ANY COLOR OF PAPER AND THREAD.

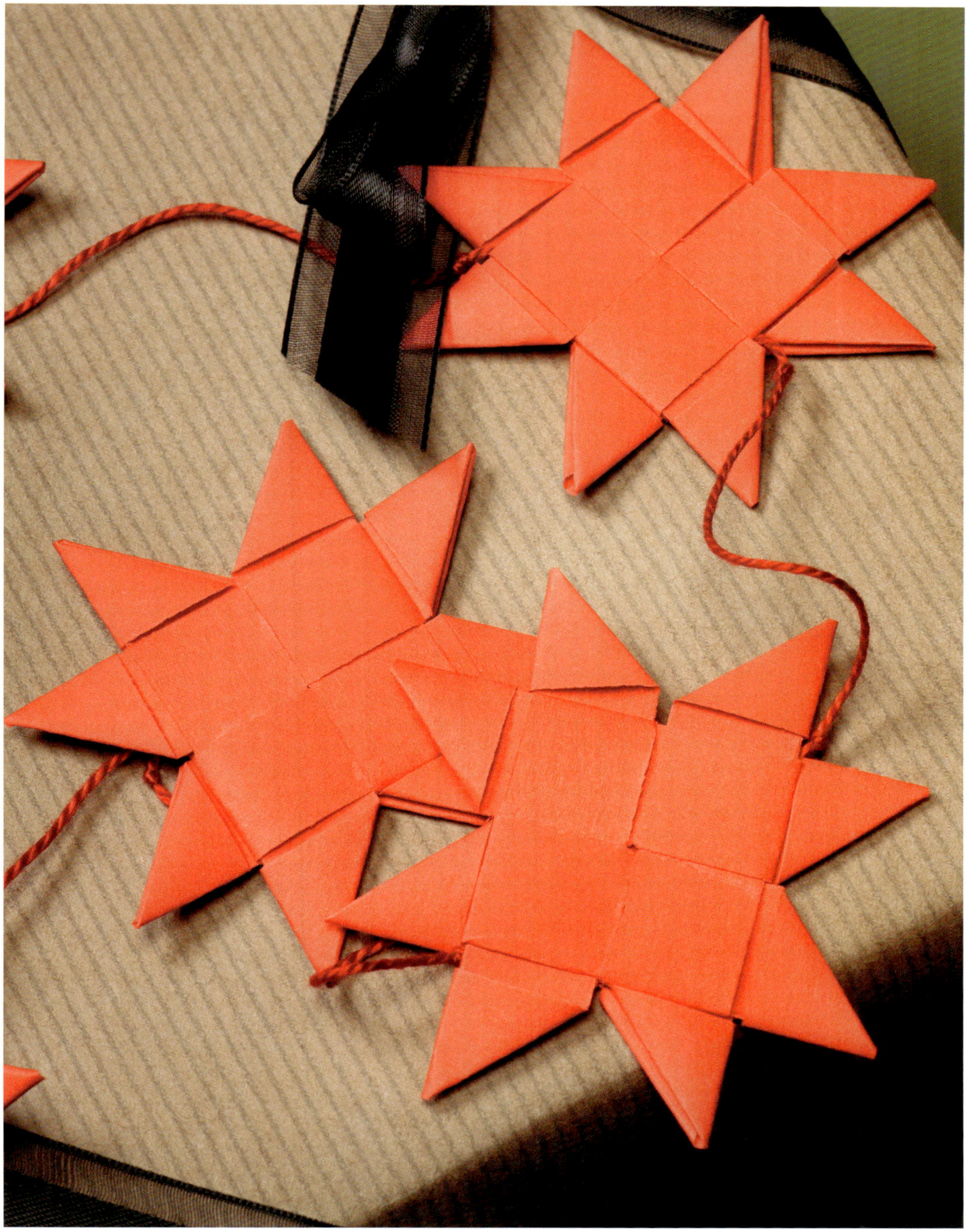

Paper-Star Garland

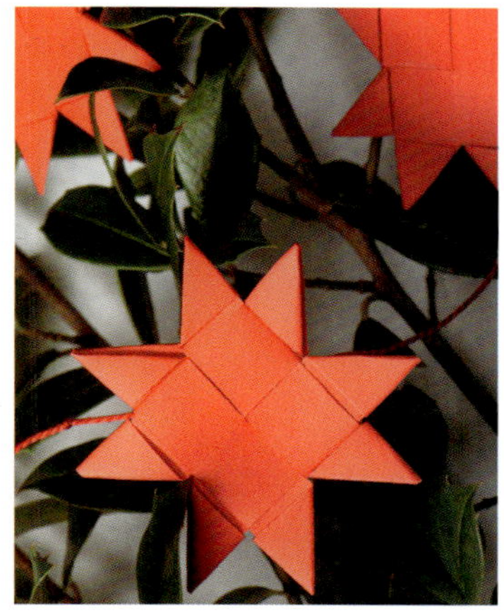

WHAT YOU NEED:

Paper, 8 1/2 x 11 inches
Matching pearl cotton floss, size 3
Ruler
Pencil
Scissors or rotary cutter
Long needle (like a doll needle)

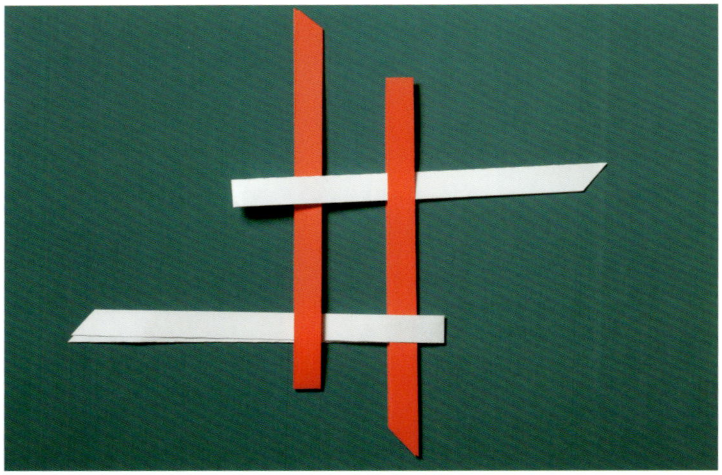

Illustration 1

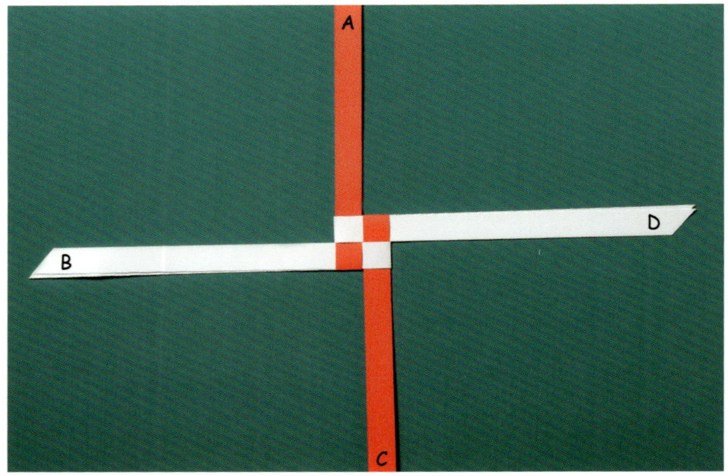

Illustration 2

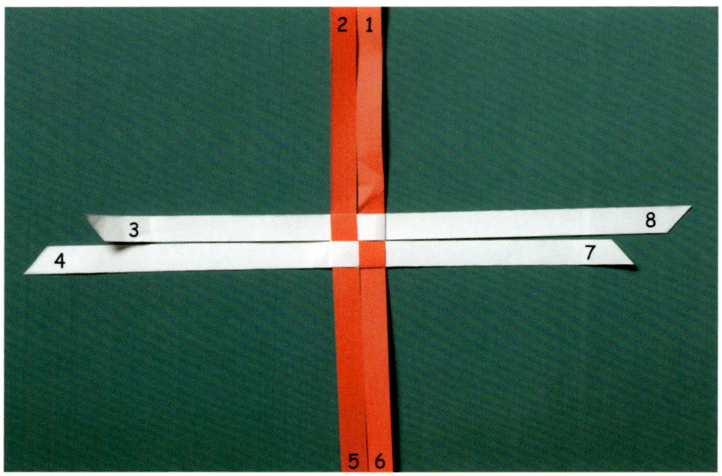

Illustration 3

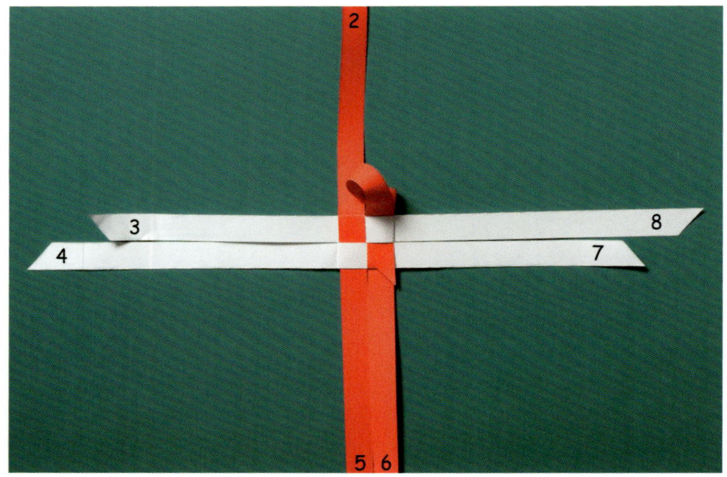

Illustration 4

INSTRUCTIONS:

Measure and mark off 1/2 x 8 1/2–inch strips on the paper. Cut the strips. Snip each end to create a point. You will need four strips for one star.

Take four strips and fold them in half. On a flat surface, interweave them as shown in illustration 1. Note that when two ends of one strip go through another strip, the two ends do not split; they stay together. (We used two different colors in the illustrations to make them easier to follow.) Once all four strips are interwoven, gently push them together so they are tight and form a four square in the center (illus. 2).

Mark the ends of the strips counterclockwise with the letters A, B, C, and D. Orient the interlocked strips with A at the top. Starting with A and working through D, fold the top piece of each strip back over the center square. When you get to D, as you fold it back over the square, weave the end over C and under A and pull it all the way through. This will lock the folds in place.

You now have all eight pieces of the strips visible (illus. 3). With the lettered side facing down, mark the ends, counterclockwise again, with numbers 1 through 8. Pick up the square in your hands with strips 1 and 2 at the top. Starting with 1, fold the strip

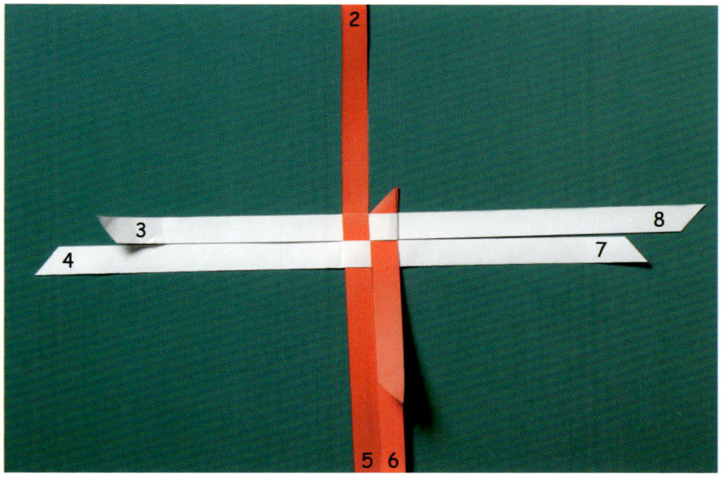

Illustration 5

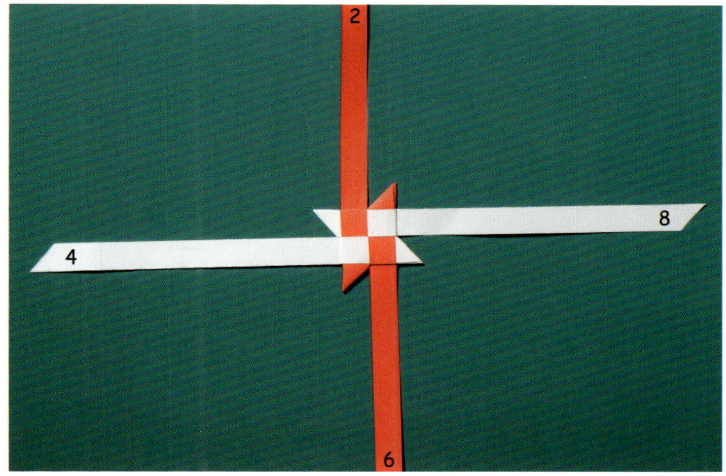

Illustration 6

down and to the side to form a triangle. Pinch the fold and then, to reinforce the triangle shape, continue to fold the same strip by twisting it to the back and then again to the front. As you fold the strip to the front, tuck the end into the square, pull it snug, and pinch the triangle flat (illus. 4 and 5). Trim the strip so that the end is hidden within the square. Fold strips 3, 5, and 7 the same way. Once 1, 3, 5, and 7 are complete, your star will look like illustration 6. Turn the star over and repeat the folding process with 2, 4, 6, and 8. Remember to trim the end of each strip after you tuck it into the square.

Consider how long you would like your garland to be and make the appropriate number of stars. We placed our stars about 3 inches apart. When you have a pile of stars ready, thread the floss onto the long needle. You will need one long continuous thread. At the end of the thread, make a loop for hanging, and knot. About 2 inches in from the knot, tie another knot in the floss. Push the needle through one side of a star and out the opposite side. Make another knot. These knots will hold the stars in place on the thread. Measure about 3 inches, tie a knot, push the needle through another star, and tie a knot. Continue this process until you have the length you want. At the end, make a loop for hanging as you did at the beginning.

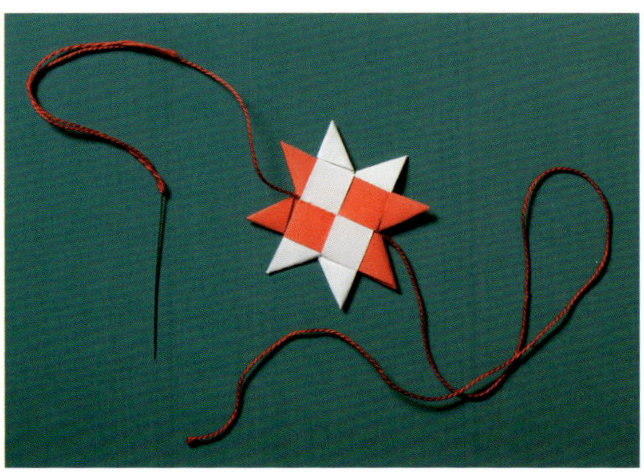

IDEAS: TRY DIFFERENT COLOR COMBINATIONS TO FIT YOUR STYLE. EACH STAR COULD BE MADE UP OF FOUR DIFFERENT COLORS IF DESIRED. FOR A LITTLE SPARKLE, ADD SMALL BEADS AS YOU THREAD THE STARS.

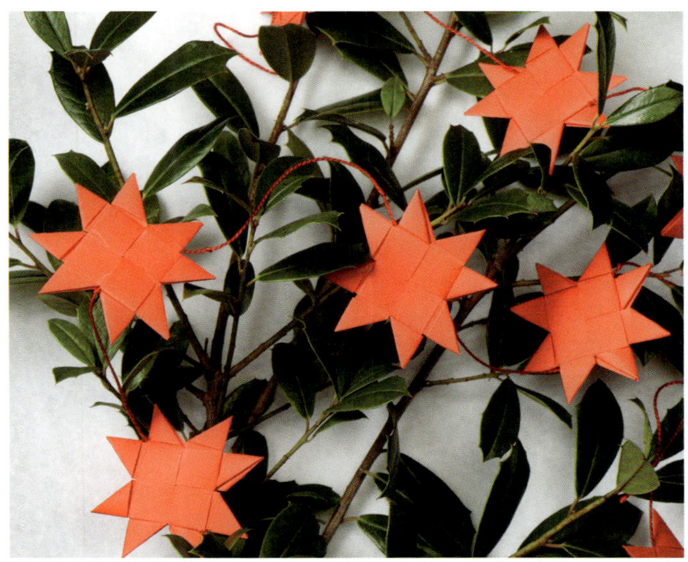

CHRISTMAS

Mattie Lou O'Kelley (1908–1997), Georgia, 1989, paint on canvas, 24" x 36", gift of Dr. and Mrs. T. Marshall Hahn Jr., 2001.101.24

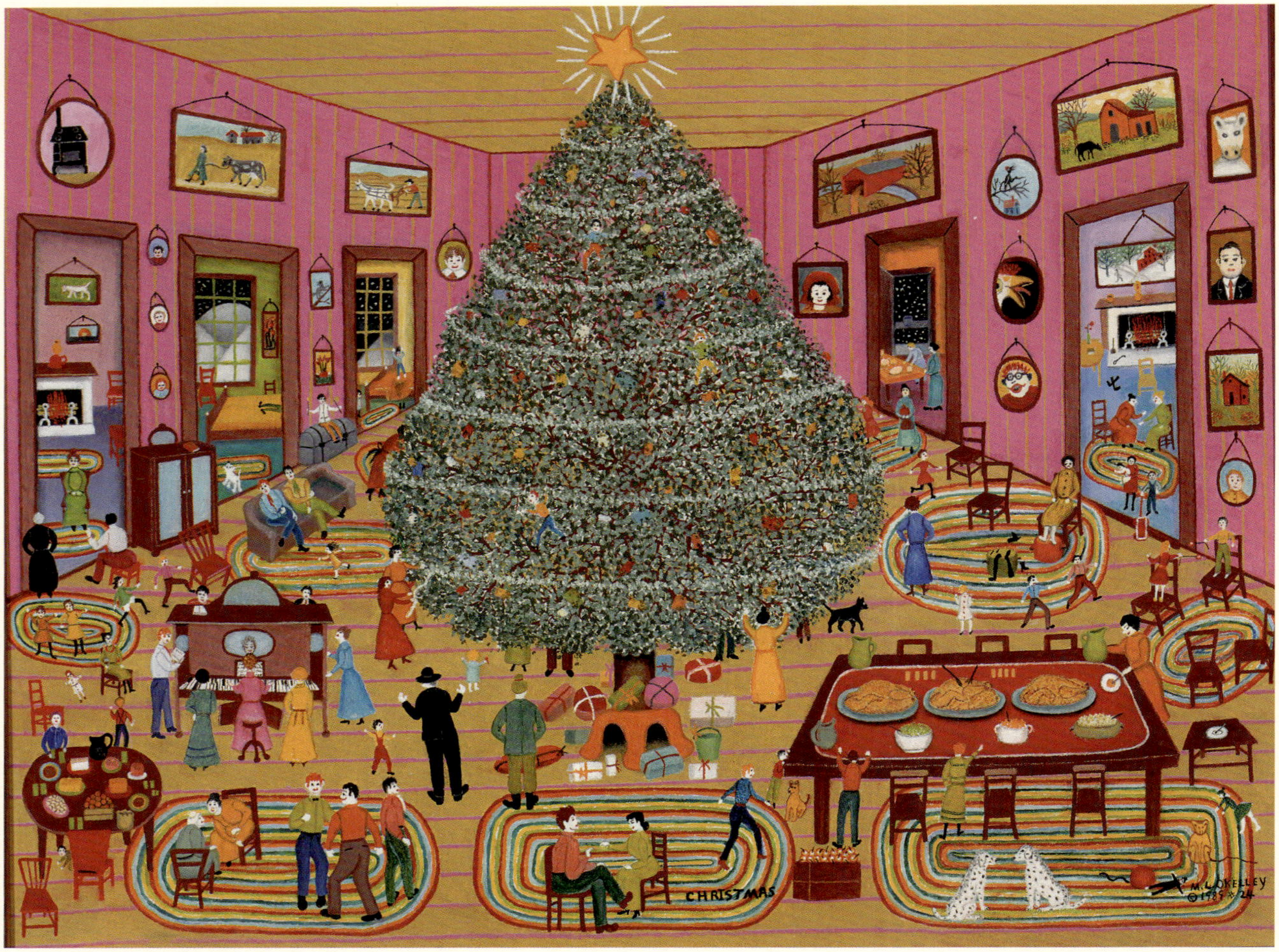

This illustration is the last in the series that Mattie Lou O'Kelley created for her book *Moving to Town*. The text accompanying this illustration captures the joy of the day as well as the relief of being back home in the country away from the big city:

> Christmas Day! What a day! Such a crowd! Lillie played the organ just like always. Papa said, "I like listening to her music even better than eating!" I got a big doll. Johnnie got a red wagon. Candy! Oranges! Good bananas! Johnnie and I just stood by the doorway with our mouths hanging open. It sure was good to be home.

The enormous tree dominates the room and dwarfs the people but does not detract from the many activities and the enjoyment of friends and family. If you look closely in the first doorway on the right, you can see Mattie and Johnnie with their new toys. You can just imagine their delight and wonder.

Gathered-Fabric Tree

LIKE MATTIE AND JOHNNIE IN THE STORY, WE WERE CAPTIVATED BY THE TREE. THIS FABRIC VERSION NICELY MIMICS THE STRIPED EFFECT OF THE TREE. THE ADDITION OF A STAR-SHAPED BUTTON ON TOP FINISHES IT OFF PERFECTLY.

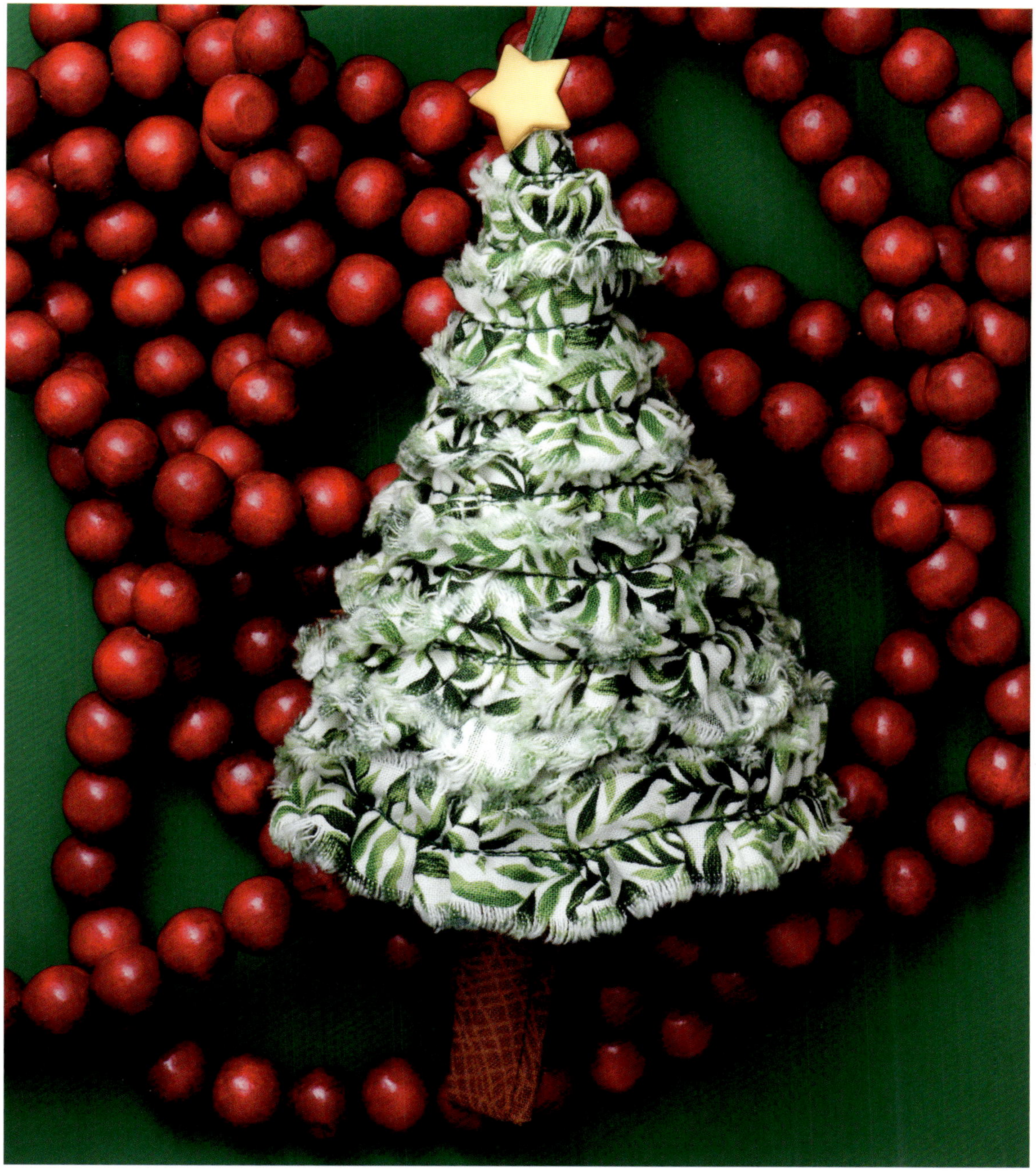

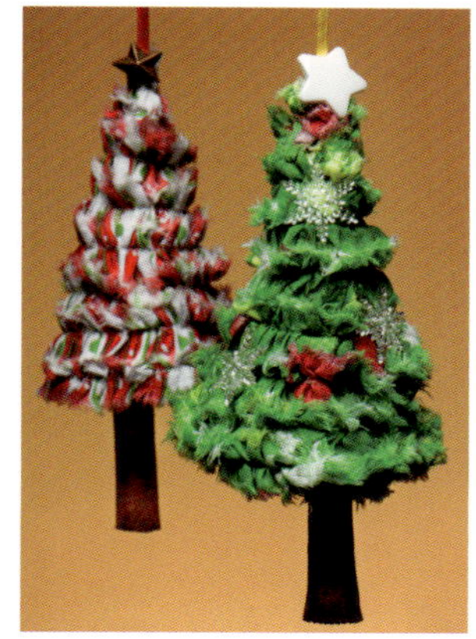

WHAT YOU NEED:

Tree template (page 133)
Festive cotton fabric, 10 x 44 inches
Matching thread
Ruler
Pencil
Scissors
Sewing machine
Green felt, $5^1/_2$ x $9^1/_2$ inches
Matching thread
Pins
Buttons, charms, beads (optional)
Brown cotton fabric, 2 x 7 inches
Matching thread
Safety pin
Star button with shank
$^3/_8$-inch ribbon, 10 inches long

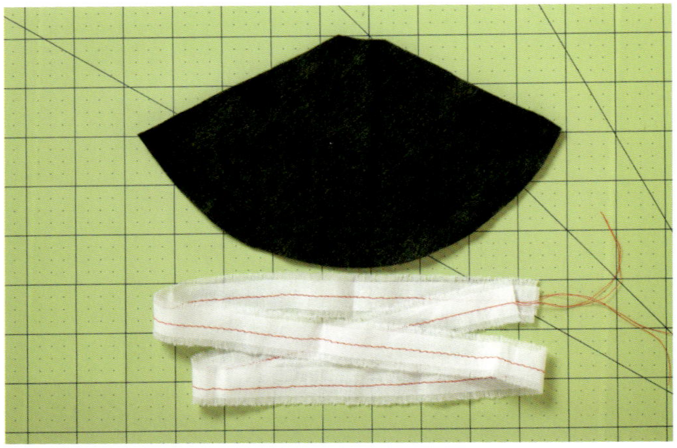

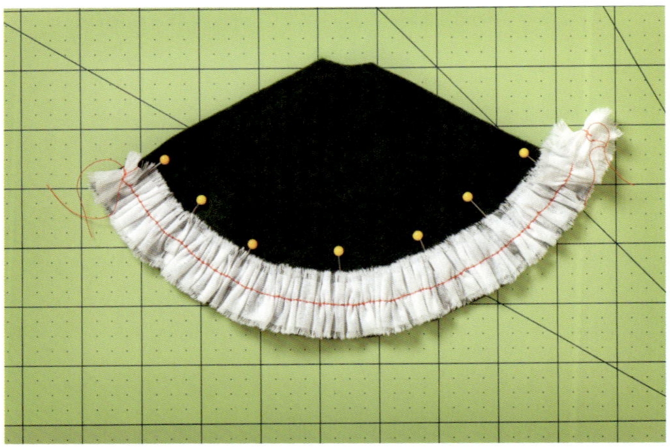

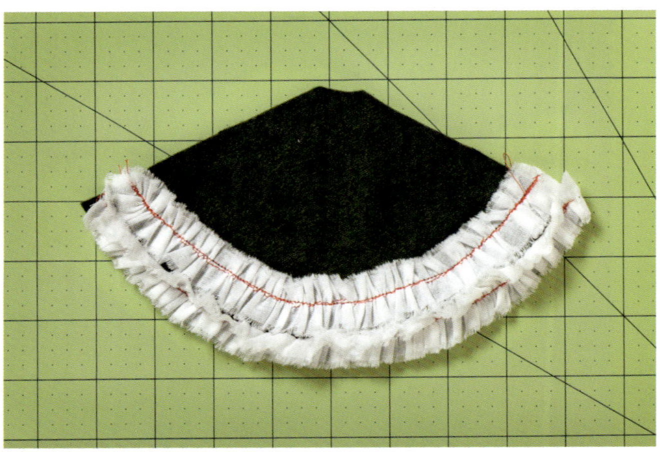

INSTRUCTIONS:

Rip the festive cotton fabric into eight strips that are roughly 7/8 x 42 inches. To do this, mark the 7/8 inch at the edge and snip with scissors. This will give you a starting point for ripping the length of the fabric. Fray the long edges of each strip by pulling out a few of the stray threads. (Note that we are using white fabric and red thread in the instruction photos to make them easier to see.)

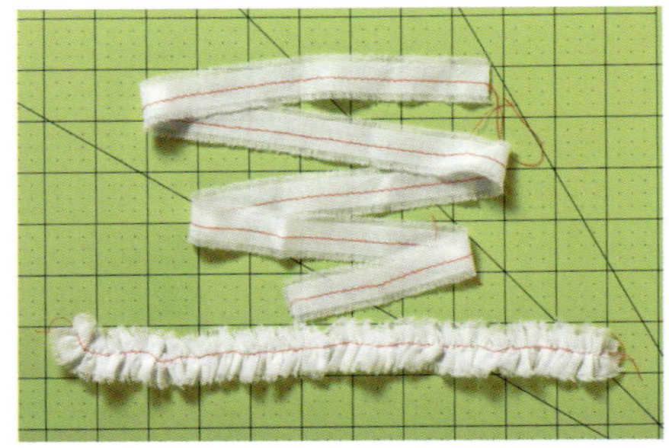

Set your sewing machine stitch length to the longest setting, and stitch down the center of each strip with the matching thread. Once you have stitched all eight strips, gather each one: Tie a tight knot in the thread at one end of each strip, and then, holding the other end of the thread between your fingers, gently slide the fabric down toward the end with the knot. Be careful not to pull too quickly or too tightly as this could cause the thread to break. Tie off each gathered strip at 11 inches so that the gathers look consistent when all the strips are attached to the tree.

Using the tree template, cut the tree from the green felt.

Pin one of the gathered strips to the bottom edge of the felt tree leaving one end of the strip overhanging the side edge of the felt tree by about 1/8 inch. Don't be concerned about any overhang on the other end of the strip. With green thread on the bobbin so that the stitching will blend in with the felt underside, machine stitch the gathered strip into place, removing the pins as you sew. Leave the one end of the gathered strip overlapping by 1/8 inch, but trim the other end even with the green felt.

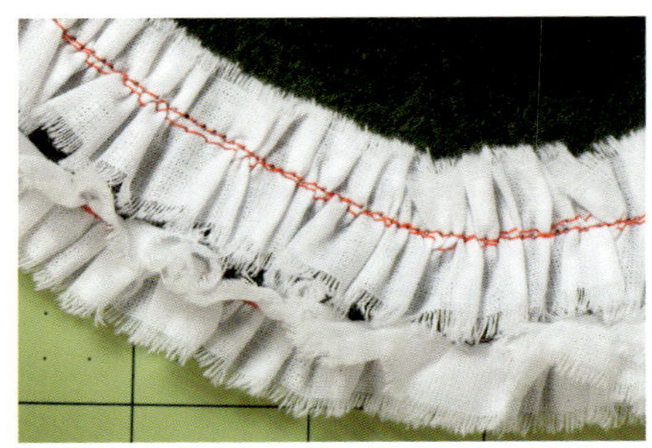

To attach the second gathered strip, press the top of the first

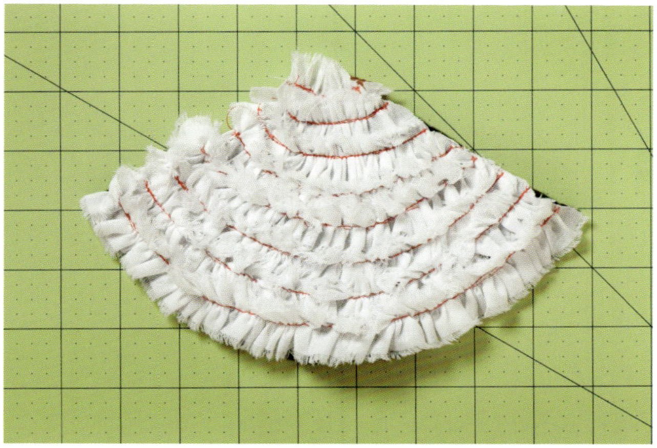

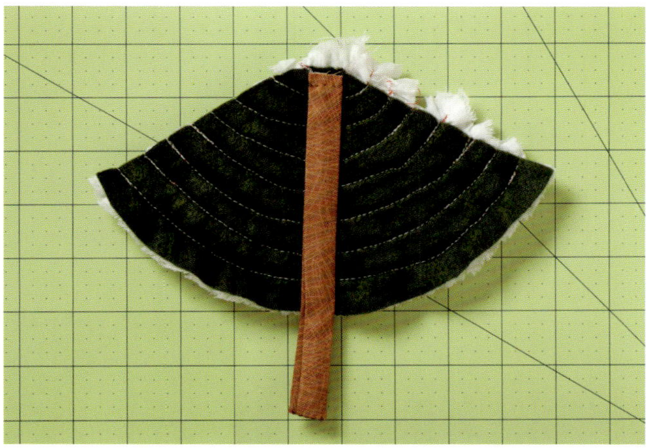

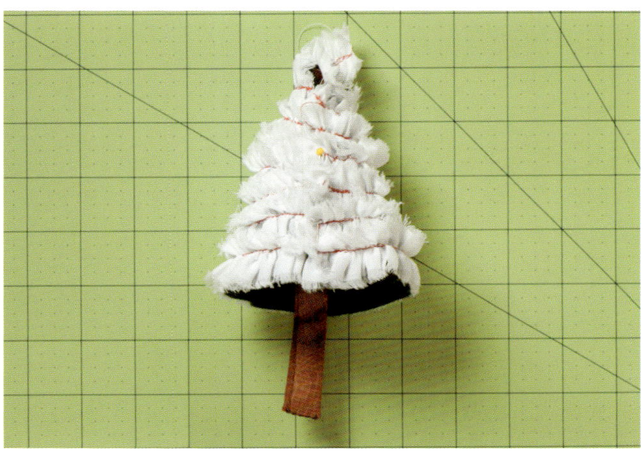

strip down with your fingers against the bottom of the strip, and pin the second strip in place by matching the edge of the gathered fabric to the stitching line of the lower strip. Machine stitch the strip into place with the 1/8-inch overhang at one end, and remember to trim the strip at the opposite end. Repeat these steps until the tree is filled. As you move to the top of the tree, you will have more excess to trim off the strips.

Now is the time to decorate the tree if you want. Sew on buttons, charms, or beads to create "ornaments" on your tree.

To make the tree trunk, fold the brown fabric lengthwise right sides together and machine stitch the long raw edges. Use the safety pin to turn the tube right side out by pinning it to one end and pushing the safety pin through the tube to the other end. Fold in the raw edges at the ends and whipstitch the bottom opening closed. Lay the trunk onto the wrong side of the tree and adjust the length so that it hangs below the bottom of the tree. You can make the trunk as long or short as you like. Stitch the trunk to the green felt, attaching just near the top of the tree so that the trunk hangs freely.

Fold the tree into a cone shape right side out, match edges, and stitch in place using a whipstitch. This seam is best sewn by hand. The 1/8 inch that you left overhanging the edge will overlap to hide your stitching. Stitch the star-shaped button to the top of the tree.

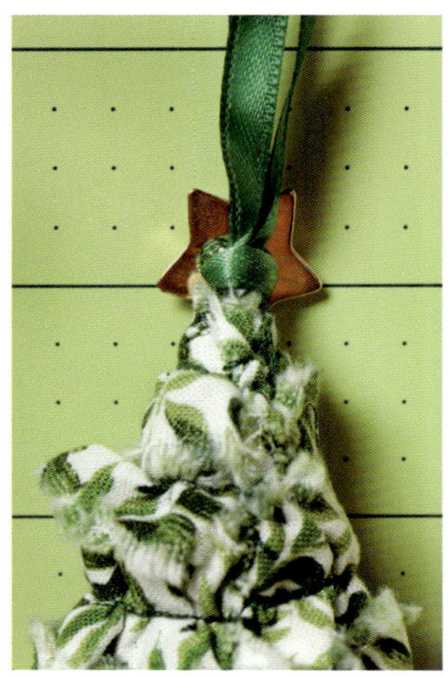

For the hanger, thread the ribbon through the shank of the button and tie off at the desired length for hanging.

IDEAS: CREATE A FOREST OF THESE TREES. EXPERIMENT WITH DIFFERENT SIZES, SHAPES (NARROW OR FATTER TREE), AND FABRICS. MAKE THEM LARGER, STUFF, AND MAKE A FOREST CENTERPIECE FOR THE HOLIDAY TABLE. YOU CAN OMIT THE TRUNK, OR JUST TUCK IT IN, IF YOU WANT THEM TO STAND RATHER THAN HANG.

What Inspires You?

Many of the folk artists represented in this book drew inspiration from their life experiences and their immediate environment. Whether it was Irwin Weil's re-creation of a cherished pet or Mattie Lou O'Kelley's scenes from her long-ago childhood, these art pieces represent captured memories that were personal to the creator and now inspirational to viewers. As a final project, we suggest you take a blank canvas and create your own miniature folk art picture that reveals something about you. Maybe it depicts a favorite vacation spot, a family pet, or just a scene outside your window.

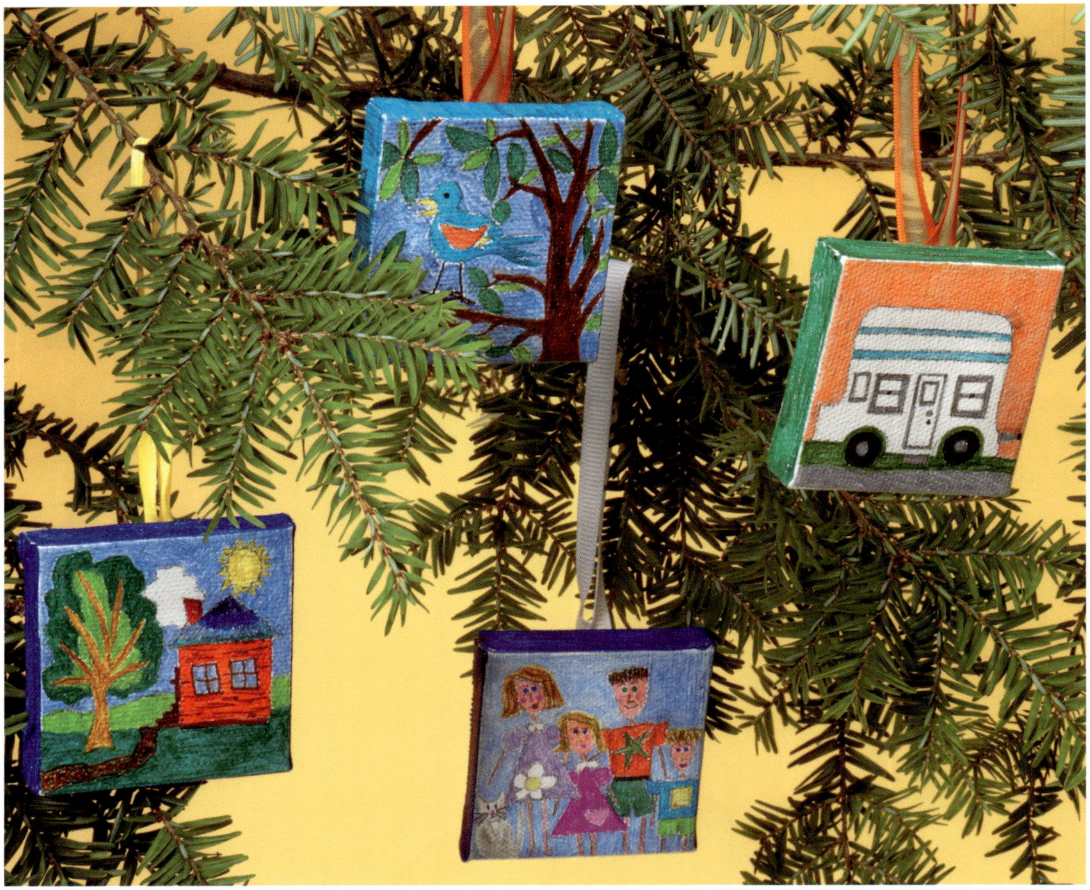

WHAT YOU NEED:

- Studio mini canvas, 2 x 2 inches or 3 x 3 inches
- Pencil
- Fine-tipped color markers
- Ribbon, about 10 inches long
- Thumbtack

INSTRUCTIONS:

Think about the picture you want to draw and the colors you want to use. With the pencil, you can lightly sketch the image on the canvas. If you are confident of your drawing, you can jump right in with the markers. We recommend covering the entire canvas with color. Consider the edges of the canvas too. They can be either part of the drawing or covered in a single color. Note: When working with markers, it usually looks better if you do not overlap the colors.

Once you have completed the picture, turn the canvas over. Fold the ribbon in half. With the thumbtack, secure the ribbon ends to the back of the canvas stretcher in the center of the top.

IDEA: At a holiday party, these would make wonderful table decorations or name cards. Wooden mini easels (3 x 5 inches) work perfectly to display the miniature art.

ACKNOWLEDGMENTS

Although this was a collaboration between two coworkers (and friends), a project like this is never just about the authors. Ron Hurst, Colonial Williamsburg's vice president for Collections, Conservation, and Museums, allowed us to pursue the idea and make it our own. We could not have accomplished the work without the support and encouragement of our supervisors, Rick Hadley and Trish Balderson. We also relied on the amazing curatorial skills of our colleagues present and past who have studied and exhibited the collection since 1957, particularly Beatrix Rumford, Carolyn Weekley, and Barbara Luck. We also thank Donna Sheppard for encouraging us to think about creating this book.

Our families deserve thanks for letting us take our work home and offering their assistance or staying out of the way during the more difficult parts. Jan thanks her parents for cultivating in her an appreciation of all types of art and encouraging her to pursue a career in the museum field. Julianne Gilliam not only gave support at home but also helped with the needlework and added her special touch. Christina thanks her husband, Michael, for his constant love, encouragement, and sense of humor and her amazing children, Cate and Zack, for understanding that mommy has to finish up one more ornament for THE BOOK. Christina's thoughts also include her darling Patty-Cat, who was her constant companion throughout the project.

At work, many volunteers happily gave their time to assist in making ornaments. We are grateful to them for all their hard work and encouraging comments. In particular, Priscilla Culkowski came faithfully every Tuesday to do whatever was asked of her. She offered thoughts about the projects and provided continuous support.

We especially want to thank Paul Aron, Amy Watson, and Helen Olds not only for their publication assistance but also for their enthusiastic response to our ideas and the continued encouragement throughout the process. Tom Green masterfully brought our ideas to life in his wonderful photographs. The images of the artwork so important to this project are courtesy of Hans Lorenz and Craig McDougal. Angelika Kuettner kindly worked with us to see that we had all of the images we needed in a timely fashion. Elizabeth Eaton took on the task of illustrating the stitch guide. Gloria McFadden willingly took on any task at the last minute to help us get those final touches in on time. Thank you to all.

And most of all, thanks to the artists past and present who created the art that inspired us to create our art.

STITCH GUIDE

Straight Stitch

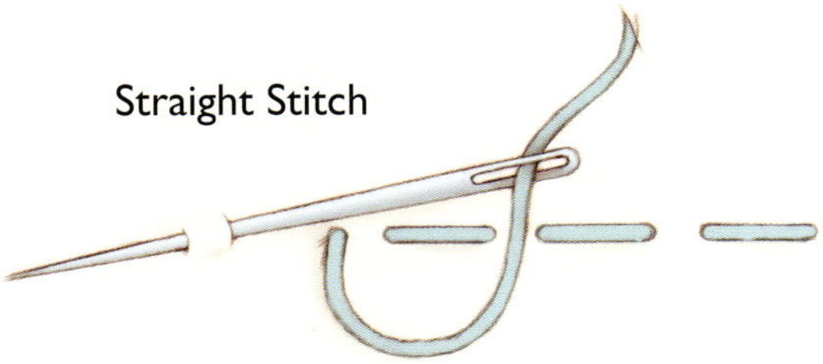

Running Stitch

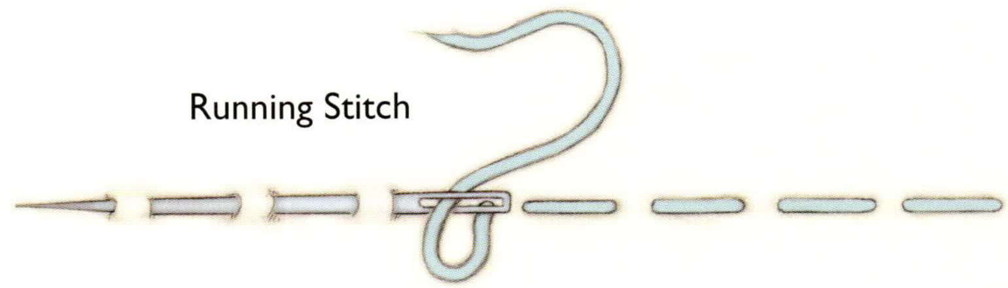

Backstitch

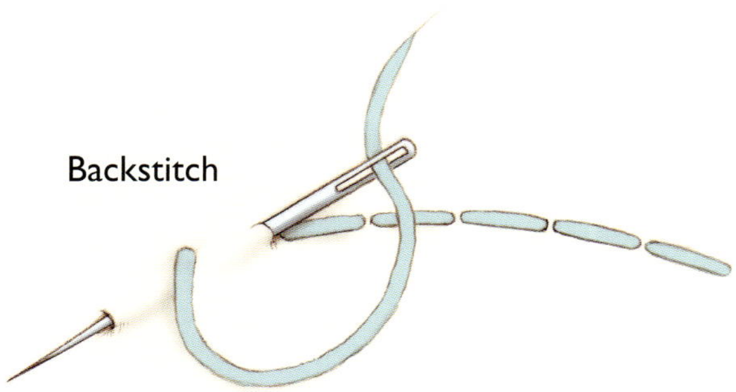

Whipstitch

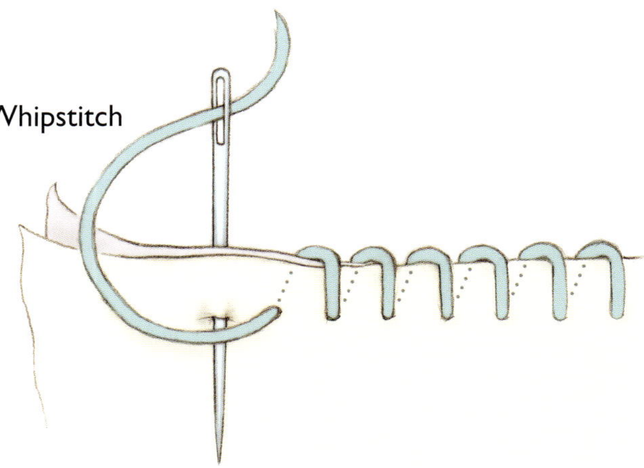

Blanket Stitch

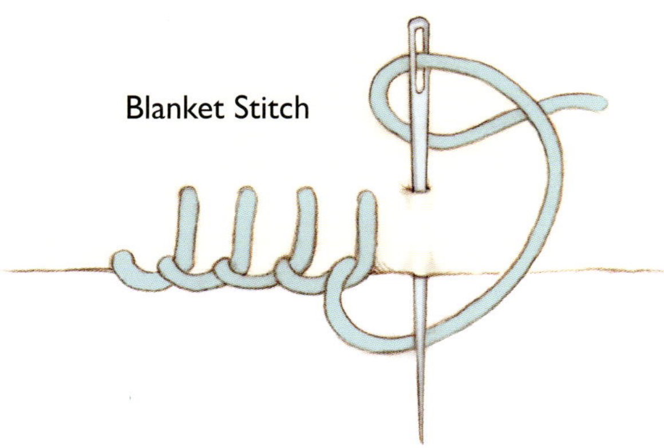

Blind Stitch

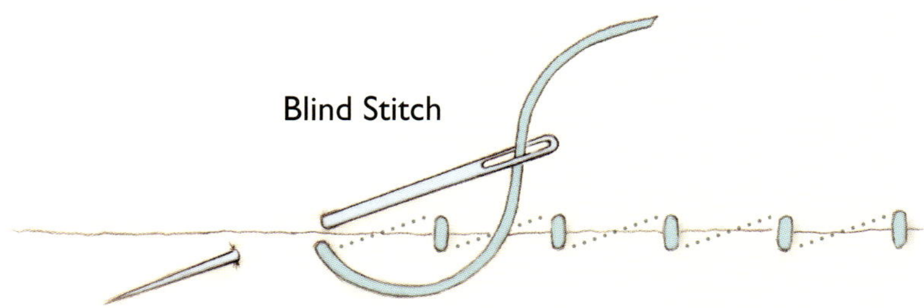

Slip Stitch

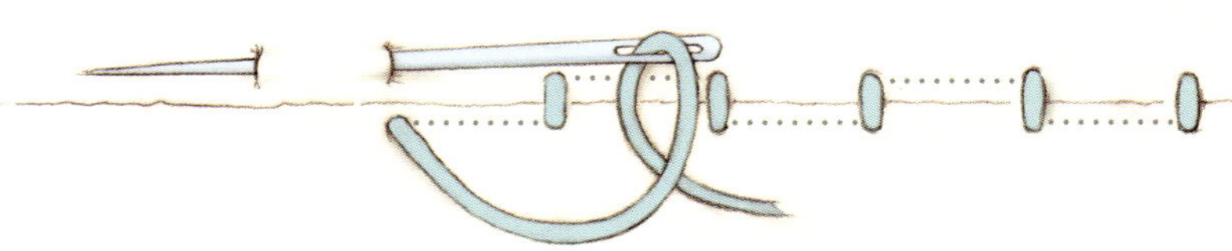

Satin Stitch

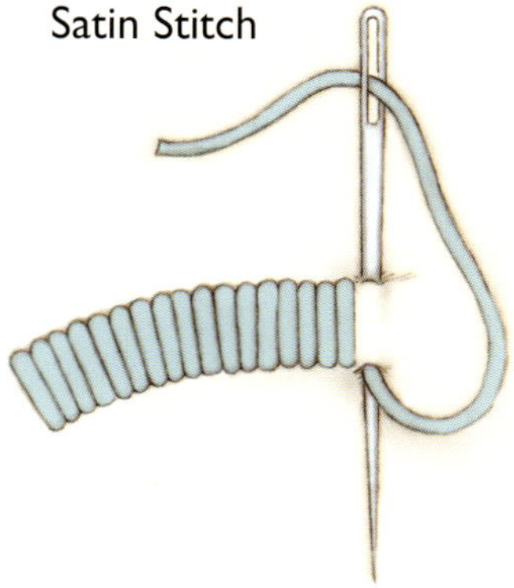

Stem Stitch

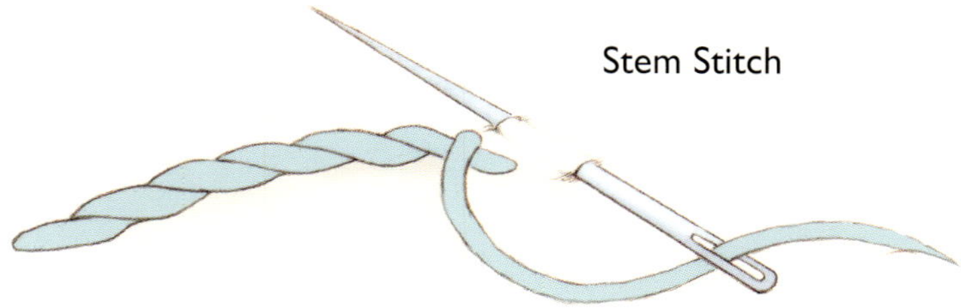

French Knot

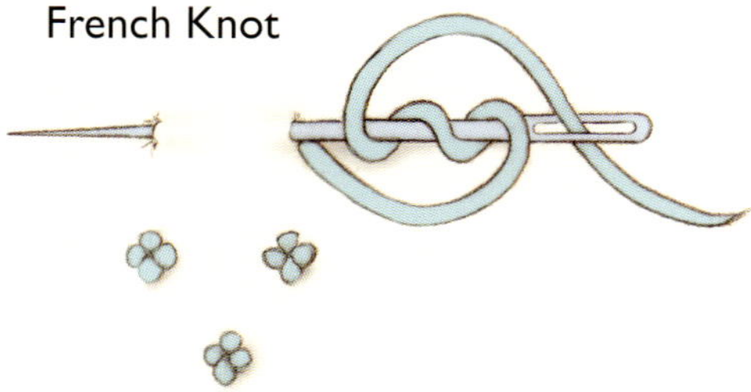

Star Stitch

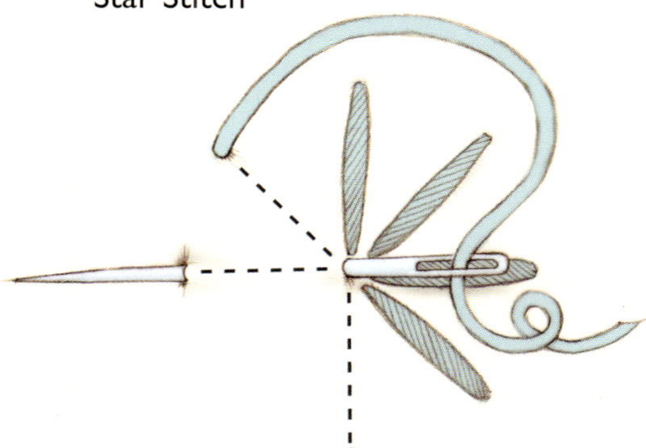

Tent Stitch

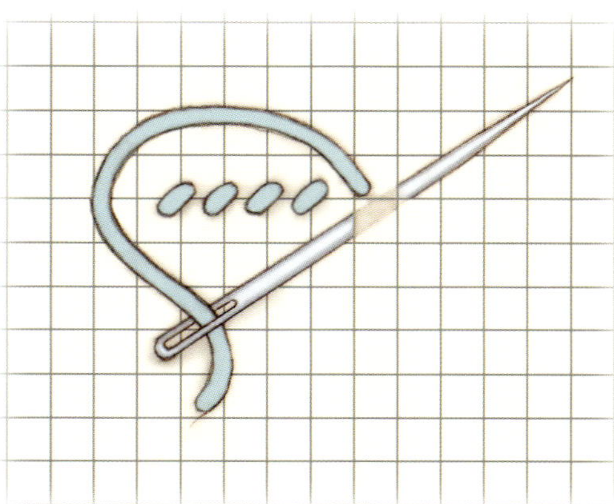

Cross-Stitch

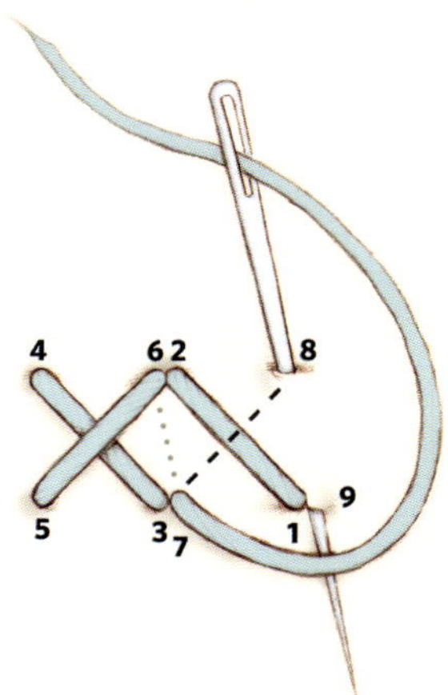

Bargello

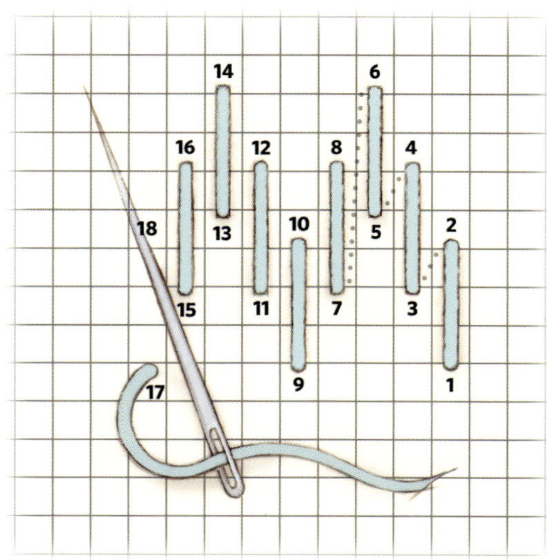

TEMPLATES

FELT SNOWMAN

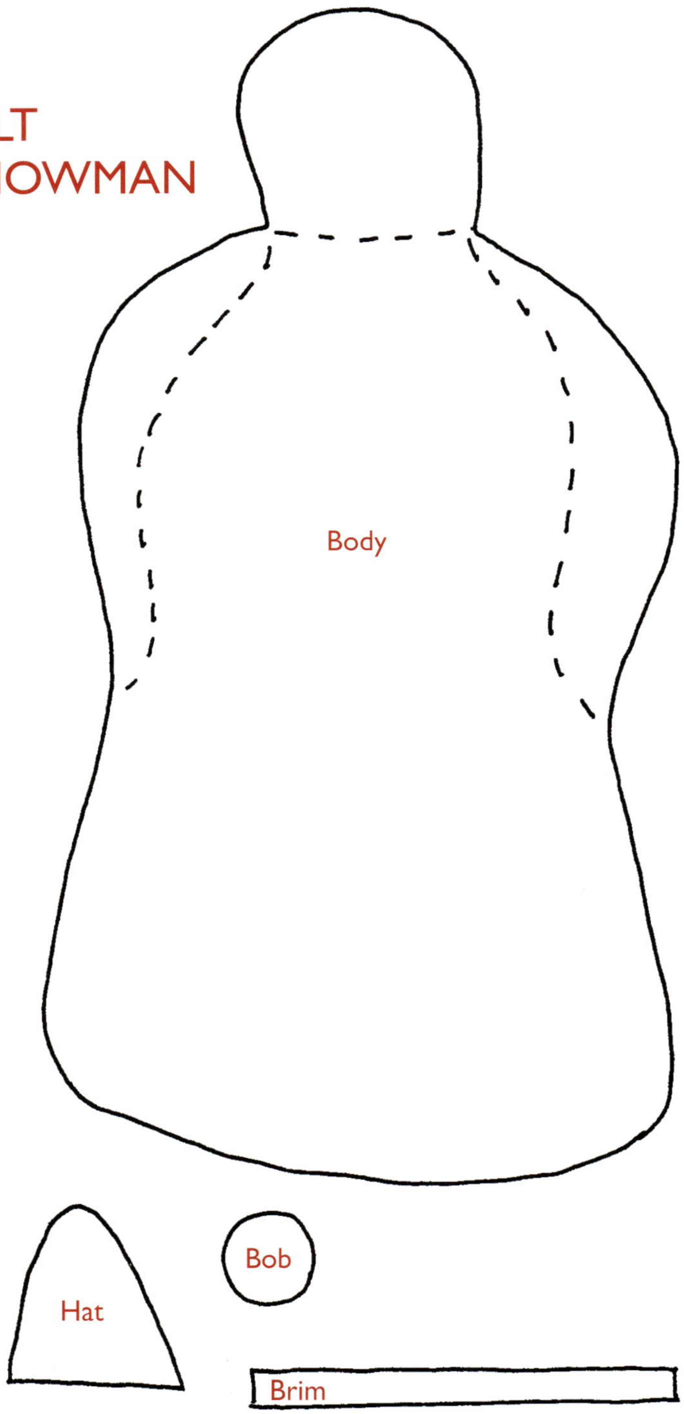

FELT BIRDS

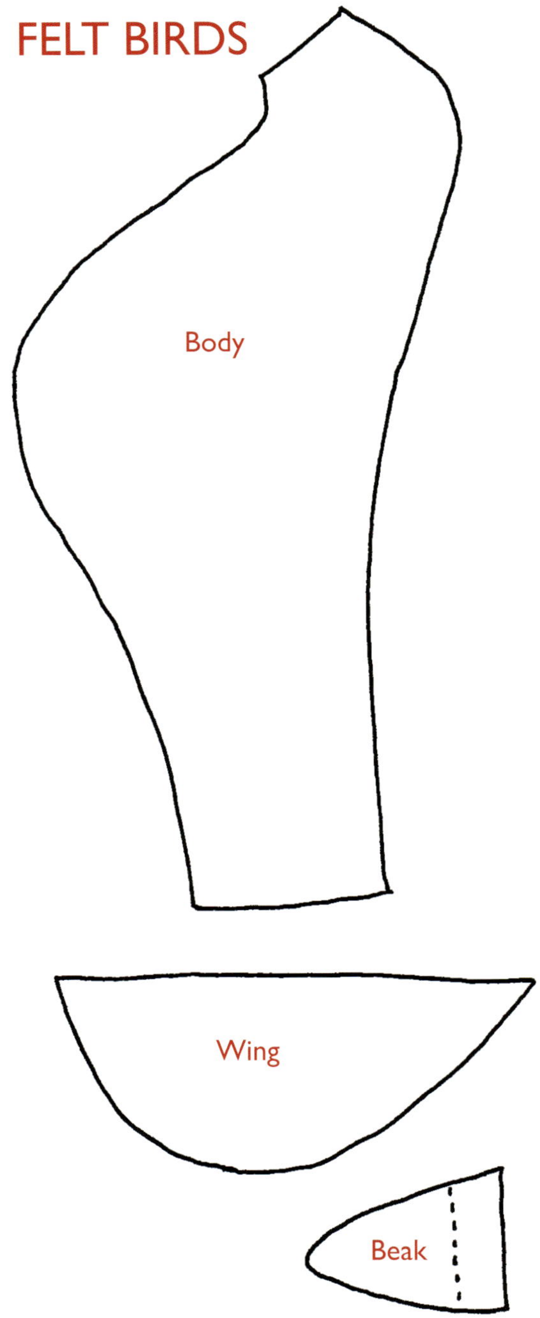

FELT DOG

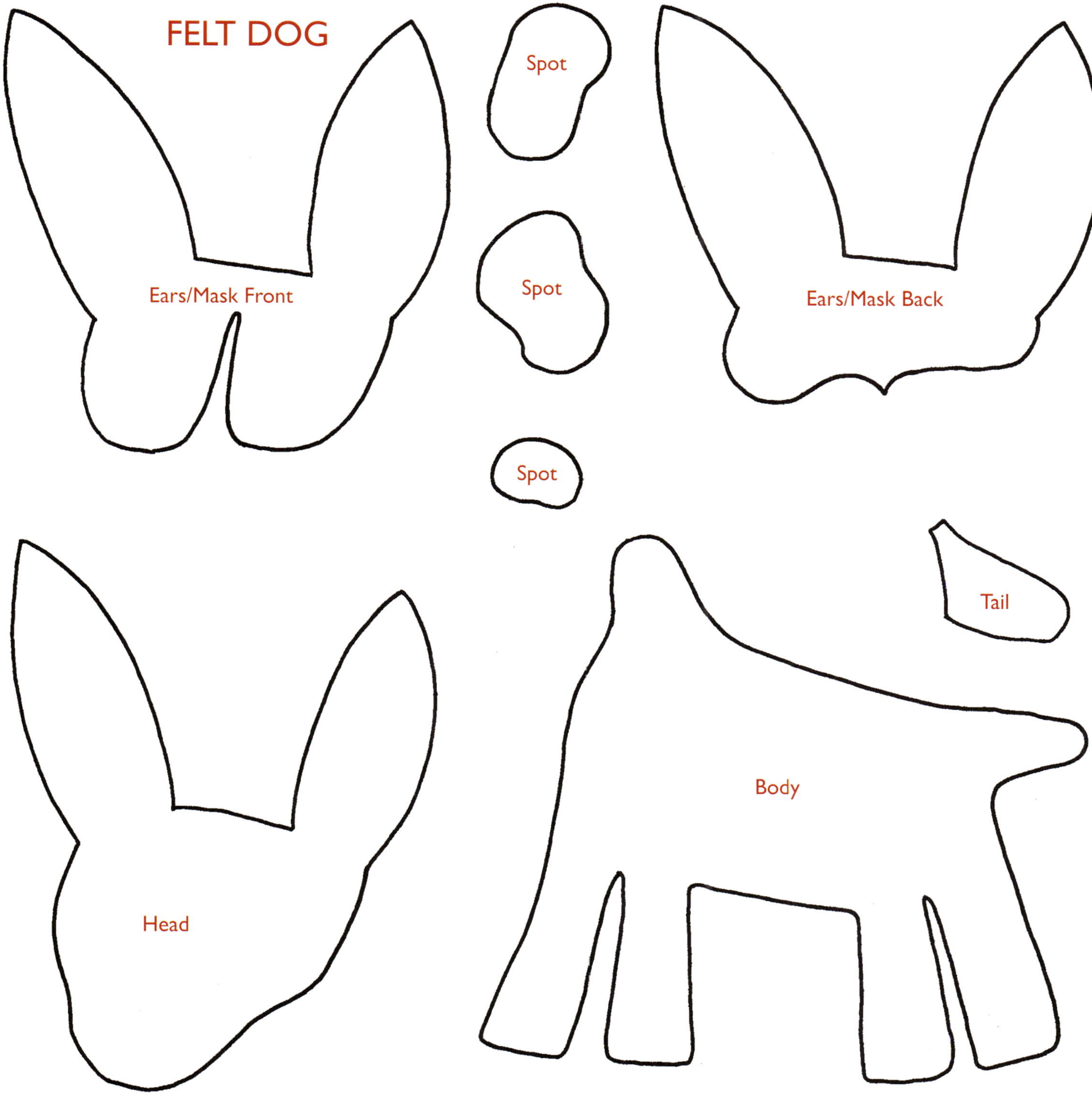

RECYCLED DENIM HEART

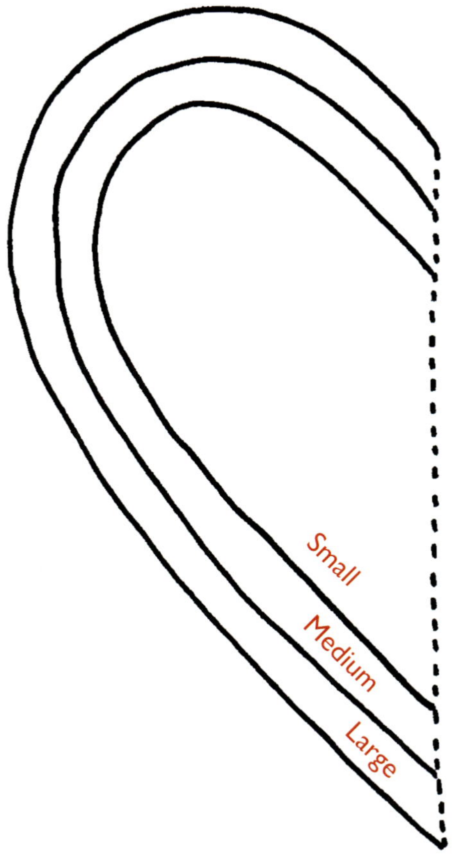

LAYERED FELT FLOWER

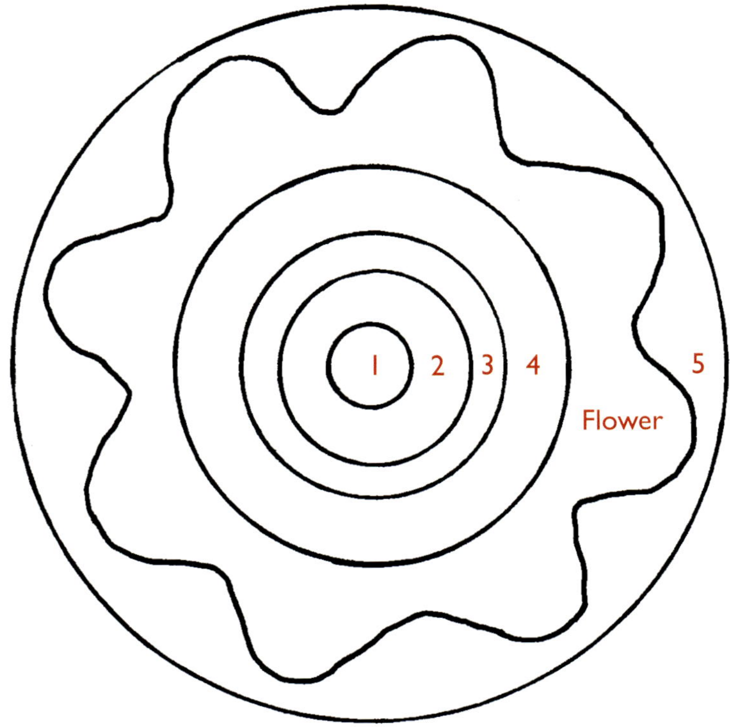

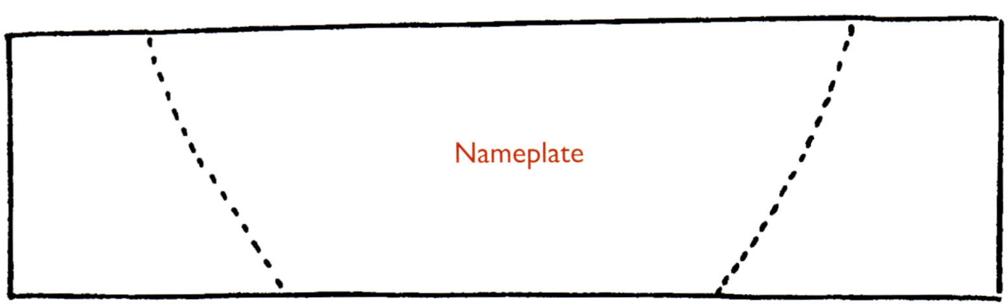

FABRIC DOLL

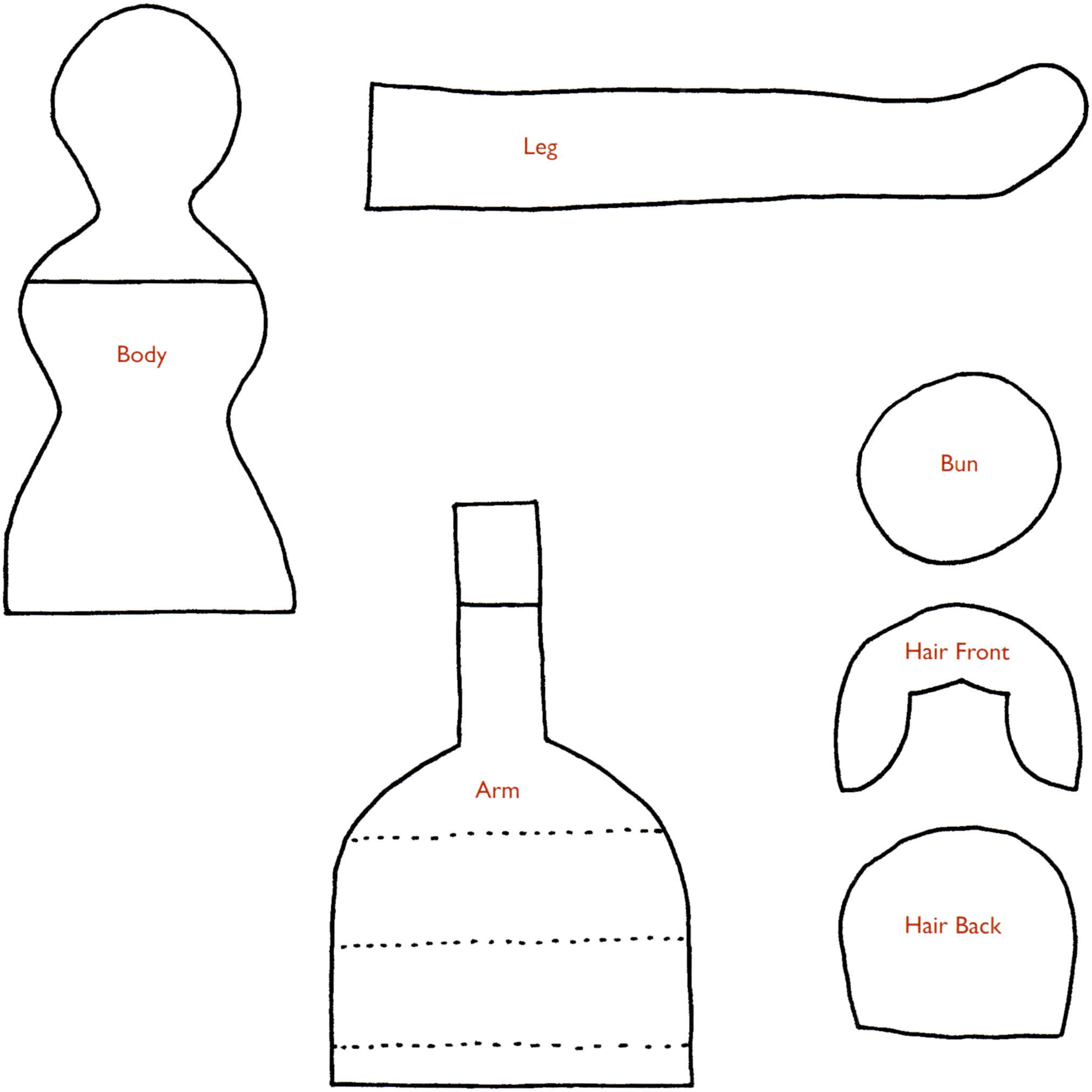

CROSS-STITCH TREE STOCKING

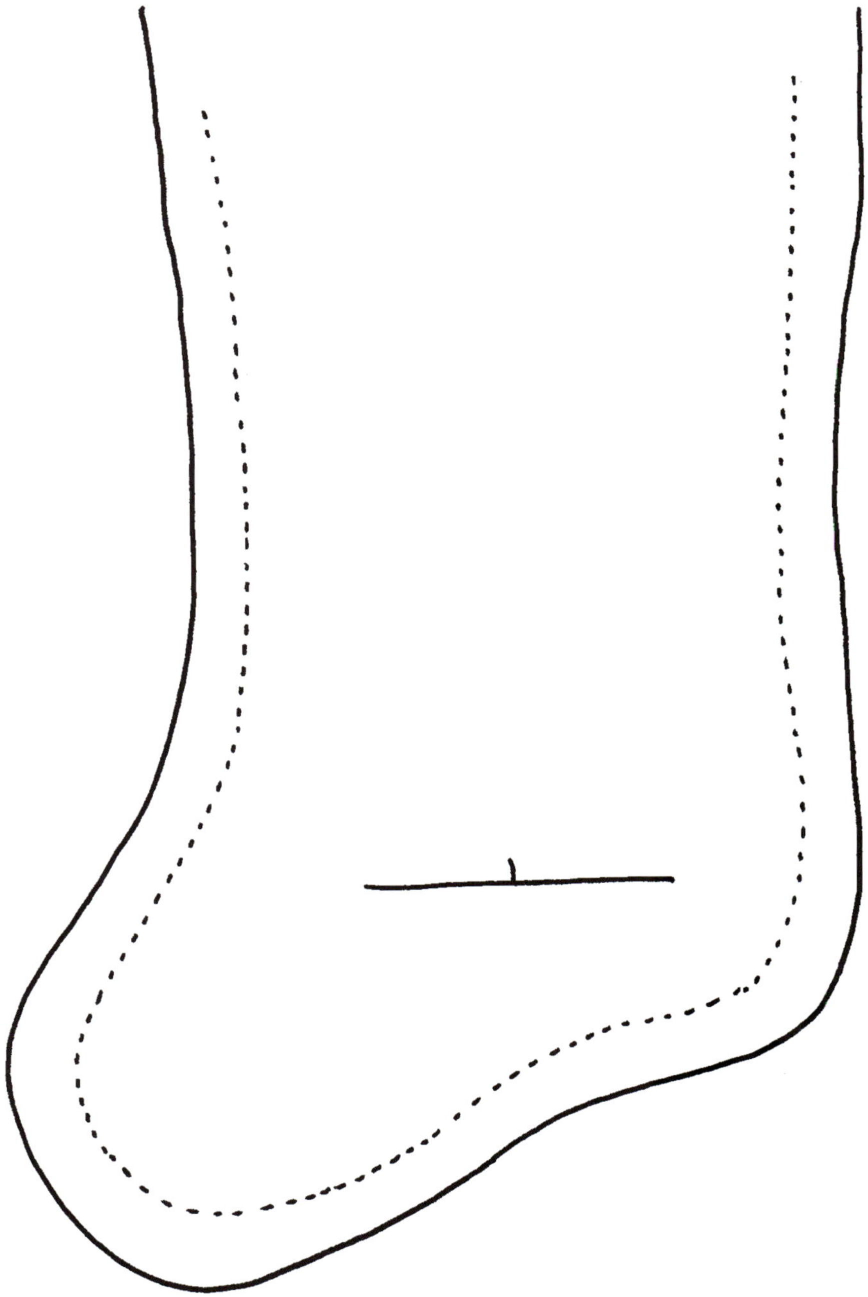

GATHERED-FABRIC TREE

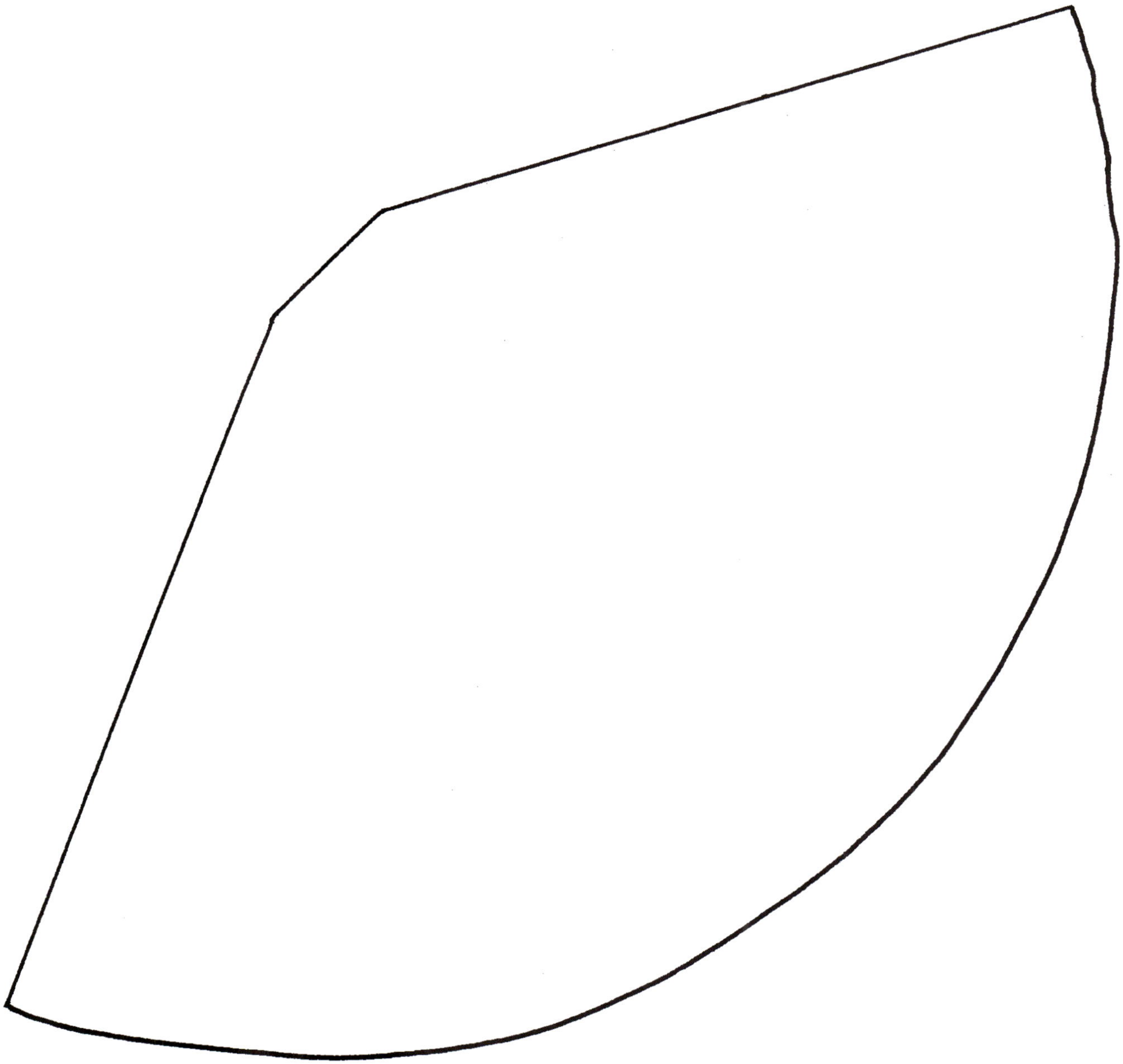

PUNCH-NEEDLE
BASKET OF FRUIT

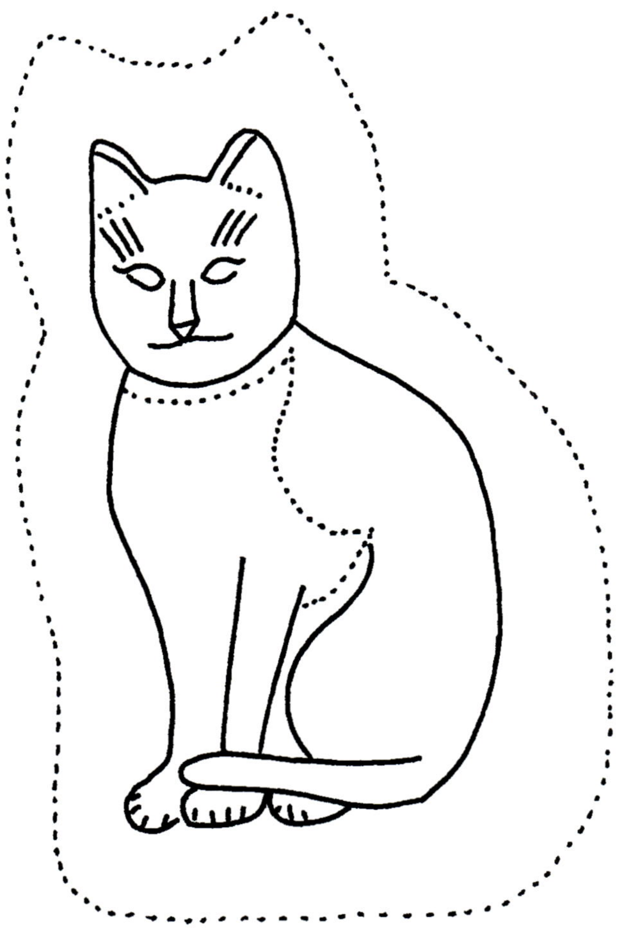

EMBROIDERED CAT

PUNCH-NEEDLE HEART

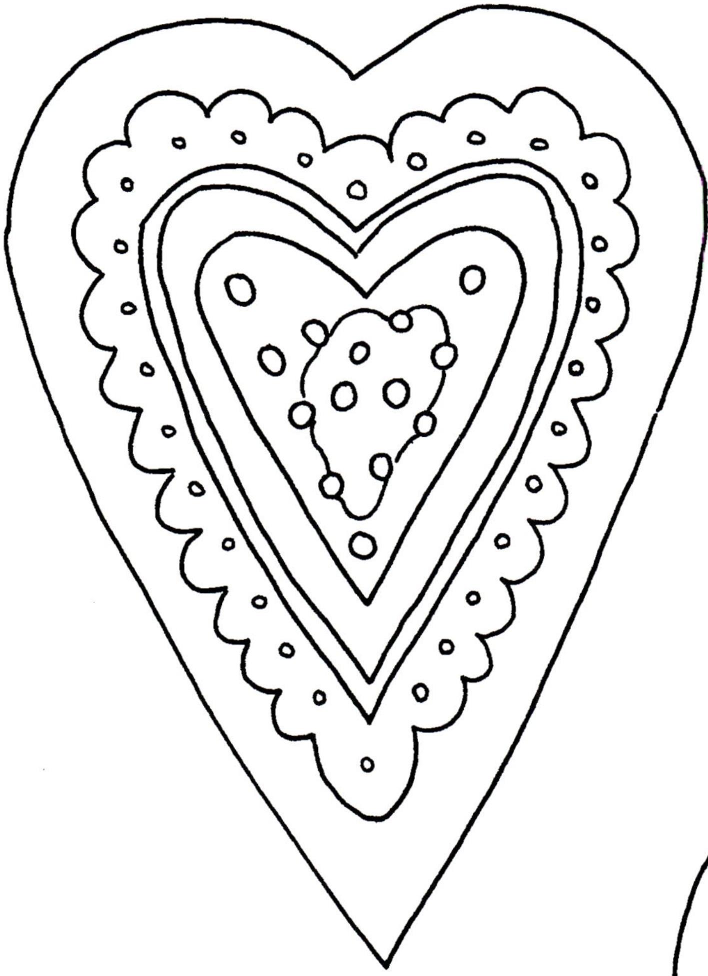

PUNCH-NEEDLE SHIP

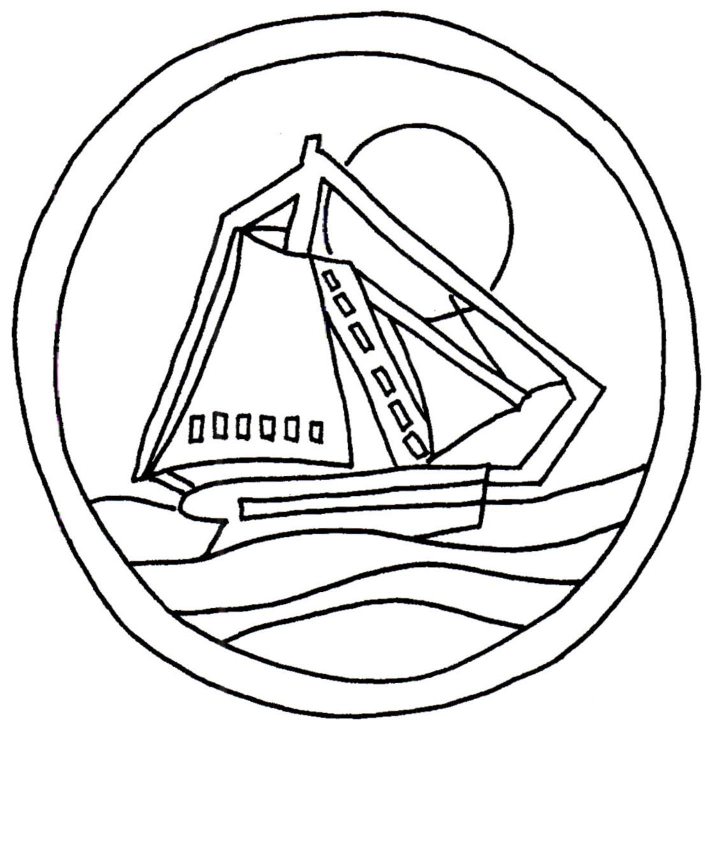

PAPER DOVE

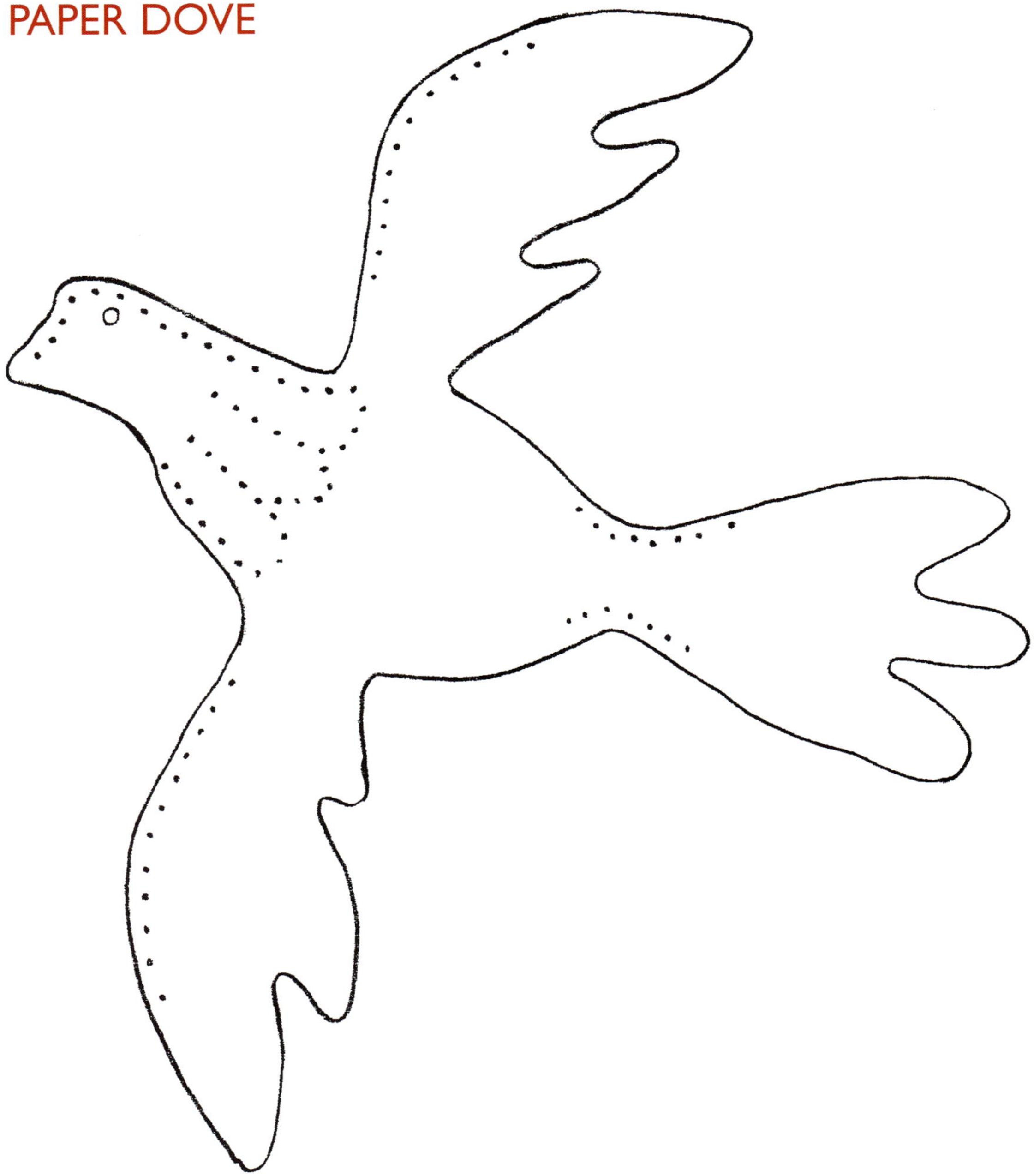

SCHERENSCHNITTE BIRDS

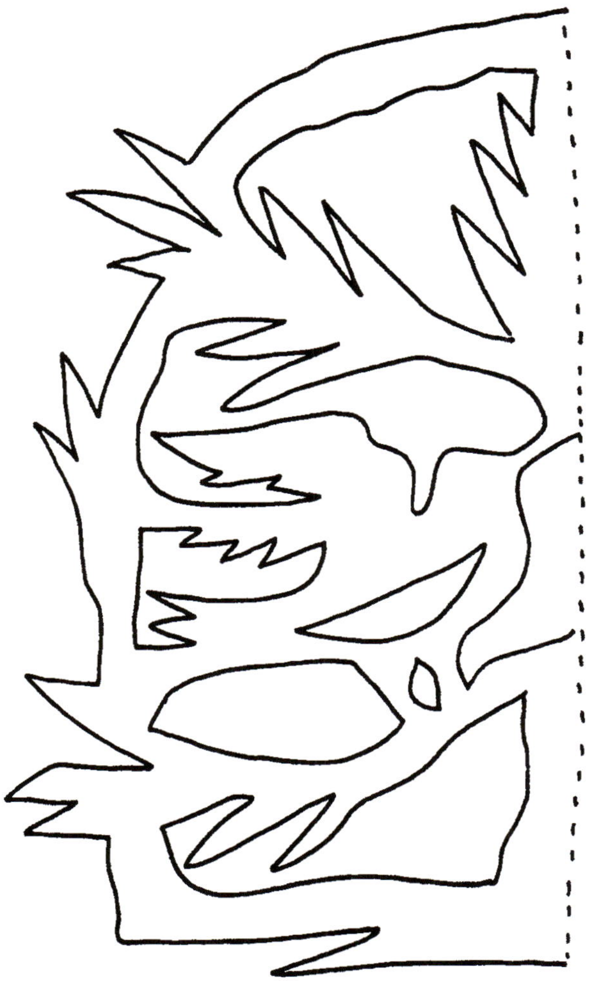

Template

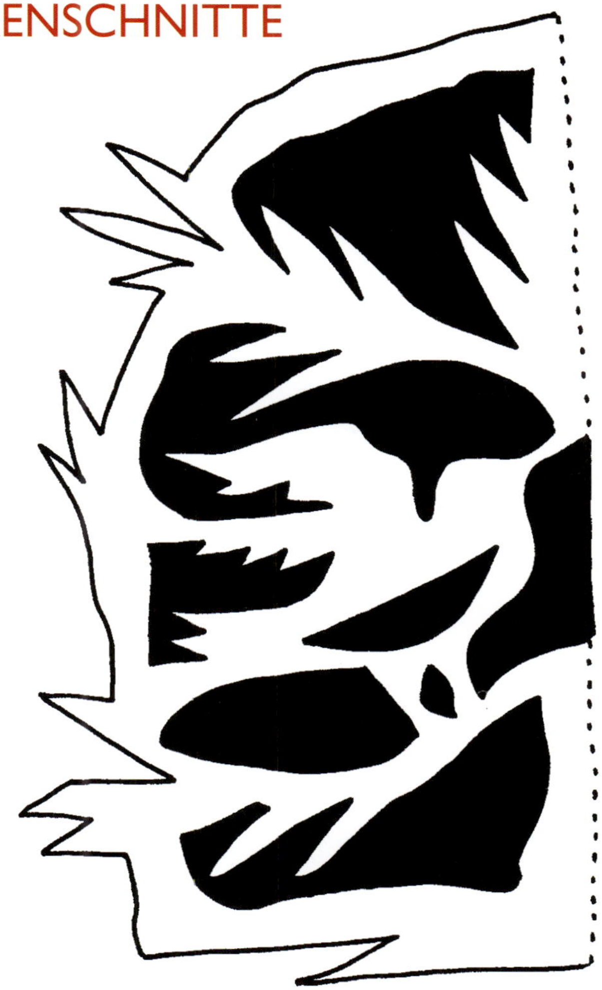

Cutting Guide

FABRIC SILHOUETTE

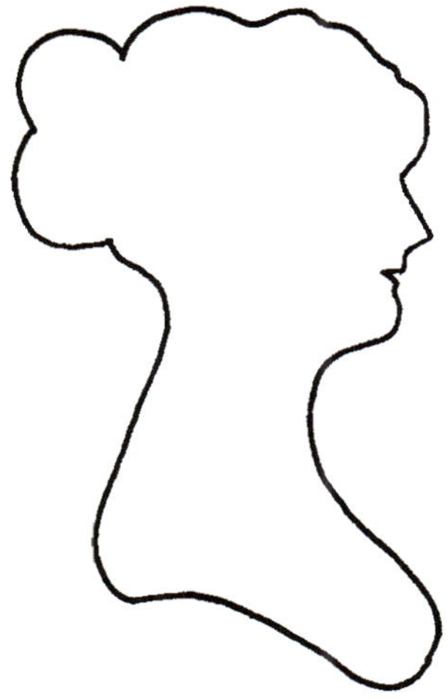

RECYCLED-CARD STAR

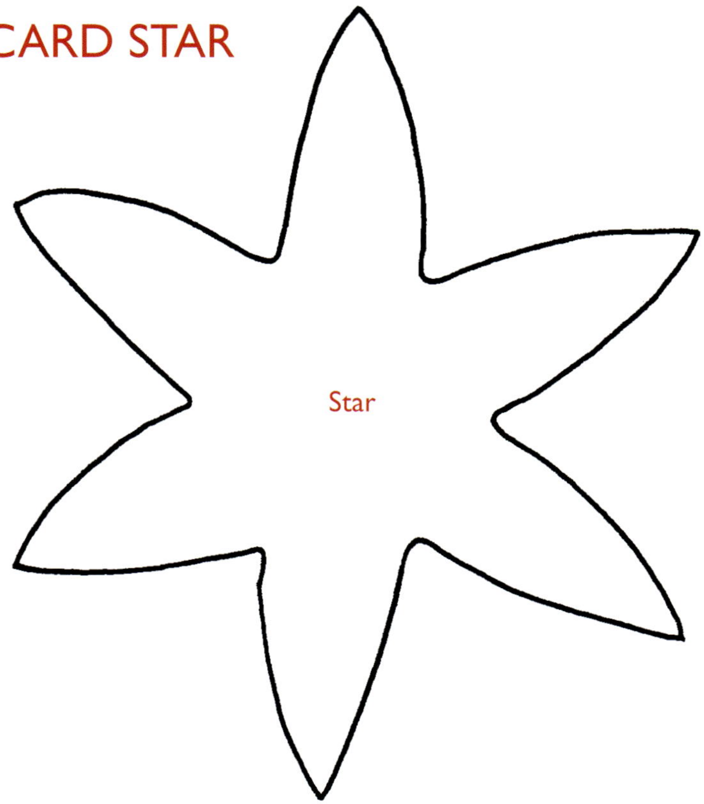

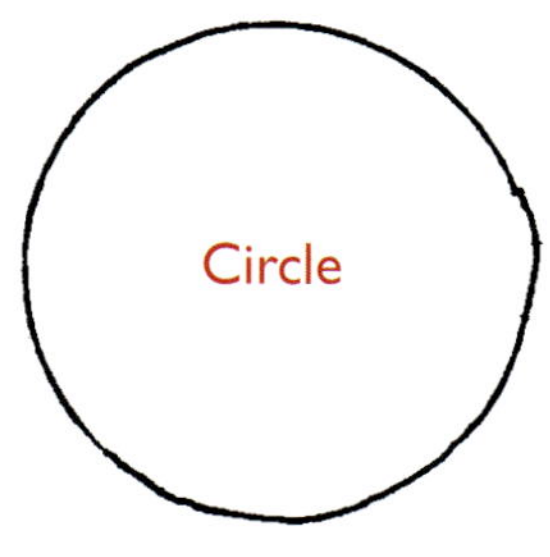

RECYCLED-BOOK SNOWFLAKE

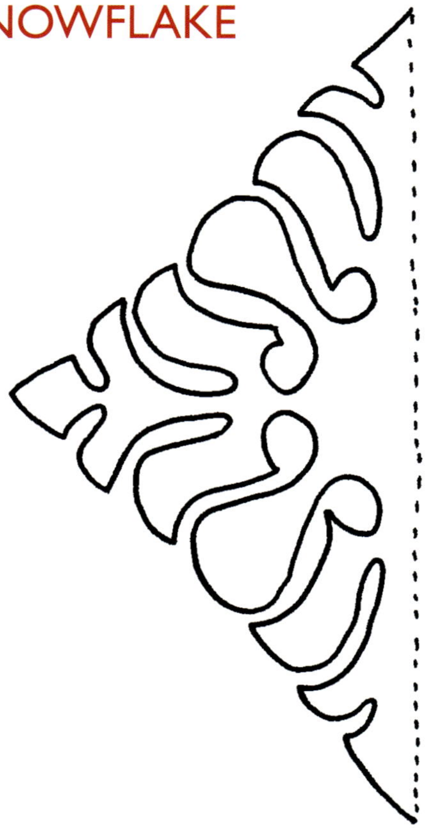

ALUMINUM ANGEL

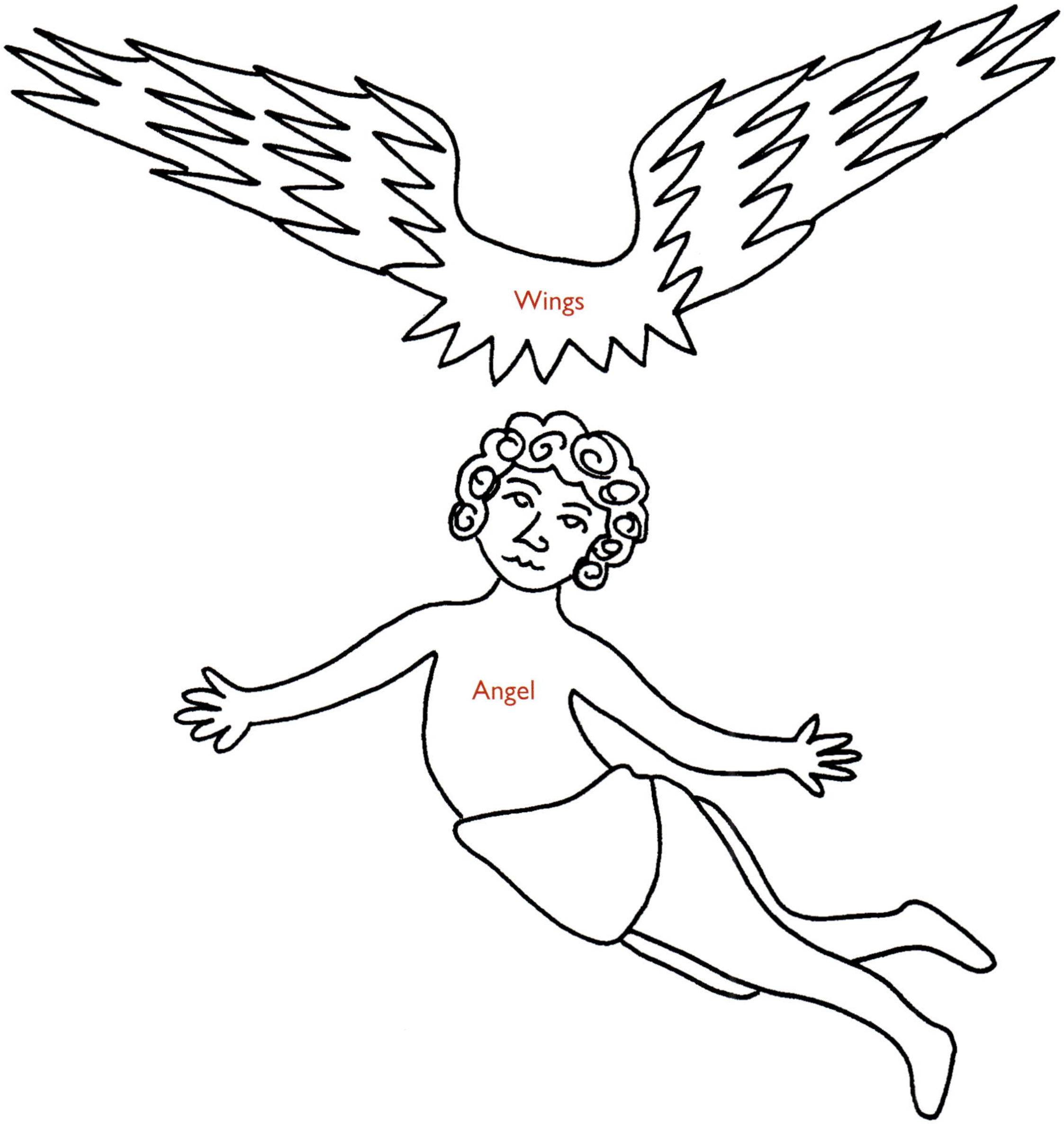

COPPER SUN

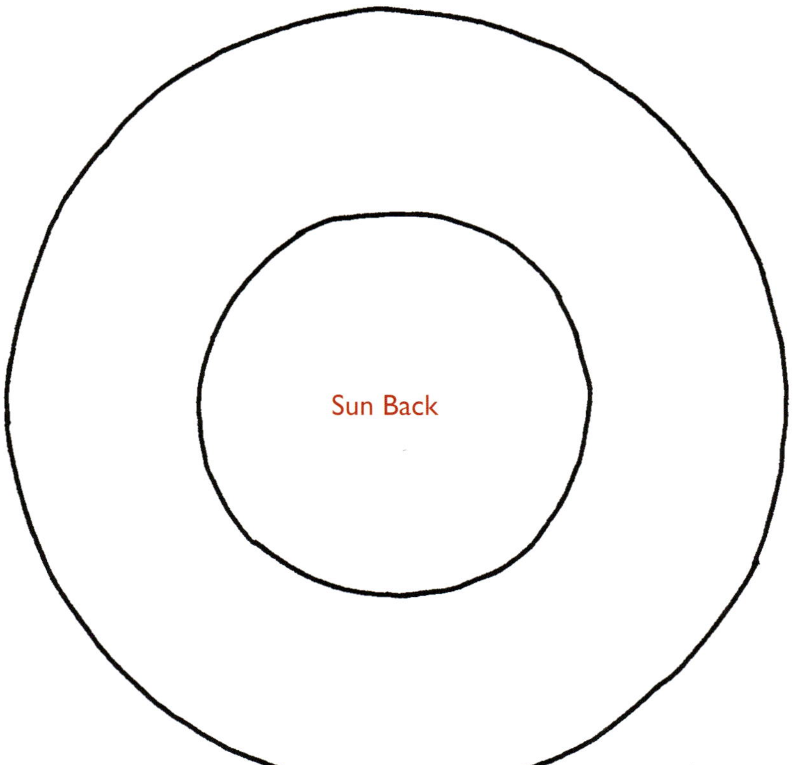

ALUMINUM AND COPPER STAR GARLAND

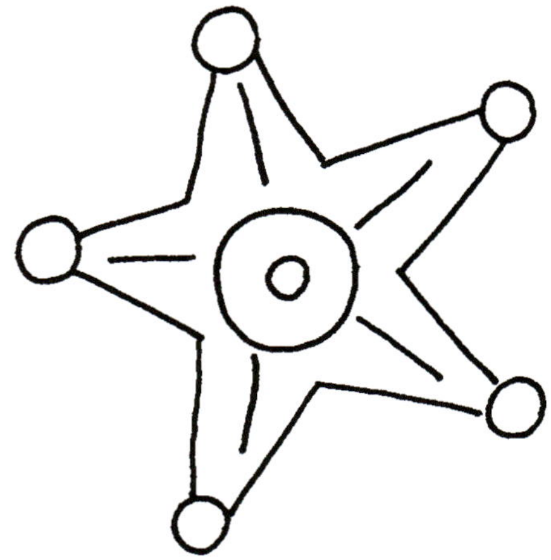

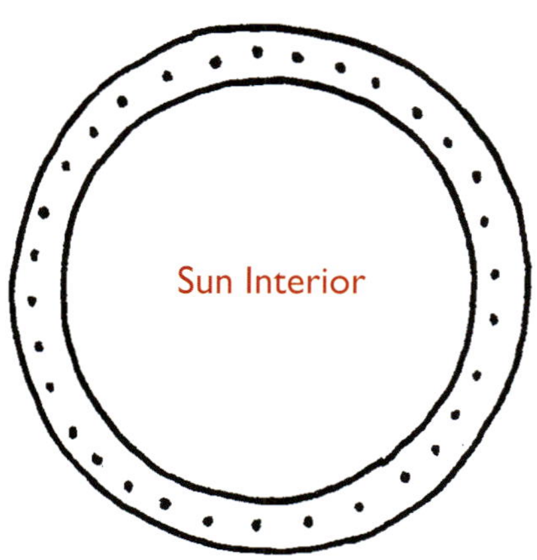

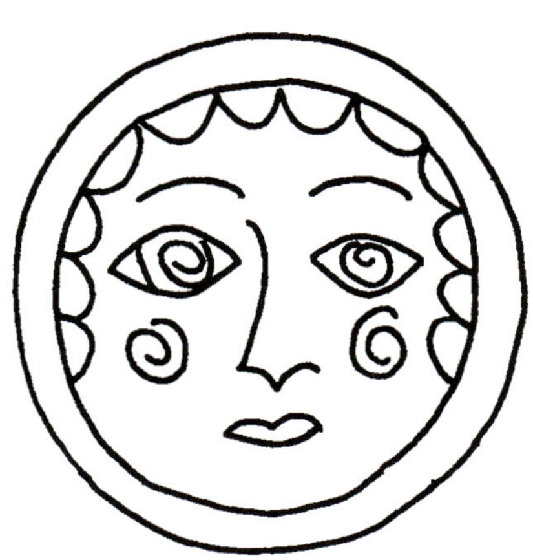

Sun Face

ALUMINUM BUTTERFLY

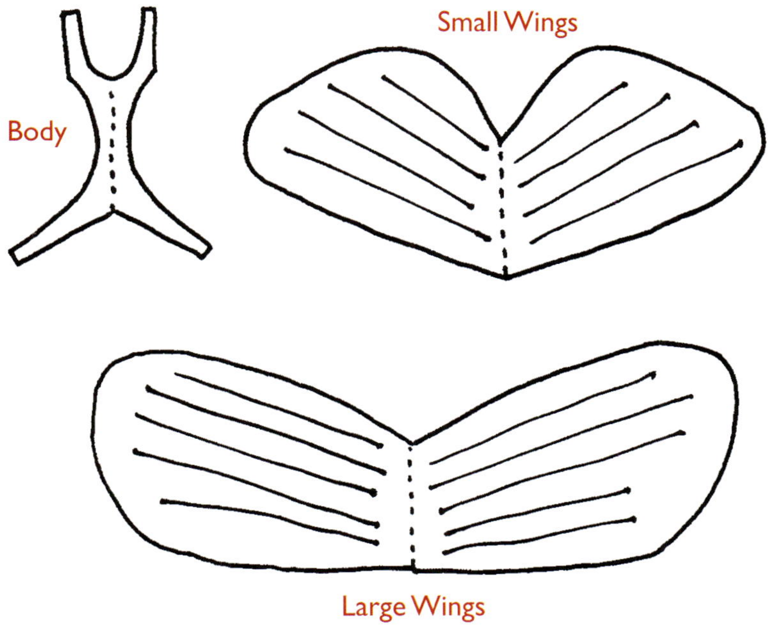

RECYCLED-METAL HEART

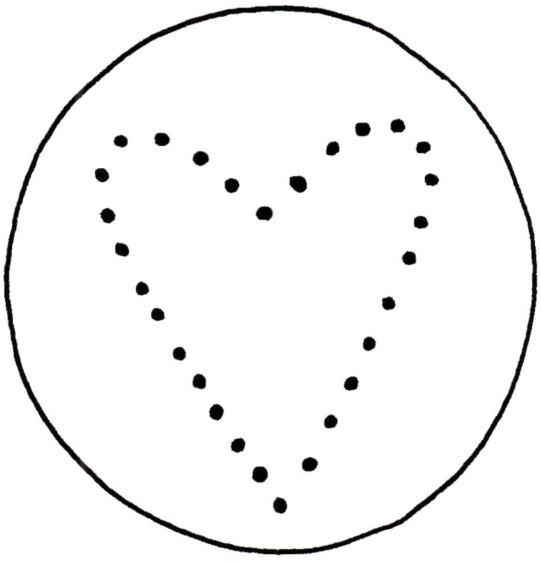

ALUMINUM FISH

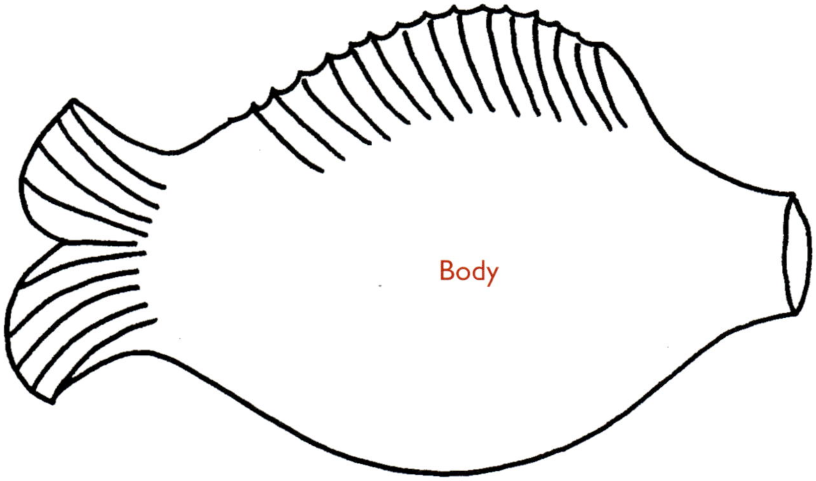

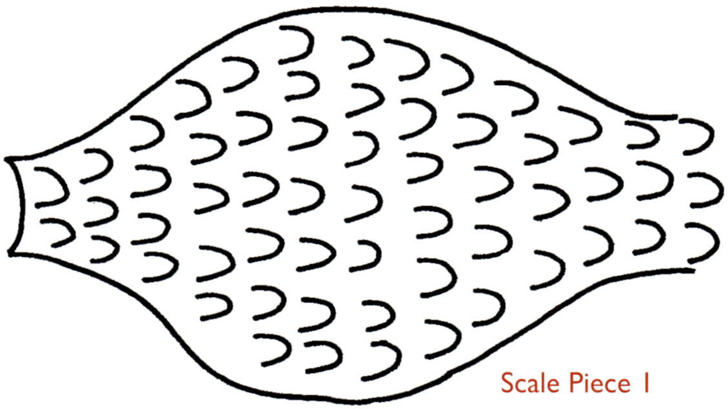

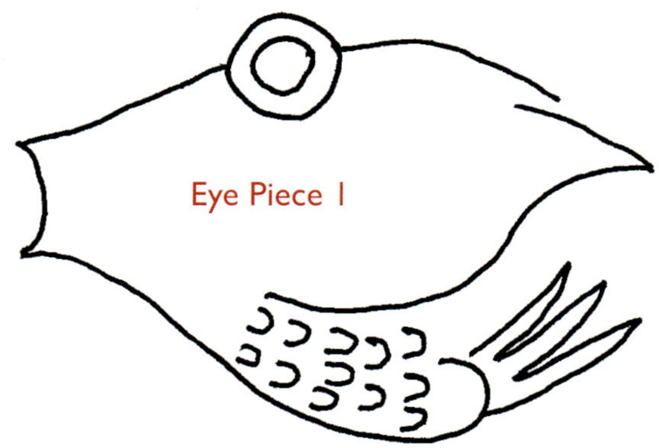

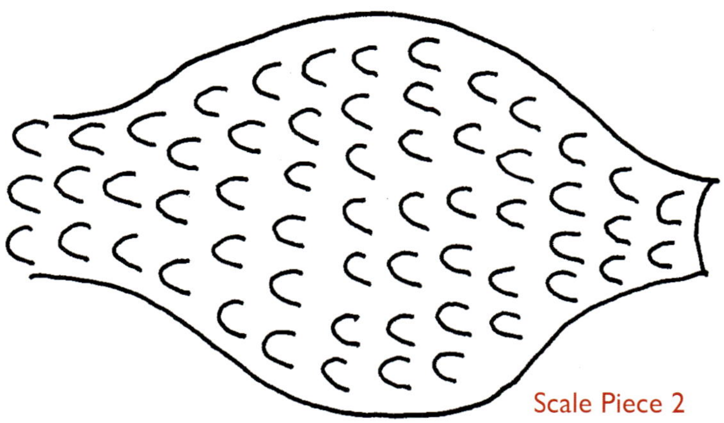

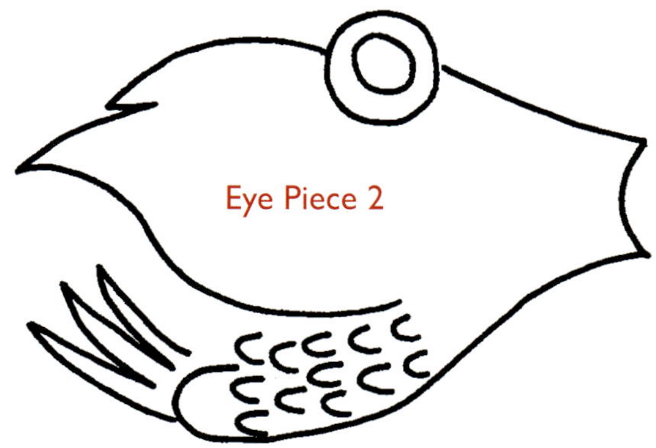

RECYCLED-PLASTIC LANDSCAPE

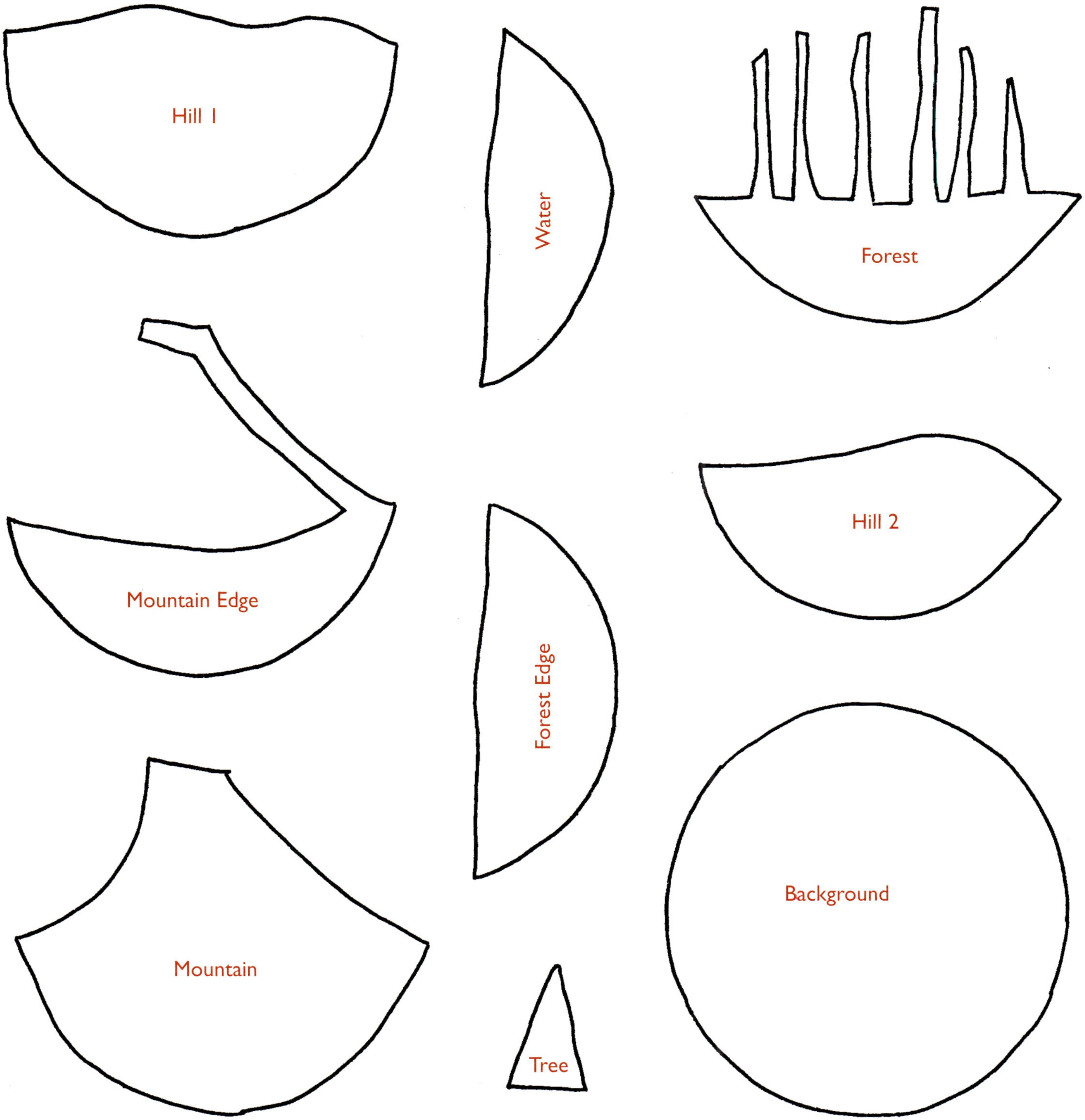

Colonial Williamsburg

The Colonial Williamsburg Foundation is a private, not-for-profit educational institution dedicated to the preservation and interpretation of the restored eighteenth-century capital of Virginia. In addition to the 301-acre Historic Area, the Foundation also operates the Abby Aldrich Rockefeller Folk Art Museum, the DeWitt Wallace Decorative Arts Museum, and Bassett Hall.

The Abby Aldrich Rockefeller Folk Art Museum, founded in 1957, was the country's first museum devoted to the subject. Folk artists usually have little or no training in fine arts practices and techniques, and their work tends to feature personal and creative use of line, color, form, and decoration. Abby Aldrich Rockefeller was a pioneer collector of American folk art in the early decades of the twentieth century. The gift of her treasures to Colonial Williamsburg began an impressive collection that spans the eighteenth century to the present and includes furniture, metalware, pottery, paintings, drawings, needlework, quilts, carvings, and sculpture in a variety of media.

The DeWitt Wallace Decorative Arts Museum displays American and British antiques, including furniture, metals, ceramics, glass, paintings, prints, maps, firearms, and textiles from the seventeenth, eighteenth, and early nineteenth centuries. Bassett Hall was the Williamsburg home of John D. Rockefeller and Abby Aldrich Rockefeller during the early restoration of the Historic Area, a restoration they financed.

Colonial Williamsburg actively supports history education in schools and homes by engaging in a wide variety of educational outreach programs and activities. These include Electronic Field Trips, which transport the story of Williamsburg and the founding of our nation to students across the country; the Colonial Williamsburg Teacher Institute, which immerses elementary, middle, and high school teachers in interdisciplinary approaches to history and government; and *The Idea of America*, a digital history program that covers the nation's history from its beginnings through the present and that prepares high school students for active citizenship.